Geoff Martin

THE POLITICAL ECONOMY OF CANADA

AN INTRODUCTION

second edition

D0165607

Michael Howlett

Alex Netherton

M. Ramesh

OXFORD
UNIVERSITY PRESS

OXFORD
UNIVERSITY PRESS

70 Wynford Drive, Don Mills, Ontario M3C 1J9
www.oup.com/ca

Oxford New York
Auckland Cape Town Dar es Salaam Hong Kong Karachi
Kuala Lumpur Madrid Melbourne Mexico City Nairobi
New Delhi Shanghai Taipei Toronto

with offices in
Argentina Austria Brazil Chile Czech Republic France Greece
Guatemala Hungary Italy Japan Poland Portugal Singapore
South Korea Switzerland Thailand Turkey Ukraine Vietnam

Oxford is a trade mark of Oxford University Press

Canadian Cataloguing in Publication Data
Howlett, Michael, 1955–
    The political economy of Canada : an introduction

2nd ed.
First edition written by Michael Howlett and M. Ramesh
Includes bibliographical references and index.
ISBN-10: 0-19-541348-2   ISBN-13: 978-0-19-541348-9

1. Canada – Economic conditions. 2. Economics – Canada.
I. Netherton, Alex, 1950– . II. Ramesh, M., 1960– . III. Title.

HB121.A2H68 1999   330.971   C99-930926-9

Copyright © Oxford University Press Canada 1999

3 4 5 6 - 08 07 06

This book is printed on permanent (acid-free) paper ∞.

Printed in Canada

Contents

List of Tables and Figures

Acknowledgements

Writing often has roots in conversation, discussion, and dialogue. The desire to write this book came from the challenges of teaching students at a number of universities, including Acadia University, McGill University, University of British Columbia, Queen's University, the Victoria University of Wellington, the National University of Singapore, the University of New England, the University of Sydney, and Simon Fraser University. In many ways, the book has been shaped by these discussions, and by these students' candour, interest, and inquisitiveness.

This book first saw the light of day as a study guide for a distance education course prepared through the Centre for Distance Education at Simon Fraser University for the university's Centre for Canadian Studies. We would like to thank Rowland Lorimer, Len Evenden, and Allen Seager of the Centre for Canadian Studies and June Sturrock, Jane Cowan, and Colin Yerbury of the Centre for Distance Education for sponsoring the initial publication. Financial support from Dean of Art's Robert Brown and Evan Alderson and Vice-President (Research) William Leiss aided the completion of that project.

The first edition of the book appeared under the McClelland & Stewart imprint, largely through the efforts of Michael Harrison, Peter Buck, and Robert Clark. Between the first and second editions, numerous comments and suggestions for change were received from a large number of colleagues, teachers, and teaching assistants who worked with the book. These include Patrick Smith, Derek Cook, Russell Williams, Aaron Laing, David Brown, Gary Teeple, David Laycock, Natalie Minunzie, Jacqui Kenney, Brad Hornick, Mary Sibierski, and Ross Mackenzie. Research assistance was provided by Ed Rouse, Wayne McIlroy, and Linda Young. Special thanks to David Skinner and David Robinson without whose help it would not have been possible for one of the authors living in Australia to work on Canadian political economy. The comments of reviewers for both McClelland & Stewart and Oxford University Press have been especially helpful. The project has also benefited from the encouragement and research support of Evan Alderson and Mark Selman of the university's Integrated Studies Program in Liberal and Business Studies.

At Oxford University Press, we have been fortunate to have the support of an excellent team, including Ric Kitowski, Euan White, Phyllis Wilson, Laura Macleod, and Richard Tallman.

Of course, many others contributed to the book, including Mandy Leena Tan, Brigitte, Robin et Jérémy, and Rebecca, Alex, and Anna.

Thank you everyone.

Chapter 1

Introduction

Over the next decades Canadians will face a number of serious challenges and crises. While the failure of efforts at constitutional reform ensure that outstanding issues such as provincial and Aboriginal rights will remain at the forefront of Canadian political discourse, these failures also call into question the ability of Canadian governments to manage a range of other problems—everything from the depletion of key natural resources and the need for environmental protection to the stresses of further sociocultural integration with the United States. In addition, the country will have to adjust its economy to the continentalist pressures set in place by the North American Free Trade Agreement (NAFTA) and to the international pressures created by the globalization of business and commerce (Banting, Hoberg, and Simeon, 1997; Anderson et al., 1998).

How will Canadian governments at various levels react to these pressures, and how will they cope with change? Can the political and economic system deal with the challenges in its present form? These are two of the most important questions facing Canadians, but there are others. If changes are required, what will they look like? Will governments allow private actors to determine what goods will be produced and how—and simply turn a blind eye to the negative consequences of such a policy? Or will governments take on even more active roles in the economic life of the country, regulating and monitoring or even supplanting the market through the use of public agencies and enterprises?

The study of political economy sets out to address questions like these and to formulate answers. Its subject matter is the regulation of social and natural resources used in the production and distribution of goods and services in society.[1] Every society has some mechanism for determining the use of its various human and natural resources: what is produced in what quantity, and how and in what manner the resources are distributed. All modern societies depend on two principal institutions for making such decisions: the state and the market. Because the state belongs to the realm of politics and the market to the realm of the economy, the study of both is an integral part of political economy.

Societies, however, differ significantly in the areas of social life organized by these institutions. Some societies rely extensively on state production and allocation of goods and services; others rely on market-based institutions. Even countries with a similar overall mix of state and market activities, moreover, can differ significantly in how they use state or market institutions to organize specific production and allocation activities. The specific mix of state and market institutions found within a nation-state constitutes that nation's political economy. Similarly, the specific mix of state and market institutions found in the relations that exist between nation-states constitutes the international political economy (Unger and Van Waarden, 1995).

The study of political economy reveals a great deal about how a particular society or an international regime operates, because different groups of people benefit in different ways from the use of state and market institutions to regulate or control the production and allocation of goods. Political economy focuses on biases in the structure and processes of state and market—biases that systematically favour some members of society over others. For instance, due to the manner in which they insulate owners of capital from the day-to-day struggle to survive, in their normal course of operation markets invariably favour the owners of firms more than workers. Similarly, democracy, insofar as it is based on secret ballot and majority rule and favours large, relatively homogeneous groups in society who tend to vote in a similar fashion, provides, at least theoretically, large groups such as workers with some political superiority *vis-à-vis* much smaller groups such as owners of enterprises.

Political economy therefore examines how the state and its associated political structures and processes affect the production and distribution of wealth. Conversely, political economy also examines how the market generates political conflicts and influences the organization and operation of the state. The objective of political economy is to discover how particular mixes of state and market activities came about and who benefits from them; to assess the capability of both state and economic actors to alter this mix; and to explore how such changes might occur. It is a study with a broad scope: investigating, describing, and explaining the mixtures of state and market activities in different countries. Thus, the term 'political economy', as William Carroll (1988) points out, is used to refer simultaneously to *an existing empirical subject*, to *a method of study* of that reality, and to *a body of theory* concerning that reality. The basis for all three facets, however, remains the particular relationship between states and markets found within and among nation-states.

Political-Economic Method:
The Study of States and Markets

State

The concept of the state is ambiguous and contentious enough to yield, according to one observer, as many as 145 separate definitions (Rosenau, 1988: 24). Thus, instead of trying to define the term comprehensively, we will highlight a feature of state activity that is fundamental to the understanding of political economy: authority. As Max Weber ([1915] 1978) pointed out, the state possesses a monopoly on the use of legitimate coercion. The state is the only institution in society that has the legal authority, or the right, to command obedience from its citizens. In the case of recalcitrance or a refusal to obey, it can maintain its decisions through force if necessary. While gangsters, for example, sometimes back up their decisions through force, they do not have the legal authority to do so. Indeed, the state usually attempts to prevent criminals from using force against others by putting them in jail or even executing them. The state is, in a legal sense, the most powerful social institution.

In this capacity the state, in theory, can determine how societal resources are allocated and distributed. It can determine what can be produced and under what circumstances; how and under what circumstances goods, services, and the various inputs such as land, labour, capital, or technology can be bought and sold; and how the resulting income is to be distributed. In theory, all it has to do is implement laws and regulations commanding a particular action, for example, antipollution and minimum wage laws or progressive taxation of income.

In practice, however, the state's ability to control societal actors is severely constrained. The availability of narcotics or sex on the market despite state prohibitions against their sale testifies to the limits of the state's regulatory capacity. The modern state is also severely restricted in its ability to control the production and distribution of societal resources and wealth, except in cases of national emergency or wartime. In the normal course of events the state is constrained from exercising its full powers by societal resistance contesting the *legitimacy* of its authority to act, as well as by the existence of other nation-states that can contest the effects of a particular state's actions on international relations (Beetham, 1991; Keohane and Milner, 1996).

Domestic resistance can have numerous sources. Certain groups with independent sources of wealth and power may object to state regulation of their activities; certain people may be ideologically or culturally predisposed to oppose state activity. An important source of domestic resistance arises from the fact that as a political institution the state makes decisions that confer benefits on certain groups in society and costs to others. When this pattern of selective costs and benefits is repeated, the groups bearing the burden of costs may begin to question the legitimacy of the state's authority (Rose, 1968). States are subject to similar constraints at the international level. Some of the constraints are imposed by international laws; some of them arise because certain states are militarily and economically stronger; others derive from more subtle factors, such as dependence on foreign states for trade and investment (Young, 1980; Risse-Kappen, 1995).

In addition, a state's internal structure and processes can place limits on the available options. For example, the Canadian state may find it difficult to develop and implement coherent national policies because of the federal-provincial division of jurisdictions, which makes it difficult to co-ordinate governmental actions in many policy areas. The state's position as the most powerful institution in the society is also at the root of a dilemma. The state can issue authoritative commands and is quite capable of resolving issues that can be addressed through a command-penalty system. But issues requiring more subtle measures are its failing. In Charles Lindblom's (1977) colourful metaphor, the state has 'strong thumbs, no fingers'.

To manage the economy efficiently without the support of the market, for example, the state must be able somehow to rank consumer priorities. Given that economic resources are finite, it is not possible to produce and distribute everything, everywhere, at the same time: there has to be a mechanism for deciding how much cheesecake, hospital care, and housing should be produced and in what order. While the state can attempt to control production and distribution by command-penalty measures, it cannot do the same with consumer demand. Despite its authority to produce whatever it wishes, the state cannot ensure that those goods and services will actually be consumed. State officials have little incentive to respond to consumer demand if their salaries and benefits are tied to production and not to consumption—as in many societies with extensive state apparatuses attempting to control production. In fact, these officials tend to face insurmountable problems in forecasting consumer demands even when they have been given some incentive to do so. The list of organizational problems the state faces in its planning of production and distribution is extensive. (See Lindblom, 1977: 66–75, for more examples.)

Hence, there is a distinction to be made between what the state can theoretically accomplish and what it is able to accomplish in practice. Yet the state's ability to organize production and distribution must not be underestimated. Despite all the limitations, various states at various points in history have successfully organized and implemented monumental projects. The construction of Egyptian pyramids and the Great Wall of China are examples of ancient state-directed projects and have their modern counterparts in vast military armament projects as well as such efforts as the contemporary Russian and US space programs.

Market

The market carries out production and distribution of societal resources in a vastly different way from the state. Rather than relying on authority, markets work through exchange. A market is an arena in which people exchange land, labour, capital goods, and services. Unlike the state's authority, which is backed by coercion, the market's exchange is predicated, at least in theory, on voluntary action by individuals. If a person wants to exchange something, that person must, at least theoretically, voluntarily want to part with the property. The other party to the exchange must want to do the same. The market, therefore, is in theory an efficient mechanism for allowing consumer wants and desires to be expressed in a way that directs subsequent decisions on production and allocation.

Exchange in a market can take various forms. People can exchange things they don't want for other commodities they do want; this is known as barter exchange. In modern markets some barter transactions take place, but the usual mode of exchange is through the medium of money. When people want something, they must sell something else—their labour or their goods or property—for money. Then they use that money to buy what they want. They don't directly exchange one thing for another; they use money as an intermediary to make the exchange. But when something is exchanged for money, there has to be a way to determine its value, which means establishing a price. The determination of price, which is a complex subject, essentially depends on how much is supplied by producers at any given point in time. The producers' search for profits and the consumers' preference for certain goods—constrained by the ability to pay—form the basis of price activity and, therefore, market exchange.

Unlike production by the state, then, production by the market does not require centralized information or co-ordination. Production decisions are taken by individual producers responding to the demands of individual consumers. There is no need for a central authority to draw up a list of priorities indicating which types and quantities of goods and services will be produced. Theoretically, consumers buy what they want and can afford. They make their decisions as carefully as possible ('rationally') because they know that the purchase of one item leaves less money for buying something else. On the other side, producers produce those items, and in such a manner, that will secure the highest profit. If the consumers or producers make a wrong choice, they absorb the cost and do their best to avoid repeating the mistake in future. This relatively simple mechanism has done wonders in organizing production in the modern world. It has led to technological innovations and a substantial improvement in the quality of material life for many people.

The voluntary nature of the market process and its ability to confer benefits on the populace, however, are open to question. Exchange presumes ownership, since one must own property (including cash) before it can be exchanged. This means that an initial endowment of property helps determine who is able to exchange what, at what times, and in what quantities, and therefore who is able to benefit the most from market exchange. This initial distribution of property is crucial to subsequent market activities and is never voluntary or conflict-free. Different groups and individuals in society possess different amounts of various items to exchange, and those with the most desirable forms of property can command higher prices and larger rewards from the market than can those who only possess less desirable forms.

This initial inequality greatly influences the sale of many items through the market, not least the sale of labour. For a starving person, the act of selling labour for wages does not represent a purely voluntary exchange between employee and employer. Similarly, the distribution of landownership in Canada derives from the forceful occupation of Aboriginal lands by European immigrants, which now gives European descendants a disproportionate ability to engage in 'voluntary' exchange with Aboriginal peoples. Market exchange can be considered voluntary and mutually beneficial only if the existing distribution of property is taken for granted. Severe inequalities in initial distributions of wealth and property can greatly distort market exchange, and if those inequalities hinder intergenerational mobility and opportunity they can lead to severe resistance on the part of groups failing to benefit from the market transactions.

States and Markets

Although, for the sake of clarity, we have referred to state and market forms of organization as separate entities, political economy presumes not the independence of states and markets but their mutual dependence and intertwining. States and markets cannot be studied in isolation. Indeed, the inseparable nature of their relationships forms the very rationale for political economy. Otherwise, the state would be studied under political science and the market under economics and the rationale for the study of political economy would disappear.

States and markets are interdependent primarily because they need each other: together they must overcome the societal and organizational constraints that each of them is incapable of facing alone. The state needs the market because of the market's efficiency in responding to consumer demands and co-ordinating an extensive production apparatus. Allocation of all resources by the state alone requires a machinery so complex that it consumes many of those same resources without significantly increasing either the quality or quantity of goods and services produced. Even in centrally planned economies (such as in the former Soviet Union, China, or Eastern Europe), a good part of the routine allocation of goods and services was carried out through legally sanctioned markets, not to mention illegal or 'black' markets.

Markets need the state because, to function at all, they need a body that enforces property rights and private contracts. Otherwise, people could sell things they do not own or refuse to honour their commitments—actions that the market by itself has no capacity to prevent. The state can perform these functions effectively because of its authority to enforce rights and contracts. In modern times, the state has gone beyond these basic functions and has established laws and built infrastructure to promote the orderly functioning and development of markets.

Both state and market forms of organizing production and allocation activities exist in all modern nation-states, although no two countries share exactly the same mix of state and market activities. The studies and theories of political economy explore the reasons for these different mixes.

The Subject of Political Economy:
Capitalism and Democracy

The modern theories of political economy have a history of no more than two hundred years. During that period, capitalism has been the dominant economic system in Western nations. Similarly, democracy has formed the basis for political organization, first as an aspiration in the nineteenth century and then as a reality in the twentieth. Capitalism and democracy have been powerful forces in moulding the relationship between state and market and, correspondingly, in moulding the political-economic theories that explain this relationship.

Capitalism

Capitalism refers to a market-oriented type of political economy. More than this, it refers to a society in which control over the property required for production (capital) is concentrated in the hands of a small section of the populace. Capitalism is a socio-economic system that originated as a corollary to the breakdown of agriculturally based societies and their subsequent industrialization in Europe towards the end of the eighteenth century. It spread rapidly to North America and most of the rest of the world in the nineteenth century. In the twentieth century many nations rejected capitalism and adopted socialism—a state-oriented political economy in which capital, or the means of production, is publicly owned and allocated—with the expressed intention of working towards the establishment of a communist political economy, in which capital would be communally owned.

Canada has always had a capitalist political economy based on a particular mix of state and market institutions, and the two general theories of political economy that have been most prominent in Canada—liberalism and socialism—have both attempted to explain this mix of state and market activities.[2] Liberal political-economic theory is very much oriented towards the 'perfection' or improvement of an actually existing capitalist political economy. Even the socialist theory—with the avowed purpose of working towards the replacement of capitalism—is a theory of capitalism in the sense that it explains how capitalism originated and operates and how and why it will be replaced by socialism.

In capitalism, production is undertaken not for direct consumption by the producer but for the purpose of sale, so the producer can use the money thus derived to purchase goods for consumption. This differs from precapitalist societies in which producers directly consumed much of what they produced, except for a small portion exchanged through barter. In capitalism, exchange takes place through markets among individuals usually unknown to each other.

Moreover, ownership of the production inputs—such as raw materials, machinery, and factory buildings—is in private hands, that is, in the hands of the capitalists. This implies that the owners of the means of production have the exclusive right to decide on their use, a right guaranteed by the state. This feature of capitalism entitles the owners to decide what will be produced and in what manner, which also establishes the capitalists as the dominant social class. The corollary of this feature is that to earn a livelihood those who do not own the means of production must work for those who do. In capitalist societies, labour is often the only productive input workers own. Consequently, workers must sell their labour to capitalists for wages in order to survive.

Another critical feature of capitalism is the need for firms to make profits, or accumulate capital, in order for the economy as a whole to survive. Profit is to capitalism what motion is to bicycles: capitalism, like bicycles, cannot properly function by standing still. If an adequate return on investment is not forthcoming, capitalists will withhold their investment or invest it somewhere else. The result can be a decline in economic activity in the society and a general lowering of the society's living standards. This imposes an enormous pressure on the democratic state to ensure hospitable conditions for investment.

Democracy

Democracy is one of the most contentious concepts in the study of politics: one survey found 311 definitions of the concept (Cunningham, 1987: 25). It is not our objective to resolve the debate. For our purposes, it is sufficient to regard democracy as a plan of political organization, a political decision-making system (Bealey, 1988: 1). Göran Therborn succinctly defines modern democracy as '(1) a representative government elected by (2) an electorate consisting of the entire adult population, (3) whose votes carry equal weight, and (4) who are allowed to vote for any opinion without intimidation by the state apparatus' (Therborn, 1983: 262).

Democracy confers entitlements on citizens to choose who they want to have represent them in government. The method of election varies among nations, but the primary purpose is always to declare the candidate with the largest number of votes as the winner in periodic competitions to staff legislative and executive institutions of governments. This condition establishes that the government will be formed by the representatives of the largest number of citizens and, depending on the type of system used, that through those representatives it will be directly or indirectly accountable to the citizens. Elections as a means of removing a government and replacing it with another were virtually unheard of until the nineteenth century, and even today there are governments that find ingenious excuses to avoid submitting themselves to the judgement of the electorate.

Towards the end of the nineteenth century Western nations began to establish democratic institutions, a process not completed until well after World War II when the franchise, or right to vote, was made universal for most adults in most Western nation-states (Therborn, 1983: 264). The intent of earlier restrictions was to limit the privilege of voting to social and economic élites. The removal of these barriers represented a major milestone in promoting social equality. From a political-economic perspective, insofar as democracy is based on the principle of secret ballot and majority rule, the non-owners of the means of production

can at least theoretically exercise their numerical superiority to pressure governments to use state authority to offset the adverse effects of capitalist ownership
of the means of production. As Adam Przeworski (1985: 11) points out: 'Political
democracy constitutes the opportunity for workers to pursue some of their interests. Electoral politics constitutes the mechanism through which anyone can as a
citizen express claims to goods and services. . . . Moreover . . . they can intervene in the very organization of production and allocation of profit.'

Democracy, by requiring that governments be elected, permits the subordinate
classes some degree of control over the state and thus helps to shape not only the
internal functioning of the state but also, through the use of state authority, of the
market. Under the influence of the democratic process, in most countries the state
has introduced income redistribution measures, in defiance of one of the basic
tenets of capitalism that the market alone ought to determine distribution of
income (Przeworski, 1991). Similarly, in many countries states have replaced
private ownership of some means of production with public, or state, ownership.

Political-Economic Theory: Old and New Debates

In eighteenth-century Europe, political economy was an established area of study.
It looked at how wealth was created and distributed and at the role of the government in the process, thus displaying acute sensitivity towards the interdependence
of states and markets. In fact, this idea of interdependence had been the general
understanding of the relationship between economy and polity since ancient times
(Staniland, 1985), and such an understanding informed the early development of
two general theories of political economy: liberalism and socialism.

Only in the twentieth century did economics and political science become
separate disciplines. Both, especially economics, developed their own orthodoxy
and spawned their own vocabulary to the extent that communication between
scholars working in the two disciplines became nearly impossible. The separation became even more pronounced in the post-World War II period. Economics
became increasingly mathematical and leaned towards a microeconomic analysis of the behaviour of individual producers and consumers in the market, with
little direct reference to the state and its role in the market.

The lack of interest in political economy was partly a result of the aplomb
that derived from the robust economic performance of most Western nations in
the postwar period. In fact, so comfortable was the era that a US scholar, Daniel
Bell, had pronounced 'the end of ideology' in politics and economy (Bell, 1960).
While the economy was humming along there was little need for anything more
than fine-tuning, for which the principles of economics were eminently suited.

All this changed with the international economic dislocations following from
the drastic oil-price hike by the major oil-exporting nations in 1973. The economic
problems of the 1970s and early 1980s—simultaneous high unemployment and
high inflation (which in the then-prevailing economic theory were supposed to be

inversely related) and declining productivity—refused to respond to the govern-ment measures that had worked so well in the previous two decades. It became increasingly apparent that the problems had their roots in the economy as well as politics and that any cure must simultaneously address both sectors. For example, the economists' solution to the problem of high inflation was reduction in govern-ment expenditures and/or money supply. What this solution disregarded was that such reductions would be extremely difficult for states to implement because of opposition from those who would be hurt by such cuts. Similarly, the purely polit-ical solution of wage and price control, even if it was possible for a government to impose, created bottlenecks in the economy and aggravated economic problems. Efforts to cope with problems such as inflation made it abundantly clear that analysts must have a broad understanding of both economy and politics and especially of the relationship between the two (Hall, 1989, 1992).

Other factors also fuelled the resurgence of political economy in the 1970s. The increasing prominence of foreign investments after World War II came under severe scrutiny from scholars in many countries who stirred fears concerning the economic dominance of major capitalist nations, often exercised through the medium of transnational corporations, and asked whether this might be a prelude to political dominance. This debate led again to a consideration of the interdependence of politics and economics (Mares, 1988). It fostered the growth of a nationalist orientation among a number of scholars in countries like Canada and Argentina who became prominent in the field of political economy.

Yet another factor contributing to the resurgence of interest in political economy was the realization in the 1970s that there were systematic differences in the performances of industrialized nations along various criteria such as economic growth, unemployment, inflation, and productivity (Goldthorpe, 1984: 3). If, after all, economic management is a simple task of applying basic economic principles, then all nations should be able to manage their economies more or less equally successfully. But in practice it turned out that nations consis-tently differed in their ability to choose and implement policies. For example, during the 1970s the Scandinavian countries were successful in keeping unemployment low and inflation only moderately high, whereas the United Kingdom and United States could do neither. In the 1980s, while Sweden encoun-tered difficulties, Japan did not. These anomalies were eventually accounted for by examining differences in the political structures of these nations (Haggard and Kaufman, 1992). It became clear that to understand economic performance it was also necessary to study politics. In a way, developments since the last century have come full circle, and political economy is fashionable once again.

Canadian Studies in Political Economy

Considering the short history of Canada as a nation, political economy has had a distinguished place in the development of the country's social sciences. In the early decades of this century Canadian scholars produced insightful and original works in the political-economic tradition. The main reason for this development, C.B. Macpherson has surmised, was the small size of the country's academic community, which meant that university teachers had to be generalists and teach courses in several related disciplines—an arrangement highly conducive to the emergence of political economy because of its general, cross-disciplinary nature (Macpherson, 1974, 1979). But as universities became larger in the 1960s, with the resulting tendency towards specialization, political economy was gradually eclipsed. The arrival of US academics and the analytical tools they brought (Wood and Wood, 1970) reinforced the departure from the political economy tradition. Only in the late 1960s and early 1970s did Canadian political economy begin to re-emerge from the shadows.

Given the international economic trends, it is more than a coincidence that the discipline was experiencing a revival in other Western nations at the same time. Much interest in Canadian political economy was fuelled by the concern voiced about the increasingly high level of US ownership of Canadian industries in the 1960s and 1970s, a concern spurred by the publication of the Watkins Report (1968) and the Gray Report (1972) by the federal government (Marchak, 1985: 673). Nationalist concerns inspired interesting studies in Canadian political economy (Levitt, 1970; Lumsden, 1970; Teeple, 1972). The greater awareness of regional economic inequalities in Canada also spawned numerous studies in political economy. The discipline's growing popularity in universities was manifested in the establishment of a political economy section under the Canadian Political Science Association at the Learned Society meetings in 1976. That was followed by the establishment of the journal, *Studies in Political Economy*, in 1979. Other academic journals in political science and sociology began to publish articles on the subject with greater frequency. As a result, the discipline became diversified and robust in the 1980s and 1990s.

For most of this century there have been three broad traditions in Canadian political economy: liberalism, socialism, and the hybrid 'staples' theory. Liberal political economists have been active since the eighteenth century, but recently they have become especially vocal with the acquisition of a formal (economic) model of politics afforded by *public choice theory*. This theory, developed in the United States in the 1960s, became immensely popular in the 1980s, securing its chief US proponent, Professor James Buchanan, a Nobel Prize in 1986. Public choice theory marked a turning point in economics because of its avowed interest in both the economy and politics. Public choice treats governments and voters in democratic societies as producers and consumers respectively and attempts to explain political outcomes as the result of the bargaining between the two. The political actors (politicians, bureaucrats, and voters) are assumed to be guided by self-interest and rationality, just like their economic counterparts (producers and consumers).

Socialist analyses of the Canadian political economy had been developed along Leninist lines after World War I by the Communist Party of Canada (CPC) and, after 1933, along social democratic lines by the Co-operative Commonwealth Federation (CCF)—the forerunner of today's New Democratic Party (NDP). Despite excellent studies by C.B. Macpherson (1953) and Stanley Ryerson (1963, 1968), however, it was only in the early 1970s that the application of the analytical tools of socialist political economy became popular among scholars in Canada.

During this earlier period, the principal opposition to liberal political economy came from a group of economic historians known as the 'staples school', due to the emphasis they placed on the export of bulk natural resource commodities—or 'staples'—such as fish, lumber, minerals, and energy in analysing the course of Canadian history and economic development. Influential in Canadian political economy between the 1920s and 1950s, staples analysis almost disappeared in the 1960s as Canada appeared poised to abandon its dependence on resource exports and become a major manufacturing economy. Continual problems encountered in Canadian industrialization, however, including its uneven regional nature and impact, led to a revival of staples analysis in the form of the 'new Canadian political economy' of the late 1960s and 1970s.[3]

Despite its recent revival in Canada, political economy is still at an early stage as an academic discipline. A decade ago students were graduated in political science or economics without being exposed to the interrelationships between Canadian politics and the economy. Textbooks on Canadian politics rarely mentioned the effect of the economy on their subject matter (see, for instance, Van Loon and Whittington, 1987); similarly, textbooks on the Canadian economy impart no broad understanding of the role of politics in the economic life of the country (see Lipsey, Steiner, and Purvis, 1987). A more systematic analysis of the relationship between the two disciplines is required, and that is what this book sets out to accomplish.

Plan of the Book

The purpose of this study is to conceptualize the structure and functioning of the Canadian political economy. It focuses on the state and market in Canada and on their broader context. But before embarking on the main study, we also discuss the existing theoretical interpretations of the subject, to show that the analyses of, and prescriptions for, the Canadian political economy derive from the theoretical assumptions of the analysts. Chapters 2, 3, and 4 examine the liberal, socialist, and staples theories respectively.

Chapter 5 studies the structure of the Canadian political economy with a view to ascertaining the constraints it imposes on state and market actors. Chapter 6 assesses Canada's place in the international political economy and shows how the destination/source of its trade and the international agreements to which it is party constrain its policy choices. Chapters 7, 8, and 9 examine the organization of the three main actors in the Canadian political economy—the state, labour, and capital—and their capacity to affect each other and the nature of the domestic and international political economies.

Chapters 10 and 11 present two case studies of the nature of state and market activity in two important areas of the political economy: fiscal and monetary management at the macro level, and industrial development at the micro level. These cases illustrate the difficulties Canadian governments face in attempting to overcome existing domestic and international constraints on effective state action in these and other policy areas. Chapter 12 summarizes and discusses the implications of our findings in relation to the questions the book set out to address.

Each study has, or should have, a methodological and theoretical framework of inquiry. This book follows an approach based on the premise that the organization of the state and society and the particular network of relationships between the two shape the political economy of a nation (Hall, 1986; Hall and Ikenberry, 1989). This modern institutionalist, or *neoinstitutionalist*, perspective attributes explanatory significance to the historical pattern of the development of both social and state institutions (Kato, 1996; Hall and Taylor, 1996).

These political-economic institutions, in the words of Leon Lindberg (1982: 24), 'constitute a historically specific constraint and opportunity structure that implies an enduring division of labour and rules of play that establishes distinctive capacities and incapacities, and that constrains the strategies any individual, economic agent, or political authority can adopt to achieve its aims.' In other words, a given set of institutions facilitates some interests and impedes others, in turn determining which interests are likely to be realized (Freeman, 1989; Ikenberry, 1988; Katzenstein, 1985). Using this approach we will show how the structure of the domestic and international political economies and the manner in which state, labour, and capital have been organized in Canada have shaped the country's particular mix of market and state structures. Ultimately, we will argue that this mix is resistant to change and leaves Canada in a poor position to adapt its political economy to deal with difficulties arising from resource depletion, internal political conflicts, and the globalization of manufacturing production and financial flows.

Notes

1. Production in this context means the amount of various goods and services produced from available societal resources. Distribution refers to, first, the apportioning of income among those involved in production and, second, the apportioning of those goods and services produced among the populace for consumption.
2. The staples theory, discussed in Chapter 4, is not a general theory but applies only to Canada and other similar economies in the 'New World'.
3. The term 'new political economy' as used in Canada refers to a school different from its counterpart in Europe and the United States. In the United States the term is also used for the public choice school. See Staniland (1985).

Chapter 2

Liberal Political Economy

Liberalism has been the dominant tradition in Canada in both the study and practice of political economy, although this often goes unrecognized by both its proponents and opponents. What is called economics and much of what is called political science in capitalist industrialized nations is in actuality liberal political economy. It is therefore important to understand both the concept and its implications. Like any broad theory in the social sciences, liberalism has analytical as well as prescriptive components. Its analytical tools have been used by most mainstream economists in this century. More importantly, its prescriptions concerning the proper role of the state in capitalist market society have been adhered to by all Canadian governments, including the provincial governments led by the social democratic New Democratic Party.

Given their particular view of the state and market, liberal analysts and practitioners in government tend to recommend the adoption of certain measures and the avoidance of others. Their analyses and prescriptions lead broadly in the same direction: to steer clear of state activity in the marketplace as far as possible. Liberals' support for free trade and reductions in social welfare or regional development payments, for example, derives not so much from the results of empirical studies—since the evidence of such studies tends to be mixed—but from their theoretical premise favouring market over state forms for the organization of a nation's production and distribution systems (Boadway, 1994). Therefore it is essential that we know what these fundamental assumptions are and how they fit into the liberal scheme of things.

Disregarding the flippant, derogatory, and incorrect sense in which the term 'liberalism' is often used in the United States to describe an anti-capitalist ideology, we will use it here to refer to institutionalized beliefs and practices that maintain and promote capitalism. Liberalism 'emerged in the seventeenth, eighteenth, and nineteenth centuries to justify and help refine the increasingly important capitalist mode of production. The opposite of liberal, then, is not a conservative but a defender of pre-capitalist social relations, on the one hand,

and post-capitalist ones [communism and anarchism, for example] on the other' (A. Wolfe, 1977: 4). Liberalism emerged in Europe as a political-economic theory partly to legitimize and partly to facilitate the development of capitalism. As capitalism matured and spread to South and North America and later to Africa and Asia, encountering new problems in the process, liberal political economy itself adapted to reflect the changes.

In this chapter we will discuss liberalism from a historical perspective, tracing the development of its theory of the market and considering its political implications, especially with regard to the role of the state in the market. As we shall see, liberal political economy has proved to be a highly flexible and adaptive theory, which perhaps accounts for its popularity and longevity. Indeed, it has proved flexible enough to permit an increasing role for the state in the economy in response to changing political and economic circumstances, without ever having to depart too far from its fundamental assumptions concerning the superiority of the market form of organization. However, as we shall also see, liberal political economy suffers from a muddled conception of the state, which leads adherents of this view to analytical inaccuracies and unrealistic policy recommendations.

Fundamental Tenets

The basic precepts of liberal political economy are a mixture of factual observations, hypothetical assumptions, and normative (ideological) prescriptions; and these precepts and their flexibility explain the theory's resilience in the face of changing circumstances.

Liberal political economy begins with the assumption of the *primacy of the individual* in society, referred to as *methodological individualism*. While all social theories recognize the individual as a distinct entity, liberalism uniquely emphasizes a person's importance and reduces all social activity to individual behaviour. Liberalism views individuals as having inalienable natural rights, including the right to own property and to enter into contracts with other individuals concerning the disposition of that property (Macpherson, 1962). These rights have to be protected from intrusion by collective social organizations such as the state, churches, or trade unions. Consequently, a good society in liberal philosophy guarantees individuals freedom to pursue their interests and realize their potentials. This freedom should be restricted only when one person's freedom erodes that of another.

In contrast to the emphasis on freedom of individuals, liberalism says little about the equality of individuals. Indeed, it treats equality as an adjunct of liberty. Equality merely means *equality of opportunity*: that all people should be free to pursue their own goals, constrained only by their own physical and mental endowments. Only such a limited form of equality is consistent with individual liberty. Liberalism rules out any measure designed to promote *equality of outcome*—that is, political measures designed to ensure that economic processes equally benefit all individuals—because this would involve imposing restrictions on some so others can benefit. Thus, liberalism disapproves of income redistribution measures (progressive taxation, for example) to advance the lot of the poor because these measures involve forcible confiscation of wealth that belongs to the rich. In the twentieth century, however, the theory has been more favourably disposed towards accepting a minimum standard of wealth distribution.

Despite its emphasis on individuals and their freedom, liberal theory recognizes that the state has to be strong, to ensure that some people do not deprive others of their freedom. Beyond protecting freedom, however, in the liberal view the state has only a few other functions; it undertakes aspects of social life that individuals operating in the marketplace will not undertake, such as providing public goods, maintaining internal peace, and protecting society from external aggression. But this strong state itself must be restricted, lest it encroach upon the private realm of individuals. Liberalism therefore provides for a complex mechanism to keep the state in check. Representative government, whereby the government is chosen by the people, is one such control mechanism, as is the notion of the division of powers between different branches of the state whereby one branch 'checks and balances' the activities of the others.

The primacy of individuals is reflected in the liberals' view of the economy as well. Freedom to pursue the livelihood of one's choice and to accumulate wealth is sacrosanct. The mechanism through which individuals can pursue their interests in an unencumbered fashion is, of course, the market. Here, all individuals selfishly pursue their own interests according to their own abilities and preferences. Unlike other social philosophies that frown on this kind of self-centred behaviour, liberalism celebrates it. Liberals see exchange in the marketplace as benefiting everyone who engages in it, and the net result of this activity is the enhancement of society's welfare as a whole.

A related economic assumption is that individuals are rational or calculating actors. They decide rationally what they want and choose the least costly way of achieving it. This is not to say that the end result of their choice is rational, but simply that they arrive at their choice through reasoning. People can rationally decide what they want to produce or consume, and hence they should be allowed to do so. Restrictions on individual preferences and actions are viewed as harmful to the individual as well as to society, because such restrictions prevent the realization of the benefits of free exchange. For this reason, liberal political economy is sometimes referred to as a *laissez-faire* ('leave it alone', referring to the economy) theory.

The Market: From Classical to Post-Keynesian Theory

Liberal economic theory was formulated in the late eighteenth century. Until then there were two approaches, too crude to be called theories, that enjoyed a substantial following in Europe: *mercantilism* and *physiocracy*. The mercantilists saw the primary economic objective of any nation as maximizing its international balance of trade. They recommended government efforts to assist exporting industries and protect home industries from imports. The physiocrats believed that agriculture was the only economic activity that generated an economic surplus (return over cost) that could be used to pay for other amenities of civilization. This line of reasoning led adherents of this school of thought to recommend policies to support agriculture and the activities of landowning classes. While mercantilism continues to have some influence, physiocracy as a school of thought has all but disappeared.

Historical Foundations

Classical Political Economy

The origin of classical political economy coincided with, and indeed aided, the emergence of capitalism as a decisive force in Europe, especially England (Wolfe, 1981). The main theorists associated with the classical school—Adam Smith (1723–90), David Ricardo (1772–1823), Thomas Malthus (1766–1834), James Mill (1773–1836), and Mill's son John Stuart Mill (1806–73)—laid down the framework that still forms the cornerstone of liberal political economy.

Adam Smith's *Wealth of Nations* (1776) was the first book in political economy to lay out a complete, abstract model of the nature, structure, and workings of the capitalist system. According to Smith, the self-serving behaviour of individuals—deriving from the natural and universal human instinct for self-preservation and self-advancement—benefits not only those concerned but also the whole society. In his most famous passage Smith states: 'It is not from the benevolence of the butcher, the brewer, or the baker, that we expect our dinner, but from their regard to their own interest. We address ourselves, not to their humanity but to their self-love' ([1776] 1987, Book 1, ch. 2). According to Smith, each individual pursuing his own selfish interest is 'led by an invisible hand to promote an end which was no part of his intention' (Book 4, ch. 2). The underlying reasoning here is that if all individuals were better off as a result of advancing their own separate interests, the society they formed would also be better off. Smith argues that this process should take place without outside intervention, which would only discourage individual enterprise and thus diminish economic well-being. As such, Smith advocated policies designed to minimize interference by authority—Church or state—with individual freedom. In the more than 200 years of its subsequent development, liberal theory still retains the essence of these teachings.

Classical liberal political economists saw the *accumulation of capital* (profits) and resulting new investment in productive capacity as the growth-propelling force in the economy. What is actually accumulated is the 'surplus' left after paying for the costs of production. Liberal political economy postulates that the accumulation of capital is helped most by the establishment of conditions for making profits, which can be reinvested continuously to make even more profit, with the process leading to the increased material well-being of the entire society. The liberal theory thus originally focused on suppliers and the supply side of economics, unlike later developments in the theory that would attribute equal importance to both demand and supply.

Another important feature of classical political economy is its authors' varying degree of adherence to the *labour theory of value*, an idea developed formally by David Ricardo, though Smith had pursued it as well. This theory states that the prices of goods are strictly proportional to the value of labour embodied in them; a natural object has no value until human labour is applied to it, transforming it into a usable good or commodity. While capital goods (such as machinery) also contribute to value, they are themselves, like other consumer goods, embodiments of labour. As shall be discussed in Chapter Three, in developing the labour theory the classical economists created the noose upon which Karl Marx and other socialist political economists would try to hang the political-economic system liberals so assiduously nurtured. Not surprisingly, the labour theory was abandoned by later liberal political economists.

The theory of *income distribution* in classical political economy states that income is a function of whether an individual owns labour, land, or capital. Labour is paid wages according to what is required for its 'subsistence', defined as those commodities needed for the physical survival and reproduction of the workforce. Landowners receive rent, defined as the produce over and above the production costs of cultivating the least productive land (marginally productive land, in later parlance). The classical economists were, however, confused about profit. They could understand rent for the landlord and they could explain wages, but they could not explain that if labour created value, then for what reason did profit accrue to the capitalists? The implication was clear that profit was theft by another name.[1] While the classical economists recognized the unfairness of income distribution in capitalism, they did not oppose it because of their belief that the accumulation of profits was essential for expanding production, and that the benefits of this accumulation were spread by the market right across society, even though profits benefited the capitalists more than others.

The *theory of comparative advantage* developed by classical political economists still forms the basis of much modern international trade theory. While Smith referred to it, again it was Ricardo who developed the theory in its most sophisticated form. Extending the principle of free exchange to the international arena, the theory states that free international trade benefits both countries involved in a trade relationship. Competition resulting from free international trade confers benefits similar to its counterpart in the domestic economy because of the greater efficiency that competition engenders. So even if a country were more efficient than its trading partners in every type of economic activity, it would still be beneficial to concentrate on those goods in which its efficiency was the greatest and import the rest. This theory has been refined over the years—and is known as the Heckscher-Ohlin-Samuelson model in its present incarnation—but the underlying reasoning remains the same. It is on this ground, for example, that most liberal political economists support Canada's free trade agreement with the United States.

Marginalism and Neoclassical Economics

The publication of separate books with similar implications by Stanley Jevons (1965) and Carl Menger (1950) in 1871 and Leon Walras (1965) in 1874 marked the beginning of *marginalism* in liberal political economy. While little in their works was entirely new, these authors offered a new approach to the kind of liberal economic theory developed by the classicals. They theorized about the determination of prices, a question that had vexed their predecessors, and after stating the answer they explained the entire economy based on their postulates.

Marginalism argues that people receive utility (that is, pleasure or satisfaction) from consuming commodities (or services). However, the consumption of each additional unit gives increasingly less utility until a point of 'marginal utility' is reached, when further consumption yields no additional utility. So it is important to find out the marginal point at which consumption stops. Thus, a cup of water that normally has no value becomes exceedingly valuable when the stock of water has been depleted—during a drought, for instance—and only a cup remains. It is the value of the last unit of a product still sought by consumers that determines its price. Thus, the utility of any good or service diminishes with increasing availability, and, as such, it is the utility of the least wanted, the point of marginal utility, that sets the value for all units. The marginal value is the price of the product or service in question.

This apparently simple concept applies not only to consumers but also to producers. Producers continue to hire (demand) factors of production (that is to say, land, labour, and capital) until they reach the point when the hiring of an additional unit will provide no additional utility, and this point of marginal utility determines the overall level of rents, wages, and interest. These simple hypotheses about consumers' and suppliers' behaviour are meant to explain what is consumed and what is produced and how income is distributed in society.

The implications of this formulation are more serious than might first appear. Unlike the classical economists, who were searching for an answer to what 'created' value, the marginalists avoided the question altogether by simply assuming that value was the same as price, which was determined by the subjective preferences of producers and consumers. Using this theory meant that mainstream liberal political economists no longer had to wrestle with the revolutionary implications of the idea that labour was the source of value (Dasgupta, 1985: 15).

After the publication of *Principles of Economics* by Alfred Marshall in 1890, *neoclassical economics* quickly became the dominant mode of economic thinking and continues to form the essence of what we know as economics today. Neoclassical economics was nothing more than a formalized and technically refined statement of the marginalists' ideas, which for the most part were an extension of what had been said by the classical political economists. In neoclassical economics, economic decisions are viewed as representing the point at which demand and supply intersect, just as cloth is cut at the point—in Marshall's graphic analogy—where the blades of scissors meet. The understanding of how the prices of commodities and factors of production are determined answers all questions concerning what is produced and consumed and how income is distributed. The theory is indeed remarkable in its brevity, simplicity, and elegance; a few simple assumptions explain the operation of the entire economy.

In the simplified model of the economy found in neoclassical economics, the resources available to households and firms are assumed as given. The market is assumed to be perfectly competitive: that is, neither the producers nor consumers can directly manipulate prices. Consumers buy more when the prices are low, and firms supply more when the prices are high. The utility-maximizing consumers and the profit-maximizing producers are rational agents constantly juggling what they want to buy or sell in response to changes in price signals.

Prices are determined at the point at which demand equals supply; there will be a mismatch between the two at any other price. If the price is higher, supply will increase but the demand will be lower, resulting in a surplus. If the price is lower, demand will be higher but the suppliers will reduce supply, thus causing a shortage. Hence the perennially downward-sloping demand curve and the upward-sloping supply curve. In the case of changes in the level of demand or supply, the change is reflected in the price, which will adjust to a new equilibrium. When the demand and supply are at equilibrium, both consumers and firms are satisfied and there is no pressure for change. When the price of everything in the economy has been individually arrived at in this manner, the whole economy is said to be in equilibrium, and as a result neoclassical economics is sometimes referred to as *general equilibrium theory*. To reiterate, the mechanism applies not only to goods and services but also to the prices of labour (wages), capital (interest), and land (rent).

If the forces of demand and supply working through price signals in the market determine everything in the economy, there is very little role for outside intervention in the marketplace, such as by the state. This description, however, is a deliberate abstraction of a perfectly competitive market. When one or more conditions of a competitive market are not met, there is a role for outside intervention to correct the failure. As a result, liberal political economy has developed a theory of the state and requisite state activities to deal with these circumstances of imperfect competition and market failures at the micro-level of economic activity.

Neoclassical economics also has a specific vision of how the macroeconomy operates. Macroeconomics deals with the economy as a whole, especially economy-wide aggregates such as the level of employment, prices, national income, and the economic growth rate (Grant and Nath, 1984: 77). In the neoclassical conception of the macroeconomy, money flows from firms to the public in the form of wages, profits, interest, and rent. In turn, the public spends most of its earnings on consuming goods and services, thus transferring the money back to firms. What is not spent on consumption is saved. Savings in turn are invested in productive activity, and investment is the growth-propelling element in the economy. The rate of savings and the corresponding level of investment are determined by interest rates.

In orthodox neoclassical liberal political economics, the macroeconomy, like the microeconomy, exists as an efficient system in which the different economic components rest in perfect balance. There might be some maladjustments, but those problems are purely temporary because the market will eventually clear in the long run. According to this view, for example, in a competitive market the unemployment of capital or labour is not possible in the long run. If unemployment exists it is because workers are refusing to work unless they are paid more than the value of their marginal productivity. In other words, unemployment is voluntary. As such, there is no role for government intervention in the macroeconomy. The British economist John Maynard Keynes disagreed with this neoclassical conception of the macroeconomy and developed a new theory and new instruments to deal with macroeconomic market failures. Many liberal economists, however, continue to stick to the orthodox position, and the battle between Keynesians and neoclassical economists continues to represent a major division within the liberal camp.

In a matter of just a few decades neoclassical economics assumed a complete dominance over liberal political-economic thinking. Several factors nurtured its popularity. Primarily, it conveniently circumvented the question of what creates value, a question that had bedevilled the classical economists and dangerously suggested the importance of labour over all else in production. Its avoidance of this difficult question and its alternative focus on the question of price determination made it readily acceptable to most liberal economists. The theory also offered quantitative precision, which appealed to those searching for a 'science' of economics. The essential simplicity of the theory, combined with its ability to explain the complex interdependence of economic phenomena, made it almost irresistible. But perhaps its greatest charm was that it did not pose a threat to the status quo, as did its main alternative, socialist theory, itself an outgrowth of classical political economy but with a focus on the politics of production rather than the economics of exchange.

Welfare Economics

The interwar period (1919–39) saw the development of a new branch of economics that dealt with the conceptualization and analysis of imperfect competition. This branch is known as *welfare economics*, as it was inspired by *The Economics of Welfare*, an influential text written by A.C. Pigou towards the end of World War I. This version of liberal political economy emerged as a result of investigations taken by Pigou and others into how extensive state activities in Britain during World War I had resulted in the improvement of the economic welfare of the society as a whole. The term has nothing to do with social welfare programs *per se* but, rather, refers to the study of the conditions under which the welfare of the society as a whole can be improved.

The mainstream welfare economics theory is based on the norms of *Pareto optimality*—named after the Italian economist Vilfredo Pareto—which state that a social situation is optimal when no one person's position can be improved without worsening the position of another person. Social improvement in this sense is defined as movement from a non-Pareto optimal towards a Pareto optimal position. This matter of economic position is an ethical standard defining what is best for society, although it is not often recognized as such by adherents to the neoclassical orthodoxy. The theory derives from the branch of social philosophy called *utilitarianism* and rests on the normative assumptions that: (1) societal welfare depends on individuals' subjective sense of satisfaction, and (2) satisfaction is best achieved by letting individuals' preferences determine the use of societal resources (Rhoads, 1985: 62). Because people have different tastes there is no unique Pareto optimum, and infinite patterns of allocation are possible depending on the distribution of income and wealth in the society.

Theoretically, the prime example of a Pareto optimal situation is a perfectly competitive neoclassical market in which economic resources are allocated in the most efficient manner possible through the price mechanism. So long as the market is perfectly competitive, Pareto optimality obtains and there is no place for corrective measures, which would only upset the optimality. But when a market distortion is deemed to be inhibiting the realization of optimal results, the state should intervene to correct the distortion. The purpose of the intervention is to promote the optimal level of *economic efficiency* and hence overall social welfare.

Even Adam Smith had recognized that the market would not produce public goods such as street lighting or national defence. Because of this Smith had supported the provision of certain public goods by the state. But he saw such goods as exceptions to the general rule of production and allocation of societal resources through market mechanisms. It was only during the twentieth century that liberal economists began to discover the extent to which a market left on its own did not yield optimal results. With the passage of time, an increasingly large number of *market failures* had been detected, forming a justification among welfare economists for expanding the state's role in the economy.

One form of market failure is the emergence of *monopoly*, a condition that distorts competition and hence hampers the achievement of optimal results. In conditions of monopoly, the sellers or buyers are not price-takers—as they should be if competition is to prevail—but price-fixers. In fact, some industries such as electricity supply and telephone services (natural monopolies) are marked by increasing returns to scale, which means that a single firm can grow to dominate the industry. *Imperfect knowledge* among buyers and sellers also leads to market failure by yielding similarly non-optimal results from poorly informed consumption and investment decisions. In such situations, the welfare theorists argue, the government has a role to play in regulating monopolies and providing product and market information to buyers and sellers to facilitate the working of a competitive market, which is then expected to lead to Pareto optimal results.

Another variety of market failure is the existence of *externalities*, or spillover effects. Producers and consumers make economic decisions on the basis of how the decisions benefit themselves, but when they do so these decisions can have an adverse effect on others. For instance, a company dealing with dangerous chemicals might consider it more profitable to dump its waste in the public water system rather than paying for costly shipping and disposal. While this action would clearly be more efficient as far as the firm is concerned, it would be inefficient for the society as a whole. In such a situation, welfare economics suggests that governments intervene to contain industrial pollution. This is an example of *negative externality*, but there are also *positive externalities*, which the government is supposed to promote. Education, for instance, is a good that the market does not provide to those who cannot afford it even though the social benefits of a literate population are high; in such instances, it is argued, the government should intervene and support its provision. Later on, positive externalities requiring state intervention came to include activities such as support for infant industries and industrial adjustment.

Finally, markets cannot be expected to lead to an equitable distribution of income. People starting with more wealth will be able to secure a disproportionate amount of subsequent economic activity and economic benefits. If nothing else, the old and the infirm would find it rough going in a purely market-based society. This warrants state intervention to support some degree of income redistribution. However, this is a different form of state intervention, because it does not lead to Pareto optimality. In fact, it is a denial of the principle because it involves the improvement in conditions of the poor at the expense of the wealthy. Be that as it may, a limited degree of income redistribution is now an accepted part of welfare economics.

Keynesian Economics

The development of Keynesianism in the 1930s had an impact similar to welfare economics in detecting market deficiencies and extending the state's role in the economy. While the interventions inspired by welfare economics were of a *microeconomic nature*—that is, they dealt with particular market failures— Keynesian interventions were *macroeconomic*, aimed at adjusting the operation of the whole economy. The theory first appeared in the context of the Great Depression and was proposed by John Maynard Keynes (1883–1946) in *The General Theory of Employment, Interest, and Money* (1936).

In the process of analysing the Depression and proposing solutions to it, Keynes had to modify certain key assumptions of the neoclassical theory. The orthodox position—that in a competitive market unemployment of capital or labour was not possible, except when workers refused to work for market-determined wages—sounded like a cruel joke in the 1930s. During that decade unemployment in Europe and North America had reached between one-quarter and one-third of the workforce, and many individuals could not find employment even if they were willing to work for less than subsistence wages. But neoclassical economists and most politicians remained unswayed from their belief that allowing the market to operate freely—which would reduce wages to the level of workers' marginal productivity—was the only solution to the crisis. Keynes disagreed, arguing that the market does not always adjust automatically to create full employment of labour and capital. In cases when it does not, he said, the state must intervene to correct the situation.

Keynes said it was possible, as in the existing Depression, that aggregate demand and supply would equilibrate at a level less than optimal, leaving resources unemployed. This view, of course, contrasted with the orthodox neoclassical assumption that in the long run demand and supply were always at an equilibrium at the optimal point. Keynes saw the problem as arising from inadequate aggregate demand for commodities, capital, and labour. Inadequate demand, in turn, had its origin in the existence of savings that were not being invested because of a lack of business confidence. If businesses expect the demand for their product to be low, they cut back on their investment (which leaves unused savings) and lay off workers. The resulting unemployment reduces the workers' income, so in turn workers have to reduce their consumption, which leads to further cutbacks by businesses, thus locking the economy in a downward spiral of decline.

Keynes's solution involved the calculated use of government revenues and expenditures, or *fiscal and monetary policies*. To boost aggregate demand (for goods and services by consumers and for raw materials, labour, and capital by businesses), he argued that the government could increase the money supply, which would reduce interest rates and in turn cause firms to invest by borrowing from people's savings. The increase in demand caused by increased investment would put the economy in an upswing, and because of multiplier effects from new investment, the economy would gain momentum as it grew.

But Keynes did not believe this solution would be enough. He added that the government would also have to step in, borrow the excess savings (which businesses were not using) directly, and invest the money thus raised in public projects. These projects would create employment, which would lead to increased consumer spending and improve business confidence by promoting higher aggregate demand, which in turn would lead to increased production and higher investment by firms. Once economic growth had reached a point where it employed all the available resources, the government could cut back on its spending. Any budget deficit that might have been incurred in borrowing money to finance public projects would be paid back in the long run by the increase in tax revenues caused by increased economic activity.

Not surprisingly, orthodox neoclassical liberal political economists were suspicious of any theory that involved increased government intervention. But the outbreak of World War II vindicated Keynes. The preparations for war entailed increased government expenditures on military personnel and hardware, and the inadvertent result of this spending was the complete elimination of unemployment and the operation of the Western economies at full capacity. The increased state expenditures were financed largely through borrowings from the public (such as Canada Victory Bonds).

After the end of the war, many Western governments attempted to adopt Keynesianism as a normal theory of economic management. Keynesian tools—adjusting the level of money supply and/or public spending—were sometimes used or urged as an attempt to boost or slow the economy: governments sometimes felt the need to slow the economy to check inflation or 'overheating'. The policies came to be called the strategy of 'leaning against the wind' or 'fine-tuning', and the theory was eventually incorporated into the mainstream of liberal political economics. Nevertheless, doubts remained among some neoclassical economists, who were uneasy with any theory calling for increased state intervention in the economy.

While Keynesianism represented a major breakthrough in liberal economics, it should not be construed as a radical departure from the principles of neoclassical economics. Like its predecessors, it sees the government's role in the economy as no more than acting to correct the (macroeconomic) shortcomings of the market. Keynes had no quarrel with the microeconomic assumptions of neoclassical theory that a free, competitive market leads to the most efficient (optimal) allocation of resources or that income is paid according to the factors' marginal productivity. He did, however, reject the fundamental assumption of neoclassical economics that in the long run the market adjusts automatically to create full employment of capital and labour (Hunt, 1979: 395).

While the principles of the Keynesian proposals were not radical, the implications for the relationship between state and market were revolutionary. The maintenance of full employment provided a rationale, if only unintentionally, for the state to engage continuously in income redistribution without eroding the foundations of capitalist economies. This suited the aims of socialist and labour parties, in or out of government, very well. As Przeworski (1985: 36–7) argues:

> The fact is that social democrats everywhere soon discovered in Keynes' ideas, particularly after the appearance of his General Theory, something they urgently needed: a distinct policy for administering capitalist economies. The Keynesian revolution—and this is what it was—provided social democrats with a goal and hence the justification of their governmental role, and simultaneously transformed the ideological significance of distributive policies that favoured the working class. . . .
>
> And this was not yet all: Keynesianism was not only a theory that justified socialist participation in government, but, even more fortuitously from the social democratic point of view, it was a theory that suddenly granted a universalistic status to the interests of workers. Earlier, all demands for increased consumption were viewed as inimical to the national interest: higher wages meant lower profits and hence a reduced opportunity for investment and future development.

Transferring more income to workers was no longer seen as inimical to capitalism because the transfer gave workers more money to buy things produced by capitalists, who made profits in the process. This was surely a no-lose situation.

Or so it appeared until the 1970s, when sluggish economic growth made it difficult to pay for income-maintenance programs (Wolfe, 1977; Wolfe, 1981).

The enthusiasm of socialist governments in the West for Keynesianism is not without irony. As Anthony Arblaster (1984: 295) comments:

> Keynes was never a socialist, and did not see his policies as a strategy for socialism, but as the adaptation of capitalism that would enable it to survive crisis and retain the precious legacy of individualism. . . . Keynes [was] among many early twentieth-century radicals and liberals who did not consider themselves socialists because they were not, in the final analysis, anti-capitalist even if they were anti-*laissez-faire*.

Contemporary Debates

The contemporary debates in liberal political economy consist of three different yet overlapping strands: Keynesian-welfare, neo-conservative or neo-liberal, and post-Keynesian. The distinctions among them relate mainly to the extent to which they believe in self-regulating markets and the corresponding need or lack of a need for state action to correct market failures. The post-Keynesians propose the highest level of state intervention in the economy and the neo-conservatives the least, while the Keynesian-welfare theorists fall somewhere in between. The differences among them are significant in both theoretical and practical senses, but they are still all variants of liberal political economy that continue to promote individual property rights and the use of market mechanisms as the basic principle and instruments of political-economic organization.

Keynesian-Welfare Economics

Keynesian-welfare political economists acknowledge the shortcomings of the market and the role of the state in correcting those shortcomings, yet they would subject the state to efficiency tests before allowing it to intervene in the market process. The Keynesian-welfare analysts fully accept neoclassical assumptions regarding the operation of the market and its general superiority over the state as a mechanism for allocating and distributing economic resources. Yet they argue that there are specific circumstances in which the state might be more efficient than the market. They concede, following Keynes, that the operation of the market generates macroeconomic instabilities, which the state can and should balance. They also generally accept the principles of welfare economics as a guide for correcting microeconomic market failures.

However, the Keynesian-welfare theorists would have the state correct market failures only as a last resort. Since liberal political economy begins with the assumption of the greater efficiency of the market, there is a limit to how far any analyst working in the tradition can go in approving a permanent increase in the state's role in the economy. While Keynesian-welfare economists theoretically recognize the ability of the state to overcome certain shortcomings of the market, they are hesitant to recommend state actions in practice.

Macroeconomic stabilization meets with the Keynesian-welfare economists' approval, as do providing essential public goods, regulating the level of competition, and a certain degree of income redistribution. Beyond those basics, they evaluate government intervention in the area of externalities based on the criterion of efficiency; that is, the benefits to the society as a whole should be greater than the costs. Once the benefits have been determined, their choice of policy instrument leans towards the one that causes least distortion in the market.

Neo-conservative Economics

The neo-conservatives should more appropriately be called orthodox neoclassicals, neo-liberals, or ultraliberals given their resemblance to the early neoclassical liberals, but 'neo-conservative' is the term generally used in North America to describe them (McBride and Shields, 1993).[2] They are conservative only to the extent that they reject most of the modifications introduced in liberal economics since the turn of the century. Otherwise, except for a small minority, they do not necessarily favour Church supremacy, aristocracy, and traditional family values—the hallmarks of political conservatism. The neo-conservatives form a minority among professional economists, but their consistent reasoning and impassioned debating style (and friendly governments in certain countries) more than compensate for their small number. Some of them have gone on to win the Nobel Prize in economics, most notably Friedrich von Hayek, Milton Friedman, George Stigler, and James Buchanan.

While there are some differences within the neo-conservative school of thought—such as those among the monetarists, the supply-siders, and the new classicals—there are points on which they all agree. What distinguishes the neo-conservative economists is the supreme importance attributed to individuals and their freedom: they emphasize individual freedom even more than economic efficiency. They prefer the market to the state because the market is based on the principle of free choice among individuals whereas the authority of the state rests on coercion.

The neo-conservative economists believe in all the principles of undiluted neoclassical economics, including the principle of a self-adjusting market at both the micro and macro levels. Although they now present those principles in a more sophisticated form, the implication remains the same: keep the state out of the market. They concede that there might be instances of market failure, but they do not see state intervention as a solution. They believe that the only kind of market failure that should be corrected by the state is the provision of pure public goods (Rowley, 1983: 23), such as national defence and tax collection. They believe that other goods commonly provided by the state, such as street lighting, police, fire services, and parks and recreation facilities, can be 'partially' provided by the market (ibid., 25). Any public good that can be provided by the market, they argue, should be provided by it. The corresponding emphases on privatization and the 'downsizing' of the state are distinctive hallmarks of neo-conservative thought.

As far as the other market failures mentioned in the welfare economics literature are concerned, the neo-conservatives either disagree that they are failures or doubt that state intervention can correct them. In fact, they believe that the state is more likely to aggravate the situation because of the rigidities and inefficiencies of bureaucratic actions (Boyer, 1997). Even if the state turned out to be more efficient than the market in certain instances, many neo-conservatives would still reject state intervention in the market on grounds that this would erode individual freedom. Neo-conservatives also object to the use of the norm of Pareto optimality as a guide for state intervention because it does not explicitly forbid the state from entering areas that belong to the private realm of individuals. In the words of one ardent neo-conservative, Charles Rowley:

> Paretian welfare economics, by its concentration upon problems of market failure and by its explicit or implicit support for the notion of perfect government, has contributed not a little during the post-war period to the destruction of the liberal order in Western society. Yet further, the contributions of economists working in the field of social choice, masquerading in utilitarian guise, have encouraged the notion . . . of the 'dictatorial social decision-maker' which is totalitarian in nature and which is ends- rather than process-oriented in the best traditions of Marxist and Fascist dogmas. (Rowley, 1983: 28)

In contrast to the Keynesian preoccupation with maintaining full employment, the neo-conservatives strive towards price stability because of their belief that inflation is a greater economic evil than unemployment (Grant and Nath, 1984: 92). They view inflation as purely a monetary phenomenon that originates in the growth in the money supply, which in turn results from governments' need to finance constantly expanding expenditures. They argue that because the increase in money supply is unmatched by the growth in the supply of goods and services (that is, an increasing amount of money begins to chase a fixed amount of goods), inflation is the inevitable result. They therefore propose restraint in the money supply as a solution to inflation. The general slowdown in economic activity and the ensuing unemployment caused by the monetary squeeze are regarded as unavoidable, indeed necessary, for checking inflation.

In addition, neo-conservative economists believe that economies are characterized by a 'natural rate of unemployment'. A market economy always consists of people who at a given time are in the process of changing jobs and hence unemployed. Other people, they argue, are unemployed because of government measures such as minimum wage laws, unemployment insurance, welfare payments, and collective agreements negotiated by trade unions that inhibit job-seekers from accepting wages commensurate with their marginal productivity. Government measures to reduce unemployment, as proposed by Keynes, only serve to fuel inflation. The implication of this position is that the government is responsible for any unemployment above the 'natural' level. Accordingly, the solution to unemployment lies in eliminating the factors that inhibit the operation of labour markets, such as trade union rights, minimum wages, and unemployment and other welfare payments made by governments.

Another strand in neo-conservative economics is the focus on creating conditions conducive for expanding production. While the monetarist solution of reducing money supply works at the level of reducing aggregate demand, the supply-side measures work by expanding supply, that is, by increasing the total production of goods and services. Since it is the capitalists who organize production, neo-conservatives argue that the government should encourage them by reducing the taxes on their profits. This would lead them to expand production, which would generate not only additional profits but also more jobs and higher income for their workers.

The neo-conservative economists often go to great lengths to proclaim that their theories are 'value-free', 'positive', and 'non-ideological'. Regardless of these claims, their theories are as ideological as those they criticize. Neo-conservative theories are founded on an overwhelming faith in individualism and the universal benefits of the market and, as a corollary, on a doctrinaire opposition to state interference. Be that as it may, even the critics of neo-conservative political economy usually concede that its proponents are highly consistent in their analyses. No doubt they oppose welfare payments to poor individuals, but they also oppose subsidies to firms. What the neo-conservatives do not admit, however, is that implementation of their proposals would cause more hardship to the poor than to the owners of firms. Unlike the moderate mainstream Keynesian-welfare economists, whose theories often represent awkward efforts to reconcile market principles with extensive state intervention in the economy, the neo-conservative economists do not have to live with such dilemmas.

Post-Keynesian Economics

In contrast to the neo-conservatives, who call for a reduced state role in the economy, the post-Keynesians ask for its expansion. The origin of this line of thinking is said to lie in the works of, in addition to Keynes, Joan Robinson, Michael Kalecki, Nicholas Kaldor, and John Kenneth Galbraith (Gonick, 1987: 145). While clearly in the minority among contemporary liberal economists, this group forms a substantial force. The economic success of Japan is often cited by post-Keynesians as proof that capitalist economies need state guidance.

Post-Keynesians argue that the problems of advanced capitalism require more and not less state intervention in the economy. They argue that neoclassical economic theory was designed to account for an economy consisting of small firms and unorganized workers, which enabled market forces to operate efficiently without state intervention. With the rise of large corporations and trade unions, a self-correcting market is no longer possible. Given the changed circumstances, post-Keynesians say the market power of producer and labour, not the competitive forces of demand and supply, determines prices and wages (Cornwall and Maclean, 1984: 92).

Post-Keynesians view the manipulation of the market by huge corporations and trade unions as the source of economic problems. They say that inflation results from excessive wage increases secured by organized labour combined with the ability of firms to pass these costs on to consumers because of their monopolistic position in the market. To check this malady, post-Keynesians argue for a negotiated 'incomes policy' that would restrain wage demands in return for lower unemployment. The arrangement would be sponsored by the state and would involve a commitment by business and labour to hold back prices and wages. The corporatist political institutions in Scandinavia and Austria, and to a lesser extent in Germany and the Netherlands, are cited as models to be emulated.

In addition, the post-Keynesians propose active industrial and labour market policies. These would consist of formal co-operation among state, business, and labour to identify industries of the future and direct investments towards those industries. This would be accompanied by enhanced public subsidies for corporate research and development and retraining of workers to equip them to work in growing and new industries. In the meantime, while the industrial restructuring is taking place, it might be necessary to protect domestic industries from imports. The purpose of these measures would not be to retard market forces, but to assist them. Capital and labour would not be shielded from changing market forces but supported in anticipating the changes and becoming prepared for them (Crane, 1981).

An important variant of post-Keynesian political economy is *evolutionary economics*.[3] Adherents of this approach emphasize the role played by technological advance in economic growth and argue that complex interactions between governments, universities, and corporations lead to technological change and economic development (Dosi et al., 1988). Governments, they argue, should foster and promote the linkages existing in these 'national systems of innovation' that are ultimately responsible for employment growth and social progress (Nelson, 1993; Edquist, 1997; Anderson et al., 1998).

The post-Keynesian understanding of the market is not without its problems. It presumes that it is possible to predict market trends and plan accordingly, not an easy task as even the Japanese have been finding out since 1991. Markets, however, are notoriously unpredictable and formal co-operation among societal groups and the state must be highly flexible to respond efficiently to changing market conditions. Moreover, collaboration is not as costless a process as the post-Keynesians make it appear. Firms lose their autonomy to governments and labour, which constrains and restricts their management prerogatives, and they are unlikely to give up those prerogatives without resistance or compensation.

The State in Liberal Theory

The *raison d'être* of all liberal theories of political economy has been to maintain capitalism and rationalize the dominance of the market. But to be able to do so, liberal political economy has had to allow for the reality of an increasing state presence in the market. It is essentially a theory of the market that has had to include the state on grounds of contingency to perform functions that would not otherwise be performed. Liberal political economy contains two slightly different formulations concerning the state. The first is the idea of the *supplementary* or *residual state*: the notion contained in neoclassical and neo-conservative liberal political economy that the state should only undertake those activities—such as the provision of pure public goods—that markets cannot perform. The second is the notion of the *corrective state*: the idea found in welfare-Keynesian and post-Keynesian analyses that the state can act in a variety of other areas of market activity to correct micro- or macro-level market failures.

Significantly, both analyses undertheorize the state. They treat the state as an inert subject that ought to do whatever it is that the market cannot do. The state is not considered to be in any way constrained by the society in which it exists or by its organizational capacity (Schott, 1984: 60). In fact, the capacity of the state to act and the forces that act upon the state are usually not considered at all. Instead, it is usually simply assumed that the state, out of a concern for economic efficiency, can and will act either to provide goods and services or to correct market failures. The post-Keynesians are the only liberal political economists who avoid these overly simplistic conceptions of the motivations behind state actions.

The State in Neoclassical and Neo-conservative Economics

Liberalism's opposition to the state and preference for the market, which have been its most persistent features, must be understood in the context in which it was born. The feudal state was highly active in promoting the interests of landlords and mercantilists by keeping food prices high and providing special privileges to certain companies in the form of monopoly rights, protection from imports, and the backing of the armed forces. The Hudson's Bay Company and the East India Company are prime examples of such firms. Because these measures discriminated against the emerging capitalist class, a political-economic theory opposed to state intervention in the affairs of society was developed. Adam Smith proposed an economic system based on pursuit of self-interest by individuals rather than direction by the state: 'The ordinary revolutions of war and government easily dry up the sources of that wealth which arises from Commerce only' (Smith, [1776] 1987: 520). Smith argued that state interventions tend to misdirect resources and diminish their contributions to society's economic well-being; but he thought that the state's interest in expanding its control over society would prevail unless individuals in society prevented this behaviour from occurring by consciously restricting the size and activities of the state and promoting market exchange wherever possible.

The neoclassical economists continued this line of thinking. In both classical and neoclassical economics, the role of the state in the economy is to be residual and supplementary to the market. When the understanding of what the market cannot do itself expanded in the twentieth century, leading to the corresponding prescriptions of welfare economists and Keynesians for increases in state economic activity, the state was still assumed to be a cipher as well as omnipotent: an agency that takes orders from wise economists and then implements them faithfully, unencumbered by any societal or internal state forces. The state, for instance, should know that it is less efficient than the market in most instances and hence should defer to the market's superiority in organizing social relations. After all, what objectives other than the promotion of individual freedom and economic efficiency could the state pursue? But that is not all. The state should also be aware that there are selfish interests out there in the society, which would impose additional demands for goods and services on the state. Apparently, the state should also be able to resist such demands and consciously restrict its functions to providing public goods.

Curiously absent in this innocent conception is the recognition that the state itself might not be inert—a point argued forcefully by 'statist' theorists such as Theda Skocpol (1985) and Eric Nordlinger (1981)—and that the state might initiate actions for which there are no societal pressures; or that the converse might also be true, that the state might not be able to resist societal demands placed on it. More importantly, the state might not have the capacity to carry out its decisions. Simply to assume that the state should do no more than provide public goods is not an adequate starting point for an analysis of the role the state plays in society. A more fruitful line of analysis would be to recognize that economic efficiency is only one among many objectives of a state.

The neo-conservatives display a greater awareness of the reality of the state's existence in the market. The state, far from being 'an exogenous force, trying to do good . . . is [regarded as] at least partially endogenous and the policies it institutes will reflect vested interests in society' (Colander, 1984: 2). Neo-conservatives recognize that the state has a monopoly over coercion and that democracy provides self-interested individuals with the ability to press demands on the state, which the state (through its equally self-interested politicians and bureaucrats) is forever eager to meet. Voters need material benefits, politicians need votes, and the state's coercive taxation system is required to pay for it all (Buchanan and Wagner, 1977; Brennan and Buchanan, 1980). The result, according to neo-conservatives, is unmitigated economic inefficiency as states expand their activities into more and more areas of economic activity best left to market devices.

The neo-conservatives would weed out the problem—excessive state intervention in the economy—from its roots; they would impose clear limits on what the state can do. They would replace the present constitution with a 'Constitution of Liberty' (Hayek, 1960), which would provide for limitations on the power to tax, a legal requirement for balanced budgets, and a reduction in the public provision of goods (Rowley, 1983: 55–61). However, not much hope is held out for the adoption of such a constitution because (again) vested interests in society benefit from profligate governments. As a result, many neo-conservatives (Friedman, for example) would settle for a more limited program of reforms: public expenditures determined by benefit-cost considerations, tax rates that are kept fixed, and growth in the money supply fixed at a certain constant rate (Schott, 1984: 60). These proposals imply that the Keynesian instruments of activist fiscal and monetary policies will be taken away from the government and what little money is left to spend will be used only after econometric evaluations show that projected benefits of the proposed action will exceed estimated costs. In the words of David Wolfe (1981: 71), the state will assume the role of 'a disciplinarian, restraining individuals and enterprises for the sake of their mutual long-term interest'.

While more realistic than many of their predecessors, neo-conservatives continue to conceive of the state as an instrument whose only function is to promote economic efficiency and act as a supplement to the market. Their conception of political economy exaggerates the market's efficiency while continuing to undertheorize the question of state autonomy. More seriously, it suggests a vision of a thoroughly undemocratic state, since only a state detached from democratic electoral pressures would be able to go against the wishes of the people in the name of promoting economic efficiency through market mechanisms. Imposing restrictions on the government's ability to respond to democratically expressed demands would be a repudiation of many of the political advances made this century. There is also another ominous side to neo-conservatism: it rationalizes the dominance of those who benefit disproportionately from uncontrolled markets—the business community—over those who do not— the workers and the unemployed poor.

The State in Keynesian-Welfare and Post-Keynesian Economics

Keynesians and post-Keynesians recognize that as capitalism matured it encountered new problems requiring new solutions, many of them involving state intervention in the economy to correct the shortcomings of the market (Nell, 1988; Wolfe, 1981). By the end of the nineteenth century, the logic of market competition had taken its toll on small producers, and the industrial landscape was dominated by large corporations enjoying near-monopoly positions in the market. Similarly, the new trade union movement had begun to erode the employers' superior bargaining capacity *vis-à-vis* the workers. The product and labour markets were not as competitive as they once used to be, which posed problems for a theory developed to explain early capitalist societies.

Although welfare, Keynesian, and post-Keynesian economics justify and permit a substantial degree of state intervention in the economy, the market is still the favoured mechanism for determining production and distribution, and the state is to be employed only at times when the market is found to be inadequate. Even the post-Keynesians argue only for measures, no matter how interventionist, that reinforce and do not replace the market.

Keynesians would have the state hold back on fiscal expenditures and money supply in times of economic slowdown. Without these countervailing measures, the state would be prolonging the adverse effects of both economic booms and recessions. In welfare economics, the state's role is similarly confined to achieving Pareto optimality. Once a market failure has been identified, the government should intervene to correct it. The state should check any negative externalities through taxes, subsidies, or regulations. The state should either provide desirable public goods (merit goods) directly or subsidize their provision by the market. Monopoly behaviour by firms should be tackled through regulations.

The one feature common to all these recommendations is that they treat the state's objectives as given: the pursuit of economic efficiency. Why the state would pursue this goal and not others is unclear. After all, the state itself is embedded in the society it manipulates and that manipulates it. For instance, the state might decide, either independently or because of societal pressures, to develop a particular industry by offering subsidies regardless of what welfare economists argue would constitute an economic optimum. Similarly, if business and organized labour unite and forcefully demand that interest rates be brought down, few states would have the capacity to resist the demand on the grounds that Keynesian economic theory demands the opposite. As Kerry Schott (1984: 69) cautions: 'There is little to be gained from advising a state what it ought to do about economic policy if the state in question is not equipped, either institutionally or in motive, to follow such advice.'

What the state does in the economy is determined by what it is capable of doing, and its capacity for autonomous activity is conditioned by its own internal organizational structure and the organization of the economy and society in which it exists, including its international dimensions. The character of the state—such as whether it is internally cohesive or fragmented—and the character of the main social classes—the level of unity or fragmentation within capital and labour—shape what it can and cannot do. A state that is internally cohesive and enjoys the society's support can follow a coherent policy, if it chooses to do so. If it doesn't, it becomes subject to contradictory societal pressures, which are reflected in its role in the economy. In such circumstances it matters little in practical terms whether its actions promote economic efficiency in terms of welfare or Keynesian economics.

The post-Keynesians must be given credit for understanding the organizational constraints on the state's role in the economy. Their explanation of inflation and unemployment as being rooted in the lack of social consensus and their proposal for a greater degree of co-operation among state, business, and labour in managing the economy illustrate their sensitivity towards social institutions. The same holds true of neo-Schumpeterian views of the importance of constructing effective innovation systems for continuing economic growth and development.

Yet post-Keynesianism is not without its problems. References to the example provided by the political practices of corporatism in Sweden, for example, are ironic given the debate raging in that country regarding the future of its political economy, and those accounts say little about how Swedish institutions and processes are to be re-created in other countries. Any attempt to reform the state and societal institutions along corporatist lines will be constrained by the same fragmentations that are the source of the problems those institutions were expected to address in the first place (Panitch, 1979). Weak and fragmented institutions cannot be expected to undertake the establishment of cohesive institutions. If emulating Sweden or Japan were easy we would have seen a lot of nations adopting political-economic institutions patterned after them. Thus, the post-Keynesians can be said to be more successful in explaining the success of the political economy of certain capitalist nations than in prescribing solutions for the others that are less successful.

Liberal Political Economy in Canada

The high level of state involvement in Canadian economic development does not negate the Canadian political economy's primarily liberal character, nor does it prevent liberal political economists from retaining a basic market-oriented approach in their analyses. This is because intervention in Canada has always been directed at supplementing rather than supplanting the operation of the market. The mid-1980s Macdonald Royal Commission on the economic prospects of the country was correct in its observation that: 'The "positive state" tradition in our history, which has supported an influential role for governments in the economy, has nevertheless always assumed that most economic decision making will be in private hands' (Macdonald Commission, 1985, I: 47).

The dominance of liberalism in Canadian political and economic discourse is reflected in academic research and scholarly works in the area. In terms of the sheer volume of studies on Canadian political economy undertaken by economists, the liberals have been in a clear majority. The fact that it is easier to get research funds for projects following conventional approaches only partly explains the large output. Another reason is that the theory is in tune with the ethos of the politico-economic system it describes, which makes its explanations sound more reasonable than those taken from outside the orthodoxy.

Nevertheless, liberal political economy is neither homogeneous nor monolithic in Canada or elsewhere. Instead, liberalism includes a range of widely divergent approaches allowing for different levels and types of state intervention in the economy. We can classify the contemporary studies on Canadian political economy following liberal precepts into two broad categories: Keynesian-welfare and neoclassical or neo-conservative. While there are theoretical differences between the two, in practice these differences are superficial. They both arrive at conclusions, albeit through different routes, that permit only a minor role for the state in the economy.

Keynesian-Welfare Political Economy

The Keynesian-welfare school has been the most influential in Canada, and it has formed the mainstream among the analysts and practitioners of the liberal theory in this country. While there are significant differences among individual analysts, they are all middle-of-the-road liberals, willing to compromise and live with imperfect states and imperfect markets. The now-defunct Economic Council of Canada, the Institute for Research on Public Policy, and the C.D. Howe Institute have been some of the main research institutions promoting this approach to Canadian political economy.

A statement by Judith Maxwell, formerly the head of the C.D. Howe Research Institute and later of the Economic Council of Canada, illustrates the Keynesian-welfare 'principles' for defining the government's role in the economy. As this quotation shows, Maxwell is not opposed to government intervention in the economy as such, but would have state action bound by the efficiency criterion analogous to the market:

> First, government taxation, expenditure and regulation must nurture the incentives for individuals to be productive and for corporations to be efficient.
>
> Second, governments must respect resource constraint . . . . The spending must therefore be justified by an acceptable social rate of return.
>
> Third, governments must develop incentives for greater efficiency within their own organization, so that public servants are rewarded in some way for actions that improve the efficiency of existing programs and for applying more rigorous efficiency tests on new programs. (Maxwell, 1977: 12–13)

Although Canadian Keynesian-welfare political economists, unlike neo-conservatives, are not averse to using monetary and fiscal tools to stabilize the macroeconomy (Economic Council, 1983; Macdonald Commission, 1985), the high inflation of the 1970s did veer many of them towards favouring fiscal and monetary restraint, undermining the primacy of reducing unemployment as a policy objective and drawing their analysis closer to that of the monetarists (Bradford, 1998a). Even then, however, the Keynesian-welfare analysis did not advocate containing inflation exclusively through demand-restraint measures (squeezing money supply and sharply cutting back on government expenditures) that would adversely affect the weaker sections of the society by increasing unemployment (Economic Council, 1983: 13). Instead, it was suggested that some form of moderate post-Keynesian income policy be adopted whereby the state, business, and labour work together to contain demands for increases in wages and prices to keep unemployment low without fuelling inflationary pressures (Economic Council, 1983: 16; Macdonald Commission, 1985, II: 360).

At the microeconomic level, the Keynesian-welfare analysts in Canada favour only isolated state interventions to augment market forces. They usually support state interventions to facilitate adjustment to changed market conditions—such as assistance to industries, communities, and workers faced with dislocations because of changes in demand or technology. Since they favour microeconomic interventions that assist rather than suppress market forces, they are suspicious of industrial strategy proposals that seek to 'engineer' comparative advantage through manipulation of market forces, as is arguably done in Japan, France, and South Korea. Expressing its cynicism towards the state playing an activist role in shaping the economy, for example, in the early 1980s the Economic Council (1983) re-emphasized 'the merits of letting competitive [market] forces sort out the "winners" and "losers" in the domestic economy'. For the same reason, the Council was opposed to broad measures to promote manufacturing industries to reduce the natural-resource orientation of the Canadian economy. It argued that 'Canada must be less preoccupied with the manufacturing sector and ensure that trade opportunities are pursued in all sectors.'

The Council acknowledged the need for government assistance for industrial research and development in Canada. But to ensure economic efficiency it also emphasized the primacy of the market and the need for a cost-benefit analysis of government action (Economic Council, 1987). In keeping with the desire to adhere as closely to the market principle as possible, Keynesian-welfare economists recommend that assistance for research and development should not be targeted to particular industries, but should be made generally available to all industries engaged in research and development. Similarly, they favour higher expenditures on labour training and education in science and technology because these activities do not directly distort the market, as would measures directed at promoting the technological capabilities of certain 'winning' industries. They also support co-operation between the state and social groups on efficiency grounds, although not as strongly as do the post-Keynesians.

The concern for efficiency also guides the Keynesian-welfare attitude towards regulations and public enterprises (Economic Council, 1981, 1986; Macdonald Commission, 1985). The analysts recommend the elimination of the measures that cause inefficiencies. However, they do not issue a wholesale condemnation of the use of such instruments, as in the case of neo-conservative analyses.

The commitment to economic efficiency also leads most Canadian Keynesian-welfare liberal political economists to accept the doctrine of the theory of comparative advantage. They argue that hurdles to international trade promote economic inefficiencies, increase prices, and allow domestic producers to misuse their monopoly position, without doing anything to promote the long-term competitiveness of the protected industries. In the words of the Macdonald Commission (1985, I: 50), 'Our basic international stance complements our domestic stance. We must seek an end to those patterns of government involvement in the economy which may generate disincentives, retard flexibility, and work against the desired allocation of resources.'

The fact that a nation's exports might consist entirely of semi-manufactured or crude products does not concern these analysts because such exports generate national wealth just as much as manufactured products. In fact, they derisively describe those favouring manufacturing industries as having a 'manufacturing fetish'. Following from their belief in the theory of comparative advantage is their near obsession with free trade with the United States, an attitude they share with neo-conservatives. The reciprocal reduction in trade barriers, they argue, enables Canadian producers to produce for the continental economy and specialize in certain product lines; what is not produced domestically will be imported more cheaply from the US. Similarly, they do not oppose foreign investments, which (when inspired by reasons other than avoidance of tariffs), they argue, produce lasting employment and bring much needed capital and advanced technology. They do not attach much significance to the profits repatriated by parent firms or to balance-of-payment problems, which are deemed to be resolvable through adjustments in exchange rates.

The feature that most clearly distinguishes the Keynesian-welfare economists from their neo-conservative counterparts is their concern for social equity, which coexists with their concern for economic efficiency. The Economic Council (1983: 62), for example, asserted: 'Social goals and programs are not residual to the economic system. They contribute fundamentally to the smooth functioning of our economy, and they reflect the basic values of Canadians. Our economic and social goals and programs are not separable; nor are social goals subordinate to economic goals.' But even in matters related to equity, concerns for economic efficiency are not forgotten. Recent studies continue to emphasize the need for improving the manner in which governments deliver goods and services (Courchene, 1994).

A virtually exclusive concentration on economic factors, however, leads Keynesian-welfare political economists to serious omissions. The fact that they do not include power in their analysis, for example, leads them to make sterile recommendations that are virtually impossible to implement in a democratic society. In such a society, of course, questions about who will demand what from the state and how these demands will be articulated, interpreted, and responded to are resolved through the democratic process and associated state institutions. Canadian governments are affected by these processes and cannot simply refuse proposals for action that enjoy societal support on the grounds that they are inefficient. The reverse is also true: states cannot adopt proposals for action, however efficient they may seem in theory, if they do not enjoy societal support for this action.

There is also an inherent tension between the Keynesian-welfare emphasis on efficiency and the compromise on measures to promote equity. No theoretical argument in their repertoire can indicate exactly how much efficiency can be sacrificed to promote equity. To suggest that the government ought to correct inequities up to the point beyond which the public finds the resulting inefficiencies unacceptable does not make theoretical sense. If that were to be the case, then why stop at income distribution? Why not allow the same level of state intervention in every area of society? Such inherent contradictions are reflected in their policy suggestions, which satisfy neither the neo-conservatives nor those committed to greater social equality in the distribution of wealth.

Neo-conservative Political Economy

While true neo-conservatives form only a fringe element in Canadian politics and academia, their vociferousness makes up for their small numbers. They argue for economic efficiency, stress freedom, and disparage any argument based on equality other than the equality of opportunity to engage in market exchange or cast votes. They see measures to promote equality in income distribution—such as minimum wage laws, progressive taxation, government-provided universal health care, and education—as curtailments of individual freedom. They view the extension of the welfare state as an extension of the concept of 'social justice', which gained currency in the twentieth century.

The Vancouver-based Fraser Institute is one of the most well-known proponents of neo-conservativism in Canada. It has argued that 'The basic and most destructive implication of this concept [social justice] was that long-held doctrines of individual justice could be, indeed had to be, set aside in favour of the "higher goal" of justice for some collective' (Fraser Institute, 1983: 3). The Institute blames efforts to emphasize social justice over individual freedom as the main source of problems in the Canadian political economy. Accordingly, it calls on the government to move towards 'a renewed emphasis on individualism, a deep skepticism about the ability of government to do good and a growing awareness of government's ability to cause harm' (ibid., 6).

On the macroeconomic front, Canadian neo-conservatives are unabashedly monetarist. The Fraser Institute blames the high unemployment of the 1970s and 1980s on high wages, not deficiency of aggregate demand (Grubel and Bonnici, 1986). The Institute has repeatedly attacked inflation as the main economic problem affecting Canada. Following from its opposition to any government measure, it opposed wage and price controls during the mid-1970s because of their coercive nature (Walker et al., 1976).

The analysts associated with the Fraser Institute are similarly opposed to microeconomic interventions. They are vehemently opposed to industrial policies that would promote manufacturing industries (Watkins and Walker, 1981; Palda, 1979, 1984). Commenting on Alberta's industrial strategy, for example, Fraser Institute director Michael Walker stated: 'The economic structure of the province is predominantly reflecting the efforts of market forces and not a conjunction of factors the effects of which the actions for the provincial government can offset. The consequence is that intervention to foster diversification may be very expensive but in the end ineffectual' (1984: xiii). The Institute views the demand for greater spending on research and development as no more than a selfish ploy by the Canadian scientific community to improve its income and employment opportunities at public expense (Palda, 1979).

One of the chief targets of neo-conservative attacks is the trade union movement, which is viewed as developing coercive organizations that prevent market forces from setting wages. In the neo-conservative view, trade unions artificially bid up wages, which causes economic inefficiencies and fuels inflation. The neo-conservatives are not, however, opposed to monopolies—which would also seem to bid the prices of outputs above market levels—because they believe that even a monopolistic firm is under competitive pressure. When competition is lacking, it is because of government policies inhibiting competition.

Another popular subject of neo-conservative attack is government debt and any kind of deficit government budget. Fundamentally opposed to Keynesianism, neo-conservatives argue that government deficit financing restricts the amount of capital in the economy, driving up interest rates and removing a ready source of consumer spending and private-sector investment (Grubel et al., 1992). The solution proposed involves privatization of public enterprises, contracting out of many public services, and large-scale general cuts in government employment and expenditures (Richardson, 1995).

One of the more creative applications of neo-conservative theory centres on government measures to promote non-discrimination in the workplace (Block and Walker, 1985). Neo-conservatives argue that employers with the proclivity to discriminate have to pay more to hire workers of their preferred race, sex, or colour. This leads those employers to become uncompetitive with the companies that do not discriminate and hence do not have to bear the additional wage costs. Ultimately, the discriminators will stop indulging in their prejudices or be wiped out by competition. Among other things the analysis does not address how this process will occur in an economy that has more than enough unemployed workers from the employers' preferred group looking for jobs.

On international trade, the neo-conservative position is similar to that of the Keynesian-welfare liberals. The Canada-US and North American free trade agreements were supported equally fervently by both the schools; indeed, enlarged free trade was backed by virtually all liberal political economists (Globerman, 1991).

Unlike the mainstream liberals who are constantly haunted by their conflicting adherence to economic efficiency through the market and their recognition of the need for state intervention to deal with social problems, the neo-conservatives have no such dilemmas. Nor do they need to cope with the difficulties of managing state planning, having ruled that out in the first place.

Post-Keynesian Political Economy

The post-Keynesian school emerged in Canada in the 1970s for the same reasons as it did in other industrialized nations: the simultaneous existence of high rates of inflation and unemployment at the macroeconomic level and problems faced by many declining industries at the microeconomic level. These problems refused to respond to measures inspired by Keynesian and welfare economics— measures that, as we have seen, came under attack from neo-conservatives as being at the root of the problem. The post-Keynesian solution of enhanced state intervention appealed to liberal analysts who found the neo-conservative prescriptions unacceptable because of the hardships they imposed on the weaker sections of society. Post-Keynesianism also appealed to many social democrats and staples theorists because it offered solutions to reduce US dominance of the Canadian economy and further the interests of the subordinate classes without overthrowing capitalism. Many of the scholars associated with the Canadian

Institute for Economic Policy, Science Council of Canada, New Democratic Party, and Canadian Labour Congress can be classified as post-Keynesian in their approaches to political economy.

After identifying high levels of unemployment and slow economic growth rates as the main problems of the Canadian economy in the early 1980s, John Cornwall and Wendy Maclean, two prominent post-Keynesians in Canada, offered this 'package' of solutions:

> First, an incentive incomes policy, preferably with some measure of real wage insur-
> ance, must be designed that will receive widespread support from labour. Second, a
> stimulative aggregate demand policy is needed as evidence of a commitment to full
> employment, coupled with assurances that there will be no cutbacks in the welfare
> state. Third, there must be an industrial policy that incorporates as a long-term
> strategy the development of institutions and attitudes fostering cooperative indus-
> trial relations. Fourth, programs must also be included that greatly assist research
> and development, and encourage investment in the manufacture of goods with high
> income elasticities of demand, so that new products and processes will allow faster
> productivity growth and the development or expansion of international markets for
> Canadian manufacturers. (Cornwall and Maclean, 1984: 96)

They expected adoption of these recommendations to stimulate economic growth, thus reducing unemployment, without fuelling inflation. Post-Keynesians, however, are aware that adoption of these policies would require fundamental changes in attitudes among existing interests in society: 'These changes involve a vastly different attitude by capital, labour and the general public towards the federal government and its role in ensuring the proper functioning of the Canadian economy, and a radical change in attitudes that employers and labour groups now hold towards each other' (ibid., 97).

Post-Keynesians see public opposition to expansion of the state's role in the economy as a problem that must be overcome. Similarly, capital and labour must give up their antagonistic attitudes towards each other. Exactly how this change in attitudes is going to come about remains a mystery.

The Canadian Institute for Economic Policy promoted similar policy options (Rotstein, 1984). It opposed monetarism and trade liberalization and, instead, proposed an incomes policy and some protection for domestic import-competing industries. It also called for an interventionist industrial policy to channel invest-ments away from declining industries towards growing industries and research and development. As a part of its industrial policy it recommended restrictions on foreign firms operating in Canada. It recognized that its comprehensive battery of measures would require a broad 'social consensus' lacking in Canada, but again it offered no concrete proposals for overcoming this problem.

Many former members of the New Democratic Party have also proposed post-Keynesian solutions to Canada's economic problems in opposition to the NDP's more orthodox Keynesian programs and policies. In *Rethinking the Economy*

(1984) James Laxer argued the post-Keynesian position strongly. He located the problems faced by the Canadian economy in the country's weak manufacturing sector and high levels of US investment. To rebuild the economy, he proposed a concerted effort to reduce the influence of US capital, especially through the mobilization of domestic savings by the federal government to promote investment in 'those sectors of the economy where domestic and export markets have great potential'. This effort would be led by public enterprises and would involve restrictions placed on the activities of foreign corporations operating in Canada. Laxer, like other post-Keynesians, suggested that the labour movement would have to abandon its historical reliance on the adversarial system and learn to co-operate with government and business in accepting technological change. The union movement's emphasis should shift from preservation of working conditions and jobs to aiding labour adjustment through retraining (Crane, 1981, 1992).

More recently, the federal Liberal government has endorsed several aspects of the neo-Schumpeterian emphasis on science and technology as driving forces in the economy (Canada, Industry Canada, 1994a, 1994b). Focusing on weaknesses in Canada's national innovation system that arise from poor performance in research and development (Niosi, 1991a), the government has committed itself to make substantial investments in research infrastructure and to provide tax incentives to corporations to undertake similar investments (Liberal Party of Canada, 1993)

Once again, however, this version of a post-Keynesian analysis has little to say about the resilience of political and social institutions and their capabilities for resisting change. The analysis ignores the fact that Canada does not have the institutional base required for the co-ordination and co-operation of the state, labour, and capital in establishing government policy directions—no matter how imperative it is for the growth and development of Canadian society that they do co-operate (Howlett and Ramesh, 1993). Similarly, it fails to appreciate the manner in which national innovation systems are embedded in international ones (Niosi and Bellon, 1994), as well as the need for both the federal and provincial governments (into whose jurisdiction falls education) to co-operate in this area (Niosi, 1991b).

Notes

1. The classical economists were surprisingly candid in admitting how people derived their income in capitalism and how the arrangement discriminated against labour. On various occasions Smith said that rent and profits were 'deductions' from the produce of labour, that landlords 'love to reap where they never sowed', and that their profits 'bear no proportion to the quantity, the hardship, or the ingenuity of the capitalist's labour of inspection and direction.' He observed that in a contest between capitalists and workers for higher income, the workers always lose because they do not have the savings to hold out for long against the

capitalists. Although Ricardo was a much more detached scholar than Smith, even his theory showed the inverse relationship between profits and wages. Furthermore, he was aware that the introduction of machines in the production process reduced the wages available to pay labour while increasing the level of profit. John Stuart Mill went further than the others and saw private property as the result of conquest and violence. He was appalled by the 'suffering and injustices' of capitalism but at the same time believed that it could be improved by limiting population growth and making education universally available.

2. Europeans tend to use 'neo-liberalism' and Australians 'economic rationalism' to refer to what is known as neo-conservatism in North America.

3. This approach is sometimes referred to as 'neo-Schumpeterian', after the Austrian-born Harvard University economist Joseph Schumpeter. In his work during the 1930s on business cycles, Schumpeter stressed the role played by technical innovations in triggering new cycles of invention and social change (Schumpeter, 1964; Nelson and Winter, 1982).

Chapter 3

Socialist Political Economy

If liberal political economy has been dominant among the industrialized nations at the level of both theory and practice, socialist political economy has served as the dominant model for many of the remaining nations of the world throughout most of the twentieth century. Over a third of the world's population has been ruled by governments calling themselves socialist. Even in capitalist nations, especially in Europe, there are or have been governments that profess to be socialist. In Canada, the New Democratic Party—which at various times has governed British Columbia, Saskatchewan, Manitoba, and Ontario—professes a form of socialism. In nations where there has been no socialist party in government or forming a strong opposition party, a good number of intellectuals and workers have worked towards this end.

Socialist political economy is a critical theory: it developed out of the same roots in classical political economy as liberalism did, but it has always maintained a guarded distance from capitalism. Unlike liberal political economy, socialist political economy has never embraced capitalism as a model but has instead focused on the inequities of a market system of exchange and how that system operates to the benefit of some groups and individuals in society at the expense of others.

This has been socialist political economy's greatest strength and its greatest weakness. It has been its greatest strength because from the very beginning it has pointed out the gaps between liberal theory and the actual practices of market societies. Unlike liberal political economy, socialist political economy has never endorsed the neoclassical model of a perfectly competitive economy and has not had to debate the validity of incorporating market failures into abstract models of market behaviour. For similar reasons, socialist political economy from the outset has recognized the importance of the state's extensive activities in the market. It did not require a major 'revolution' in socialist thinking to incorporate state actions into its theory of political economy, as was the case with twentieth-century liberal political economy. Socialist political economy, then, fared much

change oriented

better than did liberal political economy in its description of the actual workings of a capitalist political economy. From the outset socialist political economy could deal fully with questions about monopolies, market failures, and state 'interventions', questions that continue to perplex liberal political economy.

Nevertheless, that same critical stance proved also to be the theory's greatest weakness, because the general condemnation of capitalism led inevitably to the proposal that capitalism be replaced with an entirely different system of organizing production in society: a socialist or communist system based on extensive if not complete state control over productive activities. Rather than propose reforms to capitalist economies or engage in extensive empirical investigations into how such economies have developed, many socialist political economists have chosen simply to criticize the existing system and to suggest that the problems can only be solved by capitalism's complete replacement. Exactly what this replacement would look like is unclear, and so is the method by which capitalism would be overthrown and socialism achieved. Much work in socialist political economy, therefore, has concentrated on these questions,[1] for the most part forfeiting the field for suggestions about moderate or piecemeal reforms to liberal political economy. Not surprisingly but somewhat incongruously, many moderate socialists have been heavily influenced by liberal political economy and have embraced many of the analyses and positions put forward by Keynesian-welfare liberals calling for limited increases in state-led economic development. In fact, in Canada and elsewhere, the positions and reforms advocated by the most moderate socialists—social democrats—are virtually indistinguishable from those of mainstream liberal welfare-Keynesians discussed in Chapter Two.

As a theory, socialism is an alternative to the liberal theory, with its own comprehensive explanation of the interrelationships between politics and economy. Moreover, socialist theory does not rest on the study of the allocation and distribution of resources by an abstract market mechanism, as does the liberal theory, but also inquires into the historical, social, and political conditions under which markets operate, whom they benefit, and how they can be changed. While this approach provides a better understanding of political economy, it also presents problems for students trying to understand the theory itself. Problems of understanding are further increased by the substantial differences existing among the various socialist theorists themselves.

Nevertheless, a core of interrelated concepts informs all socialist political economy. These concepts are based on the works of Karl Marx (1818–83) and his long-time collaborator Friedrich Engels (1820–95), especially on the critique of capitalism put forward by Marx in *Capital* (*Das Kapital*). The first volume of *Das Kapital* was published in 1871, at about the same time marginalist and neoclassical economics were being established. Volumes two and three were published posthumously by Engels.

Socialist political economy must be understood in the context of its beginnings in the mid-nineteenth century, when capitalism was already a dominant economic system in many European nations. While capitalism increased the nations' total wealth wherever it spread, earlier expectations that this would improve general living conditions began to appear increasingly illusory. Instead, capitalism created an ever-expanding working class dependent on the capitalists for meagre wages. The extreme disparities in wealth between the capitalists and the working class led many early socialist thinkers to develop ideas about improving the living conditions of the working poor. Their recognition that the individualism fostered by capitalism was at the root of the problem led them to propose social co-operation instead of market competition as a solution. They believed that once the unfairness of the system was pointed out, the capitalists would show compassion and curb their excesses. Marx, however, believed that it was not the attitude of the capitalists but the nature of capitalism itself that was at the root of the problem and that the only solution was its replacement by socialism. Thus, just as liberal political-economic theory can be understood as an attempt to maintain and promote capitalism, the socialist theory based on the works of Marx can be seen as an effort to demonstrate capitalism's weaknesses and accelerate its demise.

After Marx's death various efforts were made by socialist political economists to apply his methodology and conceptual analysis of the structure and dynamics of a capitalist economy to the investigation of the continuing development of capitalism. Discussing the development of socialist political economy after Marx, however, is a daunting challenge; writings in this area have been many, and many of them are inconsistent. The task is made somewhat simpler, however, by a focus on the institutions of states and markets and their effects on the production and distribution of societal resources. Many of the writings in the socialist tradition since Marx have been concerned with other elements of his writings, such as their methodological, philosophical, ontological, and epistemological bases, rather than with questions pertaining to the production and distribution of wealth in society (Jay, 1973; McLellan, 1979). Nor, since the Canadian political economy is a capitalist market economy, do we need to examine the plentiful works of those scholars working in socialist countries who have grappled with the complexities of applying Marxist principles to actually existing socialist economies (Berry, 1977; Nove, 1986; Brus, 1973; Horvat, 1982).

Two post-Marx socialist theories are, however, relevant here. The first concerns efforts made by communists such as Vladimir Lenin and Rosa Luxemburg prior to World War I to expand Marx's insights to the global level in their evaluation of the workings of the then imperial-colonial international political economy. These writings and insights in turn had a great influence on the development in Africa, Asia, and Latin America of theories of *dependency* or *underdevelopment*, which once again, following the demise of the old international system during World War II, attempted to link developments in peripheral countries with economic activities originating in the industrialized world.

The second strain of socialist political economy is a *social democratic* variant concerned with theorizing the transition of capitalist economies from a competitive to a 'monopoly' stage. Such writings and theories focus attention not on the extension of capitalist relations from Europe throughout the world but on the implications for domestic politics of the increasing concentration of capital and the decline of the competitive capitalist economy that Marx had so thoroughly analysed. These analyses of the development of *monopoly capital* have had a great influence on the development of contemporary European and North American socialist thought.

Fundamental Tenets

Socialist political economy is based on Marx's historical analysis of economic institutions and processes. Marx criticized liberal economists for lacking a historical perspective, which led them to view capitalism as a timeless, universal economic system. Had they studied history, Marx argued, they would have found that capitalism was preceded by other forms or *modes of production*, such as feudalism and slavery, each of which grew out of a previous form of political-economic organization. It follows that capitalism itself is subject to change and eventual replacement by another system, which Marx argued would be socialist or communist in nature—that is, in which property and production would be socially or communally owned and controlled.

For Marx, the specific details of the various modes of production vary across nations and time because of the particularities of each nation's history. Marx was also aware that in the period of transition from one mode of production to another, the economy and society will exhibit the features of several modes. Because different modes of production may coexist for lengthy periods of time, the form of society existing at any particular point in time, or *conjuncture*, is sometimes referred to as a *social formation*.

Marx viewed history as humankind's struggle with nature to improve its living conditions. Unlike animals, human beings do not adapt to nature as they find it. Instead, they constantly seek to change it and improve their living conditions. According to Marx, the material or economic structure of production was the 'base' of other aspects of the society—such as laws, politics, ideology—which formed a secondary 'superstructure'. These attributes of human society vary according to the particular nature of the social formation present in any given country. The fundamental 'base-superstructure' relationship, however, always exists and is captured in Marx's reference to the superstructure as the *relations of production*. The relations of production have their roots in, and are determined by, the material conditions or *means of production*. In Marx's own words, 'The mode of production of material life conditions the social, political, and intellectual life process in general. It is not the consciousness of men that determines their being, but, on the contrary, their social being that determines their consciousness' (Marx, [1859] 1974a: 182). This statement must not be understood in terms of economic causes and superstructural effects, which would amount to a crude form of economic determinism or 'economism' that Marx himself rejected. Rather, Marx merely intended to indicate, without denying that the two are mutually interactive and interacting, that the economic structure is more fundamental than political and social institutions and ideas in the analysis of human history. Recognizing the common misunderstanding of Marx's position and its reduction to economism, Engels explains it thus:

> According to the materialist conception of history, the *ultimately* determining element in history is the production and reproduction of real life. More than this neither Marx nor I have ever asserted. Hence if somebody twists this into saying that the economic element is the *only* determining one, he transforms that proposition into a meaningless, abstract, senseless phrase. The economic situation is the basis, but the various elements of the superstructure . . . also exercise their influence upon the course of the historical struggles, and in many cases preponderate in determining their form [though not the substance]. (Engels, [1890] 1972: 640)

In fact, for Marx and Engels and all socialist thinkers influenced by their works, the motive force in history is essentially political—as suggested by Engels's reference to the importance of 'historical struggles'.

For Marx, the nature of social groups is intimately linked with the means and relations of production found in society. At least theoretically, each mode of production involves the differentiation of the populace into those who control economic surpluses and those who generate them. These two groups or *classes* are engaged in a constant struggle with each other over the division of surplus. The exact character of class stratification and the nature of class conflict in any given society, however, differ in the different modes of production, depending on the innate characteristics of each mode. Thus feudalism generates its own unique classes and class struggle, as does capitalism. The number of classes and their relationship to each other are made more complex by the fact that different modes of production can coexist in different social formations, making the analysis of the class content of any society a complex and difficult matter.

Each mode of production has its own technology and social relations for organizing production, and these have a pervasive impact on every aspect of the society. Marx regards the history of humanity as a succession of different modes of production. Each was appropriate in its time but gradually lost its usefulness and was eventually replaced as a result of *class struggles*. Thus, for example, feudalism was marked by a technology and landlord-serf/tenant relationship suitable for agricultural production, and the social, political, ideological, and religious ideas and institutions of the time were geared towards its maintenance. Over time, the feudal mode of production and especially the feudal relations of production became a barrier to increased production because they prevented the reorganization of production and the introduction of more productive technologies. Struggles between the peasantry, the aristocracy, and the emerging urban trading and manufacturing class led to the demise of the old system and its replacement with a new system, capitalism, in which the relations of production corresponded more closely with the ability of society to produce commodities.

Private property, labour mobility, economic and political dominance of the capitalists, and the extensive use of machines and a specialized division of labour all were features of the capitalist mode of production and were reflected in liberal theory, government policy, and an ideology that served to legitimize and rationalize the existing political-economic order.

In Marxist theory, then, 'class' is understood somewhat differently from its meaning in everyday use. The term is often used to distinguish between the rich and the poor, the classes of 'haves' and 'have-nots'. It is also used to refer to those wielding power and those excluded from it, the classes of powerful and powerless (Ossowski, 1963). Marxist theory is only indirectly concerned with wealth or power. It refers directly to the 'groups of people sharing a common relationship to the means of production'. In every mode of production (except the 'primitive' mode in ancient times and the post-capitalist 'communist' mode) there are people who own the tools and facilities of production and those who work for them. Therefore, owners are in a unique position to exploit the workers. In feudalism, the landlords owned land, which serfs or tenants tilled, and a part of the resulting produce accrued to the owners. Capitalism, too, is marked by the existence of two broad classes, the capitalist class and the working class; the former owns the means of production, the latter works for wages. Within the two broad classes, there are numerous subclasses or 'class fractions' that occupy intermediate positions. These include managers, who do not own factories but act as the representatives of the capitalists at the factory. There are also small-time capitalists, such as corner-grocery-store owners, who own their own means of production but do not usually employ workers. Marx sometimes referred to this broad grouping of capitalists and those sharing similar economic interests as the *bourgeoisie*. Correspondingly, there are unemployed, poor, and self-employed artisans who neither work for anyone nor exploit others and generally have interests in common with the working class. Marx sometimes referred to this broad category of workers and those sharing similar economic circumstances as the *proletariat*.

The existence of classes at the polar ends of the production process (as well as at positions in between) breeds class conflicts. As Marx puts it in the *Communist Manifesto*: 'The history of all heretofore existing societies is the history of class struggles.' The existing distribution of the ownership of the means of production and the wealth and power that go with it are opposed by those who are denied the benefits and defended by those who gain. At times this precipitates open revolts or revolutions. More often, the struggles manifest themselves in more subtle forms, such as political, ideological, and religious conflicts. Examples of such struggles include the support for liberalism by the bourgeoisie and opposition to Sunday-shopping laws by small-store owners or to minimum wage laws by all employers. Similarly, the support for socialism, old age pensions, unemployment insurance, progressive taxation, and collective bargaining rights by the proletariat can also be seen as a manifestation of class struggle. Marx does not attribute the source of the conflicts to the heartlessness of the landlords or capitalists but to the intrinsic nature of a mode of production.

Historical Foundations

Marx's Political Economy

Like the classical economists, Marx set about to inquire into the origin of value. When a commodity is produced, he asked, what gives it a value? This is an issue that liberal economists from the marginalists onward have sidestepped, assuming that value was the same as price, which is determined by the forces of demand and supply. But Marx, and Ricardo before him, faced the question head on and concluded that labour is the source of all value. Marx uses several hundred pages in *Das Kapital* to explain how he arrived at his *labour theory of value*, and here we will simply note the major strands in his reasoning.

Unlike Smith and, especially, Ricardo, Marx was not concerned about showing labour as the common element in all products, which would enable labour to be the key for determining the exchange ratio of goods. For example, two chairs exchange for one desk or a chair sells for five dollars and a desk for ten dollars because it takes twice as much time in labour to produce a desk compared to a chair. Marx went beyond this distinction to show that the creation of value entails the creation of *surplus value*, which, under capitalism, accrues to capitalists as profit.

Marx argued that in the long run the value (or *true* price) of a commodity is equal to the amount of direct and indirect labour embodied in it; the surplus labour (which is what yields profit) is included as a part of direct labour. While the concept of direct labour (which Marx calls 'variable capital') is the same as what we commonly understand by the word 'labour', indirect labour ('constant capital' in Marx's phraseology) is understood as the labour embodied in the various capital and intermediate goods involved in the production of a commodity, for example, machinery and raw materials. Marx regarded capital as indirect labour because, as in Ricardo's theory, it embodies 'frozen' labour or labour that was performed in the past. For Marx, surplus value, which is something akin to profit, was the result of the surplus labour employed in production.[2]

Marx recognized, as did the classical economists, that profit is the engine of economic growth in capitalism. He therefore made it the centrepiece of his analysis, although he rarely uses the word. Instead, he speaks of surplus value, because he regarded profit to be part of a surplus over and above what the capitalist pays for labour's contribution to production. In capitalism, the means of production (machines and raw materials, for example) are owned by the capitalists while the workers own labour power, or the capacity to work. Lacking ownership of the means of production, the workers cannot engage in production on their own and, hence, must sell their labour to the capitalists or starve. While the capitalists need labour just as much to carry out production, they are not faced with starvation if they interrupt it. The relative weakness of the workers allows capitalists to exploit them by denying them a full reward for their contribution to production. As Adam Smith notes in *The Wealth of Nations*, 'In the long-run the workman may be as necessary to his master as his master is to him; but the necessity is not so immediate' (Smith, [1776] 1987: 169).

Building on these assumptions, Marx argues that capitalists pay the workers not an amount equivalent to their creation of value but an amount necessary for the workers' subsistence; and capitalists appropriate the rest as profit. By *subsistence*, Marx meant some socially defined consumption norm rather than physical subsistence, even though at times he appeared to suggest the latter. Marx was aware that it was theoretically possible for workers to bid for wages above subsistence levels because of their indispensability to production, but he argued they were not usually able to do so over the long term because of the existence of a large pool of unemployed workers (the 'reserve army of the unemployed', as he called it) who are instrumental in driving wages down to a subsistence level.

To understand how surplus value is created and appropriated, imagine a worker who has to perform six hours of work to subsist. A capitalist who owns the means of production can compel that worker to work for ten hours while paying for only six. The value of what is produced during the extra four hours is a surplus over and above what the worker is paid and accrues to the capitalist as 'surplus labour', or profit.

In Marx's theory, the employment of capital itself creates no additional value and hence no surplus value, because the surplus value created in its production had already been appropriated by the original capitalists. Thus, the only way a capitalist can increase surplus value is by increasing the productivity of labour or by forcing workers to work longer hours, that is, through the generation of *relative* and *absolute surplus value*, respectively.

Once the capitalist mode of production is established, it gradually spreads to every sphere of economic activity because of its efficiency in organizing production and generating surplus value. The capitalists do not, however, consume the entire income derived from appropriation of surplus value. The logic of capitalism is such that they must save a good part of the surplus to be able to invest in expanding production, in hiring more capital, more sophisticated technology, and more labour, so they can accumulate yet more surplus. The nature of competition is such that the capitalists must be increasingly competitive or face extinction at the hands of their competitors. The resulting increase in the accumulation of capital, while essential for the maintenance and growth of capitalism, also sets in motion forces that undermine its existence. According to Marx, the unrelenting competition and accumulation have four consequences: economic concentration, the tendency of the rate of profit to fall, sectoral imbalances, and the alienation and growing misery of the working class. Together these tendencies cause crises of capitalism and its eventual demise.

As capitalism develops and becomes more competitive, only the strong firms survive, while the weak are either absorbed or decimated by the strong. Moreover, as technology improves, so, too, does the cost of starting a new business or operating an existing one. New firms cannot enter the market because of the high start-up costs, and the weaker existing firms disappear because they do not have the accumulated capital to finance the purchase of new technology. What remains are large firms, which are more competitive because of their lower per unit costs (referred to as 'efficiency of scale' by economists) and their greater ability to finance the purchase of the latest technology. This process is referred to as *economic* or *industrial concentration*.

The increasing capital-intensity of production creates additional problems. No doubt a firm introducing a new technology can make additional profits; but this increase is only temporary, lasting only until competing firms adopt the same or better technology and whittle away the windfall profits. The process continues, and no firm comes out better as a result. Another, and more ominous, consequence is the increase in the capital-to-labour ratio. The decreasing proportion of labour to capital yields a declining rate of profit because each new investment, unless accompanied by increases in labour productivity, generates the same amount of surplus value as before, simply replacing 'living' labour with the 'dead' labour congealed in machinery. Thus, when profits are compared to investments, higher investments produce only a similar amount of value and therefore the ratio of profit to investment declines. This leads Marx to conclude that capitalism is inherently marked by *the law of the tendency for the rate of profit to fall*. The tendency can be offset, or even reversed, however, by counteracting measures.

Capitalists can prevent the rate of profit from falling by increasing the exploitation of the workers, which can be done by increasing the hours or intensity of work—for example, by speeding up assembly-line production. These measures increase the level of surplus value. Similarly, an increase in the number of unemployed, partly caused by labour-displacing technology, may temporarily allow capitalists to pay wages below subsistence levels, thus also building up surplus value. Another factor offsetting the tendency of the rate of profit to fall is any decline in the price of capital goods due to increased demand, which allows economies of scale to be realized in the production of these goods. This decline enables firms to increase the volume of machinery employed in production without raising the capital-to-labour ratio. The final counteracting influence is an increase in foreign trade, which enlarges profits by opening new markets. Foreign trade also allows cheaper imports, which can reduce the cost of subsistence. Imperial expansion, so prominent until the 1950s, creates a captive market and, like international trade, increases the level of surplus value in the metropole through the exploitation of labour in the periphery.

The increasing capital-to-labour ratio in production also creates *sectoral imbalances and disproportions in the economy*. Replacing workers by machines means reducing workers' incomes, even though the level of production continues as before. The upshot is reduced total consumption compared to total production (called 'underconsumption'), which causes economic recessions. Yet another serious impact of increasing capital-intensity in production is the disproportionate growth of the capital goods sector compared to the consumer goods sector: productive capacity expands because of the introduction of new machines while the level of consumption declines because of the increasing unemployment generated by the introduction of the labour-saving technology.

The *alienation of workers* is yet another feature of capitalism. While alienation refers to a psychological state, the condition ultimately derives from the material conditions of capitalism. Human labour is not just a mass of energy but a creative force, and it should give a sense of satisfaction to those who engage in it. But in capitalism, human labour ceases to be creative and personal. It becomes just another commodity to be bought and sold. Even the product of labour does not belong to the worker but to the employer. There is a separation between workers and their labour, which breeds an alienation that intensifies as capitalism becomes even more competitive and less personal. The flip side of the rising concentration of capital, according to Marx, is 'the law of increasing misery' for the proletariat. As he puts it:

> Labour produces works of wonder for the rich but nakedness for the worker. It produces palaces, but only hovels for the worker. It produces beauty but cripples the worker; it replaces labour by machines but throws a part of the workers . . . to a barbaric labour and turns the other part into madness. It produces culture, but also imbecility and cretinism for the worker. (Marx [1844], *Economic and Philosophical Manuscripts*, in McLellan, 1972: 136)

In statements like these, Marx was not simply referring to a decline in wages or purchasing power, though he did use the word 'pauperization' in his earlier pamphlet, the *Communist Manifesto*. He was also referring to an increase in alienation and general misery, understood in a psychological sense.

Before Marx, other scholars and pundits had predicted the demise or increasing crises of capitalism. Some classical political economists, such as Thomas Malthus, prophesied that the growth in production and income would cause a growth in population, which would impose increasing strains on natural resources and eventually lead to a stagnant or declining economy. Utopian socialists, such as Robert Owen (1771–1858) and Simonde de Sismondi (1773–1842), had similarly predicted that competition among capitalists would bring wages down far enough to cause a crisis of underconsumption. Marx's prediction differed in that it was based on concrete historical analysis. He had no patience with conjectural theories of increasing population based on the assumption of the lack of sexual discipline among the poor (Malthus) or the evil intentions or ignorance of the capitalists that led them to exploit workers (Owen). Marx regarded the problems of capitalism as inherent in its very nature. The purpose of production in capitalism is to make profits, not to satisfy social needs. In the words of Marx and Engels:

> For many a decade past, the history of industry and commerce is but the history of the revolt of modern productive forces against modern conditions of production . . . . The productive forces at the disposal of society no longer tend to further the development of the condition of bourgeois property; on the contrary they . . . bring disorder into the whole of bourgeois society. (Marx and Engels [1848], *Manifesto of the Communist Party*, in Tucker, 1972: 340)

This is undoubtedly very different from Adam Smith's view that the pursuit of private interests in capitalism promotes the interests of an entire society.

According to Marx, the efforts of capitalists to counter declining profit levels by increasing the exploitation of workers foster increased alienation of the proletariat, which can burst into open class war. In certain conditions the working class will unite and overthrow capitalism, which it correctly views as the source of its problems and misery. Marx says little about the final state of the collapse of capitalism, except that it would involve violent revolution because the capitalists, supported by the state, would use repressive forces to quell the working-class challenge, which would in turn fuel working-class violence.

By placing economics and politics in a broad historical and social context, the Marxist theory performs brilliantly as a theory of political economy. But its insights into broad trends have been at the expense of explaining the operation of the micro-level political economy. The Marxist theory does not precisely explain—perhaps is incapable of explaining—movements in prices, profits, employment, and inflation, the incidence of taxation, or the impact of technology. These are exactly the areas in which neoclassical economics excels.

It is also difficult to reconcile Marx's notions regarding the increased impoverishment of workers and his prediction of the imminent collapse of capitalism with later historical developments in which worker-led revolutions in modern industrial states did not occur. Socialist political economists after Marx have grappled with these later developments in capitalist societies, especially with the notion that the competitive capitalist economy that Marx described no longer exists and has been replaced by *monopoly capitalism*, in which a few large companies control production and are able to manipulate markets to their advantage.

The theory of monopoly capitalism is that the logic and functioning of capitalism inherently lead to the development of ever larger firms that control greater and greater amounts of production. These producing firms are integrated horizontally and vertically within their sectors and, more importantly, across sectors as well. They come to dominate the economy and can draw state apparatuses into supporting their activities. This leads to a merger of financial and production companies and governments in what the Austrian social democrat Rudolph Hilferding called *finanzkapital* and what later US theorists, following on the heels of élite theorist C. Wright Mills, termed the *military-industrial complex* (Hilferding, 1981; Baran and Sweezy, 1966). Two approaches to post-Marx socialist political economy attempted to deal with the development of monopoly capitalism in the years up to and including World War I. These are the approaches put forward by the Russian revolutionary leader Vladimir Lenin and the social democratic approach developed by trade union leaders in continental Europe.

Leninist Political Economy

Lenin's two major contributions to socialist political economy were his formalization of a theory of imperialism and his analysis of the role of the labour process in capitalist society. However, his writings on the labour process were to remain less significant than his writings on the imperial system, although his analysis of the introduction of mass production and assembly-line techniques influenced the writings of the Italian socialist Antonio Gramsci in the interwar period (Gramsci, 1972). When those labour writings were rediscovered in the 1970s by US and European academics, they were integrated into an effort to revitalize socialist political economy by 'returning to the basics', much the same way neo-conservative liberal political economy returned to marginalist and neoclassical thought for its own inspiration during the crisis of that period.

The analysis of the international political economy found a much more prominent place in Lenin's work. Writing from what was then a peripheral nation, Lenin was concerned with understanding the location and role that Imperial Russia occupied in the international system of states and theorizing about the implications for Russian political and economic practice of this location. He was especially interested in the rapid expansion of the colonial trading networks of European powers in the late nineteenth century into African and Asian territories and wanted to understand both the causes of this development and its consequences for the pre-capitalist economic formations or political economies of the colonized territory. As he argued in *Imperialism, The Highest Stage of Capitalism*: 'Imperialism emerged as the development and direct continuation of the fundamental characteristics of capitalism in general . . . imperialism . . . represents a special stage in the development of capital' (Lenin, [1916] 1939b: 88).

Lenin defined imperialism as a stage of capitalist development marked by the decline of competitive firms and the rise of monopoly corporations. He said that imperialism as a system of production had five principal features:

1. The concentration of production and capital has developed to such a high stage that it created monopolies which play a decisive role in economic life,
2. The merging of bank capital with industrial capital, and the creation, on the basis of this 'financial capital' of a financial oligarchy,
3. The export of capital which has become extremely important as distinguished from the export of commodities,
4. The formation of international capitalist monopolies which share the world among themselves,
5. The territorial division of the whole world among the greatest capitalist powers is completed. (Ibid., 89)

Imperialism, in Lenin's view, was intimately tied to the development of monopoly capitalism and especially to the issue of foreign investment. He argued that at earlier stages of the development of capitalism, companies had exported goods to the periphery and benefited from the high returns they could earn on this type of exchange. In the imperialist stage, however, capitalist firms penetrated foreign markets through investment, taking over and manipulating existing firms and production relations to earn higher profits. He stated: 'as long as capitalism remains what it is, surplus capital . . . will be used for the purpose of increasing . . . profits by exporting capital abroad to the backward countries. In these backward countries profits are usually high, for capital is scarce, the price of land is relatively low, wages are low, raw materials are cheap' (ibid., 63). Rosa Luxemburg, a German socialist writing around the same time as Lenin, had a similar analysis. Unlike Lenin, she stressed the role that a competitive and not a monopoly capitalist economy plays in creating imperialism. For Luxemburg, pressures resulting from competition in the home market drive capitalist firms to seek out foreign markets (Luxemburg, 1964).

Regardless of the mechanism at work, Lenin's conclusions are shared by both authors, as well as by others. That is, at a certain point in capitalist development, to maintain profitability firms require access to cheap raw materials and expanded, secure markets for their finished products. Having outgrown the domestic marketplace, these firms enlist the state's coercive machinery to undertake foreign adventures and establish large protected trade blocks. This inevitably creates two phenomena: first, *the uneven development of core and peripheral countries*; and, second, *intercapitalist rivalry and world war* (Lenin, 1939b; Luxemburg, 1964).

These two conclusions concerning the operation of the global economy had significant implications for political practice in peripheral and metropolitan countries. First, development in the periphery was not possible within the existing colonial system and such development awaited the overthrow of the colonial regime. Second, the working class had no interest in world wars caused by intercolonial or intercapitalist rivalries. These wars were aimed not at improving the conditions of either the metropolitan or colonial working class but simply at bettering the lot of one group of monopoly capitalists over another. Based on this analysis, following the Russian Revolution of 1917 Lenin withdrew the Soviet Union from World War I. The same analysis justified Lenin's and Stalin's later efforts to promote autarkic development in the Soviet Union. It also justified the Soviet government's continued support under both Lenin and Stalin for anticolonial struggles in many nations in Africa, Asia, and Latin America and formed a major part of the political-economic analyses proffered by socialists and nationalists in these countries.

Social Democratic Political Economy

A second important variety of post-Marx socialist political-economic thought also involves the analysis of the demise of competitive capitalism and the transition to a new stage of monopoly capitalism. This is the social democratic analysis of monopoly capitalism developed by individuals such as Karl Kautsky, Eduard Bernstein, and other trade union leaders in continental Europe and Scandinavia prior to World War I (Bottomore, 1978; Przeworski, 1985).

Unlike Leninism, this analysis was put forward by theorists located in the most advanced capitalist economies of the day and focused virtually exclusively on the implications of this development for political practice at the domestic level. While variants of Marxism-Leninism informed the practices of revolutionary parties in many industrializing countries, social democratic theory has served as the basis for the kind of parliamentary socialism practised by socialist and social democratic parties in many industrialized nations (Boggs and Plotke, 1980; Esping-Andersen, 1985).

Dismissed by Lenin as 'revisionists', social democrats like Bernstein and Kautsky insisted that in fact they, and not Lenin, were following the analysis put forward by Marx in *Das Kapital*. In their writings they argued that the continuing expansion of capitalism in individual nation-states would inevitably lay the foundations for its overthrow and replacement by socialism by increasing the ranks of the working class until that class became a large majority in capitalist society. Unlike Lenin, who argued that capitalists would never accede to a peaceful transition of power to the workers, social democrats maintained that workers could gain political power through the democratic process as long as they were organized to vote as a block and support workers' parties in parliamentary elections. As such, they placed a great deal of emphasis in their analyses on links between the trade union movement and workers' political parties operating in a democratic electoral system. As Kautsky put it in his work, *The Class Struggle*: 'The more unbearable the existing system of production, the more evidently it is discredited . . . the greater will be the number of those who stream from the non-proletarian classes into the Socialist party and, hand in hand with the irresistibly advancing proletariat, follow its banner to victory and triumph' (Kautsky, [1892] 1971: 217).

The appropriate mechanism through which this growing strength would manifest itself in the overthrow of capitalism was the democratically elected legislature or parliament, which Kautsky argued could be used by workers to liberate themselves in the same fashion that capitalists had used it to exploit them. 'Whenever the proletariat engages in parliamentary activity as a self-conscious class, parliamentarism begins to change its character. It ceases to be a mere tool in the hands of the bourgeoisie' (ibid., 188).

For early social democrats, the workers would use parliamentary institutions to achieve the transition to socialism through the nationalization of private property by the state. However, over time social democrats gradually abandoned the proposal for the eventual replacement of the market by the state and instead developed a theory and practice of market-state coexistence based on careful state monitoring and regulation of market activities. Most social democratic parties in Western Europe and North America, as a result, were early adherents to, and remain enthusiastic supporters of, Keynesian welfare state policies.

Social democrats have a different view of the welfare state than do most liberal political economists, however. Throughout the twentieth century, social democrats developed an analysis of the development of modern political economies based not on the concepts of individual rights and freedoms but on the assumption that the inherent tendency of such economies is to generate large non-capitalist classes that can use the democratic parliamentary process to curb and offset the advantages capital enjoys in the marketplace. As Michael Shalev argues, this analysis seeks to explain the development of 'welfare capitalism' in Western capitalist nations not through technical analyses of the strengths and weaknesses of markets but through four basic political propositions:

1. The welfare state is a class issue. Logically and historically, its principal proponents and defenders are movements of the working class.
2. Like other dimensions of public policy, the parameters of the welfare state are defined largely by the choices of governments.
3. In the capitalist democracies the most significant partisan cleavage (in terms of both voter alignment and policy positions) is that between parties of the working class and other parties. For the most part, only reformist (social democratic or 'labour') working-class parties have been serious left-wing contenders for governmental power in these polities.
4. The capacity for reformist labour parties to emerge and grow to the point of coming to power is a function of the extent and coherency of institutionalized working-class mobilization in trade unions and political parties. The potential for such mobilization is largely predetermined by certain historically given structural characteristics of a society. (Shalev, 1983: 320)

Both Marxist-Leninists and social democrats shared many of the same fundamental assumptions about the nature of a capitalist economy, assumptions firmly grounded in Marx's analysis of capitalism. They differed in their orientation (Leninists towards the international system and social democrats towards the nation-state); in their prescriptions for political action drawn from their economic analyses (Leninists favoured revolutionary action and social democrats favoured a peaceful, parliamentary transition to socialism); and in their attitude towards the market (Leninists supported its abolition or replacement by the state and social democrats supported its regulation or control by the state). These differences have their roots in the different analyses of the class structure of monopoly capitalism put forward by each theory and in the very different interpretations of the state each made.

Contemporary Debates

Dependency and Regulation Political Economy

In the post-World War I era Leninist analysis, with its emphasis on the exploitative aspects of European imperialism, figured prominently in the liberation movements of many African and Asian nations (Nkrumah, 1965; Mao Tse Tung, 1961; Fanon, 1965). It also had a major impact in long-independent Latin American countries in the post-World War II era as theorists worked at understanding why those countries had failed to develop in the same fashion as other independent countries.

The Latin American theorists focused on the Leninist insight that imperialism had perpetuated the uneven development of metropolitan and peripheral countries, as surplus earned from the peripheral countries accrued to metropolitan nations. They argued that despite their political sovereignty Latin American nations became tied economically to metropolitan nations through foreign ownership either of companies or of the capital and technological resources required for industrial development. This placed peripheral countries in a position of dependency *vis-à-vis* advanced industrial nations and, dependency theorists argued, resulted in a kind of truncated industrial structure in these countries. They usually referred to this as a process of *underdevelopment* (Furtado, 1964; Frank, 1970; Cardoso, 1972). As André Gunder Frank explains in *Latin America: Underdevelopment or Revolution* (1970: 4):

> The now-developed countries were never underdeveloped, though they may have been undeveloped. It is also widely believed that the contemporary underdevelopment of a country can be understood as the product or reflection solely of its own economic, political, social, and cultural characteristics or structure. Yet historical research demonstrates that contemporary underdevelopment is in large part the historical product of past and continuing economic and other relations between the satellite underdeveloped and the now-developed metropolitan countries. Furthermore, these relations are an essential part of the structure and development of the capitalist system on a world scale as a whole.

Although they shared a Leninist heritage, dependency theorists were divided on a number of issues. There were disputes, for instance, concerning the empirical question of whether or not industrialization was proceeding at all in many peripheral countries or whether these countries were 'sliding backwards' (Warren, 1973; Smith, 1979). There were also theoretical disputes concerning the nature of the mechanism by which metropolitan countries dominated the affairs and development of countries on the periphery—a significant debate that directly influenced political practice in many developing countries looking to promote indigenous economic development. Some dependency theorists followed an orthodox Leninist line, arguing that the mechanism of control was the multinational corporation based in the metropole. They argued that multinationals transferred surplus from the periphery to the metropole through unequal trade relations: companies used their market dominance to buy resources at below market value in the periphery and sell processed goods back to the peripheral country at inflated prices (Prebisch, 1968; Amin, 1974; Arrighi, 1978).

Others reasoned that at least part of the blame for underdevelopment lay in peripheral countries themselves. They pointed to the nature of the social formation present in many of those countries as root of the problem. That is, they argued that because of colonization and prohibitions on indigenous economic activity enacted and enforced by imperial military authorities, many developing countries had their economies disrupted and transformed into capitalist forms of economic activity; but this happened without the growth of an indigenous capitalist class, as had occurred in the course of the capitalist transformation of the economies of the metropolitan nations. Instead, peripheral countries developed only a small bourgeoisie involved in trade relations with the metropole. This *comprador* fraction of the colonial capitalist class relied on its connections with the metropole to build up its wealth and power and continued in the postcolonial period to resist any local efforts to sever links with the former imperial power. While multinational corporations remain the primary vehicle linking metropolitan and peripheral countries, in this view the social and political structure of peripheral countries facilitated, if not actively promoted, dependent relations (Poulantzas, 1974; Murray, 1978). As Fernando Cardoso, now the President of Brazil, argued:

> In countries like Argentina, Brazil, Mexico, South Africa and India, and some others, there is an internal structure connecting the most 'advanced' parts of their economies to the international capitalist system. Separate although subordinated to these advanced sectors, the backward economic and social sectors of the dependent countries then play the role of 'internal colonies.' (1972: 90)

Although disputes over these and other issues remained unresolved, dependency theory itself was challenged from within the Leninist tradition by many analysts who felt that its insights relied far too heavily on critiques of trade and international relations and ignored significant changes in global industrial organization. This led many socialist political economists to return to Marx and Lenin's focus on *production relations* rather than *exchange relations* (Jenkins, 1981). A new version of socialist political economy developed in the 1980s and 1990s concentrated on the relations of production or *labour process* present in capitalist societies, and especially on the changes that have occurred in those relations since the writings of Marx and Lenin, in explaining the pattern of capitalist development found in both the 'developed' and the 'developing' world.

The labour-process approach to socialist political economy is based on a careful evaluation of how capital and labour interact in the production of surplus value in capitalist society and especially on the techniques used by capital to control the workforce. The 'labour process' indicates the means by which raw materials are converted to products having use-values, which may be exchanged for each other as commodities (Braverman, 1974).

Following Marx, theorists of the labour process note that there are only two ways in which surplus value can be created or increased—either as *absolute surplus value*, in which workers work longer hours and create additional value, or as *relative surplus value*, in which work is intensified so that it takes less time to produce an equivalent amount of goods. As analysts note, once a country has developed legislation limiting working hours, any increase in surplus value must come from relative surplus value or productivity increases, which arise mainly from the reorganization of work (Palloix, 1976).

Marx initially remarked on these changes in his discussions of the introduction of steam-powered machinery into factories, which completed the transition from the cottage 'putting-out' system of hand production to the factory system of 'manufactories'. Following Lenin and Gramsci, labour-process theorists argue that two and possibly three major changes to the organization of work have occurred in more recent times. The first change was the dismantling of the craft system of production of individual goods by skilled workers and the introduction of unskilled mass-production techniques. The second was the introduction of assembly lines to speed up production even more. These two developments in the labour process are known respectively as *Taylorism* and *Fordism* after the two individuals most responsible for their implementation in the United States: Frederick Winslow Taylor in the steel industry and Henry Ford in the automobile industry (Gramsci, 1972).

Pioneering work in this field was undertaken by Harry Braverman in his *Labour and Monopoly Capital* (1974). Braverman noted that capitalism is founded on the ability of capitalists to extract surplus labour from production activities and that in the process of the development of capitalism, any vestiges of worker control over production that might give them the ability to regulate how much surplus value is produced have been removed. The primary technique that has accomplished this has been the gradual transfer of knowledge over the production process from workers to managers. As Braverman (1974: 82) put it:

> The capitalist mode of production systematically destroys all-around skills where they exist, and brings into being skills and occupations that correspond to its needs. Technical capacities are henceforth distributed on a strict 'need to know' basis. The generalized distribution of knowledge of the productive process among all its participants becomes, from this point on, not merely 'unnecessary,' but a positive barrier to the functioning of the capitalist mode of production.

As a result, skilled labour is 'deskilled', a new strata of managers comes to control the production process, and individual workers are rendered powerless and inert in the face of capitalist expertise: 'Every step in the labor process is divorced, so far as possible, from special knowledge and training and reduced to simple labor. Meanwhile, the relatively few persons for whom special knowledge and training are reserved are freed so far as possible from the obligations of simple labor . . . . This might even be called the general law of the capitalist division of labor' (Braverman, 1974: 82–3).

Although many labour-process theorists limited their analysis to the examination of changing modes of organizing production in various countries (Braverman, 1974; Edwards, 1979; Littler, 1982; Edwards, Reich, and Gordon, 1975; Price, 1984), later theorists have expanded these insights to a general theory of global economic development based on the concept of a regime of production or *regime of regulation*. This analysis, popularized by Michel Aglietta, Alain Lipietz, and others associated with the French research institute CEPREMAP, is often referred to as the *Regulation School* (Aglietta, 1979; Boyer, 1985; Lipietz, 1984a).

The regulation approach argues that a particular and specific set of political-economic relationships exists for each different stage in the labour process. Each set of relationships constitutes a *regime of production* or *regime of accumulation* designed to facilitate capital expansion and avoid the economic and political crises associated with this process. Each 'regime', therefore, involves application of the coercive powers of the state to control labour and aid in the reproduction and expansion of capital. In the modern era, a regulatory regime must also maintain a certain consumption norm to ensure that the mass production of commodities does not result in oversupply and a decline in prices and profits. Hence, in this theory, Keynesianism is seen as a regulatory regime that is an outgrowth of, and consistent with, a modern, Fordist regime of production (Brenner and Glick, 1991; Robles, 1994).

Regulation school political economy shifts the focus of investigation away from the emphasis on the implications of the development of monopoly capitalism found in Marxism-Leninism and dependency theory and back to an analysis of the mechanisms by which surplus value is produced and appropriated in capitalist society. As Michel Aglietta argues in *A Theory of Capitalist Regulation* (1979: 21), such an approach provides

> a theoretical foundation to the periodization of capitalism into successive stages of historical evolution. The criterion for this periodization is furnished by the changing content of relative surplus value: in the first stage, the transformation of the labour process without major alteration in the conditions of existence of the wage-earning class; in a second stage, the simultaneous revolutionization of both the labour process and the conditions of existence of the wage-earning class . . . we reject the idea that the concentration of capital is the most fundamental process in the history of 20th century capitalism. The key theoretical process rather lies in a radical change in the conditions of reproduction of capital in general.

This analysis sets up a theoretical dispute between dependency and regulation socialist political economy, and efforts to integrate the two approaches have not been entirely successful (Rowlinson and Hassard, 1994). There are also continuing internal disputes within the labour-process approach. One concerns its ability to aid the analysis of microeconomic and political behaviour as well as that at the macrolevel (Jonsson, 1993). Another concerns the characterization of the contemporary labour process. Many labour-process theorists see a third stage emerging, with robots and electronic control devices being introduced into the workplace and traditional mass-production techniques being replaced by specialized manufacturing (Morris-Suzuki, 1984; Sabel, 1982; Reich, 1983). In this view, a new regime of regulation better suited to the modern conditions of production is emerging in which labour markets restructure to match the flexibility of production. The 'Schumpeterian warfare state', as Bob Jessop (1993) has called it, is centred on temporary and part-time work and a low social wage. But not all labour-process theorists agree that this is a new stage of *post-Fordism* in which robotics and other labour-saving devices may liberate workers from the day-to-day drudgery of the assembly-line system of mass production (Clarke, 1990b). Some suggest that it is merely a variation on the Fordist model, or *neo-Fordism* (Murray, 1979).

Alain Lipietz has made an effort to synthesize the dependency approach with the regulation approach. Although empirical studies of the labour processes in different countries have led to the conclusion that Fordism or mass production has been extended around the world—generating the concept of 'global Fordism' (Lipietz, 1982)—it is generally acknowledged that conditions and regimes vary in developed and developing countries (Gordon, 1988). Lipietz uses this insight to point out that in the most developed countries the expansion of capital results from productivity increases that generate increased relative surplus value, with the goods produced being consumed on the home market. Workers, therefore, require a high consumption level, which is provided by governments following Keynesian demand-management techniques and by financial institutions providing easy credit. In many developing countries, however, the regime is based on the generation of absolute surplus value, because workers lack political rights and surplus is generated through the export of manufactured products to developed countries. Workers in these countries are provided with minimal consumption norms, and surplus is expropriated almost exclusively by capital, leading to social unrest and political instability (Lipietz, 1984b, 1997).

Social Democratic Political Economy

The main opposition to both the Leninist-inspired dependency and regulation schools of socialist political economy has continued to come from the analyses of social democrats. These analyses tend to lack the micro-level focus on shifts in production processes that characterizes regulation school approaches and ignore questions about imperialism and neocolonialism that characterize dependency analyses. Contemporary social democratic thought retains its traditional focus on the development of monopoly capitalism and its effects on the domestic political arena in developed capitalist nations.

The primary area of concern for contemporary social democrats continues to be the democratic class struggle, that is, the democratic process and the theorization of the impact that changes in class structures brought about by the development of monopoly capitalism have had on domestic class formation and voting behaviour. Unlike its traditional precursors, however, contemporary social democratic theory is no longer passive—merely awaiting the further development of capitalism to produce more workers and hence electoral success—but is concerned with obtaining political power to further the potential for the achievement of socialism and the replacement of capitalism. This has led social democratic theory into two main areas: first, the theorization of class formation and class solidarity; and second, the development of practical political, policy, and electoral strategies designed to achieve success at the polls and within legislatures.

Following some elements in Eduard Bernstein's works, contemporary social democrats have rejected the notion implicit in Marxism-Leninism that there are ultimately only two classes characteristic of the capitalist mode of production: the working class and the owners of capital. Social democrats argue that the development of monopoly capitalism has generated at least one more class, the middle class. Although the exact membership in this class is contentious, all social democrats agree that, at a minimum, it is composed of managers and administrators and other individuals who neither directly own productive apparatuses nor struggle for wages (Esping-Andersen, 1985).

In most countries this class has expanded rapidly since World War II, with its fortunes closely tied to the development of bureaucracies in both large public sectors and large private-sector corporations. Social democrats have been concerned with the effects of the growth of this class on the 'democratic class struggle' between capital and labour they see being waged in parliamentary institutions. Just as social democrats before and immediately after World War I were preoccupied with the idea of forming coalitions between labour and other classes, such as farmers, peasants, and small shopkeepers and manufacturers, in the postwar period they started to concentrate on defining the new middle class and other class fractions or elements and to discuss means of attracting these into alliances with workers (Korpi, 1983; Wright, 1985; Erikson and Goldthorpe, 1992; Breen and Rottman, 1995). This stands in sharp contrast to those working in the Leninist vein, who have tended either to deny separate class status to 'middle elements' in society or to argue that coalitions including those elements simply reduce the possibility for meaningful change in capitalist relations.

In some cases this focus on social alliances has led contemporary social democrats away from the analysis of class altogether and towards the theorization of *new social movements*, such as the peace, environmental, gay and lesbian, and feminist movements. Much recent effort has gone into analysing the social origins of these movements and into determining whether and to what extent such movements are 'progressive', that is, compatible with the aims and ambitions of the working class (Esping-Andersen, Friedland, and Wright, 1976). Claus Offe, for example, has argued that these movements represent the political expression of 'de-commodified' social groups, which rely on state expenditures in areas such as pensions and education, and no longer are subject to the discipline and exigencies of commodity-based market forces (Offe, 1987). Others, however, have argued that new social movements exist beyond class boundaries and deal with other fundamental divisions in society such as race and gender (Carroll, 1992). Such alliances, it is argued, do not provide the basis for the achievement of social democratic aims (Esping-Anderson, 1985).

A second major debate found in contemporary social democratic political economy revolves around the question of whether or not the nationalization of industries and the implementation of state-sponsored welfare and other social security programs have achieved their aim of reducing the dependence of workers on capitalist-dominated market mechanisms for their income. Some social democrats argue that these activities should be continued until markets have been rendered completely superfluous. Others say that markets remain inherently more efficient than state-sector activities in allocating goods and services in society and should be allowed to function effectively. As Gosta Esping-Andersen (1980: 258) points out:

> Such Social Democrats . . . have claimed that genuine socialism may be achieved through a blend of welfare state reforms, taxation policies, and a sophisticated use of Keynesian economic management techniques. Yet as a number of . . . Social Democrats have argued, political and social citizenship rights are only meaningful forms of working class participation if they are supplemented with full economic citizenship, which essentially implies a democratic form of control over the means of production (that is, a total redistribution of economic power).

In practice, most social democratic party governments have substituted industrial democracy for economic democracy. That is, they have concentrated their efforts on securing some worker control over the management of productive enterprises rather than on the abolition of private property and the complete elimination of wage and income disparities (Esping-Anderson, 1985). Although this has often been accompanied by proposals for various 'wage-earner' funds that promise to turn workers into share-owners over the long term, these funds have tended to adopt more or less passive *rentier* investment roles promoting worker savings rather than an active role in the management of firms. Nevertheless, some social democrats continue to hold out hope that such funds can exercise a 'locational commitment' to communities and offset some of the worst excesses of capital mobility associated with globalization (Laxer, 1995).

Any dependence on the market, as Przeworski acknowledges, creates a problem for the reformist aspirations of social democrats because it places the working class and the working-class state at the mercy of capitalists.

> Without nationalization of the means of production, increases of productivity require profitability of private enterprise. As long as the process of accumulation is private, the entire society is dependent upon maintaining private profits and upon the actions of capitalists allocating these profits. Hence the efficacy of social democrats—as of any other party—in regulating the economy and mitigating the social effects depends upon the profitability of the private sector and the willingness of capitalists to cooperate. (Przeworski, 1985: 42)

More significantly, the continued operation of markets under social democratic governments can alter the social structure and hence the system of class alliances upon which social democratic electoral strength depends. Herbert Kitschelt, for example, has argued that the continued development of capitalist economies under the welfare-Keynesian regimes established by social democratic parties in many countries has led to an increase in both capitalist and libertarian political orientations. This is because a reliance on technologically literate knowledge workers provides individuals with these skills with higher pay levels and a great deal of autonomy and flexibility in their work relationships (Kitschelt, 1993a, 1993b). Attempts by social democratic parties to gain the allegiance of these workers may well undermine their ability to retain the allegiance of their traditional bases of support in the ranks of the less-skilled 'mass worker'. Ultimately, these two groups can split with each other, supporting, on the one hand, liberal and liberal-reform parties that promise greater individual 'freedom' and, on the other, authoritarian parties that promise to 'roll back the clock' and restore the traditional political order, that is, to undercut the privileges accruing to the new knowledge workers. In the process, social democratic parties, of course, can find themselves squeezed into the middle of a shrinking political spectrum (Kitschelt, 1994).

The dilemma of social democratic political economy, therefore, is very real, and the debates have significant implications for political practice. Forming alliances with new social movements may dilute working-class demands and ambitions, while continued reliance on market mechanisms may thwart further reforms required for the transition to socialism. In pursuing these contemporary issues, social democratic theory finds itself at a crossroads, and it must come to some resolution of these questions if it is to influence the nature of future social democratic political and economic practice (Weitzman, 1993).

The State in Socialist Theory

All variants of socialist political economy integrate political and economic variables in a fashion that liberal theories do not. That is, socialist political economy has never adopted, even for heuristic purposes, the separation between states and markets that liberal political economy espouses. Socialist economic theory never considers markets without also considering the impact of governments on those markets and the impact of market actors on governments and state activities. Nevertheless, the theorization of the role of the state, and especially the role of the democratic state in capitalist society, has caused major difficulties for socialist political economists.

The question of the role of the state in socialist political economy is made more difficult by the fact that Marx himself never completed his intended work on the question, and many early Marxists assumed that after a socialist revolution the state would simply wither away or emerge in a new form. Therefore, they saw either no need or little need prior to the revolution itself for extensive analysis of this question (Bobbio, 1987).

All socialist theories of the state are based, in one way or another, on the Marxist conception of the state as an institution of class domination. Although there are numerous disagreements on questions such as the extent of economic domination of the state by large capital or the mechanisms by which capitalist economic power is translated into political power, most socialists tend to subscribe to either an *instrumental* or a *structural* view of the role of the state in capitalist society.

The instrumental view of the state posits that the state in capitalist society tends to make decisions and develop policies that favour capital because it is thoroughly dominated and staffed by representatives of these interests (Mandel, 1970; Castells, 1980). This view of the state in capitalist society has dominated both Marxist-Leninist and social democratic political economy.

The structural variant of socialist state theory, unlike the instrumentalist conception, is a 'high-level' theory in the sense that it abstracts from mundane and observable phenomena to make generalizations about the systemic or structural 'imperatives' of a capitalist economy. According to this view, a capitalist economy has to fulfil certain functional requirements to operate effectively; and these imperatives drive political decision-making and exist outside of, or independently of, the will of political and administrative decision-makers (Althusser and Balibar, 1977).

Adherents of the structural view assume that because of the tendency of the rate of profit to fall, companies are constantly looking for methods of reducing production costs. One way to achieve this is to socialize many expenditures. Instead of a firm providing training, education, and health protection, for instance, these costs can be passed onto the population as a whole through their provision by the state. Regardless of who actually staffs the state—that is, regardless of their personal or class nature—the state must respond to the needs of capital to ensure the reproduction of the social system. Thus, for example, structuralists would explain the rise of the welfare state and welfare state expenditures by saying they aid the reproduction of capital in a capitalist political economy (Gough, 1979). Although there are debates on the extent to which states can afford to provide such 'subsidies' to business (O'Connor, 1973), the theorists usually argue that such expenditures are necessary for the preservation of monopoly capital and that the state makes them because, although 'relatively autonomous' of capital, it is structured in a way that ensures the reproduction of the dominant political-economic system.

Although this view has interesting things to say about the development of social programs and state expenditures associated with the modern welfare state, its reliance on a kind of functional determinism has led to it being criticized for being too high-level—that is, too simplistic, economistic, or teleological (Thompson, 1978). Although the functional or structural interpretation of the capitalist state appears to continue to hold out the socialist promise of a future system of production relations replacing capitalism, it is difficult to see how this would occur because the theory lacks a precise conception of 'agency'. Instead, the state is viewed as responding to the systemic needs of capitalism, which in fact it must do because that is its function or role in capitalist society. This means that political activities involving the state are not likely to alter existing social relations and radical change must instead originate outside of the state, presumably in the economic sphere. However, it is not clear how these developments are expected to result in the eventual overthrow of a capitalist system. As a result, this structural interpretation of the nature of the capitalist state has been challenged by socialist political economists working in the Leninist and social democratic traditions, since both hold out the possibility for change in capitalism occurring through the capture and use of state institutions by workers and workers' parties.

Both Leninist and social democratic political economic analyses have most often shared an instrumental conception of the state as a tool of the dominant social class. They differ in many respects, including most notably their analysis of whether liberal democratic states can be captured by other classes through the democratic process or must be overthrown through revolution. However, both these analyses avoid the mechanistic and technological aspects of structural approaches by concentrating on the relationship actually existing between the state and class actors in society.

The Leninist and social democratic analyses of the nature of the state in capitalist society have significant implications for political practice and, unlike liberal political economy, justify the extensive use of state apparatuses to promote political goals. Like liberal political economy, however, both approaches to socialist political economy tend to undertheorize the state and hence fail to explain adequately many aspects of its role and activities in modern capitalist societies.

Marx's Theory of the State

Several different conceptions of the state can be located in Marx's writings, including *Capital*, the *Grundrisse*, the *Communist Manifesto*, *The Civil War in France*, and *Class Struggles in France*. In addition, early writings found in the *Economic and Philosophical Manuscripts of 1844* and in *Critique of Hegel's Philosophy of Right* also contain ruminations on the origins and purpose of states and governments in Western society. Engels, of course, also touched on the state in many of his works, including most notably *Origins of the Family, Civil Society, and the State*.

Although these writings are often cursory, fragmentary, and contradictory, it is possible to glean a general conception of the state implicit within them. This is a notion of the state as a coercive apparatus established to perpetuate the political domination of society by an economically dominant class. The state is part of the superstructure, which also includes religion, ideology, art, and culture, constructed on the economic base of a specific mode of production. Thus, different states exist for each current or historical mode of production (for instance, a slave state, a feudal state, or a capitalist state), and some kind of new state is expected to exist in any post-capitalist socialist or communist society.

Although there are many aspects to this argument (including distinctions that can be drawn between dominant and ruling classes or the possibility of an autonomous state developing when opposing classes are of equal strength), the key philosophical concept is of the state as an instrument of class rule, with its origins in the class structure of society and responding to changes in that structure brought about by movements of the economic base. As Marx remarks in *The Civil War in France*, the state is both the location of much of the class struggle and the prize that this struggle fights over. Thus, at a particular point in time the state can be used by an emerging social class to overthrow the previous ruling class:

> The centralized State power, with its ubiquitous organs of standing army, policy, bureaucracy, and clergy and judicature . . . originates from the days of absolute monarchy, serving nascent middle-class society as a mighty weapon in its struggles against feudalism. Still its development remained clogged by all manner of mediaeval rubbish, seigneurial rights, local privileges, municipal and guild monopolies and provincial constitutions. The gigantic broom of the French Revolution of the eighteenth century swept away all these relics of bygone times, thus clearing simultaneously the social soil of its last hindrances to the superstructure of the modern state edifice. (Marx, 1974b [1871]: 289)

Once conquered and staffed by the new class, however, the state can also take on a repressive role in society, preventing or delaying other classes from attaining political power:

> During the subsequent régimes, the Government, placed under Parliamentary control . . . became not only the bone of contention between the rival factions and adventurers of the ruling classes; but its political character changed simultaneously with the economic changes in society. At the same pace at which the progress of modern industry developed, widened, intensified the class antagonism between capital and labour, the State power assumed more and more the character of the national power of capital over labour, of a public force organized for social enslavement, of an engine of class despotism. (Ibid., 284)

Thus, for Marx the state was an instrument of class domination, but not inherently so. Rather, it was an instrument that could be, and usually was, used in the course of class struggle by the dominant class to maintain its hold on the subordinate classes. The actual form this domination would take, and the question of whether the state would be used at all, depended on the level of class struggle, that is, on the strength of the various classes and the extent of antagonism between them. Thus, the nature of the state was contingent on the political ramifications of underlying economic processes, in keeping with Marx's fundamental concept of base and superstructure. The questions of whether and how state structures could be used by subordinate classes to secure their control over the political economy were left open, sparking a debate between socialists who felt a revolution was necessary to overthrow the capitalist state and others, such as social democrats, who argued that a transition from capitalism to socialism could be achieved through existing state institutions and political practices.

Leninist, Dependency, and Regulation Theories of State

In the effort to transfer Marx's analysis of the social, economic, and political conditions of advanced capitalist nations such as France, Germany, and England to the less developed Russian Empire, Lenin made several critical elaborations premised on the idea that a revolution was a necessary prerequisite to the achievement of socialism. Lenin's ideas, of course, were implemented in the Russian Revolution and in succeeding revolutions in countries such as China, Cuba, Vietnam, Ethiopia, Yemen, Angola, and Mozambique. These concepts and the experience of the state in the Soviet Union were also transferred by force of arms to other countries in Eastern Europe, the Baltic states, Korea, and Mongolia. With some further variations, they have informed the political practice of dependency theorists and revolutionaries in countries such as Cambodia, Peru, and Iran.

Leninist theory is premised on the notion that the capitalist class will not willingly relinquish its control over the state and will use its coercive powers— the military and the police—to attempt to retain control. Lenin argues that consequently only violent revolutionary action can bring about the transfer of state control from the capitalist to the working classes. Although many other socialists influenced by Marx, such as Rosa Luxemburg, felt that this revolution could be led spontaneously by the working class itself in the form of a mass or general strike, Lenin rejected this analysis, arguing that the working class tends to pursue only economic objects such as improvements in wages and working conditions if left to itself and that it requires the assistance of intellectuals and other progressive elements of society to achieve the political consciousness required to create and maintain a successful revolution. This, he argues, is the role of the Communist Party: to act as an institution capable of organizing and maintaining the revolutionary leadership of the working class.

In *The State and Revolution* (1917) and *What Is To Be Done?* (1902) Lenin elaborated a theory of political action based on this instrumental concept of the state. Lenin argued that in the monopoly capitalist stage of development, existing state structures had been captured and staffed by representatives of capital and were used by capital to exploit workers in both the metropole and the periphery. He argued that workers left to their own devices would probably conduct individual struggles with individual capitalists through trade union activities and fail to develop the political activities necessary to overthrow capitalist states. This, he says, is especially true in peripheral nations, where repressive state military and police activities actively prevent even the development of trade unionism among the working classes.

Lenin argued that the appropriate and necessary vehicle for achieving socialism in most countries was an élitist revolutionary political party; thus, it was crucial to develop a political party dedicated to advancing the interests of the working class through both economic (trade union) and political activities. The strategy he proposed involved a party-led mass revolution that would overthrow existing state personnel and allow the party to capture the state apparatus and institute workers' rule. After the revolution was successful and the working class had seized power, the appropriate form of government required to bring about the transition to socialism would be a *dictatorship of the proletariat*—a governmental structure dominated by the party. In the case of the Russian Revolution, this involved replacing a Czarist aristocracy with a federal system of governments and local councils, or 'soviets', but in other countries this 'dictatorship' was put into practice using existing parliamentary or republican institutions under party control.

Once in power, the workers' government would move to consolidate its economic power by nationalizing industries and agriculture, a move that also consolidates its political power by destroying the economic base of the capitalist and landowning classes. After destroying the basis for a market-based allocation of goods and services, the Leninist state would establish direct state allocation through the institution of central (state) planning of the economy. In the Soviet Union this series of steps in the development of the socialist state occurred in a rather ad hoc fashion and was intimately tied into specifically Soviet conditions such as the outbreak of civil war and the reconstruction of the military and state hierarchies under war communism. However, in many other countries this model was adopted holus-bolus, and the wholesale nationalization of industry and collectivization of agricultural activities were key features of most post-revolutionary state activities.

This analysis of the revolutionary politics of socialist political economy had a great impact not only on nations that fell into the Soviet orbit during and after World War II by military force but also on peripheral countries that wished to emulate the economic growth and success of the Soviet Union, then the only existing example outside Japan of a backward nation that had successfully industrialized and overtaken many advanced industrial nations. The Leninist formula presented an analysis of social and economic circumstances prevalent in many developing nations as well as a ready blueprint for political action and the creation of a post-revolutionary state, which made its appeal very great indeed.

Although some developing nations emerging from the confines of the European colonial system adopted this model of the state and the political concepts behind it, many did not, preferring instead to develop their own forms of government and state structures based on the models of their former colonial masters. Most social democratic parties and movements in the developed countries also rejected the Leninist model after arriving at their own interpretations of Marx's writings and of the political practice and theory of socialism. Difficulties encountered by Soviet-style states in co-ordinating economic activities once industrialization had been achieved, and in renewing the party system and bureaucracy, led to a transition in many of these countries towards multi-party democratic processes in the late 1980s and early 1990s (Nee and Stark, 1989; Przeworski, 1991). Although many of these countries moved towards increased reliance on market mechanisms for economic purposes, the extent of political and economic change varied greatly by country. Several centrally planned single-party states, such as China, Vietnam, North Korea, and Cuba, continue to exist. Several other countries that moved towards democratic and market-based reforms, such as Romania and Slovakia, have also slipped back into their old habits (Carpenter, 1997; Comisso, 1997; Hellman, 1998).

These developments have led to some attempts to reformulate the theory of the state found in socialist political economy. However, for the most part these analyses have retained the essentially instrumental conception found in socialist theory and have focused on the need to reformulate the manner in which workers can actually control the state apparatus. That is, abandoning the notion of party control, they have begun instead to attempt to discern other methods by which workers' interests can be made manifest by government apparatuses (Miliband, 1990; Bull, 1993). As Simon Clarke (1990a: 29) has argued:

> The lesson for socialists of the fate of state socialism, in both its Soviet and social democratic variants, is that socialism cannot be imposed on society through the alienated form of the state, but can only be achieved by building on the self-organization of the working class. The conquest of state power, far from being the immediate ambition of a socialist movement, is a poisoned chalice so long as the working class has not developed alternative forms of democratic organization to replace the alienated forms of state power.

The democratization project includes efforts to revitalize trade unions from their current bureaucratic form, as well as proposals to democratize the administrative system through various forms of popular control of bureaucratic behaviour (Panitch, 1992; Albo, Langille, and Panitch, 1993). In all these cases, however, the logic remains the same—democratization should occur in order that the working class may effectively transform the capitalist state into an instrument of its class interest.

Social Democratic State Theory

An important aspect of the Leninist theory of the state is the notion that the mechanism for attainment of worker control over the state is the revolutionary political party. This idea was not shared by social democrats. Lenin believed in the need for an élite, 'vanguard' party, that is, a party composed of intellectuals and 'advanced elements of the working class' that could transcend trade unionism and realize the 'true' interests of the working class in achieving socialism. Social democrats, while agreeing with many aspects of Lenin's theory of the state, argued that the conception of a vanguard party reversed Marx and Engels's emphasis on the state responding to changes in the economic base and would fail to usher in an era of true socialism.

Social democrats viewed the appropriate mechanism for attaining state power to be a political party, but they insisted that this party should be linked to and grow out of the trade union movement and participate in existing legislative bodies, form coalitions with other parties, and peacefully obtain power in order to usher in the transition to socialism. Social democrats argued that the Leninist vanguard party at best could obtain power through a *coup d'état* and would not have the links with the working class required to create a true socialist state. They argued, quite accurately, that such a party would be forced to rely on the coercive power of the state to attempt to bring in socialism and would more likely transform the state into a 'dictatorship of the party' than into a 'dictatorship of the proletariat'.

Given that social democrats believed the continued development of capitalism generated a multiplicity of classes including a substantial middle class (Nicholaus, 1967), they argued that capital can rule only with the allegiance of other classes and cannot simply rely on force or coercion to impose its will. In social democratic theory, then, the state becomes the focus for class struggle as the democratic franchise, or right to vote, is extended: first to legitimize capital's support among the middle classes, and later as property restrictions are removed to bring the working classes into the electorate (Therborn, 1977; Korpi, 1983). Eventually, through the political organization of the working class and the construction of electoral and party alliances with the middle classes (Esping-Andersen, 1980; Esping-Andersen and Friedland, 1982), the capitalist state can become a socialist state. Following this logic, social democrats see the adoption of Keynesianism and associated large public expenditures in the modern welfare state as a manifestation of this democratic class struggle for control of the state, as workers force concessions from capital that alleviate the threat of unemployment and enhance the social wage through the operation of the democratic process (Shalev, 1983; Esping-Andersen, 1981).

While social democratic analysis represents a sophisticated appreciation of how states and markets are interrelated in capitalist democracies, it does not entirely explain the timing or content of the different welfare state programs adopted in different countries or jurisdictions. This is because while the analysis is sensitive to different configurations of political and partisan organization in different societies, it is not sensitive to the variations in state structures and organizations (Skocpol and Finegold, 1982). Compared to Leninist or regulation political economy, both of which tend to have purely instrumental conceptions of the relationship between states and societal actors, social democratic political economy grants more autonomy to the state (Skocpol, 1985).

But in viewing state policy-making as characterized by begrudging capitalist accommodation to working-class militancy, social democrats overlooked the important role played by states and state officials in the adoption of—or failure to adopt—social welfare and other policies (Hall and Ikenberry, 1989; Nordlinger, 1981; Migdal, 1988; Granatstein, 1982). Similarly, social democrats have been very slow in coming to terms with international factors related to the globalization of capital and its ability to shift production and investment rapidly around the globe in response to changes in the prices of factors of production—-including labour rates and government regulatory and tax burdens. Without examining such factors, however, it is very difficult to understand the industrial crises that many social democratic countries have faced, and the adjustment strategies—including job cuts, deregulation, and privatization of public enterprises—with which they have responded to those crises (Smith, 1995).

Socialist Political Economy in Canada

In the early era of Canadian industrial history, the dominant tendency in socialist political economy was a kind of pre-Marxist Utopian socialism or anarcho-syndicalism, which attempted to construct a new social order based on co-operatives and large, multi-industry trade unions (Lipset, 1971; Wood, 1975; Sacouman, 1979; Robin, 1968; Palmer, 1986; Palmer and Kealey, 1982). By the end of World War I and following the Russian Revolution of 1917, however, much socialist political economy in Canada had adopted a distinctly Marxist flavour. For example, it accepted the need for a class analysis of Canadian society and the tenet of the leading role played by the economy and production relations in determining the nature and direction of political life (Avakumovic, 1975; Frank and Reilly, 1979).

A strong Leninist line was brought into Canada with the creation of the Communist Party of Canada (CPC) in 1919 (Avakumovic, 1975), while evolutionary social democratic principles emerged in the farmer-labour-intellectual coalition of the Co-operative Commonwealth Federation in the 1930s (League for Social Reconstruction, 1935).

Although the CPC shifted its analysis several times in accordance with the positions and analysis of the international scene provided by the Soviet-led International of Communist Parties, the party always focused on the close relations existing between the United States and Canada and emphasized the need for Canadians to break away from the domination of the United States before socialism could be achieved at home. Therefore, the CPC supported the establishment of nationalist trade unions and ran candidates in federal elections espousing a nationalist line. Although it successfully influenced the direction of the union movement in Canada—until it moderated its nationalist line in the late 1930s and 1940s to support the war effort and endorsed the affiliation of Canadian industrial unions with the US-based Congress of Industrial Organizations (CIO) (Abella, 1973)—the CPC-backed Labour Progressive Party (LPP) was much less successful at the polls. In a bitter struggle with the CCF for electoral support, the CPC-LPP was never fully committed to the democratic process and was unable to attract large numbers of voters to its ranks.

Leninist, Dependency, and Regulation Political Economy in Canada

From 1919 to about 1969, the CPC and its political line dominated Canadian Leninist political economy. By the early 1960s concerns about continually increasing foreign penetration of the Canadian economy and the apparently concomitant loss of Canadian political sovereignty led to a gradual shift in emphasis among both party supporters and academics towards a re-emphasis on the question of imperialism, resulting in the emergence of a distinctive 'dependency' slant in many analyses of the nature of the Canadian political economy and a separation of this variant of socialist political-economic analysis from that of the Communist Party of Canada.

This trend was obvious in many works that were highly critical of foreign investment in Canada, especially US investment, and its adverse consequences for Canadian indigenous development (Laxer, 1973; Hutcheson, 1978).[3] The resulting dependency approach infused the analysis of the Canadian political economy put forward by the so-called 'Waffle' faction within the NDP and was the theoretical base of the group's 'Waffle Manifesto' (Watkins, 1970) and other writings in the late 1960s and early 1970s. This approach brought about the consolidation of some nationalist liberals and most socialists in the country by stressing the constraints Canada's position in the international political economy placed on Canadian political life (Kellogg, 1989). It resulted in a powerful political movement, but by the mid-1970s many analysts were already concerned that the dependency analysis was empirically flawed and based on a misreading of Canadian economic development. They argued that it was theoretically weak in its neglect of careful class analysis and its overemphasis on elements such as geographical location, foreign ownership, and trade relations (Veltmeyer, 1978; Carroll, 1988).

Two authors working within the dependency approach summarized the debate in 1975:

> Is Canada a colony or an imperialist country? Is Canadian nationalism progressive or reactionary? Is the Canadian bourgeoisie comprador or independently imperialist? These are key questions facing the Canadian Left. They are not academic questions; for their answers determine the strategy for socialism in Canada.
>
> Those who view Canada as a U.S. colony with a comprador, non-imperialist bourgeoisie usually argue that the main contradiction is between the Canadian 'people' and American imperialism. Usually, this position favours a two-stage revolution and alliances with the 'non-imperialist' bourgeoisie. Since Canada is viewed as an 'oppressed' nation, nationalism plays a progressive role in the class struggle . . . . On the other hand, those who view Canada as a monopoly capitalist, imperialist country with an independent imperialist bourgeoisie argue that the main contradiction is between the Canadian working class and the Canadian bourgeoisie. (Moore and Wells, 1975: 7)

Although some socialist political economists continued with a dependency analysis of the national economy, fewer and fewer did so in the 1980s as criticism of the applicability of this model to the Canadian situation grew (Veltmeyer, 1979). Instead, dependency analysis concentrated on metropolitan-hinterland relations within Canada itself, arguing that the Atlantic, western, and northern regions of the country existed in a state of dependency and truncated development as a result of the actions and activities of central Canadian capital (Sacouman,

1981; Leadbeater, 1984; Sager, 1987). Other former supporters of dependency theory began to use regulation theory in their analyses of the Canadian case (Boismenu and Drache, 1990; Boismenu, 1989). In this they were supported by labour historians working in Canadian universities, many of whom have attempted to integrate a historical analysis of the labour process with the historical development of the Canadian economy and politics (Palmer, 1986; Kealey, 1981). In doing this they provide not only much-needed insights into the social history of Canada and its process of class formation (Pentland, 1981; Kealey, 1985) but also empirical studies of the development of the labour process in the Canadian manufacturing and resource industries (Heron and Storey, 1986). The studies fit neatly with works in a regulation vein chronicling the effects that different international regimes of production have had on Canadian social and political structures (Houle, 1983; Cameron and Houle, 1985; Marchak, 1986).

Although it is far from clear that the Fordist model, with its emphasis on the mass production of durable consumer products, is applicable to the resource-dependent Canadian economy, several recent analyses attempt to venture beyond the analysis of economic and production relations to apply a Fordist analysis to contemporary Canadian political life (Bradford and Jenson, 1989). As Rianne Mahon (1991: 325) has argued:

> Canada's model Fordism was both dependent on, and different from, American Fordism. Although mass consumption played a part in Canada's postwar economic expansion, the accelerator was not so much investment in the consumer durables industries but the inflow of foreign capital related to the extraction and export of Canada's staples resource industries, whose product was destined primarily for the American market.

In the contemporary period, however, limitations have begun to appear in this system as capital has become increasingly mobile and the production of commodities such as computers and computer software requires far less inputs in terms of natural resources than did earlier mass commodities such as automobiles (Gonick, 1992). In such circumstances, it is argued, a new regime of accumulation is emerging in Canada based on the extraction of absolute rather than relative surplus value. That is, employers everywhere seek to reduce wages and extend working hours, often via decertification of trade unions or extension of part-time employment. As Daniel Drache (1991: 266) has argued:

> The globalization of work and employment practices has an unmistakable character. Not only does it mean more low-paying work for large sections of the workforce but, increasingly, it relies on job ghettoes, the gender gap and highly competitive labour markets. The return to the cruder assumptions of economic liberalism also presupposes greater freedom for employers to utilize labour only as the new technologies dictate. Thus the new standards of work are premised on a subsistence minimum that allows the labour market to function with less interference.

While many Canadian staples political economists have concentrated on the denunciation of the Canada-US and North American free trade agreements as the 'constitutionalization' of this new labour process and social order (McBride and Shields, 1993), Canadian regulation school political economists have suggested that these agreements are merely part of the transition from Fordism to post-Fordism occurring in most industrialized states (Kaplinsky, 1993) and that this opposition represents the last vestiges of a misplaced and no longer progressive nationalist project (McNally, 1991). Somewhat paradoxically, given the attention formerly paid by Leninist political economy to international factors, most suggestions for improvement to the status quo today focus attention on the need to reform the internal structures of Canadian democracy in order to bypass the party system and bring the views and ideas of workers directly into the operation of the Canadian state (Albo, Langille, and Panitch, 1993; Bartholomew, 1993). How and why the Canadian state should be open to these efforts at re-democratization, and exactly how this will be achieved over the opposition of groups, such as business, which, it is argued, currently control the state, is never addressed.

Social Democratic Political Economy

Except for a brief period in the 1960s and early 1970s, the Leninist, dependency, and regulation approaches to socialist political economy have always been in the minority, labouring against both the confines of a capitalist economy and liberal political-economic theory and, within socialist political economy, against the more dominant social democratic tradition of political economic analysis.

Emerging out of the early pre-World War I socialist, labour, and workers' parties and gaining strength through the forging of electoral and partisan alliances with dissident farmers' groups in the 1920s and 1930s (Morton, 1950; Brodie and Jenson, 1988), Canadian social democrats embraced a moderate model of state planning and nationalized industrial and financial sectors based on the proposals of the British Labour Party and the Fabian Society (Young, 1969a; Zakuta, 1964) and Middle West American agrarian populism (Laycock, 1990). They did not broach the question of international dominance of the Canadian economy; instead, they looked at the failures of the existing market and governmental system to provide for a reasonable standard of living for the workers, farmers, and middle-class elements who were expected to form the basis of electoral support for a socialist party.

In the 1933 Regina Manifesto, which signalled the formation of the social democratic Co-operative Commonwealth Federation, and in the 1935 document, *Social Planning for Canada*, the CCF and its intellectual wing, the League for Social Reconstruction (LSR), outlined a program of public works, nationalization, and creation of state planning machinery premised on the election of social democrats to power through the existing democratic process (Whitehorn, 1992). This strategy was based on a nine-point proposal first set out by the LSR in 1931. The initial steps 'towards the realization of a new order' advocated by the League were:

1. Public ownership and operation of public utilities connected with transportation, communications, and electrical power, and of other industries as are already approaching conditions of monopolistic control.
2. Nationalization of Banks and other financial institutions with a view to the regulation of all credit and investment operations.
3. The further development of agricultural co-operative institutions for the production and merchandising of agricultural products.
4. Social legislation to secure to the worker adequate income and leisure, freedom of association, insurance against illness, accident, old age and unemployment and an effective voice in the management of his industry.
5. Publicly organized health, hospital and medical services.
6. A taxation policy emphasizing steeply graduated income and inheritance taxes.
7. The creation of a National Planning Commission.
8. The vesting in Canada of the power to amend and interpret the Canadian constitution so as to give the federal government power to control the national economic development.
9. A foreign policy designed to secure international co-operation in regulating trade, industry and finance, and to promote disarmament and world peace. (LSR, 1935: x)

The CCF program was directed at overcoming the problems of late monopoly capitalism and providing for a more efficient allocation of resources and wealth and production of goods and services in Canadian society. As in the cases of many European social democratic parties, this analysis quickly led the CCF and its adherents to endorse and adopt Keynesianism in the post-World War II era. In fact, the analysis made in *Social Planning for Canada* presaged this development by several times approvingly citing Keynes's analysis of the failures of a capitalist market economy.

Having opted for a Keynesian strategy if elected, Canadian social democrats turned their attention to the question of the appropriate electoral strategy for the party. The strategy of constructing alliances with farmers' organizations and trade unions proved successful in helping the CCF gain power in Saskatchewan in 1944 and become the official opposition in Ontario and British Columbia in the postwar period. As Canadian society became increasingly urbanized and industrialized after World War II, however, the farmers' role in electoral and partisan politics dwindled everywhere outside of the prairie provinces and Prince Edward Island, leading to a decline in CCF electoral fortunes. In response, Canadian social democrats undertook two actions. First, they attempted to reinforce their links with the trade union movement; and second, they began a search for some other social group to form an electoral coalition. Links with the trade union movement were solidified in 1961 when the CCF transformed itself into the New Democratic Party in a formal alliance with the new Canadian Labour Congress (CLC). The alliance gave CLC unions the right to send delegates to NDP conventions and otherwise influence internal party affairs (Brodie and Jenson, 1988; Black and Myles, 1986; Myles and Forcese, 1981; Schreiber, 1980).

These changes did not bring the NDP success at the polls, however, and many Canadian social democratic political economists in the 1970s looked for inspiration towards European and US social democratic analyses of monopoly capital, arguing that foreign investment and a history of affiliation of Canadian unions with their American counterparts had resulted in truncated industrial development and a weak trade union movement (Panitch, 1977; Grayson, 1980; Moscovitch and Drover, 1981). Others, however, returned to the old social democratic emphasis on the analysis of domestic institutions, state policies, and class relations. Rather than concentrating on external causes for Canada's failure to develop a socialist system, these social democrats paid much more attention to internal factors and especially to the links between state policy and class structures (Mahon, 1979, 1984; Cuneo, 1978, 1980).

These analyses focused on the manner in which social structures in Canada have been changed by economic development and state actions to the point where a very large proportion of the Canadian electorate is, or views itself as, middle class. Bolstered by state spending on social programs in areas such as health care, education, unemployment insurance, and pensions, significant elements of the population no longer have a direct link to the production relations of capitalism and tend to be concerned with a host of 'post-materialist' issues, such as identity, the environment, and quality of life, rather than the traditional social democratic concerns with employment and incomes (Clement and Myles, 1994). Social democratic parties in Europe, like the NDP in Canada, sought to capture these voters by adopting policies related to human rights and anti-discrimination measures, as well as by endorsing a 'green' agenda (Rosenblum and Findlay, 1991; Gonick, 1987). But, as George Ross and Jane Jenson have argued, this coalition-building is not without its quandaries for class-based political economic theory and practice:

> The politics of the peace, ecology and other movements and their electoralist propensities are often radical and progressive—in the sense of being change oriented—while simultaneously harbouring deep anti-working class feelings. At best such new middle strata politics seeks, in an interesting historical change of focus, to subordinate the workers' movement to its goals. At worst it simply disregards workers and their needs . . . . It follows from all this that a political position which advocates that the labour movement strike a deal with the 'new politics' as is, invites new problems. To the degree to which the labour movement is sufficiently strong to insist upon pro-working class priorities in the alliance, the alliance will be unstable. To the degree to which out of organizational or ideological weakness it ends up 'tailing' such new middle strata movements simply because they seem 'radical' the result is likely to be very dangerous for workers. (Ross and Jenson, 1986: 43)

Although the coalition strategy resulted in some NDP electoral successes in Ontario, Saskatchewan, and British Columbia in the 1990s, none of these governments was able to move very far towards the attainment of traditional social democratic objectives of industrial or economic democracy (Watkins, 1994; Cohen, 1994; Hansen, 1994). At the federal level, on the other hand, as Kitschelt had predicted, Canadian social democrats were singularly unsuccessful at the polls and found themselves squeezed between the neo-liberalism of the Progressive Conservative and Liberal parties and the authoritarianism of the Reform Party. For the most part, Canadian social democratic political economists have failed to grapple with the consequences of these developments and alter their understanding of the Canadian party and state systems or, more generally, of the nature of the contemporary Canadian political economy. Most social democratic analyses continue to advocate the perpetuation of Keynesian welfare state programs despite the fact that the economic and political structure of the country has moved well beyond Keynesianism (Panitch, 1992b).

Notes

1. This is true, for instance, concerning the extensive literature that addresses the question concerning how 'actually existing socialism'—that is, the system of central planning found in most socialist countries organized along the lines of the former Soviet Union—operates. See, for example, Nove, 1983; Brus, 1973.
2. The unit of labour Marx used in determining the value of each commodity is the 'average' or 'abstract' amount of labour required to produce all commodities in the economy. To determine the labour needed to produce a commodity he averaged the different skill levels required in various industries to arrive at an abstract standard of measurement. In this computation, every instance of skilled labour is reduced to a simple multiple of unskilled labour.
3. This new emphasis on metropolitan-hinterland relations or centre-periphery relations in Leninist political economy accorded very well with the older Canadian tradition of a staple political economy and in fact allowed a 'radicalization' of this primarily inductive, empirical approach to Canadian history and Canadian development (see Chapter 4).

Chapter 4

Staples Political Economy

The insights of a third method of studying Canadian political economy—the staples approach—have furthered our understanding of the Canadian situation and significantly influenced the work of both liberal and socialist political economists. Unlike the other two theories, this is only a partial theory—hence our use of the term staples 'approach'. It can be applied only to the examination of the political economies of Canada and other countries, such as the US, Australia, New Zealand, Argentina, and Chile, that at various times shared similar characteristics. These included: (1) a relatively sparse population prior to settlement by European colonizers, and (2) a reliance on bulk commodity exports—'staples'— to generate wealth in the economy.

While liberal and socialist political economists both rely on general models of the economy and political-economic relations that are then applied to the particular circumstances of the Canadian case, in contrast, the staples approach adopts a more inductive methodology. Its conclusions are based on the results of careful investigations into the particularities of the Canadian process of economic development carried out, in the main, by economic historians who wrote in the 1930s and 1940s. Significant differences between these early authors over their analysis of the trends and trajectory of Canadian economic development still colour the analyses made by contemporary adherents of the staples approach.

Fundamental Tenets

The staples approach was developed primarily by Canadian economists and historians whose works were rooted firmly in the empirical study of the actual conditions that prevailed during the historical development of the Canadian political economy from the sixteenth century onward. Writing in the 1930s, economic historians Harold Innis, Arthur Lower, and W.A. Mackintosh described a process whereby many, if not all, aspects of Canadian social and political life were affected by the reliance of the economy on staples industries. The school derives its name from the emphasis on staples, which Gordon Bertram (1963: 75) defined as 'agriculture and extractive resources, not requiring elaborate processing and finding a large portion of their market in international trade'. Staples theorists viewed Canadian political economy as having been distinctly shaped by the export of successive staples—fish, fur, lumber, minerals, wheat, and energy—over the course of Canadian history from the earliest colonial times to the modern era.

Following Gordon Laxer, four main 'analytical assumptions of the staples school' can be identified (Laxer, 1989b: 180–1). First, staples theorists believed that the key to understanding Canadian history is to discover the export commodity that the economy depended on in each era. They argued that the Canadian state and Canadian capital devoted themselves single-mindedly to discovering and extracting bulk resource commodities or staples that have a ready export market. The money thus derived was used to pay wages to Canadian workers and finance imports of goods demanded by Canadian consumers. Canadian economic growth, then, was intimately linked to the demand for staples in foreign markets, and this demand has indirectly shaped the economic development of Canada. This is because any shift in demand for a key staple in foreign markets, while usually inconsequential for the importing country, has a pervasive impact on the local export-based economy. This can be a positive phenomenon, as when new demand increases prices and leads to increased economic activity in the exporting country, but it can also have very negative consequences. Examples of the latter include the fading away of the fashion for beaver-felt hats in Europe in the nineteenth century, a phenomenon that had a serious, debilitating effect on the early Canadian economy, which was at the time almost completely dependent on the export of furs (Innis, 1956).

Second, staples political economists argued that Canadian political life is heavily influenced by the country's staple export-dependent economy because economic wealth and political power are concentrated in Canadian business and political élites—often the same people—who act as the instruments of interests in the industrialized countries importing the staples. The Canadian business community, in the view of many staples analysts, was more interested in promoting continued and expanded staples-resource exports than in acting as entrepreneurs developing an industrialized Canadian manufacturing economy (Naylor, 1972, 1975a). This, it was argued, had serious consequences for the structure of the Canadian economy, which has tended to develop trade and commercial enterprises and activities rather than industrial ones.

Third, the staples school emphasized that understanding history was the key to understanding the nature of the contemporary Canadian political economy. A study of the actual history of Canadian economic development, it was argued, enabled analysts to overcome the limitations of liberal and socialist theories developed primarily to understand and evaluate the operation of the mature economies of industrialized Europe. Staples theorists argued that Canada and many other New World economies had unique features that the two traditional theories could not account for (Jenson, 1989).[1]

Fourth, analysts in this school argued that the need to overcome geographical impediments to the expansion of staples exports helps explain the state's role in a staples-dependent economy. They noted that confronting the harshness of the Canadian terrain and the physical distances that had to be traversed to get staples from the hinterland to ocean loading ports required large capital expenditures on transportation and communications infrastructure, which Canadian business could not afford to make. Instead, projects such as canals and river improvements, railway construction, and the establishment of telephone, electrical, and airline systems were all undertaken by the Canadian state (Innis, 1972).

Not all staples theorists placed equal weight on all of these aspects, and significant debates existed, and continue to exist, between different groups concerning questions such as the historical time periods that the analysis can cover (Bertram, 1963) or whether the construction of transportation infrastructure amounts to industrial development or not (Eden and Molot, 1993). The most contentious question, however, one that divides staples political economy into two schools, is whether the reliance on staples exports rather than industrial manufacturing was positive or negative in terms of the contemporary status and potential of the Canadian political economy.

Historical Foundations

The staples approach has its origins in research into Canadian social, political, and economic history carried out in Canadian universities, roughly between 1920 and 1940, by members of what were then known as departments of political economy. The two most prominent scholars following this approach were Harold Innis and W.A. Mackintosh. But numerous other scholars during the same era arrived at similar conclusions regarding the significance of the resource industries and their impact on Canadian settlement (Fay, 1934). These included, most notably, Arthur Lower, a Queen's University historian; S.A. Saunders, a Dalhousie University historian; and Donald G. Creighton, a University of Toronto historian, as well as others scattered across the country. Lower (1938) explored the origins and impact of the lumber industry on Canadian development, while Creighton [1937] (1956) adopted several staples tenets in developing his 'Laurentian thesis' of Canadian history (Berger, 1976). Saunders examined the development of the Maritime provinces using a staples framework (Saunders, 1939).

Enough scholars were working in a similar vein by the mid-1930s to allow the publication between 1934 and 1938 of a nine-volume *Frontiers of Settlement* series on the history of Canadian economic, political, and social development. This series of books contains some of the finest writings in this tradition, including work by Lower (1938), Innis (1938), Mackintosh (1934), and A.S. Morton (1938). In 1939, major submissions by Saunders and Mackintosh to the Royal

Commission on Dominion-Provincial Relations (the Rowell-Sirois Commission) presented the development of the Canadian economy in staples terms, and in 1941 V.W. Bladen relied on a staples framework to write the first textbook on Canadian political economy (Bladen, 1956).

The two dominant thinkers in this tradition, however, were Innis and Mackintosh. While the two shared common theoretical premises in their emphasis on staples, they followed different lines of analysis and arrived at different conclusions in their works. Most later writings in the staples tradition can be classified according to whether they share Innis's pessimistic outlook on Canada's future or Mackintosh's more optimistic analysis.

The Innisian Approach

Harold Innis, an economist at the University of Toronto and one-time head of the American Economics Association, wrote a series of books from the 1920s to the 1940s discussing the significance of various early resource industries to the development of different parts of Canada. These included the classic works *A History of the Canadian Pacific Railway* (1923), *The Fur Trade in Canada* (1930), and *The Cod Fisheries* (1940) as well as numerous essays and edited works on related topics.

Innis argued that the political economy of Canada was shaped by the successive concentration on exports of cod, fur, lumber (and pulp and paper), agricultural products (principally wheat), and minerals, which all went to the metropolitan economies of Europe and later the United States. As Innis summarized his staples thesis:

> The economic history of Canada has been dominated by the discrepancy between the centre and the margin of western civilization. Energy has been directed toward the exploitation of staple products and the tendency has been cumulative. The raw material supplied to the mother country stimulated manufacturers of the finished product and also of the product which were in demand in the colony. Large-scale production of raw materials was encouraged by improvement of technique of production, of marketing, and of transport as well as by improvement in the manufacture of the finished product . . . . Agriculture, industry, transportation, trade, finance, and governmental activities tend to become subordinate to the production of the staple for a highly specialized manufacturing community. (Innis, 1956: 385)

According to Innis, Canada's export of staples products in unprocessed or semi-processed form was necessitated by the lack of technological capability to process them within the country; as well, exports were desired by the local populace in order to support the promise of an improved standard of living that had brought Europeans to Canada in the first place. The exportation of staples and the importation of consumer goods, while satisfying the needs of the immigrants, primarily benefited the interests of the industrialized nations, which secured cheap and reliable supplies of raw materials in exchange for captive markets for their manufactured goods. The domestic commercial interests involved in the movement and financing of the export-import trade also benefited from their position as middlemen or brokers in this process.

With the passage of time, Innis argued, increasingly larger local resources had to be devoted to resource exports in order to continue to increase living standards as more and more immigrants entered the country. This increase in the scale of resource exploitation exacerbated the staples-orientation of the political economy in several ways. First, increasing reliance on staples exports necessitated ever greater investments in transportation infrastructure as easily accessible sources of raw materials became more difficult to locate and bring to market. The heavy debt-servicing charges that such investments involved diverted funds away from other areas of the economy, including manufacturing. In addition, the railways built to transport wheat and lumber to ports not only often could not pay for themselves, but provided unused capacity that made it possible to transport and export other products, such as pulp, paper, and minerals (Innis, 1956).

Second, the dependence on staples export also exposed the Canadian economy to the vagaries of price-setting in international commodity markets. These tend to witness violent fluctuations as new capacity comes onstream in different countries, lowering world prices and resulting in lay-offs and closures in exporting countries until world demand catches up with global supplies. When that happens, prices suddenly rise, leading to boom conditions in exporting countries until capacity again increases and the 'boom-bust' cycle begins anew.

Third, the increasing dependence on staples correspondingly widened Canada's technological backwardness, since only limited technology is required to extract and ship raw materials to foreign markets. The failure to adopt and develop new technologies would deepen and reinforce the country's dependence on unprocessed or semi-processed raw materials.

The cumulative impact of all this, according to Innis, was that the Canadian economy became caught in what Mel Watkins (1963) would later call a 'staples trap'. Innis noted that some countries, like the US, had managed to avoid this trap, but argued that this was due to significant differences in resource endowments and other geographical factors between the two countries. Climatic and topographical difficulties prevented Canada from undergoing a similar process of development to that of the United States, where a less harsh geography allowed a large and prosperous agricultural sector to develop, one capable of supporting a large domestic population. This, in turn, allowed a substantial industrial sector to develop to serve the growing domestic market.

In Canada, however, the virtually complete dependence on staples exports, according to Innis, doomed Canada's chances of developing a domestic industrial base. This form of economic life could provide relatively high standards of living to citizens of exporting countries, but only as long as domestic resource supplies and world demand remained constant or increased. Any declines in demand or increases in supplies would have drastic consequences for the domestic political economy, which would be poorly placed to respond to the challenge of finding a new economic base. As a result, Innis and most staples political economists following his lead were very pessimistic about Canada's future as a reasonably wealthy 'developed' country (Williams, 1986).

The Mackintosh Approach

W.A. Mackintosh, a Queen's University professor of economics and adviser to the federal Liberal government of William Lyon Mackenzie King, had more impact on practical political economy than most academics ever will. He served as a key researcher for the Rowell-Sirois Commission in the late 1930s, looking into problems caused in Canada by the Great Depression, and was one of the most powerful bureaucrats in the federal government during World War II—at a time when the government itself was very powerful as a result of the federal military and production activities to promote the war effort (Ferguson, 1993; Granatstein, 1982). Mackintosh was instrumental in introducing Keynesianism to Canada, and that approach formed the basis for Canada's postwar strategy of economic growth, but with the twist that full employment was to be secured through increased staples exports and an inflow of investments in further resource extraction and branch-plant manufacturing.

In his theoretical writings Mackintosh argued that in a 'new' country, dependence on the export of staples is an essential stage in economic growth. In his first article on the subject, in 1923, he stated: 'The prime requisite of colonial prosperity is the colonial staple. Other factors connected with the staple industry may turn it to advantage or disadvantage, but the staple in itself is the basis of prosperity' (Easterbrook and Watkins, 1967: 3). In a report to the Rowell-Sirois Commission in 1939 he stood by this position: 'Rapid progress in . . . new countries is dependent upon the discovery of cheap supplies of raw materials by the export of which to the markets of the world the new country may purchase the products which it cannot produce economically at that stage of its development' (Mackintosh, 1939: 13).

Mackintosh presented economic development as a linear process in which each nation has to pass through a series of stages (Williams, 1986: 131–2). For him, Canada's dependence on staples reflected the nation's early stage of development, when staples were the only area in which it enjoyed a comparative advantage internationally. Unlike Innis, he argued that eventually the technology acquired and the profits accumulated from the extraction and export of staples would lead to investment in manufacturing industries. The expansion of the domestic population and the availability of foreign capital and technology in setting up manufacturing plants to supply the growing domestic market would further facilitate the process, as occurred in the United States. If Canada had not yet been as successful as the United States, it was because its harsher climate and smaller population only inhibited or slowed, but did not prevent, the establishment of efficient manufacturing industries. The implication of his analysis was clear: there was nothing wrong in depending on staples exports, for eventually industrialization would arrive in Canada as the population continued to grow.

Following World War II, Vernon Fowke (1946) and Kenneth Buckley (1958), among others, followed Mackintosh's line of reasoning. Both pointed out the tremendous economic spin-offs to the Canadian economy that had accrued as a result of booming wheat exports between the 1890s and 1920s. As John Richards (1985) observed:

> To Fowke and Buckley, the wheat boom was necessary to Canadian industrialization because it alone provided a sustained high level of demand necessary for the Canadian manufacturing sector to 'take off.' Without wheat Canada would have had a much smaller domestic market and, given serious barriers to any new manufacturing exporter, manufacturers could not easily have substituted export for domestic markets; their level of activity could have been seriously curtailed.

Fowke and Buckley's work supported Mackintosh's theory. They noted, however, that the growth occurring in Canada had a significant regional dimension. That is, a large proportion of the benefits did not flow to the western wheat producers but to Canadian manufacturers, most of them located in central Canada. The application of staples analysis to the internal workings of the Canadian economy was to become an important aspect of staples political economy in Canada in the 1970s and 1980s (Richards and Pratt, 1977; Marchak, 1983; Frank, 1984; Nelles, 1974; Basran and Hay, 1988). In the 1950s, however, many different aspects of Canada's resource-dependent economy were being investigated (Easterbrook, 1959) using a Mackintosh-inspired staples approach. These included studies of topics such as the impact of resource dependence on provincial development (Dales, 1957) and the impact of US investment in key resource industries (Aitkin et al., 1959; Aitkin, 1961). The high point in the staples analysis, in a practical political sense, occurred in the late 1950s when the federal Royal Commission on Canada's Economic Prospects (the Gordon Commission) accepted Mackintosh's version of the staples thesis and focused its efforts on planning for, and controlling, the various effects on Canadian society of resource-led economic growth (Canada, Royal Commission on Canada's Economic Prospects, 1957).

Contemporary Debates

By the 1960s, both variants of the staples approach to Canadian political economy were being challenged on a number of fronts. The historical generalizations of the staples tradition were being subjected to detailed scrutiny and to a demand for empirical verification by means of quantitative economics and econometrics (Bertram, 1963; Chambers and Gordon, 1966). At the same time, the significance of the historical approach to understand contemporary economic and political phenomena was being undermined by alternative methodologies in contemporary political science, such as the systems and behavioral approaches, which promised greater insight into discovering solutions for contemporary political problems (Easton, 1965; Charlesworth, 1962). Although the staples approach would receive its finest formulation at this point (Watkins, 1963), it would be increasingly relegated to the sidelines in academe as a conceptualization of the early developmental stages of a relatively new economy, an approach without much relevance to contemporary life.

Nevertheless, because most significant historical works on Canada's development had been fashioned by staples theorists, the approach could never be completely eliminated. Any researcher delving into Canada's past was bound to encounter the staples theorists and their powerful, inductively developed model of the Canadian political economy. This, in fact, occurred at the end of the 1960s as many scholars, in Canada and elsewhere, rejected what they viewed as purposeless quantification and modelling of economic and political phenomena in favour of the broader insights offered by a synoptic staples perspective.

The staples approach to Canadian political economy was revived at a time, towards the end of the 1960s, that was unusual in North American history, a time that had a pervasive impact on inquiries in social sciences. Civil rights activism in the United States and anti-Vietnam War protests across North America had rendered the intellectual milieu fertile for challenging established beliefs, while the anticolonial nationalist struggles in the Third World in the years following the end of World War II had given a new impetus to nationalism. It was also a time when the emerging evidence of the increasing strength of multinational corporations was inculcating fears that these corporations would enable the former colonial powers to once again dominate the world.

In Canadian staples political economy, an enhanced nationalism and a scepticism about the validity of established liberal and socialist theories led to the search for alternative analyses, for an approach that would be more in tune with the realities of Canadian history and provide a more pertinent guide to political practice than the deductive application of general liberal or socialist principles. Not surprisingly, this search led to a renaissance in staples theory.

However, the staples approach did not provide a clear guide for political action. Unlike the liberal and socialist theories, the staples analyses of both Innis and Mackintosh provided what were essentially descriptive evaluations of the pattern of Canada's economic growth. Moreover, as we have seen, the two differed in the prescriptions they proposed for influencing the course of Canada's development and in whether they felt the process had been harmful or beneficial to Canada. Before their analyses could be used to develop plans to improve Canada's lot, it was necessary to synthesize their various writings, observations, and insights into a general model of economic growth.

When this was attempted, it became obvious to most observers that staples political economy did not have the theoretical status of liberal and socialist political economy. That is, it did not reflect a completely separate theory outside of the liberal and socialist models but existed simply as a specific case, a somewhat unique example of national development, or lack of it, within the more general theories. This led to two different revised versions of staples theory: one combined the pessimism of Innis *vis à vis* the future of the Canadian resource economy with the pessimism of socialist political economy *vis à vis* the future of capitalism. The other, drawing on the optimistic writings of Mackintosh concerning the future direction of Canadian development, was compatible with liberal optimism about the efficiency and creativity of capitalism. The first, *neo-Innisian*, perspective is sometimes referred to as the 'new political economy',[2] while the second approach can be termed the *new staples political economy*. Debate between the two continues to the present day (Pal, 1989; Laxer, 1989b).

The Neo-Innisian Approach

The neo-Innisian staples political economy combined, or attempted to combine, the work of Harold Innis with the theories of socialist political economy, especially the Leninist dependency school. The resemblance of the Canadian economy to economies in the Third World—especially with respect to the high degree of foreign ownership—made such a line of analysis seem appropriate.

Two elements from Innis's thinking hit a particularly harmonious cord with scholars attempting to develop a new Canadian political-economic theory. One was his conclusion that dependence on staples exports inhibited independent industrial development. The second, expressed in his later writings, was the fear of US dominance of Canada. The first element allowed the neo-Innisians to adopt dependency theory in their analysis of Canadian political economy (Levitt, 1970; Teeple, 1972; Laxer, 1973; Hutcheson, 1978). The second fostered the development of economic nationalism, which in the Canadian context necessarily involved a certain degree of anti-Americanism.[3] The two together almost inevitably led to the conclusion that the Canadian economy was suffering because of overly high levels of US investment and that, more importantly, protectionist measures should be taken to reduce it. In other words, the 'staples trap' could only be overcome through resort to economic nationalism. In the words of Daniel Drache, a significant figure among neo-Innisians, 'Anti-imperialism, anti-capitalism and Canadian independence are an inseparable unity.' However, as the country moved closer to integration with the US through the creation of long-term trade and investment treaties such as the Canada-US Free Trade Agreement (FTA) and the North American Free Trade Agreement (NAFTA), neo-Innisians became more and more pessimistic about the possibilities of Canada ever escaping from its staples trap (Clement and Williams, 1997).

Neo-Innisian analyses have a number of common features. First, the scholars in this tradition attribute heavy emphasis to the need for an advanced manufacturing sector, a feature characteristic of economic nationalism (Gilpin, 1987). As Glen Williams points out, there is a 'pervasive concern with the overdevelop-

ment of the resource export sector of the economy at the expense of the industrial sector' (1986: 138). As a corollary, they assert that the dominance of the
resources sector has stifled the growth of indigenous manufacturing in Canada.

Second, the neo-Innisians believe 'that foreign direct investment in Canadian
manufacturing, among its other negative effects, inhibited our capacity to
develop an export trade in industrial products' (Williams, 1986: 138). The reference here is to US investments, which have formed a majority of all foreign
investment in Canadian manufacturing since the 1920s. This area of Canadian
economic history has generated some of the finest work in the staples approach
(Naylor, 1972, 1975b; Watkins, 1977; Levitt, 1970; Laxer, 1989a, 1989b). The
theorists argue that foreign subsidiaries have been more interested in making
quick profits for their parent firms than in attempting to be innovative, export-
oriented, or internationally competitive. Ironically, much of the US investment
arrived in Canada to evade tariff barriers against imports, which were inspired at
least partly by Canadian nationalism (Eden and Molot, 1993).

Third, neo-Innisians warn that 'a failure to address and correct these trade
problems will result in decreasing living standards or even a descent toward
"economic underdevelopment" ' (Williams, 1986: 138). Pessimism about Canada's
social and economic prospects is indeed an enduring feature of neo-Innisian analyses, and it received a fresh boost with the signing of the free trade agreements,
which neo-Innisians argue merely cement Canada's position as a resource
warehouse for US industry (Cameron, 1988; McBride and Shields, 1993).

Finally, the neo-Innisians are acutely concerned about Canada's cultural
identity, and they fear its assimilation by US culture (Christian, 1977b; Lumsden,
1970). They take considerable pride in the fact that Canadians are not Americans
and do not practise the same kind of heartless capitalism. They argue that
Canada has developed a superior social welfare system and activist state tradition due to the sense of community engendered in Canadians' attempting to
create a modern country in the context of a harsh and difficult climate. Closer
economic integration with the United States, it is argued, will undermine this
sociocultural distinctiveness and rapidly lead to assimilation (Audley, 1983).

The publication of Kari Levitt's *Silent Surrender* in 1970 marked the beginning
of a series of works building on Innis's conception of Canada as a staples-
producing nation on 'the margin' of Western capitalism. Levitt argued that US
multinational corporations 'organized the collection or extraction of the raw
material staple required in the metropolis and supplied the hinterland with
manufactured goods, whether produced at home or "on site" in the host
country' (Levitt, 1970: 25).

Direct investments in Canada by the multinationals had enabled them to
drain Canada of profits and, worse still, to buy into the economy from profits
made locally. Levitt was especially critical of Canadian capitalists who had
allowed this to happen so they could make money managing or representing US
firms. As she put it, 'The Canadian entrepreneurs of yesterday are the coupon
clippers and hired vice-presidents of branch plants of today. They have quite

literally sold out the country' (ibid., 40). She described this as a 'silent surrender' on the part of Canada because the adverse effects of the branch-plant
economy were cumulative, as Americans came increasingly to dominate the
economy because of their superior technological and capital base.

Levitt's argument had an electrifying effect on the Canadian politicians and
scholars on the left of the political spectrum (Drache, 1977). Her description of
Canada as the 'world's richest underdeveloped country' was radical and echoed
many elements contained in contemporary socialist political economy, particularly its dependency approach. As William Carroll points out, however, Levitt's
radicalism was not socialist since it was 'based not on a concept of class
exploitation but of national oppression' (Carroll, 1986: 5). Her pessimistic
nationalism was much closer to Innis than it was to Marx.

Another influential work in the emerging neo-Innisian literature was Tom
Naylor's detailed two-volume *History of Canadian Business* (1975), which
reinterpreted Creighton's (1937) earlier work on the role played by central
Canadian commercial and financial interests in the development of the country.
Naylor's primary thesis was that the dominance of the merchant class, which
later controlled banking and finance, stifled the growth of the manufacturing
sector in Canada. The profits accumulated in the staples trade assisted the establishment of a robust indigenous banking sector in Canada. But these banks did
not extend credit to nascent industries because of the higher risks and the longer
pay-back period involved. Instead, they were content to invest in staples trade
and railways. As Naylor argued, the strength of Canadian capitalism in the
commercial sector 'was not matched by its industrial efforts. Rather the strength
of the commercial sector went hand-in-hand with industrial weakness, by virtue
of the absence of funds due to the twisting of the capital market so that funds
flowed freely into commerce and staple movements, and away from industry,
and because of the absence of independent innovative capacity' (Naylor, 1975b,
II: 282–3). The industrialization of Canada was left to foreign investment. The
tariffs on imports imposed at the foreign investors' behest erected barriers to
foreign goods, not to capital. This marked the beginning of branch-plant
manufacturing, which only grew as years progressed, while the commercial
sector was left to Canadian capital.

In his conclusions Naylor is entirely pessimistic about the prospects for
Canada breaking out of this situation, as were Innis and Levitt before him. He
expected the American dominance of the Canadian economy to increase and
Canadian capitalists to be willing accomplices in the process. As he remarked in
an earlier article, 'A Canadian capitalist state cannot survive because it has
neither the material base nor the will to survive, the former contributing
substantially to the latter' (Naylor, 1972: 36).

Naylor's historical study was complemented by Wallace Clement's analyses
of the actual staffing and operation of modern Canadian businesses. Clement
(1975, 1977), in his analysis of corporate interlocks between Canadian and
American businesses, showed that the modern Canadian political economy is

dominated by indigenous capitalists in finance, transportation, and utilities and a comprador group that manages US branch manufacturing plants. The dominance of these groups has shut out Canadian entrepreneurs from manufacturing because they lack access to credit from banks. Support for indigenous industrialists from the government was also not forthcoming because the state itself—a view shared by Innis, Levitt, and Naylor—was an instrument of the dominant commercial-financial sector.

The most systematic version of the neo-Innisian approach was developed by Daniel Drache (1977, 1982). Arguing that underlying Innis's approach was a 'theory of rigidities', Drache developed a model 'to account both for the incomplete nature of Canada's industrial revolution and the inability of Canada to pursue a path of integrated development and become a centre economy in its own right' (Drache, 1982: 36). According to Drache, the staples mode of development has the following features:

1. The staple mode of development is defined by its commercial orientation . . . .
2. Resource development is based on monopoly . . . .
3. Infrastructure projects such as railways are designed to link the domestic market to the imperial centre, with the result that the external market dominates industry and other core areas of the economy.
4. Direct investment gives foreign capital perpetual control of key industrial and resource sectors.
5. The rate of capital accumulation is persistently high . . . ; nonetheless [there is a] chronic capital shortage due both to the constant backflow of profits and dividends and to the capital intensive nature of resource exploitation . . . .
6. In economic matters, the Canadian state is autonomous neither in a relative nor an absolute sense; rather, as the creation of the imperial state, it functions as the instrument of foreign capital . . . .
7. The traditional neo-classical instruments of growth such as the tariff, resource exports, technology transfer and foreign investment become structures of dependency in a satellite economy . . . .
8. [Finally,] incomplete development is not a passing stage but a permanent condition of the periphery. (Ibid., 53–4)

The links of neo-Innisian theory to dependency theory, however, began to be questioned in the late 1970s (Macpherson, 1979; Panitch, 1981; McNally, 1981). Socialist critics argued that the staples theorists' focus on the exchange relationships of domestic and international capital ignored production relations and class conflict. The debate quickly became polemical, with the neo-Innisians arguing that circumstances peculiar to Canada warranted the rejection of universal Marxist formulas developed in the European context (Drache and Clement, 1985; Drache and Kroker, 1983; Parker, 1977; Watkins, 1982).

Nevertheless, by the 1990s most neo-Innisians had abandoned dependency theory in favour of a 'regulation' approach focusing on the labour process. The principal aspect of Canada's political economy to be investigated was the nature of Canada's regime of accumulation. Although some neo-Innisians argued that Canada simply reflected a variant of Fordism in which investment flows across borders 'permeated' this regulatory regime (Jenson, 1989), others argued that Canada had moved closer to a new, post-Fordist or neo-Fordist mode of accumulation (Mahon, 1991; Kreklewich, 1993). In this view, Canada no longer existed as simply a branch plant of foreign, and especially American, capital but had become an integral part of a new continental system of accumulation in which, under the terms of treaties such as NAFTA, Canadian capital, as well as American and Mexican, enjoyed unprecedented mobility and freedom from government restraint.

While this analysis has opened up a new space for neo-Innisians to deal with contemporary questions such as the rise of the service sector and the ecological limits of resource-based economic development (Myles, 1991; Clement and Myles, 1994; Phillips, 1991), it has not reduced the pessimism neo-Innisians have consistently displayed towards Canada's political economic prospects. Although the analysis is now based on different premises from earlier neo-Innisian thought, it has the same pessimistic conclusion: that Canada has moved from 'colony to nation to colony', as Innis had argued. Thus, the neo-Innisian view of the inevitable demise of Canada, its underdevelopment, and its incorporation into the American ambit remains virtually unchanged. As Stephen Clarkson has put it:

> If for the continental regime of accumulation there is no satisfactory mode of regulation with sufficiently articulated institutions to give the component parts adequate weight in decision-making for the Canadian region as a whole, then the whole system is bound to remain in a continual condition of instability. As it stands, the FTA has neutered the Canadian state of much of its economic-management and cultural-development capabilities. Apart from tariffs, federal and provincial governments are forbidden to pass laws controlling foreign investment or regulate banking, energy or services to the advantage of Canadian-owned corporations. At the same time the American government's sovereign capacity to legislate in the economy is barely affected. (Clarkson, 1991: 119)

The New Staples Approach

Mackintosh's staples political economy did not receive the same reception as that of his counterpart, Harold Innis. His optimism that staples exports would eventually enable Canada to industrialize drew little sympathy from socialists, who saw no evidence of this occurring (Drache, 1982). However, his views did influence liberal nationalists concerned about Canada's apparent failure to develop into a diversified, industrialized economy following World War II (Ferguson, 1993). It was within a Mackintosh-inspired framework that the most systematic model of staples-led growth was developed by Mel Watkins.

Watkins's theory of economic growth rests very much within the assumptions of liberal political economy: it focuses on the role played by entrepreneurs in the marketplace as a key determinant of economic development (Watkins, 1963). Although Watkins later adopted a more neo-Innisian perspective on Canada's economic development and endorsed many of the dependency arguments concerning both regional and national underdevelopment (Watkins, 1977), his early work represents an excellent synthesis of the various conceptions of staples-led growth found in the Mackintosh-inspired staples literature.

Watkins made it clear at the outset that he felt the staples approach applied only to 'new' countries, and those in North and South America, Australia, New Zealand, such as which were distinguished by their favourable ratio of natural resources (staples) to labour and capital. He argued that because of this condition, staples exports would necessarily form the cornerstone of their economies.

> The limited . . . domestic market, and the factor proportion—an abundance of land relative to labour and capital—create a comparative advantage in resource-intensive exports, or staples. Economic development will be a process of diversification around an export base. The central concept of a staple theory, therefore, is the spread effects of the export sector, that is the impact of export activity on domestic economy and society. (Watkins, 1963: 53–4)

The extent to which the spread effects would be realized depended on three kinds of 'linkages' in the export of particular staples: 'backward linkage, forward linkage, and final demand linkage' (ibid., 55). The forward linkage involved investments in further processing of the staples, such as lumber into pulp and, preferably, paper. The backward linkage involved investments in production of the inputs required by the staples sector, such as railways to move wheat or machinery used in mining and logging. The final demand linkage would be created by the expenditure of incomes generated in the production and export of staples; it exists to the extent that those incomes are used to invest in manufacturing of the goods consumed in the home country.

The establishment of these three linkages, Watkins argued, cannot be taken for granted. Much depended on the nature of the staple itself. Cod fishing afforded few linkages, for example, because at the end of the season the fishermen tended to return to their homeland after they had caught and cured their fish; they didn't invest in backward or forward industries. Wheat, in contrast, attracted permanent immigrants who established, for example, an agricultural machinery industry (backward linkage) as well as food milling, processing, and preserving industries (forward linkage). Wheat production also automatically led to some degree of final demand linkage as industries were established to supply basic needs such as clothes, shoes, and toiletries to farmers and other members of the agricultural community.

The importance of final demand linkage is clearly the greatest if the economy is to diversify away from staples dependence. But the full realization of this linkage remains elusive if, as Innis argued, the staples exports are in the hands of foreign investors who siphon off their profits to their home countries, leaving little behind to invest in local manufacturing. Besides, it is usually easier and more profitable for foreigners to supply manufactured goods to the local economy from their home country, thus making profits for an indigenous commercial class in both the export of staples and the import of manufactured goods. The most significant problem, however, according to Watkins, was that staples dependence can foster an 'export mentality, resulting in an overconcentration of resources in the export sector and a reluctance to promote domestic development' (Watkins, 1963: 62). If this happens the economy can become ensnared in a staples trap, whereby it becomes increasingly dependent on the economies that receive its imports and supply its manufactured goods.

While this analysis shares much with the neo-Innisian approach, Watkins was much less pessimistic about the prospects for avoiding or overcoming a staples trap. Sharing some of Mackintosh's optimism, Watkins argued that eliminating the 'inhibiting export mentality' is within the means of policy-makers who can support indigenous manufacturing through a variety of policy instruments, including tariffs, taxation, subsidies, public enterprises, and regulations of various kinds.

This more optimistic new staples political-economic analysis was taken up in the 1970s by many Canadian governments. It inspired new government regulations limiting foreign investment in Canada and the creation of new policies designed to promote Canadian manufacturing and industry. The Science Council of Canada, for example, enthusiastically endorsed the model, which was used in several of its key publications (Britton and Gilmour, 1978). The Science Council was particularly emphatic about the need for Canada to regain its 'technological sovereignty' so the country would not have to rely on proprietary foreign technology in core areas of the economy. To push for this objective the Science Council continued to recommend a host of interventionist measures to promote indigenous Canadian research and development efforts. In its 1984 policy proposal, for example, it called for subsidies and protection from imports for domestic manufacturing (Science Council, 1984). After the mid-1980s, however, the Science Council watered down its proposals, perhaps because it realized that its interventionist proposals were not appreciated by a federal Conservative government committed to reducing the role of the government in the economy (see, for example, Science Council, 1988). Very soon afterwards, it was abolished.

The privately funded Canadian Institute for Economic Policy also endorsed a new staples approach to Canadian political economy in the late 1970s and early 1980s. The Institute's submission to the Macdonald Commission in 1984 represents a good example of its analysis (Rotstein, 1984: 50–4). In typical new staples political economy fashion, it pointed out the perverse effects of high levels of foreign investment on Canadian economic development and the need for their reduction. It argued that an interventionist industrial policy to promote manufacturing industries under Canadian control could help resolve these problems.

Like the neo-Innisians, adherents of the new staples political economy were opposed to the negotiation and conclusion of the Canada-US Free Trade

Agreement, which, it was argued, limited the ability of Canadian governments to adopt the positive policy measures required to break out of a staples trap (Barlow, 1990; Hurtig, 1991; Cameron and Watkins, 1993). One current in the new staples political economy has continued to decry the post-FTA situation and demand the abolition of the trade treaties or their successor documents like the Memorandum of Agreement on Investment (MAI).[4] A more interesting variant, however, is concerned with the analysis of what it terms the 'post-staples' political economy.

The progression of most of Canada towards a post-staples economy; both supports and contradicts key suppositions of the new staples political economy analysis of Canada's future economic development. From the latter perspective, hinterland areas supply resource commodities to the more industrialized and urban core areas, limiting their own development. As Thomas Hutton (1994) has observed, 'mature, advanced' staples economies have the following features:

1. substantial depletion of resource endowments;
2. well-established export markets for principal staple commodities;
3. increasingly capital- and technology-intensive resource extraction processes;
4. increasing competition from lower-cost staple regions;
5. evolution of development from 'pure' extraction to increased refining and secondary processing of resource commodities;
6. increasing diversification of the industrial structure, with manufacturing, tourism, and local administration and services;
7. evolution of settlements both within and outside the metropolis;
8. increasing pressure from 'environmental' groups to inhibit traditional modes of resource extraction and stimulate development alternatives.

Thus, while these political economies may still be characterized as 'resource dependent', their economies are more diffused and diversified than in the past (Hessing and Howlett, 1997). Factors that have affected these changes include severe pressures on critical resource sectors and the prospect of even more substantial contractions in the near future, as well as the development of significant new non-resource-based information and other technologies (Wolfe, 1991). These pressures are often accompanied by rapid sectoral shifts in the structure of the staples economy, including a shift to services, rapid tertiarization, and significant industrial expansion in regional centres.

Post-staples analysis examines the consequences of these changes for the structure and operation of affected political economies. These include an *internal* reconfiguration of growth and development, with a significant increase in metropolitan shares of population and employment, the emergence of regional economic centres, and the decline of smaller resource-dependent communities, as well as an *external* reorientation of key international relationships, characterized not merely by increasing trade and global markets but by a rapid integration within new markets, networks, and societies[5] (Hutton, 1994; Britton, 1996).

Economic restructuring of post-staples political economies has been associated with changes throughout the country: with the movement of capital offshore, global competition, and technological innovation, all of which have resulted in the downsizing of the workforce and extensive job loss. The loss of existing jobs and the inadequate creation of new jobs are increasingly problematic (Heron and Storey, 1986; McBride, 1992), driving the need for increased diversification and especially the growth of the tertiary sector. This implies the creation of more jobs with proportionally less direct resource reliance. Although the creation of alternative employment has been slow and itself subject to global competition, the post-staples variant of the new staples political economy is generally optimistic that government policies that directly or indirectly foster the growth of emerging services can overcome many of these problems. In this view, governments should pursue a wide range of activities in areas such as environmental industries and services, resource restoration and recycling, value-added resource industries and products, new products from industrial residues, alternative energy sources, and the tourism and convention industry (Hutton, 1995).

The State in Staples Political Economy

The most fundamental criticism of classical staples theory is that it lacked a sense of the political. That is, although sometimes working as political economists in government, who almost by definition must maintain a watchful eye on the numerous ways in which the political and the economic interact, these theorists somewhat paradoxically frequently undermined the importance of political factors in shaping the Canadian political economy (McNally, 1981). In their analyses of Canadian development they virtually never addressed the importance of political institutions, political parties, elections, public policy-making, or any other of the basic subjects of traditional political investigation.

Many of the early staples theorists were, in fact, economic, geographical, or technological determinists. In their work there was no autonomous role for the state. State actions were assumed to flow from certain economic or geographic, and primarily technological, imperatives. Its functions were defined by the exigencies of the staples trade. Policy options were limited by the constraints imposed by frontier conditions, and policies were chosen automatically by the objective requirements of staple exports (Whitaker, 1983). As Gregory Albo and Jane Jenson (1989) argue: 'The nature of the state—and the particular function it performed in specific spatial and temporal locations—were derived from the needs of the staples commodity. These needs included the provision of transportation infrastructures and credit guarantees and liquidity and the promotion of staples exports in general.'

Neo-Innisian staples political economists, in their own concern that Canada has not developed into an industrialized economy and that it appears to be caught in a vicious cycle of underdevelopment, did attribute some significance to political factors such as the nature of the Canadian capitalist class and especially its commercial, as opposed to industrial, orientation. As we have seen, their analyses suggest that a major part of the problem facing Canada lies in the conscious decision of the state and business élites to foster an economic struc- ture in which the dynamics of the international economy impede Canadian industrialization. The explanations of Naylor and Clement about why the state had adopted policies that suited staple exports, for example, are explicitly politi- cal: the commercial-financial class, which controlled and benefited from those exports, has always staffed and controlled the state, thus ensuring that govern- ment policies would favour its interests (Naylor, 1975; Clement, 1975, 1977).

In this sense, like much of the socialist political economy that influenced it, neo-Innisian political economy explains the role of the state in Canadian society using a theory that is fundamentally instrumentalist in nature. The neo-Innisians portray Canada's industrial backwardness as a result of the dominance of the financial-commercial sector over the state. Like other theories that rely on such a view of the state, however, neo-Innisian analysis has difficulty explaining the role of, among other things, democratic elections in the political process. Neo- Innisian analysts simply assume that the economic dominance of the commer- cial-financial élites is transformed automatically into political decisions favourable to this class. As such, and unlike new staples political economists, neo-Innisians generally do not expect the state to be able, or to desire, to adopt policies capable of extracting Canada from its staples trap.

The new staples political economists, on the other hand, attribute more autonomy to the state, but, again, usually without an extensive analysis of what the state is actually capable of accomplishing. That is, new staples theory allows for the possibility of overcoming the staples trap through actions of the state that can affect the behaviour of business in ways that it might not otherwise wish to adopt. Unfortunately, the new staples political economists often appear to have more confidence in the ability of the state to shape the economy than is warranted by its record to date. Along with examples of strategic thinking and great success, the history of state intervention in the Canadian economy is replete with examples of corruption, wastage, and mismanagement. As such, there is no guarantee that nationalist policy initiatives such as protecting and subsidizing domestic producers to promote industrialization will necessarily lead to economic growth and development. In some cases, it could be argued, such actions will merely reinforce non-entrepreneurial staples behaviour such as when a *rentier* mentality overtakes industry if indigenous capitalists are completely sheltered from competition and remain content to supply a protected domestic market at artificially high prices. In such cases, state action simply passes costs on to the consumers who ultimately pay higher prices for goods and services than otherwise would be the case (Richards, 1985: 58).

Perhaps most significantly, many of the proposals put forward by the new staples political economists for state action to regain control over the economy and promote industrialization do not take into account the fact that the

Canadian state might be too weak to be able to heed their advice. Unlike neo-Innisians, who argue this is due to the nature of the Canadian capitalist or ruling class, for new staples theory the problem tends to lie in the lack of understanding of the capacity of Canadian governments to control elements of the international political economy. Those who would advocate high tariffs on various imported goods and services—whether investment, manufactured goods, or cultural products—often assume that Canada can take whatever measures it chooses to advance its own interests. This is simply not the case. Canada is bound by international agreements it has willingly entered into in order to secure market access for its own goods and services, and the government cannot simply violate these agreements at whim without suffering retaliation from trading partners. Similarly, international financial agreements and the more or less free flow of capital throughout the world have placed many constraints on the ability of Canadian governments to alter many aspects of the Canadian political economy.

Notes

1. A strength of staples political economy is its insistence on following an inductive methodology, which largely avoids the propensity of both liberal and socialist political economy to force the world into pre-established moulds. Most staples analysis has used this same methodology to argue that Canada is in some manner 'exceptional'. If staples political economy is to contribute further to an understanding of how the Canadian political economy operates, however, it must abandon its emphasis on Canadian exceptionality. Harold Innis, the founder of the staples approach, clearly understood this point. As William Christian (1977a: 21) notes: 'Innis treated Canada not as a unique phenomenon but as a particular one . . . . He worked inductively and not deductively. He drew his theory from the facts that he studied; but there was always an interpretation of facts and theory, each refining and modifying the other.'

2. The Canadian 'new political economy' is to be distinguished from its US counterpart, which refers to the application of public choice theory, the fundamentals of which are the same as those of neoclassical economics, to the study of politics.

3. Reference to Harold Innis by the neo-Innisians as a nationalist is ironic, given his frequent invectives against it. In particularly strong language he once remarked: 'Warm fetid smell of nationalism, the breeding ground of the pestilences of the west, the worship of which kills its millions' (Christian, 1977b: 62). In another instance he noted, in an inversion of Lord Acton's dictum, that 'Nationalism is still the last refuge of scoundrels' (Williams, 1986: 137). Yet it cannot be denied that Innis was acutely aware of Canada's peripheral position in world capitalism, and in his later works he pointed out that Canada had exchanged British for US dominance (Christian, 1977b: 62), moving 'from colony to nation to colony', as he described it. Ignoring his antinationalist diatribe, his followers in the staples

school emphasize his anticolonial sentiments (Drache, 1969; Watkins, 1982) because it bolsters their case against US dominance of Canada.

4. The MAI, a proposal to extend free trade rules to foreign investment, has been promoted by the Organization for Economic Co-operation and Development (OECD) but continues to face strong resistance from many countries (Clarke and Barlow, 1997).

5. In the forestry industry, for example, there has been increased exploitation of second- and third-growth timber and increased reliance on less accessible forest resources (Barnes and Hayter, 1994). In provinces like British Columbia, which formerly relied extensively on such staples resources, several significant transitions are occurring (Davis, 1993; Davis and Hutton, 1991).

Chapter 5

The Structure and Organization of the Economy

All of the approaches and theories of political economy discussed so far have this feature in common: they undertheorize the role of political institutions and processes in creating and shaping economic relationships. This is particularly problematic in the study of Canada's political economy because the Canadian state has historically played a very active role in the development of the economy (Easterbrook and Watkins, 1967; Ryerson, 1968; Lower, 1977). In this chapter we will discuss the role of the Canadian state in economic development and how this has shaped Canada's contemporary political economy.

Although each theoretical approach notes the interrelationships that exist between states and markets in capitalist economies, they all assume a certain role for the state based on particular assumptions of how the economy functions. For instance, the liberal approach foregrounds market relationships, downplaying the role of governments in helping create both national and regional economies and generally ignoring the fact that different social actors have different resources as they approach the market. Socialist political economy tends to focus on class relationships, highlighting how state institutions and political processes often work towards reinforcing those relationships. And the staples approach emphasizes how a dependence on particular types of commodities tends to direct economic growth and influences state activities. Consequently, all of the theoretical perspectives we have examined primarily consider the activities of the state as flowing from the fundamental characteristics of a functioning capitalist, market economy. As such, they fail to investigate the rather complex relationships between politics and economics that actually characterize the manner in which states operate and make decisions or policies. Instead, based on the assumptions they make as to what interests or processes should govern economic development, they simply assume that governments will (or should) implement policies that are theoretically optimum. Whether states actually operate in the theoretically prescribed manner, or, indeed, whether they are capable of doing so, is often outside of the scope of their consideration.

In assessing the role played by the Canadian state in the country's political economy, it is important to focus on the general nature of the constraints on, and opportunities for, state activity posed by the structure of market relations. Many of the constraints have roots in the domestic economy, society, or polity, while others emanate from international sources. In this chapter we will concentrate on the structure of the domestic economy, leaving the international forces shaping the Canadian political economy to the next chapter.

On the domestic front, the existing system of market-based production and allocation of wealth, coupled with the way the domestic political economy is integrated into the international political economy, generates severe inequalities in incomes, opportunities, and quality of life between different social groups and regions of the country. These inequalities are generally unacceptable to citizens, who use democratic institutions to demand that the state use its authority to alter market arrangements so the disparities are eliminated or reduced. Indeed, much of the factionalism that characterizes Canadian domestic politics at the federal level is the product of competition between the country's regions and provincial governments over the ways in which the wealth generated by the Canadian economy as a whole is to be distributed (Brodie, 1997).

Whether or not the state recognizes these demands or eventually acts on them remains to be seen. In Canada, as elsewhere, many citizens benefit little from the operation of a market-based economy and want to see its alteration, while others receive a larger share of the benefits and don't want to lose their privileges. Thus the state is pressured to both retain and reform the status quo; and how the state responds ultimately depends on the strengths of the groups advocating various positions, the ability of the state to identify and assess the various options available to it, and the ability of the state itself to resist societal pressures.

The question of *autonomy* of the state and its *capacity* to undertake policies and activities is complex and can be adequately answered only after a study of a large number of domestic and international factors. In the Canadian context the study must take into account at least four significant aspects of the domestic political-economic situation. First, the production of wealth in Canada has been and remains dependent on the production and export of resource commodities to international markets, increasingly the United States. Second, the different regions of the country depend on export of resources to varying degrees, which affects their vulnerability to international economic conditions as well as their prosperity. Third, Canadian governments can and do attempt to offset regional inequalities through massive public expenditures. However, the governments' ability to make a substantial difference is limited by the nature of international resource trade and by the commitments Canadian governments have made to maintaining and indeed expanding capitalist liberal trade and investment relations at the international level. Finally, the interest groups that attempt to influence policy processes enjoy varying degrees of access. Those groups that are able to muster the political and economic resources for sustained strategic campaigns to influence the direction of public policy, such as those representing industrial interests, generally have a much better chance of success than those that are not as well organized and lack reliable sources of income, such as those representing women, indigenous peoples, and economically disadvantaged sections of the population (Evans and Wekerle, 1997).

The Canadian Economy in Comparative Perspective

An analysis of the economic structure of a country usually starts with a description of how many and what kinds of different goods and services are produced in that country—information that says a great deal about what people do, how wealthy they are, and, by implication, which industries and productive activities are most significant to the nation's political economy as a whole. Examining the structure of a solitary domestic economy does not reveal whether or not, or to what extent, that economy is typical or atypical of modern nation-states. Nor does it illustrate the degree to which one country is dependent on markets in other national jurisdictions. To obtain this type of information, we need to compare the nation's performance with the record of other countries.

The best indicators of aggregate national economic performance are measures known as gross national product (GNP) and gross domestic product (GDP).[1] These are closely related figures that indicate the total value of production of all goods and services in a country in a given year. They include all wages paid out, all investments made, and all the profits taken by all the companies and individuals producing goods or services in the country. As such, they are very large figures that can be broken down by region or by production activity, as need be.

Using GNP, column one of Table 1 shows that the total value of production in Canada is large by international standards, outranking all but eight countries in the world. The Canadian economy, though much larger than that of most countries in the world, is about one-quarter the size of the Japanese economy and less than one-tenth the size of the US economy. The figures indicate roughly where the Canadian economy stands in the world: somewhere in the middle. This middle position accounts for the fact that there are a variety of interpretations of Canada's economic capabilities. Whether the Canadian economy is viewed positively or negatively depends, to a certain extent, on the countries to which it is compared.

The aggregate GNP figures are somewhat misleading as an indication of economic well-being: they reveal a great deal about general economic performance but little about the standard of living in a country, which must be measured not against overall economic activity but in relation to the size of the population. To evaluate a country's standard of living we use GNP or GDP per capita: the country's aggregate value of production divided by its population. This figure gives an idea of the wealth of individual citizens as compared to people in other countries.

As columns 2 and 3 of Table 1 illustrate, while Canada is not one of the largest economies in the world, it is, relatively speaking, a very rich one. Canadian per capita GNP ranks among the highest in the world, higher than all but 16 nations (column 3). However, since the cost of living varies across nations, recent data

Table 1: Canadian Economy in Comparative Perspective, Select Countries, 1995

	Total GNP, US$ million (rank)		GNP Per Capita, US$ (rank)		GNP Per Capita, Purchasing Power Parity*
United States	7,100,007	(1)**	26,980	(7)	26,980
Japan	4,963,587	(2)	39,640	(3)	22,110
Germany	2,252,343	(3)	27,510	(6)	20,070
France	1,451,051	(4)	24,990	(10)	21,030
UK	1,094,734	(5)	18,700	(20)	19,260
China	744,890	(7)	620	(117)	2,920
Brazil	579,787	(8)	3,640	(46)	5,400
Canada	573,895	(9)	19,380	(17)	21,130
India	319,660	(15)	340	(137)	1,400
Mexico	304,596	(16)	3,320	(50)	6,400
Singapore	79,831	(36)	26,730	(9)	21,030
Mozambique	1,353		80	(165)	1,353

*Adjusted to purchasing power in the United States.
**Figures within parentheses indicate the country's rank.
Source: World Bank, *World Development Indicators,* 1997.

refer to 'purchasing power parity' (PPP), which adjusts for what a given amount of money buys in different countries. By PPP measure, Canada comes out even further ahead because of its somewhat lower cost of living. Comparison with Germany illustrates the point well: its nominal per capita GNP is substantially higher than Canada's but somewhat lower than that of Canada when PPP is taken into account because goods and, especially, services are generally more expensive in Germany. In the case of developing countries, the PPP figures are many times their nominal GNP, as the examples of China and India indicate. The case of Singapore, moreover, shows how some so-called Third World countries now have income levels that are higher than those of most First World countries.

Although per capita income reveals little about the quality of life in a country or about such aspects of everyday life as the levels of crime or pollution that citizens must endure, it provides a more accurate comparison of national wealth than does simple aggregate GNP. But even per capita GNP or GDP reveals little about the creation of wealth in society or its distribution among the members of that society. To discuss these important aspects of a country's political economy, other measures are needed.

Income Distribution

A good aggregate measure of the distribution of wealth in society is arrived at by taking the total income of the country and determining how many families or unattached individuals received what share of that income. The usual method adopted by national statistical agencies—such as Statistics Canada—is to rank resident persons by their income and then determine how many individuals or families fall into each 20 per cent group, or quintile, of total national income. Table 2 presents the before- and after-tax Canadian figures for 1993, indicating a wide disparity in incomes.

As column 2 of Table 2 illustrates, before taxes the top 20 per cent of the population earns 44 per cent of total income while the bottom 20 per cent earns less than 5 per cent. The fourth column shows that the tax system does very little to alleviate this disparity. While nominal income taxes are no doubt lower for those on lower income, the rich have access to many tax concessions, and the ability to take advantage of them, that the less well-off are unable to use. The Goods and Services Tax (GST), charged for virtually every purchase, is particularly regressive in this respect because poorer people consume most of what they earn, unlike the well-off who save a significant portion of their earnings. The practical implication of this difference is that poorer people pay a higher percentage of their income in the form of GST compared to their richer counterparts. Although some countries have a much worse record, these figures reveal the inequities of Canadian income distribution: 40 per cent of the Canadian population earns about 66 per cent of the country's total income even after 'progressive' redistributive tax measures are taken into account.

Incomes also vary significantly in Canada by region, ethnic origin, age, and gender. Families headed by women are much more likely to live below the poverty line[2], as are families headed by members of the country's Aboriginal peoples (Gunderson, Muszynski, and Keck, 1990; Statistics Canada, 1990; Evans and Wekerle, 1997). Statistics compiled by the National Council of Welfare illustrate that in 1995, 57.2 per cent of all families headed by women under 65 years of age and with children under 18 were classified as poor (National Council of Welfare, 1997). Elderly persons, and especially elderly women, also suffered

Table 2: Aggregate Pre-Tax and Post-Tax Income Distribution in Canada, 1993

Quintile	% Total Pre-tax Income	Cumulative*	% Total After Tax Income	Cumulative*
Top 20 per cent	43.9	43.9	41.1	41.1
20–40 per cent	24.7	68.6	24.7	65.8
40–60 per cent	16.4	85.0	17.2	83.0
60–80 per cent	10.2	95.2	11.4	94.4
Bottom 20 per cent	4.7	100.0	5.7	100.0

* Numbers do not add up to 100 due to rounding.
Sources: Statistics Canada, *Income Distribution by Size in Canada, 1993*, Cat. No. 13–207 (Ottawa, 1995); Statistics Canada, *Income After Taxes, Distribution by Size in Canada, 1993*, Cat. No. 13–210 (Ottawa, 1995).

from high poverty rates. Over 43 per cent of elderly single women lived below the poverty line in 1995, more than twice the very high rate found among retired men. The plight of single people under 25 is even worse, with a poverty rate of 64.1 per cent in 1995. Recent immigrants also suffered very high rates of poverty. Perhaps most alarming, however, is the fact that poverty rates continued to climb despite the improvement in economic growth after 1995.

Income Distribution by Region

The regional, spatial, or geographic distribution of production is a particularly important aspect of political-economic analysis due to the fact that most democratic political systems—including Canada's—are structured so as to better represent territorially specific issues and grievances rather than national ones. Some countries have a more or less equal spatial distribution of production throughout the national territory and hence a more or less equal distribution of incomes, occupations, and political issues. Most do not, however, and Canada certainly has a marked inequality in its spatial distribution of productive resources and activities, which results in significantly different demands being placed on governments in different parts of the country. For instance, in the mid-1990s the closure of the Newfoundland cod fishery and the boom in Alberta's petroleum industry contributed to a marked disparity of incomes between those two provinces.

To investigate these regional differences we will look at the regional distribution of aggregate production and at the regional distribution of incomes. The figures in Table 3 provide a breakdown of GDP by province and the percentage that each province contributes to the national total.

Table 3: Provincial GDP and Share of National GDP, 1996 (constant [1986] dollars)

	GDP ($000,000)	Share of National Total %
Canada	617,795	100.0
Newfoundland	8,038	1.3
Prince Edward Island	1,980	0.3
Nova Scotia	14,947	2.4
New Brunswick	12,730	2.1
Quebec	137,044	22.2
Ontario	259,098	41.9
Manitoba	20,986	3.4
Saskatchewan	20,576	3.3
Alberta	75,067	12.2
British Columbia	74,001	12.0
Yukon/NWT	2,644	0.4

Source: Statistics Canada, *Provincial Economic Accounts: Annual Estimates, 1996*, Cat. No. 13–213 (Ottawa, 1997).

The figures show a wide range of GDPs among provinces. More significantly, about 65 per cent of Canadian economic activity takes place in the two central provinces of Quebec and Ontario, and Ontario alone accounts for two-fifths of the total. In comparison, the four provinces of Atlantic Canada account for only 6 per cent of total production, while the four western provinces account for about 30 per cent. In other words, almost two-thirds of Canadian production occurs in central Canada and about one-third in the western provinces. This means, of course, that the two central Canadian provinces are Canada's economic hub.

As we saw in comparing Canadian GNP to that of other countries, however, these aggregate statistics can be misleading for estimating the relative wealth of different jurisdictions, because they do not take into account variations in size of population. All things being equal, we would expect Ontario and Quebec, with their large populations, to produce more than other less populated provinces. However, on further examination, we find marked disparities in income among those living in different regions of the country.

Provincial per capita incomes vary by as much as 14 per cent below and 16 per cent above the national average after the government's corrective measures have been taken into account. Without the federal transfers the variations are more severe, with people in Newfoundland averaging only two-thirds of the per capita income of those living in Ontario.

These figures illustrate an important characteristic of Canada's political economy: production, wealth, and poverty are unequally distributed across Canada. While 17.4 per cent of the Canadian population lived below the poverty line in 1995, this percentage was not evenly distributed among the provinces, as more than 19 per cent of the families in Newfoundland lived below the poverty line, compared to 14 per cent in Alberta and British Columbia (National Council of Welfare, 1997).

In democratic societies, these inequities can and do lead to demands for political or state action to alter the situation, and Canadian governments have responded to these demands by using a variety of redistributive means to bolster individual and regional incomes. In Canada, these measures generally take the form of *transfer payments* from the federal to the provincial levels of government, whereby the federal government deploys its powers of taxation to redistribute—and to some degree, equalize—income among the provinces. These measures include provision of welfare and social security payments to individuals, transfers of federal tax revenues to provincial governments, and the provision of regional development grants and subsidies to corporations willing to locate in depressed regions (Bakker and Scott, 1997).

Column 4 of Table 4 indicates the per capita amount of federal transfers to each province in 1996–97. Some of these transfers have been reasonably successful, while others have not succeeded in altering the existing situation. In 1995, such programs only succeeded in raising the average provincial per capita income in the Atlantic provinces from 71 per cent to 77 per cent of that in Ontario. Again, other countries have much worse records in distribution of income, while still

Table 4: Provincial Per Capita Incomes, 1995–1996

	Gross Incomes	% of Ontario's	Per capita Federal Transfers	Net Without Transfers	% of Ontario's
Newfoundland	17,877	74.4	2,547	15,330	66.2
PEI	19,015	79.1	2,092	16,923	73.1
Nova Scotia	19,083	79.4	2,010	17,073	73.7
New Brunswick	18,471	76.9	1,974	16,497	71.2
Quebec	21,404	89.1	1,495	19,909	85.9
Ontario	24,011	(100)	852	23,159	(100)
Manitoba	20,773	86.5	1,729	19,044	82.2
Saskatchewan	19,424	80.9	1,040	18,384	79.4
Alberta	23,187	96.6	801	22,386	98.6
BC	23,991	99.9	836	23,155	100

Source: Department of Finance, *Economic Reference Tables* (Ottawa: Minister of Supply and Services, 1996); Department of Finance, *Federal Transfers to Provinces and Territories* (Ottawa: Department of Finance, 1997).

others enjoy much more equitable arrangements. Nevertheless, as these statistics illustrate, there are significant distributional inequities in Canada, and certain people and groups in Canadian society benefit more than others from the operation of the contemporary political economy. To understand the basis of these inequalities we must take a closer look at the structure of the Canadian economy.

Sectoral Structure of the Economy

While the distribution of production and income in a country at the aggregate level provides important insights, an understanding of its sectoral composition is vital for understanding how the political economy operates and the constraints and opportunities the state faces. An analysis of the sectoral structure of a country's economy reveals a great deal about why certain areas of a country or certain strata of its population are rich or poor and about the types of demands governments handle when determining the extent of state involvement in the functioning of the economy.

The best way to look at the sectoral structure of the economy is to consider the amount and nature of goods and services produced in each of the three major sectors of the economy: primary, secondary, and tertiary (Fisher, 1966; Wolfe, 1955). The *primary sector* of the economy is composed of all economic activities associated with the extraction and production of natural resources. According to the United Nations system of Standard Industrial Classification (SIC)[3] these activities include agriculture, forestry, fishing, mining, and oil and gas exploration. The *secondary sector* is composed of activities associated with what the staples tradition terms 'forward linkages', that is, those involved in the further processing of natural resources and manufacturing. The *tertiary sector* comprises what staples theorists refer to as 'backward' and 'final demand' linkages, that is, production of the various goods and services necessary to support or organize the primary and secondary sectors. These tertiary goods and services include construction and transportation, finance, real estate and insurance, public administration, the wholesale and retail trades, and the various service industries that draw their income from that of the workers in the primary and secondary sectors (Watkins, 1963, 1997).

In Canada, as in most countries, the historical trend has been for economic activity to shift from the primary to the tertiary or service sector (Kuznets, 1966). Over the last century, both the amount of goods and services produced and the numbers of people employed in each sector have shifted decisively towards the tertiary or service sector. On a national basis, the primary and tertiary sectors have shifted locations as sources of economic production. This change has been caused primarily by a rapid decline in agricultural activity and employment, which fell from 32 per cent of GNP and about 46 per cent of employment in 1880–91 to between 3 and 4 per cent respectively by the early 1980s (Buckley and Urquhart, 1965; Statistics Canada, 1984). Most of this economic activity and employment has been picked up in the tertiary sector, especially in the provision of various kinds of services. As Table 5 illustrates, this trend has continued in recent years. In 1995–6, the provision of services in all sectors of the economy accounted for 70 per cent of employment and 66 per cent of GDP (*Canada Year Book*, 1997).

This is not to say that the Canadian economy is now any less reliant on resource-based production to generate its wealth than it was in the past. Much of Canada's manufacturing base consists of processing resource-based commodities such as lumber, pulp and paper, and various mineral and oil-based products, which are all commonly thought of as 'primary production', although the SIC system classifies them as 'manufacturing industries'. In 1994, $102.9 billion or about 30 per cent of Canada's domestic manufacturing capacity was accounted for by the wood, paper, and allied products industries along with the primary metal, non-metallic, and petroleum and coal products industries. Other areas of

Table 5: Distribution of GDP and Employment by Sector, 1961–1995

	GDP		
	1961	*1975*	*1995*
Primary	22.3%	18.1%	15.8%
Secondary	19.1%	20.1%	19.1%
Tertiary	58.6%	61.8%	65.0%

Source: Statistics Canada, *Canadian Economic Observer*, Cat. No. 11–210–XPB, 1995–6.

economic activity, such as the rail and truck transportation of resources and resource products, as well as many construction projects, are closely related to these activities. In addition, as the staples approach emphasizes, resource activities generate indirect effects, from banking and financial arrangements associated with large-scale capital projects to the food, transportation, and other expenditures made by consumers who earn their salaries in the resource sector. In all, resources and resource-related activities generate as much as 50 cents out of every dollar produced in this country (Hessing and Howlett, 1997: 25).

This continued reliance of the Canadian economy on primary resources and resource-based manufacturing puts it at odds with the situation in many other industrialized nations and has important consequences for the operation of the Canadian political economy. Three aspects of this resource dependence are particularly significant. First, because many of these resources and resource-based manufactured goods are exported, their primary markets are outside of the country, making the Canadian economy highly dependent on international trade. Second, because not all parts of the country are equally reliant on resources, there is an important regional aspect to the resource economy. Third, given its significance to the economy, the Canadian state relies on resource-based activity, directly or indirectly, to generate many of the tax revenues and royalties required to fund its activities.

Significant Aspects of the Resource-Based Economy

The International Structure

Canada has a marked dependence on international trade for the generation of wealth. As the figures in Table 6 indicate, Canadian trade dependence is high compared to other industrialized nations and, significantly, has increased over the past 20 years. Countries such as the United States and Japan, on the other

Table 6: Canada's Export Dependence in Comparative Perspective (Exports as % of GDP)

	1973	1983	1992
Canada	21.3	23.4	33.8
France	16.0	20.2	25.5
Japan	6.3	10.5	11.8
UK	20.3	23.5	27.3
US	6.5	7.2	11.6
Australia	12.4	14.0	20.4

Source: World Bank, *World Bank Tables, 1995* (Baltimore: John Hopkins University Press, 1995).

Table 7: Exports by Commodity Group

	1960	1995
Agricultural goods	18.8%	6.9%
Crude materials	21.2%	9.8%
Fabricated materials	51.9%	31.7%
Manufactured goods	7.8%	49.4%

Source: Canada, External Affairs, *A Review of Canadian Trade Policy* (Ottawa: Minister of Supply and Services, 1983), 26; Canada, Department of Finance, *Budget Plan Reference Tables, 1996* (Ottawa: Minister of Supply and Services, 1996).

hand, depend relatively little on exports, despite the fact they are the world's two largest exporters, because of the massive size of their aggregate economies.

Canada's exports of manufactured goods rose rapidly between 1960 and 1995 (Table 7). However, what the figures in Table 7 do not show is that most of this increase occurred in a single sector, the automobile industry, which accounted for about 27 per cent of Canadian exports in 1994. A special trading arrangement, the Canada-US Auto Pact, governs automobile trade between the two countries and facilitates not only exports to the US but imports from it as well. The large exports are thus offset by similar levels of imports, leaving a small balance of trade. Much of Canada's positive balance of trade thus continues to come from exports of natural resources.

In fact, as Table 8 illustrates, the total primary processing sector generates an annual trade surplus of over $56 billion—a sum sufficient to pay for all the deficits incurred importing manufactured goods as well as a significant yearly deficit on services trade incurred chiefly as a result of the large sums flowing out of the country in dividend and interest payments, as well as in areas such as tourism.

Although in the past Canada had two major markets for its exports—the US and the United Kingdom—trade with the latter has declined precipitously over recent decades (Table 9). Since 1940, the US market has emerged as the main destination for Canadian exports. The same is true for imports, with the United States alone accounting for more than three-quarters of our total imports (Table 10).

Table 8: Canadian Merchandise Trade Balances, 1996 ($ billions)

Agricultural and fishing products	8.2
Forest products	31.4
Energy products	16.5
Metals and minerals	−5.7
Automobiles and parts	10.7
Other consumer goods	−17.3

Source: Statistics Canada, CANSIM *matrix 3652* (Ottawa, 1997).

Table 9: Direction of Canadian Exports, 1950–1996

	1950	1960	1970	1993	1994	1995	1996
United States	64.5%	55.8%	64.4%	79.9%	81.4%	79.6%	81.2%
Japan	0.6	3.4	4.9	4.5	4.3	4.5	3.9
European Union*	18.7	25.8	16.5	6.1	5.2	6.3	5.7
Other countries**	16.2	15.0	14.2	9.4	9.1	9.6	9.1

*Includes UK before it joined the EEC in 1972.
**Countries not included above.
Sources: Statistics Canada, *Historical Statistics of Canada*, 2nd edn (Ottawa: Minister of Supply and Services, 1983); Statistics Canada, CANSIM *matrices 3685*, 3652 (Ottawa, 1997).

As we will see in later chapters, the effects of this growing dependence on the US market are far-reaching, and the rules of the international trading system that govern this trade have a very significant impact not only on domestic economic policy but on practically all areas of Canadian public policy, including labour, environmental, and social policy.

The Regional Distribution of Sectoral Activity

Although the Canadian economy as a whole never did experience the shift into manufacturing industries envisioned by the orthodox theory of economic development, the economies of Ontario and, to a lesser degree, Quebec were able to make the move.

The figures in Table 11 indicate the unequal distribution of sectoral economic activities by region. The western provinces have a high share of Canadian primary production; 61 per cent of Canada's total agricultural and natural resource production took place in the West in 1996. Central Canada, on the other hand, completely dominates manufacturing activities, producing 78 per cent of the country's total manufactured goods in 1996. The Atlantic provinces, with their relatively small

Table 10: Direction of Canadian Imports, 1950–1996

	1950	1960	1970	1993	1994	1995	1996
United States	65.2%	67.3%	71.1%	73.2%	74.7%	75%	75.7%
Japan	2.9	2.0	4.2	4.9	4.1	3.7	3.1
European Union*	14.5	16.1	11.2	8.1	8	8.9	8.7
Other countries**	17.4	14.6	13.5	13.9	13.3	12.5	12.6

*Includes UK before it joined the EEC in 1972.
**Countries not included above.
Sources: Same as Table 9.

Table 11: Distribution of Sectoral Economic Activity by Region, 1996

	Primary	Secondary	Tertiary
Atlantic	4.7	3.6	6.6
Central	23.0	78.1	60.7
West	61.3	18.3	32.7

Source: Statistics Canada, *Provincial GDP by Industry 1984–1996*, Cat. No. 15–203–XPB (Ottawa: Minister of Industry, 1997).

economies, not surprisingly remain marginal in all three sectors of the national economy. As Tables 12 and 13 show, however, the Atlantic provinces still rely on their natural resources to generate economic wealth. Similarly, the western provinces all depend on resource activities for their economic well-being. Only Quebec and Ontario have diversified economies that are not entirely resource-dependent—although even in those provinces substantial economic activity is still directly associated with resource extraction and processing.

The inhabitants of the Western and Atlantic provinces tend to gain their wealth from natural resource and agricultural activities, which, because of their dependence on uncontrollable foreign markets and the large amounts of capital invested in them, are inherently less stable than the manufacturing activities located in central Canada. Canada has a monopoly or near-monopoly on the production of only a few resources or agricultural goods, and Canadian producers must sell at prices set by international conditions of supply and demand. That is, Canadians are not 'price-makers' but 'price-takers' in international markets. While international demand for most resources—outside of wartime—has increased at a relatively steady but low rate, world supplies of certain primary products are highly variable. A good harvest, the discovery of significant

Table 12: Primary-Sector Component of Provincial GDP, 1996

Province	%
Newfoundland	6.7
PEI	10.6
Nova Scotia	4.8
New Brunswick	5.1
Quebec	3.1
Ontario	2.4
Manitoba	6.7
Saskatchewan	24.5
Alberta	24.6
BC	6.3

Source: Same as Table 11.

Table 13: Regional Resource-based Manufacturing Activity, 1992

Region	% Resource-Based
Atlantic	50.5
Quebec	42.6
Ontario	34.4
Prairies	45.0
British Columbia	75.5
Canada	42.9

Source: Hessing and Howlett, 1997: 34.

new reserves of minerals or oil, or the addition of new production capacity in the fishery or forest products sectors can greatly add to world supplies and quickly drive down world prices. Those prices stay down until demand catches up and surpasses supplies, resulting in sudden price increases that spur additional exportation and production, and so on. These fluctuations in international supplies account for the boom-and-bust cycles seen in most resource industries and, by implication, in most resource-based economies.

As the collapse of the Atlantic cod fishery in the mid-1990s dramatically illustrated, the instability of regional resource-based economies generates personal and regional disparities in incomes. Resource-dependent regions of the country can enjoy periods of high or low incomes, depending on the sustainability of their particular resources and/or international supply and demand factors. Since most resource exports go to the US market, to a large degree this means depending on the state of international supplies and US demand, and given that the Canadian supply of a particular staple remains constant, any increase in international supplies or decrease in US demand can devastate a regional economy. The reverse situation can bring on a wave of new-found prosperity.

While the government has taken measures in some sectors to provide some stability to international demand for Canadian resources—such as the grant to the Canadian Wheat Board of what amounts to a monopoly in the international sale of Canadian wheat—these aspects of regional economic health remain largely outside the control of Canadian governments. Those same governments, though, receive demands for ameliorative action from residents of affected regions whenever economic downturns occur. Because the governments rely on taxes and royalties generated from these same resource-based activities for the majority of their revenues, any funds required to offset adverse economic conditions in the regions must come from outside the region. This in itself serves as a major constraint on state activity. The Canadian state is not well suited to respond to these demands because in a federal system regional demands for additional funds have the effect of pitting different governments against each other—whether it is provincial governments urging the federal government to redistribute funds from one region of the country to another, or governments of 'have' regions resisting transfers to 'have-not' regions for fear that those transfers might be permanent rather than a temporary means of getting through until the next upswing in resource prices.

Public-Sector Reliance on Resource-Based Activity

The third aspect of Canada's resource-based economy is the heavy reliance of the Canadian state on natural resources for taxes and royalties to fund expenditures. The public sector in Canada is large, although not overly so by international standards. In 1994 expenditures by federal, provincial, territorial, and local governments accounted for approximately 46.7 per cent of GDP. A much larger percentage of economic activity is subject to some form of government regulation or administration.[4] By international standards the size of the Canadian public sector is about average for market economies, as shown in Table 14.

While government expenditures are an important part of Canadian economic activities, employment with government is also an important element of the Canadian occupational structure. As Table 14 illustrates, about 20 per cent of the workforce is employed directly or indirectly by the government, including the military and Crown corporations; about 6.5 per cent of the workforce is employed directly in government departments and agencies. Once again, in comparative perspective the Canadian figure is not exceptionally large when placed against the experience of other similar political economies. Table 15 indicates the numbers of government employees in recent years.

Table 14: Government Current Expenditures in International Comparison, 1994

	% Government Share of GDP*	% Government Share of Total Employment
Canada	46.7	19.6
US	35.8	14.0
UK	42.3	14.4
Japan	27.0	6.0
France	50.9	24.8
Germany	46.7	15.9
Sweden	66.4	32.0
Australia	36.2	16.6
Spain	42.6	15.2
OECD average	44.5	

*Total government expenditure, excluding capital expenditure.
Note: Figures for France, Germany, Sweden are for 1995; figures for the United States are for 1993.
Sources: Organization for Economic Co-operation and Development, *OECD in Figures* (Paris: OECD, 1997); Organization for Economic Co-operation and Development, *National Accounts* (Paris: OECD, 1997).

Revenues to pay for public expenditures and employees are generated from fees, royalties, and taxes—the largest being personal and corporate income taxes and sales taxes, including the federal Goods and Services Tax (GST)—and from government borrowings on both domestic and international financial markets. While governments can carry large debt loads for long periods of time—in 1995, 34 cents of every dollar in federal government revenue went to pay interest on government debt—payments of both interest and principal must eventually come from taxes. Taxes and royalties paid to governments for the use of public lands and resources—amounting to about 85 per cent of the Canadian land base—largely originate in the wages and profits generated by resource-based activities. The ability of Canadian governments to undertake the delivery of goods and services to Canadian citizens, then, is subject to the health and vigour of the resource-based primary and secondary manufacturing components of the economy. Like everything else in Canadian political economy, these activities are subject to international constraints and regional variations in economic activities.

Political Implications of the Economic Structure

An important political consequence of the resource orientation of the economy is the strong demand it generates for government relief in times of low resource prices. The response to demands for relief from both resource industries and workers tends to be temporary and to involve different types of insurance schemes, such as government-administered unemployment insurance or crop insurance. Small resource producers have also sought out government assistance in preventing both large companies and foreign producers from manipulating prices, particularly in domestic markets. Government action in this vein has traditionally involved the creation of marketing boards in areas such as grains, fish, fur, and pulpwood, although recent international trade agreements have made these measures increasingly difficult to maintain, as shall be discussed in Chapter 6.

The demand for state-sponsored redistribution also originates in the general shift in employment from agriculture to services. Although the service sector is large and encompasses a whole range of activities from finance to transportation and communications, employment gains have been concentrated in the whole-sale and retail sectors and the business and personal service sectors (Baldwin and Rafiquzzaman, 1994; Riddle, 1986). Employment in these sectors tends to be low-wage and part-time or 'casual', and rarely comes with the benefits enjoyed by workers in the industrial sector of the economy, such as employer-paid health care premiums and company pension plans. In 1995, one out of every five jobs in Canada was classified as part-time, up from one out of 10 in 1975 (Picot, Myles, and Wannell, 1990). Women and youth, especially, are more often employed in these types of jobs than in what has usually been considered to be 'standard' employment (Ghalam, 1993; Gunderson, Muszynski, and Keck, 1990; Statistics Canada, 1990).

Table 15: Government Employment in Canada by Level of Government, 1992–1995

	1992	1993	1994	1995
Total	719,500	710,200	703,600	688,400
Federal	272,100	266,100	264,700	252,100
Provincial	236,400	236,900	231,700	228,900
Local	211,000	207,100	207,200	207,500
All industries*	10,246,900	10,271,400	10,447,100	10,673,600
Public-sector employment % of all industries	7.0	6.9	6.7	6.4

* Excludes agriculture, fishing and trapping, religious organizations, owners or partners of unincorporated business and professional practices, the self-employed, unpaid family workers, persons working outside Canada, military personnel, and casual workers for whom filing of T4 tax form is not required. The armed forces employed 117,461 in 1992 and 109,470 in 1994.
Source: Statistics Canada, Cat. No. 72F0002 (1997).

Not surprisingly, workers in these categories, and especially women, are increasingly demanding action from the state that would help them obtain the same standard of living available to employees of high-wage resource and resource-manufacturing activities: for instance, permanent increases in income through public provision of essential services or the creation of a 'social wage' in the form of government-funded health insurance, pensions, education, public housing, subsidized electricity, and day cares (Arscott and Trimble, 1996; Clement and Myles, 1994). Because incomes and profits in most activities associated with services are generally low, governments must redistribute income earned in other sectors of the economy to improve the conditions of service-sector workers. Traditionally, such government redistributive measures in Canada have taken the form of taxing incomes and profits earned in the high-wage primary and secondary sectors and funnelling them to the populous low-wage workforce in the tertiary sector. However, since the early 1990s such programs have been in decline and it is estimated that in 1998–9 federal spending in this area will reach its lowest level since 1949–50.

The health of the primary and secondary sectors, then, is of great importance not only to regional economies but also to the operation of the whole political economy. These activities must provide both a reasonable return for the people engaged in them and a return high enough so that governments can undertake programs to improve the standards of living of people who are unemployed, unemployable, or underemployed. In Canada the demands for interregional, intersectoral, and interpersonal redistribution of fiscal resources are specific manifestations of the more general tendency in all democratic market systems for the electorate to demand redistributive action from the state to offset market-based inequalities in incomes and opportunities. Conditions and circumstances vary in different countries concerning the nature of these demands for action and the ability and willingness of the state to respond to them. At a very basic level, both the demands placed on Canadian governments and their capacity to respond to these demands are seriously constrained by the economy's increasing reliance on international trade and the resource-export-dependent nature of the production of wealth in this country.

Notes

1. GNP includes the value of production as well as investments made outside the country and investments in the country made by non-residents, whereas GDP measures only the production that takes place within a particular jurisdiction. Because GDP is a measure of production, it does not include government pensions, unemployment insurance, and other transfer payments. These moneys are counted at the point they enter the market as expenditures on food, clothing, rent, etc. As the United Nations notes, GDP is the better measure of production within a given territory, although the difference is usually small enough that the two can be used interchangeably. Canada switched from using GNP to GDP as the primary economic measure in 1986. However, as a measure of 'economic performance', GDP is often criticized for what it doesn't include. For instance, GDP does not measure the value of goods and services that people provide for themselves or each other outside of market transactions, such as unpaid housework, child care, meal preparation, and community service. Neither does GDP measure the impact of industrial production on the environment, such as pollution or resource depletion. Consequently, GDP can only be taken as a measure of market-based economic performance, not as an indicator of the quality of life (*Canada Year Book*, 1997: 266).

2. The calculation of cut-offs defining 'poor' and 'poverty' are by no means simple or straightforward. The current Statistics Canada low-income cut-off measure defines poverty as that point at which a family spends 58.5 per cent of its income on food, shelter, and clothing, with some differentiation being made for family size and urban-rural location. When these measures were first developed in the 1960, the cut-off was 70 per cent. In 1969 this was revised downward to 62 per cent before arriving at its present level in 1978 (Wolfson and Evans, 1996).

3. The UN SIC system will be replaced in North America over the next several years as Canada, Mexico, and the United States adopt a new North American Industrial Classification System (NAICS). The NAICS is very similar to the SIC system but includes several new categories for service-sector activities. It is expected that these changes will lead to similar changes in the UN system in the near future (Statistics Canada, 1996).

4. These figures actually underestimate the extent of government activities. Not only do they ignore government regulatory activity, but they also account only for government expenditures made from revenues actually collected. Canadian

governments also strongly affect economic activities through decisions not to collect certain taxes or royalties if individual or corporate taxpayers undertake specified activities. Although it is extremely difficult to measure this type of tax expenditure, and few studies exist on the extent of such activities in Canada, a reasonable estimate places the cost of tax expenditures at the federal level alone at about 50 per cent of federally budgeted expenditures. This means, of course, that Canadian economic activities, either accounted for directly or heavily influenced by government activities, amount to a figure closer to 60 or 70 per cent of GDP (Canada, Department of Finance, 1979, 1980, 1985; Woodside, 1983).

Chapter 6

Canada and the International Political Economy

The opening up of international trade—led by Britain in the nineteenth century and the United States in the twentieth century—continues to affect every industrialized nation, albeit in different ways and to different degrees. This has been especially true since the establishment of the new political-economic order under the aegis of the General Agreement on Tariffs and Trade (GATT) and the International Monetary Fund (IMF) immediately after World War II. More recently, the restructuring of the GATT to form the World Trade Organization (WTO) in 1994 and the creation of large regional trade agreements such as the North American Free Trade Agreement (NAFTA) and the European Union (EU) have not only fostered increasing interdependence among nations but also created imperatives for both nations and trading blocs to resist the adverse effects of this interdependence while maximizing the benefits (Hoekman and Kostecki, 1995). While the result has been a decidedly greater degree of openness in the world economy, the extent of this 'economic globalization' has often been overstated (Hirst and Thompson, 1992; Whalley, 1993). Despite the growth of world trade in recent decades, the leading industrial nations' share of exports as a percent of GDP is not significantly higher than it was in 1913. For Canada, however, this new order has fostered greater economic interdependence than at any other time in the postwar era.

The International Economic Order and Canada

The contemporary international political economy is both an economic and political order and does not neatly conform to any one of the theoretical perspectives examined earlier. On the economic side it is informed by the liberal doctrine of 'comparative advantage' or 'free trade', which, as we saw in Chapter 2, postulates that each nation should export the products it can produce most efficiently and import the rest. This doctrine presumes the primacy of market forces, which are deemed to deliver maximum economic benefits to all participating nations. On the political side, however, most policy-makers acknowledge that market forces do not benefit all nations equally and that governments play a key role in providing form and structure to markets. For instance, labour legislation, environmental regulation, tax policies, and international investment rules can all have major impacts on the structure of market relationships and the production and distribution of wealth within national boundaries. Consequently, the nations that benefit the most from open trade arrangements promote the doctrine of free trade in its purest form while the remainder manipulate and live with the rules as best they can. But even the states avowedly committed to the doctrine of comparative advantage intervene to check the adverse effects of open trade and to gain economic advantage over their trading partners through political means.

Canada's participation in the new international economic order has been no different from that of other countries: professing faith in reduced barriers to trade, largely abiding by the principles but also conveniently ignoring them, even manipulating them, when both convenient and possible. As the 1985 Macdonald Commission noted in a study that laid the ground for the Canada-US Free Trade Agreement, 'Governments do not serenely observe the operation of international market forces without concern for their impact on their society, economy and people, and indirectly, therefore, on the status and power of individual states in the international system.' The Commission also observed: 'It is misleading, therefore, to view the post-war liberal international economic order as a market order. It is a political order within which national governments are prime actors in a system where they have allowed market forces considerable freedom to operate' (Macdonald Commission, 1985, I: 31). In modern political economy, market forces coexist with state intervention, and this is as evident on the international scene as it is domestically.

The concept of *international political economy* (IPE) as understood here is broader than international trade relations. While the focus is on formal treaties and agreements governing the terms of trade among nations, such as the World Trade Organization and the North American Free Trade Agreement, IPE is also concerned with the relative economic and political standing of nations in the world. The sheer size of the US and Japanese economies, for example, gives these two nations more power and influence to shape the international economy than smaller countries, such as, say, Fiji or Iceland. Attracting investment from major corporations based in one of these economic powerhouses can be key to generating jobs and tax revenues, while access to their consumer markets can provide domestic companies with rich trade opportunities. Canada, though no match for the United States or Japan, is more powerful economically than most other nations of the world and possesses some capacity to manipulate trade in its favour. In other words, Canada is a 'middle power', not in the laudatory sense in which the phrase is at times used to describe its supposedly benign international role (Glazebrook, 1947; Ropp, 1963; Wood, 1988), but as a description of its middle position in the world.

Because the terms and conditions of international trade agreements can have far-reaching effects on international investment patterns and the markets for domestically produced goods and services, they can also have tremendous implications for a national government's control over its domestic political economy. Regional development programs, income transfer arrangements, and the funding for social programs and education are all, to varying degrees, dependent on the abilities of national governments to control patterns of investment and the jobs and tax revenues they realize (Porter, 1990). In Canada, for instance, the development of the domestic political economy has been tied to the federal government's manipulation of international trade relationships. Tariffs—or taxes on imported goods—have been a key vehicle for financing the development of transportation and communication systems as well as, to a degree, encouraging an East-West pattern of economic development (Eden and Molot, 1993). Consequently, as barriers to international trade fall, the ability of nation-states like Canada to use such tools to determine the structure and character of their domestic political economy has been undermined.

Another significant aspect of IPE is the historical pattern of a nation's trade, which establishes relationships that impose constraints on, and provide opportunities for, national policy-makers on an enduring basis. For example, the open order established after World War II enhanced trade opportunities for the highly competitive Canadian resource industries, but at the same time it constrained the Canadian government from protecting its vulnerable consumer products industries from imports (Young, 1957; Ostry, 1992). As we saw in Chapter 5, the result of this pattern of development is a reinforcement of Canada's heavy dependence on the export of resource products. In turn, the income—from taxes, royalties, wages, and so on—generated by these exports finances the large-scale importation of manufactured goods.

The structure of IPE is, however, far from monolithic. Historically, there has been no basic body of law at the international level, such as a constitution, governing the relations among nations. International agreements, such as the GATT, have generally been voluntary in nature, and the loose character of IPE has provided some countries with opportunities for manipulating agreed upon rules to their advantage, depending on their relative economic, political, and military strength. Recognizing this problem, recent agreements tend to be broader in scope and provide for mechanisms for enforcing agreed rules. In Europe, trade agreements forged in the immediate postwar period have provided the ground for increasing political integration, the establishment of the European Parliament, and proposals for a common currency among member states. In 1994, expansion of the GATT gave rise to the WTO and a quasi-judicial body equipped with powers for adjudicating trade disputes and issuing binding trade decisions. NAFTA, too, is equipped with a binding dispute resolution mechanism. Enforcement of the decisions of these bodies, however, is generally limited to trade sanctions, and the more economically powerful nations still retain a distinct political and economic advantage over smaller states (Hoekman and Kostecki, 1995).

Canada's position in the international economic order, as noted above, is one of a middle power (Fox and Jacobson, 1973; Fox, 1977; Lyon and Tomlin, 1979; Wood, 1988, Mares, 1988). The main implication of this is that Canada is quite powerless in its ability to impose its interests directly on the dominant powers such as the United States, Japan, and the European Union. In short, Canadian producers have a greater dependence on access to large international markets than international producers have on access to Canadian markets and products. Yet, set on the doorstep of the most powerful economy in the world and equipped with a trade agreement that offers unprecedented access to that economy, Canada is in a unique position in terms of both being an attractive site for international investors seeking access to the American market and having a ready market for the resource products that form the basis of the Canadian economy. The question is, however, what price must be paid for exploiting these advantages?

Perhaps the most critical feature of Canada's political economy is the country's historic dependence on international trade. European nations colonized this northern half of the continent so they could sell its natural resources in the world market. Indeed, Canada established its Trade Commissioner Service as far back as 1892, long before the establishment of its own diplomatic service (Canada, Department of External Affairs, 1983: 4). The importance of international trade to the Canadian economy has fostered the government's keen participation in most major international trade institutions, such as the GATT/WTO, the International Monetary Fund (IMF), and the World Bank, as well as in the United Nations and its various specialized agencies.

As was discussed in Chapter 5, an overwhelming and increasing proportion of Canada's trade is now with one country, the United States. In 1996 the United States absorbed more than 80 per cent of our merchandise exports, while almost 76 per cent of our total imports also came from that country (Statistics Canada, 1997c). Canada has traditionally maintained a trade surplus on its 'merchandise account' with the United States (that is, it has exported more goods than it has imported), but it has run even larger deficits on its 'non-merchandise account', which includes trade in services and the transfer of profits by subsidiaries of US firms (Canada, Department of Finance, 1988a). Meanwhile, the United States is not dependent on Canada to anywhere near the same extent; only about 18 per cent of its total trade is with Canada, even though Canada remains its single largest trading partner (Schwanen, 1997).

The dominance of resource products in its exports also affects Canada's international economic objectives. Until the end of the nineteenth century, the Canadian economy was based on exports of fish, fur, timber, and wheat. In the twentieth century, as industrialization swept the world at an unprecedented speed, the demand increased for Canada's natural, especially mineral, resources, making the country one of the world's largest exporters of many such commodities. Today, well over half of Canada's forest products and 80 per cent of its mineral products are exported (Clement and Williams, 1997: 46). In total, only 49.4 per cent of Canadian exports (more than half of them automobiles and parts going to the United States) are fully manufactured goods. The remaining exports are semi-manufactured products (euphemistically called 'fabricated materials' in government statistics), unprocessed crude materials, and farm and fish products (Statistics Canada, 1995, Cat. No. 65–001). These figures, however, mask the fact that many Canadian manufactured exports are, for the most part, based on the domestic availability of raw materials. Thus, for example, Canadian exports of paper, steel, and processed food depend on the abundant availability of forestry, iron, and agricultural products.

In contrast, Canadian imports have increasingly consisted of manufactured goods. Manufactured goods accounted for 60.6 per cent of all imports in 1976 and 67.2 per cent in 1995 (Bank of Canada, 1996: Table H3). Canada has traditionally experienced huge trade deficits in the high-technology and capital goods sectors—sectors that are often regarded as being essential to the long-term competitiveness of Canadian industries, indeed, of the economy. In large part, these deficits have been the result of the federal government pursuing a policy of *import substitution*, whereby 'the federal government was involved through setting tariff levels high enough to make feasible domestic production of goods that would otherwise be imported' (Clement and Williams, 1997: 54). This policy was pursued vigorously in the late nineteenth century and for most of the twentieth. On the one hand, the policy encouraged direct foreign investment in manufacturing in Canada, enabling rapid industrialization and job creation for Canadians. On the other hand, however, it led to a process of *technology transfer*, whereby the subsidiaries of foreign, mainly American, multinationals, as well as Canadian entrepreneurs, imported much of the technology supporting the Canadian manufacturing industry. Consequently, there was little incentive for Canadian manufacturers to develop export markets, as many of the products produced in Canada were produced more cheaply elsewhere. As a result, import substitution made almost no difference to the overall strength of the Canadian manufacturing sector, except in a few specific industries such as automobiles and telecommunications.

Together, the dominance of staples in Canada's economy, import substitution, and technology transfer have played critical, if contradictory, roles in shaping Canada's international economic objectives. Right from the beginning, the abundance of marketable natural resources in Canada determined that this sector would be the cornerstone of the Canadian economy and that the reduction in foreign trade barriers to those exports would be Canada's main foreign economic policy objective. This presented a problem, though, as Canada's demands for reductions in foreign barriers on staples products generated corresponding demands from other countries for Canada to lower its own barriers on manufactured goods. Meeting this demand was difficult if Canada wanted to grow out of its role as 'the hewer of wood and drawer of water' by nurturing its manufacturing industries behind tariff walls until those industries were strong enough to take on the world market. But over the years many industries—including, for example, textiles, clothing, and footwear—failed to grow out of their 'infancy' and needed continued protection. The large number of workers employed, often in economically depressed regions in Ontario and Quebec, made the removal of protection very difficult. For much of the twentieth century Canadian policy-makers were thus led to pursue somewhat contradictory goals: negotiating reductions in barriers to exports while attempting to retain Canada's own barriers to imports.

Since World War II especially, Canada has been under increasing US pressure to lower its import barriers as the price for gaining increased access to the American market for Canadian exports. Much of the debate surrounding the FTA and NAFTA has focused on the ability of the Canadian economy to withstand the effects of such reductions, as well as the subsequent impact of changes in the economy on the abilities of governments to fund and deliver social programs. For those based in the liberal camp, reducing trade barriers is seen as leading to increased economic efficiency and productivity. For many socialist writers, any further integration with the US reduces the possibility of Canada adopting a non-capitalist path of economic, social, political, and cultural development. More critical writers, such as those who subscribe to elements of the staples tradition, point to the important historical role government intervention has played in Canadian economic development and argue that liberalizing trade barriers will only lead to increased economic uncertainty and social instability.

From the GATT to the World Trade Organization

When the GATT was signed in 1947, it was intended to be a provisional measure that would eventually be replaced by a more wide-ranging and permanent entity, the International Trade Organization (ITO). After American President Harry Truman failed to secure congressional approval for the ITO treaty, however, the GATT signatories agreed that the General Agreement and its secretariat would assume the proposed functions of the ITO in the interim. It would take more than four decades and eight rounds of negotiations before a permanent trade secretariat, the World Trade Organization (WTO), would finally be established. The key events related to the evolution of the WTO are listed in Table 16.

Since GATT was created, the number of member nations has expanded from 23 to 132. The original provisions have remained essentially intact, although over the years a number of supplementary codes and agreements have been adopted to strengthen, extend, or clarify the original rules. Until the last round of negotiations concluded in 1994, the GATT text was a loosely worded document, reflecting its original provisional character. The flexibility resulting from this looseness permitted the practical resolution of many trade frictions among its members; but that same flexibility also allowed members, especially the economically powerful ones, to bend the rules in their favour.

In 1986, the eighth and most ambitious round of multinational negotiations of the GATT began in Uruguay. An agreement was due to have been concluded by

Table 16: The Postwar Trading System: A Chronology

Year	Event
1947	Twenty-three countries, including Canada, sign the General Agreement on Tariffs and Trade (GATT).
1948	The GATT comes into force on a provisional basis. Trade representatives draft a charter (Havana Charter) for the International Trade Organization (ITO) that was to incorporate and oversee the GATT.
1948	Canada and the United States reach a tentative agreement establishing free trade. Prime Minister William Lyon Mackenzie King refuses to ratify the deal.
1950	The US administration abandons efforts to win congressional approval of the ITO Charter.
1957	The Treaty of Rome establishes the European Economic Community (EEC).
1964	The United Nations Conference on Trade and Development (UNCTAD) is created to promote trade measures that will benefit developing countries.
1964	The Kennedy Round of the GATT negotiations begins (concluded in 1967).
1965	Canada and the United States sign the Auto Pact, a trade agreement covering the automobile sector.
1973	The Tokyo Round of the GATT negotiations is initiated (concluded in 1979).
1986	The Uruguay Round of the GATT negotiations begins (concluded in 1994).
1987	Canada and the United States conclude negotiations for a comprehensive free trade agreement.
1989	The Canada-US Free Trade Agreement comes into force.
1989	The Asia-Pacific Economic Co-operation forum (APEC) is created to promote trade liberalization among its members, including Canada and the United States.
1990	At the GATT negotiations, Canada formally introduces a proposal to create an international trade organization to oversee and enforce agreements of the Uruguay Round.
1991	Trilateral free trade talks between Mexico, the United States, and Canada begin.
1993	The Maastricht Treaty comes into force, creating the European Union (EU). The treaty establishes a single European market among members and provides for monetary union by 1999.
1994	The North American Free Trade Agreement (NAFTA) is implemented.
1994	The World Trade Organization (WTO) is created and embodies the results of the Uruguay Round.
1995	Members of the Organization for Economic Co-operation and Development (OECD), including Canada, begin negotiations to establish a Multilateral Agreement on Investment (MAI) intended to liberalize foreign investment rules and regulations.
1997	Canada negotiates free trade agreements with Chile and Israel.
1998	Representatives of North and South American nations begin discussions in Santiago, Chile, aimed at drafting a Free Trade Agreement of the Americas (FTAA).

Sources: Whalley, 1985; Hoekman and Kostecki, 1995; Merret, 1996.

1990, but serious disagreements delayed the completion of talks until 1994. The Uruguay Round culminated with the creation of the WTO to oversee and enforce the GATT and other multilateral agreements. The original 1947 GATT text, extended and modified, was incorporated into the WTO agreements as GATT-1994. The WTO, however, is not a simple extension of the GATT. Whereas the original GATT was never officially ratified by members and therefore remained largely ad hoc and provisional, the WTO and its agreements have been adopted by the legislatures of member nations. This gives the WTO a far more solid legal basis in international law than the GATT ever had (Hoekman and Kostecki, 1995).

The WTO agreements are also much broader in scope. The GATT dealt exclusively with tariffs on products, trade in agricultural goods, and other non-tariff trade restrictions such as quotas and government subsidies. What was left out was the international trade in services. As we have seen, however, most modern economies rely on the service sector to generate employment, and services account for over 60 per cent of GDP in the OECD countries (Hoekman and Kostecki, 1995: 127). Spurred on by innovations in communications technology and government deregulation, the trade in services has grown faster than merchandise trade throughout the past decade. In 1996 alone, Canada exported $38.9 billion and imported $48.3 billion worth of services (Statistics Canada, *The Daily*, 28 Feb. 1997). Recognizing the growing importance of such trade, the WTO agreements include a General Agreement on Trade in Services (GATS), covering trade in transportation, travel, banking, insurance, and telecommunications.

The WTO agreements also expand on the GATT by including far-reaching provisions governing intellectual property. The Agreement on Trade-Related Aspects of Intellectual Property Rights (TRIPS) establishes international rules that cover copyright, trademarks, industrial designs, and patents. The TRIPS Agreement establishes standards of protection for these rights and outlines procedures and remedies available for member states to enforce rights. For developing countries, the inclusion of intellectual property rights could be particularly burdensome. Apart from some general exceptions, developing countries will no longer be able to treat medicine and agricultural products as exempt from national patents as they have done in the past. While that is good news for Western-based manufacturers of pharmaceutical drugs and genetically engineered seeds, patent protection will place an added cost on the ill, farmers, and others in the South (Instituto del Tercer Mundo, 1995: 14).

Finally, the WTO dispute settlement system is more automatic and binding than the old GATT system. Countries can no longer ignore the findings of arbitration panels, as they could under the GATT. Although decisions can be appealed, the ruling of the appeals panel is final. Countries that fail to comply with WTO rulings face authorized trade sanctions. In the first two years of its existence, the WTO dispute settlement panel received 62 complaints (World Bank, 1997b: 134).

Drawing largely on the liberal doctrine of comparative advantage, the basic philosophy of the WTO is that open markets, competition, and non-discrimination in international trade are good for the welfare of all nations. The purpose of the WTO, therefore, is to promote a liberal international economic order. The agreements establish reciprocal rights and obligations among WTO members to reduce barriers to international trade and offer exporters opportunities to sell in the markets of member nations. But the WTO also imposes obligations not to erect barriers to imports, except under special circumstances provided for in the agreement. These are the principal provisions of the WTO agreements:

- The Most Favoured Nation (MFN) clause guarantees the principle of non-discrimination as 'immediate and unconditional' in the conduct of the international trade in goods and services. It specifies that any concessions or favourable treatment offered to one member nation must be made available to other members as well. There are, however, some clearly specified exceptions to this principle: nations entering into free trade agreements (for example, NAFTA) or customs union (the EU, for example) are not obliged to offer the same concessions to others; selected trade measures of developing nations; and specifically exempted trade arrangements such as the Canada-US Auto Pact. The GATS applies the principle of MFN treatment to the service sector, but in a more restricted way than the GATT. The GATS contains an annex that allows countries to invoke exemptions to MFN, although these exemptions can only be made once and are to be phased out over 10 years.

- The concept of national treatment applies to the GATT but not to the GATS. This provision states that once a product enters the domestic market and the applicable tariffs are paid, the product must be treated the same as similar domestically produced products. The intent is to prohibit governments from discriminating against imports in favour of domestically produced goods in forms other than tariffs. The national treatment principle is very wide-ranging in its scope and has often been invoked in dispute-settlement cases brought to the WTO.

- A provision in the GATT 'binds' tariffs to the existing level, which can be reduced but not increased, except after undergoing a formidable process of negotiation with the principal exporters of the product(s) in question. In the Uruguay Round, an average tariff reduction of 35 per cent was adopted. Developing countries agreed to a large number of binding tariffs, increasing their share of bound industrial products from 22 per cent to 72 per cent (Hoekman and Kostecki, 1995: 90).

- The Multifibre Agreement under the original GATT is to be eliminated over a 10-year period. The Multifibre Agreement permitted industrialized countries to impose quotas on textiles and clothing imported from industrializing countries. The WTO agreements will phase out this special arrangement and in return developing nations have agreed to offer greater access to their agricultural markets.

- A general prohibition has been established against quotas or other quantitative restrictions on imports (and exports), except in cases of certain clearly specified goods under specific circumstances. The exceptions include some agricultural products and the restrictions imposed on Third World nations and other nations facing a serious balance-of-payment difficulty. Another crucial exception is the Emergency Action clause contained in Article XIX of the GATT, which permits temporary limitations on imports to mitigate unforeseen hardships caused by imports. These restrictions cannot be imposed in a selective or discriminatory manner.

- A provision exists for countervailing and anti-dumping duties against subsidies and dumping. In the case of a government subsidy that gives exporters an unfair advantage *vis-à-vis* the producer in the importing country, the importing country is entitled to impose *countervailing duties* to the extent of the subsidy. The GATT made a distinction between different types of government subsidies. Subsidies that have a broad impact on the economy (education, infrastructure, and research and development) or that have a non-commercial function (income support programs) are allowed. Countervailing duties can only be applied if it is proven that a domestic industry is suffering because of subsidized imports. Similarly, if exporters sell goods abroad at a price lower than the price they sell at in their home market, and it is proven that producers in the importing country are adversely affected as a result, the good is deemed to be dumped, and the importing nation is entitled to impose *anti-dumping duties*. The WTO Anti-Dumping Agreement stipulates that anti-dumping measures are to be terminated within five years of imposition, unless a review shows the injury is likely to continue if the duties are lifted. Duties may not be imposed if dumping margins are below 2 per cent or if the market share of a dumping firm is less than 3 per cent. A good is not regarded as being dumped just because the imported product is cheaper than the comparable domestically produced product, although the word is sometimes used in this way.

- A dispute settlement mechanism has been created to provide a stronger and more formal institutional basis for administering trade disputes than the GATT. After the Uruguay Round, a permanent Dispute Settlement Body (DSB) was formed to oversee the dispute process. In the case of a dispute, members must first enter into consultations within 30 days of another member's request. If the request is turned down or if the dispute is not resolved within 60 days, the complaining party can take its case to a dispute panel consisting of named experts to examine the complaint and recommend solutions to the DSB. Panel reports are forwarded to the DSB. Under the GATT's dispute resolution process, consensus was required to accept a panel report. The WTO requires consensus to reject a panel report. A ruling may be appealed to an Appellate Body composed of seven persons broadly representative of the WTO membership. Punishment (in the form of retaliation by countries adversely affected by the exports of the offending nation) is imposed only if a party refuses to abide by the ruling.

Tariffs and the WTO

Tariffs have been reduced within the GATT/WTO system during successive rounds of negotiations among the member nations. For all practical purposes, the first

Geneva Round (which took place at the same time as the negotiation of the General Agreement in 1947), the sixth Kennedy Round (1964–7), the seventh Tokyo Round (1973–9), and the eighth Uruguay Round (1986–94) have been the most important in introducing significant changes in the regime.

In Canada the GATT/WTO talks have been preceded by intense negotiations among various competing interests to influence the positions of Canadian representatives. The exporting interests usually press the government to lower tariffs on imports as a concession for achieving reduced foreign barriers to exports. On the other hand, the import-competing industries, usually the traditional manufacturing industries, press the government to avoid tariff reductions on imports. The Canadian negotiators must pursue these two contradictory objectives. Canada's position has for the most part favoured the interests of the exporting industries, which is not surprising given their dominance in the economy (Mahon, 1984).

Tariff reductions have been an important goal during all the rounds of the GATT negotiations. The negotiations are conducted on an item-by-item basis, whereby pairs of nations bargain for reduction in each other's tariffs on particular products. The reductions agreed on are made available, under the MFN clause, to all other members. Other pairs of nations are simultaneously negotiating for similar reductions on other products of interest to them, and thus tariff reductions spread throughout the GATT system. In practice, not all members negotiate with all others with respect to every product, which would be an unmanageable process. Rather, negotiations take place only between the members that are principal exporters and importers of the product in question. Canada has thus negotiated primarily with the United States, since most of its trade is with that country.

To avoid the cumbersome nature of the item-by-item negotiations, the Kennedy and Tokyo rounds were for the most part conducted on a 'linear' basis, whereby members first agreed on a formula of across-the-board reductions by a certain percentage and then negotiated only with respect to the exceptions to the formula. Canada was exempted from the linear cuts at the Kennedy Round, but not at the Tokyo Round. The exemption was on the basis that it was primarily an exporter of resource products on which tariffs were already generally low everywhere, and hence it would have had to reduce its tariffs on manufactured imports without gaining a matching level of benefits for its exports. After the implementation of the Kennedy Round cuts, the average Canadian tariff on all industrial products was 13.6 per cent, compared to 6.5 per cent for the US, 6.6 per cent for the European Economic Community (EEC), and 5.5 per cent for Japan (US Congress, 1987: 31). After the Tokyo Round, Canadian industrial tariffs fell to 8.3 per cent, compared to 5.7 per cent for the US, 6.9 per cent for the EEC, and 6.0 per cent for Japan. The average tariff cut resulting from the Uruguay Round was 35 per cent, but Canada agreed to the largest overall tariff cut—43.2 per cent. Table 17 shows the comparative industrial product tariff rates of some nations before and after the implementation of the latest Uruguay Round cuts.

As the table illustrates, the tariffs of nations increase with the level of processing involved with the product. Raw material products (fishery, forestry,

Table 17: Uruguay Round Tariff Rates and Reductions (percentages)

Product	Canada			United States			European Union			Developing Countries' Average		
	Old	*New*	*Cut*	*Old*	*New*	*Cut*	*Old*	*New*	*Cut*	*Old*	*New*	*Cut*
Fishery products	3.2	2.1	34.4	1.2	0.9	25.0	12.9	10.7	17.1	35.2	8.1	77.0
Forestry products	0.0	0.0	0.0	0.3	0.0	100.0	0.0	0.0	0.0	0.1	0.1	0.0
Mining	2.6	1.3	50.0	1.3	0.8	38.5	1.1	0.8	27.3	11.5	9.5	17.4
Textiles	18.6	11.7	37.1	10.5	7.5	28.6	9.0	6.8	24.4	30.3	20.3	33.0
Clothing	22.9	16.6	27.5	16.7	15.2	9.0	12.6	10.9	13.5	14.6	10.8	16.0
Primary steel	7.4	0.4	94.6	4.5	0.2	95.6	5.3	0.5	90.6	8.7	6.1	29.9
Primary metals	4.9	2.7	44.9	2.9	2.6	10.3	7.2	5.9	18.1	2.7	2.1	22.2
Fabricated metal products	9.7	6.0	38.1	4.7	2.8	40.4	5.7	3.1	45.6	8.5	6.9	18.8
Chemicals & rubber	10.3	5.3	48.5	5.0	3.0	40.0	7.7	4.2	45.5	19.1	13.2	30.9
Transport equipment	8.1	5.4	33.3	4.8	4.6	4.2	6.9	6.0	13.0	27.2	17.3	36.4
Other manufactures	6.3	2.9	54.0	3.5	1.5	57.1	5.5	2.5	54.5	18.0	13.3	26.1
Total merchandise trade	7.4	4.2	43.2	4.6	3.2	30.4	5.3	3.2	39.6	13.5.	9.8	27.4

Source: Whalley and Hamilton, 1996: 41.

and mining products) have significantly lower tariffs than semi-processed goods (steel, metals, chemicals, and rubber). The highest tariffs are reserved for finished manufactures such as clothing and transport equipment. This pattern has been true for most countries since before the establishment of the GATT/WTO and reflects governmental desires to foster domestic manufacturing by protecting the sector from imports.

Non-Tariff Barriers to Trade: Quotas and Subsidies

Andre W. Moroz (1985: 262) defines non-tariff barriers (NTBs) as 'those policy measures that artificially manipulate the relative competitiveness of domestic and foreign supplies in a given market with the explicit intention of improving the competitive position and hence increasing the level of output and income of the domestic producers above that allowed by free trade.' While the types of instruments are too numerous to catalogue, the most commonly used NTBs are quotas on imports, subsidies to domestic industries, technical standards, and preferential government purchasing.

Quotas

The underlying spirit of the GATT/WTO is more opposed to quotas than to tariffs as a barrier to trade. Quotas, by setting absolute limits to the quantity of imports, establish a stronger trade barrier because imports cannot overcome a quota regardless of their competitiveness in either price or quality. Tariffs at least allow foreign exporters to keep supplying if they can despite the advantages enjoyed by domestic producers. The trade in clothing is a perfect example: the industrialized nations have not been able to stop imports despite extraordinarily high tariffs and so they have had to use import quotas as well. Despite the greater ability of quotas to impede trade, the GATT/WTO has been more successful with tariffs than quotas because of the myriad forms, some subtle and others not so subtle, in which quotas appear in international trade.

Quantitative restrictions on imports, or quotas, were generally prohibited by Article XI of the GATT, except for agricultural and fisheries products. These controls were designed to offset balance-of-payment problems (Article XII) and many barriers to trade imposed by Third World countries (Article VIII) (GATT, 1969). In addition, Article XIX allowed member nations to raise tariffs or impose quotas on imports to protect domestic industries. This was meant as an *emergency clause* to help a signatory mitigate unforeseen hardships caused by imports, and the conditions under which it can be used are highly restrictive, as intended by its authors. In return for limited imports, the country is expected to offer compensation to countries with 'substantial interest' in the product as exporters. Another restriction was that the measure must be temporary, which, while not defined, generally meant no longer than five years. Moreover, the quotas had to be applied on a global basis, that is, against all nations on a non-discriminatory basis.

Given the difficulties associated with its use, Article XIX was applied infrequently before the Uruguay Round, including 22 times in all by Canada (GATT, 1987b). Most of the Canadian applications were on agricultural, textile, and clothing products, all of which enjoyed special treatment under the original GATT. Instead of using global quotas under Article XIX, most industrialized nations imposed quotas on imports outside the provisions of the GATT. The early agreement was silent on arrangements whereby an importing nation enters into a bilateral agreement with the exporting nation to limit its exports of specified products to a certain level. Such arrangements are called *voluntary export restraint agreements* (VERAs) or *orderly marketing arrangements* (OMAs). Since they were entered into entirely outside the provisions of the GATT, they were not bound by the conditions of Article XIX. VERAs did not technically contravene the provisions of the GATT because the agreement did not explicitly prohibit such bilateral agreements. But these did violate the spirit of the GATT to the extent that they were applied on a discriminatory basis, did not involve payment of compensation, and were not temporary.

Until the completion of the Uruguay Round, Canada used Article XIX quotas or VERAs less frequently than the US or the EU (GATT, 1987b). One reason is that Canadian tariffs were generally higher than tariffs in other industrialized nations, thus reducing the need for protection through quotas. As well, Canada, unlike most other industrialized nations, has never had a large manufacturing sector, which is often the intended recipient of quota protection. Finally, the high dependence of the Canadian economy on exports ensures that Canada will use caution in imposing import controls, lest its own exports be subjected to similar controls abroad.

By the time of the Uruguay Round, opposition to VERAs had grown and negotiations to constrain the use of such import controls had begun. A major achievement of the subsequent WTO Agreement on Safeguards is that it prohibits VERAs; any such measure in place as of January 1995 must be phased out by 1999.

Subsidies

The second government instrument for controlling imports—subsidies to domestic industries—are of various kinds. All governments provide numerous varieties of subsidies to domestic producers and exporters. These can take the form of cash grants for workers' training, the purchase of capital equipment, or conducting research and development. The intended effect is to reduce the firm's cost of production. Instead of cash grants, governments sometimes provide loans at reduced interest or none at all, which again have the effect of reducing production costs. Tax credits or tax breaks have a similar impact on the recipient firms. The total cost of such subsidies provided by the Canadian government fluctuates rapidly but always runs in billions of dollars.

In certain circumstances subsidies may be desirable to develop domestic industries or encourage a more efficient allocation of resources. Consumers, of course, gain from buying subsidized products, the bill being footed by taxpayers in the country providing the subsidy. Liberal economists claim such subsidies misdirect economic resources to uncompetitive rather than competitive industries and that these inefficiencies in the domestic economy are transmitted to the world economy through international trade. Writers based in the Marxist tradition generally claim that state-sponsored subsidies to industry are really a transfer of wealth to the capitalist class as they deploy tax revenue to the benefit of owners of capital. From the staples perspective, subsidies are seen as the product of stilted economic development brought on by an unhealthy dependence on resource industries.

Attempts to deal with the issue of subsidies under the original GATT regime suffered many difficulties. The term 'subsidy' was never properly defined. Negotiators could not agree on what subsidies are most trade-distorting. These difficulties led to many disputes among members throughout the 1970s and 1980s.

The WTO agreements made some progress in this area. A subsidy was more clearly defined as a financial contribution made by a government or public body that involves any of the following:

1. a direct transfer of funds (e.g., loans, grants)
2. a potential transfer of funds (e.g., loan guarantees)
3. tax concessions or credits
4. the purchase or provision of goods or services other than general infrastructure
5. funds given to a private body to undertake functions normally performed by government
6. any form of income or price support. (Hoekman and Kostecki, 1995: 106–7).

The WTO Agreement on Subsidies and Countervailing Measures identifies three categories of subsidy: non-actionable, prohibited, and actionable. Non-actionable subsidies are permitted and include government assistance that is available generally to the population and not directed at a particular industry. For example, the US government cannot impose countervailing duties on Canadian exports on the ground that the government subsidizes the cost of producing these goods through its contribution to education and health services, employment insurance, old age pensions, and so forth. They also include some specific subsidies related to research and development and regional assistance programs. As well, subsidies for helping firms meet new environmental laws or standards are legal.

Prohibited subsidies, on the other hand, are those that directly subsidize specific exports or encourage the use of domestic over imported goods. Examples of these types of subsidies include the provision of services at lower cost for exporters than domestic producers and export credits designed to lower the costs of goods for export. Such subsidies are expressly illegal under the WTO agreements.

Actionable subsidies refer to subsidies that are not explicitly prohibited but may be countervailed if such subsidies adversely affect a WTO member. While the agreement permits the use of actionable subsidies in order to protect domestic producers from unfair foreign competition, it also permits nations to harass foreign producers. An example of the latter is the ongoing attempts by the United States to impose countervailing duties on Canadian softwood lumber exports (Percy and Yoder, 1987).

Government procurement of domestically produced goods is another means of discriminating against imports. Examples of this include prohibitions on foreign purchases (e.g., Canadian civil servants must fly with Canadian airlines); formal rules for foreign purchases (e.g., local content requirements); and informal rules that favour government purchases from local providers (e.g., selective tendering). The importance of government procurement can be better appreciated if we remember that the total purchases by federal and provincial governments in Canada account for well over 10 per cent of the total GNP. The figure rises to 20 per cent if purchases by government-owned or -controlled bodies are included (Moroz, 1985: 251). All nations use this measure to a greater or lesser extent. The WTO Agreement on Government Procurement in principle prohibits preferences for domestic firms by applying the national treatment provision of the GATT. The measures apply to government entities (i.e., ministries), subnational governments (i.e., provinces), and publicly owned utilities. Many countries, particularly those in the developing world, have concluded the agreement is too far-reaching—only 11 signatories (counting the EU as one) have signed the Agreement on Government Procurement (Hoekman and Kostecki, 1995: 122–4).

A New World Trade Regime

The Uruguay Round signalled a basic shift in the principles underlying the political economy of the world trading system. Whereas previous rounds of talks focused almost exclusively on the trade in goods, the Uruguay Round succeeded in broadening the agenda to include services and, perhaps more importantly, other complex issues such as intellectual property rights. According to S.P. Shukla, India's representative to the GATT, the inclusion of these items has important implications for developing nations in particular. While the tariff reductions contained in the WTO agreements may open up new markets for the products of developing countries, Shukla warns that the broader scope of the agreements limits their policy options. The GATT, according to Shukla, was based on a 'border paradigm' in which the sovereignty of nations was respected. Earlier talks avoided issues like property rights and investment laws because they were agreed to be legitimate measures taken by sovereign states. The new paradigm of the WTO, he contends, is one that is more 'borderless' because it sets out rules that encroach on areas of economic and social policy that were previously the exclusive domain of nation-states. In his view, this grants the developed world a greater say over the economic policies of developing countries, creating a new colonial relationship (Instituto del Tercer Mundo, 1995: 54).

Under pressure from the developed world, it is likely that future rounds of WTO negotiations will become increasingly entangled in more complex trade-related issues. In particular, a desire to create a set of binding rules liberalizing foreign investment is a goal of the United States and other developed countries, which are home to the world's largest transnational corporate investors. Thus far, however, attempts to establish a Multilateral Agreement on Investment (MAI) within the WTO have been stalled by the concerns of developing countries that insist on imposing requirements on foreign investors in order to maximize the local benefits of investment. Faced with this impasse at the WTO, the 29 industrialized countries of the OECD have been separately negotiating an investment treaty since 1996. This agreement, if successful, may prove to be the blueprint for a WTO investment treaty (Clarke and Barlow, 1997).

As well, future WTO negotiations will likely need to address growing concerns about the impact of trade liberalization on the environment, social standards, and labour and human rights. Thus far, the WTO has managed to skirt these concerns, but as the restructuring caused by trade and investment liberalization takes greater hold, political demands for creating mechanisms to offset the fallout of these economic reforms will likely increase.

Canada's International Economic Relations

Historical Background

Great Britain's move towards free trade through the repeal of the Corn Laws in 1846, with its inadvertent effect of terminating the Canadian producers' preferred access to the British market, marked the beginning of Canada's efforts to develop its own trade policy. The British action signified that Canada's interests were not a factor in the mother country's trade policies. Consequently, the five colonies forming British North America signed the Reciprocity Treaty with the United States in 1854, offering preferred access to each other's markets. The treaty was terminated in 1866 at the request of the US government for several reasons, including Canada's huge trade surplus, concerted pressures from US interests adversely affected by Canadian exports, and Britain's support for the South in the American Civil War, which caused resentment in the eventually victorious North.

The end of the treaty led Canadian policy-makers to search for alternative means of establishing assured access to a large market for Canadian producers, and one of the results of this search was the establishment of Confederation in 1867. At the same time, the newly established Canadian government continued to pursue another reciprocity agreement with the United States, but to no avail. Frustrated with the US government's lack of interest in negotiating a trade deal, the Canadian government under Sir John A. Macdonald announced the National Policy in 1879. Its cornerstone was a drastic increase in tariffs on imports. While tariffs had been deployed before in retaliation against Great Britain's moves towards free trade, Macdonald's National Policy marked the first effort by the government to position the new country in the new international political economy. It also set the precedent for the strategy of import substitution that was to frame Canada's trade relations for the next 100 years (Eden and Molot, 1993).

Even at this early stage of development, however, Canada's trade policy was characterized by contradictory motives. One reason for the tariff increases was to exert pressure on the US government to negotiate reciprocal reductions in tariffs against each other's imports. Another was to foster industrial development by protecting Canadian 'infant industries' from imports and by encouraging foreign manufacturers to establish plants in Canada so they would avoid tariffs. This second goal was by and large accomplished as many manufacturing plants, both Canadian and foreign (mostly US), were established towards the end of the century. But the goal of negotiating reciprocity with the United States remained as elusive as ever. Undaunted by the lack of interest in the United States, the Canadians continued their efforts covertly under the Conservatives and overtly under the Liberals. An offer of preferential access for British exports in 1879 remained similarly unreciprocated by the British government.

The goal of reaching a free trade agreement with the United States was almost accomplished in 1911, when the Liberal government under Sir Wilfrid Laurier announced an agreement to reduce tariffs on a reciprocal basis with the United States on a range of natural products and some manufactured products. The agreement was clearly designed to support the western and eastern agricultural and primary producers, while only marginally reducing the protection afforded central Canadian manufacturers. But 1911 was an election year. The Conservatives, in an alliance with business and labour, mounted a bitter campaign that ended in a humiliating defeat for the Liberal Party. The lesson from the election was not lost on either of the main parties, and neither dared raise the topic for several decades (Granatstein, 1985).

The anti-American, pro-British sentiments that marked the 1911 election were out of tune with the time, for the United States was emerging rapidly as the world's foremost military and economic power. Despite the rejection of the free trade deal, Canada's trade with the United States continued to expand, and increasingly large amounts of US investment continued to pour in. Canada was on the march towards closer integration with the US economy, punctuated only by the Great Depression in the 1930s. After Canadian exports suffered at the hands of the US Smoot-Hawley Tariff of 1930, in 1935 the two nations signed an agreement to lower their tariffs substantially; this was the first trade pact between the neighbours since 1854. It was followed by further attempts to reduce tariffs, and in 1938 an agreement was reached among Canada, the US, the UK, Australia, New Zealand, and South Africa to provide easy access for each other's goods. The process of multilateral reductions in trade barriers had begun, a process that gained momentum after the end of World War II.

The United States emerged from the war as the dominant technological, economic, and military power in the world, and it was in its interest to organize an open world trading order. That goal was supported by Canada, which also emerged from the war as a beneficiary in economic terms. The US efforts led to the negotiation and signing of the General Agreement on Tariffs and Trade (GATT) in 1947. Under this agreement, which has expanded considerably both in membership and scope since its inception, tariffs on industrial goods in developed countries have fallen from an average of about 40 per cent to a current average of about 5 per cent (*Canada Year Book*, 1997: 297).

In 1948, immediately after the signing of the GATT, Canadian and American negotiators reached an agreement to establish virtually free trade between the two countries, and there was pressure on Prime Minister William Lyon Mackenzie King to move forward and sign the treaty. But at the last minute King balked, later noting in his diary: 'I stressed strongly that regardless of what the economic facts might be, the issue would turn on union with the States and separation from Britain' (Whalley, 1985: 37). King's sentimentality about Britain was misplaced, however, for Canada's trade relations with the mother country had been dwindling rapidly and by the late 1940s were no match for relations with the United States.

For most of the postwar period, global trade negotiations have been characterized by *multilateralism*—that is, they have included many nations rather than just one or two potential trade partners. Canadian leaders, aware of the nation's high degree of trade dependence, have recognized that a multilateral arrangement provides the best guarantee against protectionism and the economic and diplomatic powers of the larger nations. This explains the strong Canadian participation in the GATT and other international institutions. While its commitment to multilateralism is beyond doubt, in practical terms the multilateral framework has worked mainly towards expanding Canadian trade with the United States (Dunn, 1991).

The visibility of these relations with the US is so high that it is easy to lose sight of trade with other nations. Canada, for instance, not only has free trade with the United States and Mexico under NAFTA, but has also signed free trade agreements with Chile and Israel, although the volume of trade with these latter countries is relatively small when compared to Canada's other trading partners (Dobell and Neufeld, 1993). Canada has also been very actively involved in attempts to create a hemispheric free trade pact, the FTAA or Free Trade Agreement of the Americas, and will no doubt be drawn into recent US initiatives to establish NAFTA-EU linkages (Walker, 1998).

The EU (a political and economic union that establishes a common market for goods, services, and labour among the UK, Ireland, Portugal, Spain, Italy, Greece, France, Belgium, Luxembourg, the Netherlands, Germany, Denmark, Austria, Finland, Sweden, and soon several countries from Eastern Europe) forms the world's largest trading bloc. It is Canada's second largest trading partner, although in 1996 it accounted for only 5.7 per cent of exports and 8.7 per cent of imports. Trade with the UK accounts for much of this total, with 2.2 per cent of our imports coming from that country and 2.5 per cent destined for that market (Statistics Canada, 1997c).

The Asia-Pacific region—consisting of the economic superpower Japan, the newly industrialized countries (NICs) of South Korea, Taiwan, Hong Kong, and

Singapore, and the rapidly industrializing China, Thailand, Malaysia, Indonesia, and Philippines—has formed a more loosely structured economic bloc along with Australia, New Zealand, and several Pacific Rim countries in North and South America. Many of these countries belong to the Association of South-East Asian Nations (ASEAN) but now also work within the context of the Asia-Pacific Economic Co-operation forum (APEC). With others, many of these countries have also joined in the 14-country Indian Ocean Rim Initiative aimed at creating a large trade bloc in that area of the globe. However, the regional organizations in the Asia-Pacific are still at an incipient stage and will perhaps never achieve the level of institutionalization found in the EU and NAFTA.

The Asia-Pacific region had the fastest rate of economic growth in the world over the last few decades, although by mid-1997 this growth declined dramatically in the face of over-investment in real estate and a decline in demand for the region's exports of standard-technology manufactured products. The region's wage-based competitiveness, while real, is often exaggerated. Collectively, these countries supply a small fraction of our total imports, most of which, at any rate, come from Japan, a high-wage economy. While employment in many Canadian industries—most notably in textiles, clothing, footwear, toys, and automobile parts—has been eroded significantly by imports from these countries, their success is based on the principles of comparative advantage, which Canada has supported. Indeed, these countries have been able to export despite the various discriminatory practices—such as quotas and VERAs—that Canadian and other Western governments maintain against their products. They also form an increasingly important destination for exports, especially for western Canadian producers, and bullying these countries to accept unfavourable terms of trade, which has been common in the past, has become increasingly difficult. Ongoing trade liberalization efforts under the auspices of the APEC forum indicate the growing importance of this region.

Canada's trade with Third World nations that are non-oil exporting and outside the Asia-Pacific region (which leaves most of Africa, South Asia, and South and Central America) is minuscule as a proportion of total trade. One reason for the low degree of trade with these nations is that they mainly export primary natural resource-based products, which Canada itself has in abundance. Another reason is the barriers that Canada (along with other industrialized nations) maintains against their exports: the trade-weighted Canadian tariffs on goods from Third World countries have been about twice as high as on goods from industrialized countries (Macdonald Commission, 1985, I: 257). In the early 1970s, Canada agreed to grant preferential tariffs to Third World nations, but in practice this move has been meaningless because more than 95 per cent of the total goods exported by the Third World are not eligible for those lower tariffs. While Canada's foreign aid to these nations (0.45 per cent of the GNP in 1991) is only slightly below the OECD average (0.51 per cent), it is substantially below the level provided by the Netherlands and the Scandinavian nations (Instituto del Tercer Mundo, 1995). Moreover, much of Canada's foreign assistance is tied to the purchase of Canadian goods. This approach may partly explain the trade surplus that Canada has traditionally maintained with these nations (Helleiner, 1985: 104).

Canada-US Free Trade and the North American Free Trade Agreement

The GATT, born in the context of steep pre-World War II trade barriers, was remarkably successful in reducing trade barriers and introducing a modicum of uniformity and security into the conduct of international trade. As a result, international trade is now freer than at any time in the last 100 years. As the Macdonald Commission concluded in 1985: 'The performance of GATT to date has been without historical precedent and generally satisfactory, not in any absolute sense of perfection, but in comparison with that of earlier periods. Without GATT, it is unlikely that Canadian exports would have grown at a faster pace than the national economy during the post-War years' (1985, I: 281).

While the role of the GATT was critical in promoting international trade and increasing the economic prosperity of trade-dependent nations such as Canada, before the conclusion of the Uruguay Round there were some justified fears about its future. For one thing, long delays in the negotiations made many suspect an agreement on services and further tariff reductions would not be reached. With more and more nations participating, optimism about the future of multilateral negotiations was tempered by the concern that a wider variety of conflicting interests must now be accommodated. Moreover, the gigantic US trade deficit in the late 1980s and early 1990s made protectionism politically popular in that country, even though the US was the architect of the GATT and the modern liberal trading order.

In the 1980s, the fear that the GATT might not be as effective in the future as it was in the past led the Canadian government to look for alternatives. Without abandoning the GATT, Canada's focus shifted towards solidifying and furthering the already relatively open trade relations with the United States. The reasoning behind this shift in Canadian policy was that the principal effect of trade liberalization under the GATT, as far as Ottawa was concerned, had been to increase Canada's trade dependence on the United States. As the Macdonald Commission remarked: 'For Canada, the post-War opening up of the international economic order has not been accompanied by a diversification of our trading partners. The reverse has happened: our post-War participation in the global economy has led to an increasingly continental economic integration of our trade partners' (1985, I: 58).

In fact, the recognition that dependence on the United States was an unchangeable reality dawned on Canadian policy-makers even before the Macdonald Commission reported or the Conservative government assumed office in 1984. The same Trudeau government that in the early 1970s had intended to move away from the United States and Britain and pursue a 'Third Option', in Europe, Latin America, and the developing world, had by 1983 opened negotiations, which eventually failed, with the Americans to arrive at free trade in specific sectors (Economic Council, 1988b: 4). In the context of this failure to negotiate sector-specific free trade arrangements and scepticism about the prospects of further trade liberalization under the GATT, Canadian policy-makers began to contemplate a general free trade agreement with the US. The Macdonald Commission made the point rather well:

> Thus, while Commissioners support continued efforts to work through the GATT, we are not sufficiently optimistic about the possibilities of major breakthroughs in the short term to advocate an exclusive preoccupation with the multilateral GATT system. Further, the major benefits for Canadians of a successful GATT reduction of non-tariff barriers would be increased access to the US market. The United States will be our major market, whether or not there is another successful round of GATT negotiations. The fact is, therefore, that the multilateral route which we prefer has, as a primary objective, an increase in the security of our dominant trade relations with the United States. (Macdonald Commission, 1985, I: 60)

Following the same line of reasoning, the Mulroney government soon after its election in 1984 declared its intention to pursue free trade with the United States, pending the outcome of the Uruguay Round negotiations. The Canada-US Free Trade Agreement was reached in October 1987 and came into effect on 1 January 1989 (Doern and Tomlin, 1991; Hart, Dymond, and Robertson, 1994; Ritchie, 1997). On 11 June 1990 US President Bush and Mexican President Salinas announced that they would negotiate a free trade agreement, and after a brief delay Canada joined these talks on 5 February 1991. In 1994, the Canada-US FTA was superseded by NAFTA (Waverman, 1991; Lipsey, Schwanen, and Wonnacott, 1994).

Despite the inclusion of Mexico in the latter agreement, both the FTA and NAFTA signify the *de jure* recognition of Canada's special trade relations with the United States, which have existed for almost a century, and reflect a sense of resignation among policy-makers that it is not possible to use state actions to diversify Canada's trade relations to any substantial degree and avoid the pattern imposed by the international marketplace.

When Canada initially entered into bilateral trade negotiations with the United States in 1986, the Minister for International Trade, James Kelleher, stated that Canada had four objectives:

- *security of access* to the United States market, particularly by reducing the risks inherent in the US system of restrictive trade measures (for example, quotas, surtaxes, and so forth) and the constitutional powers of Congress to pass protectionist legislation affecting Canada;
- *expanded access* to the United States market to provide Canadian industry with a market large enough to realize economies of scale and specialization and to carve out niches for specialty products;

- *a stable North American trading system* that would encourage an orderly transition in Canada towards an economy more competitive at home and in world markets and provide increased incentive for investment from all sources;
- *an ordered and more predictable system* for managing the trade relationship and resolving disputes. (Lipsey and York, 1988: 10–11)

Much of NAFTA is based on the framework of the Canada-US FTA. In fact, many provisions of the original deal are included word for word in NAFTA. However, the latter deal significantly extends their scope and application, particularly in the areas of services and investment (Canada, 1992). The main provisions of NAFTA include agreements on the following.

Tariffs
While about 70 per cent of Canadian exports to the US and 65 per cent of US exports to Canada were already exempt from tariffs in 1988 (Economic Council, 1988b: 7), the original Canada-US FTA provided for the elimination of all tariffs by 1 January 1999. This schedule remains in place under NAFTA and a new timeline is established for the elimination of trading tariffs with Mexico. Many tariffs were eliminated when NAFTA came into effect on 1 January 1994, and the rest are scheduled to be reduced in three stages, in 1998, 2003, and 2008. Tariffs on products protected by the highest levels of tariffs will be the last to be eliminated. Since Canadian and Mexican tariffs are on average higher than the comparable tariffs in the US, the adjustment pressures resulting from their removal are likely to be greater for Canadian and Mexican producers than for US producers.

National Treatment
NAFTA incorporates the same national treatment obligation as in the GATT and extends this obligation to the measures of state and provincial governments. This requires the three countries and their subnational governments not to discriminate against the others' exports. There are, however, a number of specified exceptions to this general principle. As well, this provision does not stop any country from adopting particular measures that discriminate against imports from the other country; it just requires that the adopted measure be equally applicable to goods and services from all three countries.

Agriculture
The NAFTA chapter covering agriculture is the only part that does not contain a common text for all three countries. Instead, two separate agreements are established, one on Mexican-American agricultural trade, the other on Mexican-Canadian agricultural trade. Under the latter, Canada and Mexico agreed to eliminate all tariff and non-tariff barriers on their agricultural trade, with the exception of dairy, poultry, egg, and sugar products. Canada immediately lifted import restrictions on Mexican wheat, barley, beef, veal, and margarine. In return, Mexico eliminated its tariffs on the import of Canadian cattle, beef, rye,

buckwheat, frozen blueberries, and raspberries. The two countries also agreed to phase out, within 10 years, all tariffs on fruits and vegetables.

While the NAFTA does not contain a separate section dealing with Canadian-American agricultural trade, the agreement does incorporate provisions from the FTA. These require all tariffs on agricultural products to be phased out by 1999. The FTA clauses incorporated into NAFTA also provide for termination of export subsidies in bilateral trade, exemptions from laws controlling imports of beef and veal, harmonization of some technical standards, and a commitment to make standards more uniform. Most of the non-tariff barriers remain untouched. The agreement allows the continuation of import quotas to support supply management schemes for poultry, eggs, and dairy products. This is to prevent imports from flooding the market because of high domestic prices maintained purposely by various management schemes in both countries. For the first 10 years, a special safeguard provision applies to certain agricultural products that allows each party to reapply tariffs if imports of agricultural products reach a threshold amount specified in the agreement.

Automobiles

Since 1965 there has been managed trade in automotive products between Canada and the United States under the Auto Pact. NAFTA, like the FTA, essentially maintains the pact for the existing firms covered by it but prevents its extension to new companies. Regarding Mexico, both the United States and Canada agreed to eliminate all tariffs on automotive goods over time, and in turn Mexico committed to lift its tariffs by 2003. Several provisions eliminate or reduce Canada's ability to offer incentives to foreign producers to locate manufacturing facilities in Canada. NAFTA raised the percentage of North American content required in order for automobiles to trade tariff-free, to 62.5 per cent from the 50 per cent in the FTA. NAFTA also carries forward a provision of the FTA that will phase out, over five years, Canada's ban on the importation of used cars.

Energy

Both the FTA's and NAFTA's provisions regarding the energy sector have been among the most far-reaching and contentious in Canada. The US is the world's largest energy consumer and importer, as well as producer, and Canada is its largest foreign supplier. Many of the Trudeau government's measures to Canadianize the sector in the early 1980s were major irritants for the US, and Canadian negotiators felt it was doubtful whether the US government would have signed the Canada-US FTA without an assurance that such measures would not be repeated. Yet, in NAFTA, Mexico won significant concessions from the Americans to maintain public control over its energy sector. Mexico reserved a number of strategic areas, including the oil and gas industry and the supply of electricity. Private investment in these areas is not allowed without the permission of the Mexican government.

The energy sector as defined in the agreement includes oil, natural gas, light petroleum gas, coal, uranium, and electricity. NAFTA eliminates, with the exception of Mexico's reservations, almost all barriers to trade in these commodities. It explicitly prohibits—and this is the feature that riles the critics of the agreement the most—the use of measures that make export prices higher than domestic prices, such as the export tax imposed under the National Energy Program by the Trudeau government. Moreover, while not prohibiting restrictions on the amount of energy exports in time of shortage, NAFTA allows importers to purchase an amount no smaller than the 'proportion prevailing in the most recent 36 month period'. The US government wanted this provision to make absolutely sure that in times of shortage the Canadian government would introduce cuts affecting consumers on both sides of the border equally. While this is in keeping with the provisions implicit in the WTO agreements and with Canada's obligations under the International Energy Agreement pertaining to oil, NAFTA goes further by explicitly specifying the proportion in which supplies will be shared. Critics allege that insofar as the Canadian government cannot reduce supplies to the US consumers in times of shortages without hurting Canadian consumers as well, this is a serious erosion of Canada's sovereignty.

Services

The role of services in the economies of the industrialized nations, especially in Canada and the United States, has grown rapidly in recent decades. Over two-thirds of the GNP and employment in both countries is now concentrated in this sector, which is significantly higher than the average for industrialized nations. Services also occupy an important place in the trade between the two nations. In 1996, Canada imported $18.6 billion of services from the US and exported $7 billion worth of services to it (*Canada Year Book*, 1996). Not surprisingly, the Canada-US FTA contained two long chapters covering 150 specified services, including financial, agriculture and forestry, mining, distributional trade, construction, and commercial services (Radebaugh, 1988: 27). NAFTA provisions follow on this and establish an extensive set of rules and obligations to facilitate the trade in services among its parties.

The agreement explicitly excludes air transportation and government-provided services such as health, education, and social services, and also 'grandparents'—that is, permits the continuation of—all existing laws and regulations in the covered services. Measures by local governments are not affected by NAFTA, however. The agreement does not prevent either nation from enacting new policies, so long as the particular policy applies equally to domestic producers and those in other member countries.

NAFTA treats telecommunications and financial services separately from other services. The telecommunications chapter places significant restrictions over the operation and provision of basic communications services. However, each party is obliged to make telecommunications networks available on a non-discriminatory basis for enhanced uses by firms or individuals from other NAFTA parties. These uses include the provision of value-added telecommunications services and intracorporate communication.

The financial services chapter exempts American and Mexican investors from Canadian laws prohibiting foreign ownership of financial institutions. NAFTA allows for American and Mexican investors to acquire up to 25 per cent of the shares of any Canadian trust and insurance companies as well as the chartered banks.

Investment

The investment provisions lie at the heart of NAFTA (Appleton, 1994: 79). NAFTA eliminates cross-border barriers to investments in all sectors except financial services, transportation, basic telecommunications, cultural industries, oil and natural gas, uranium mining, and the non-covered services such as child care, health care, and education. The agreement also grandparents all existing rules, except those explicitly mentioned. Under the agreement, NAFTA parties are obliged to give investors of other NAFTA parties treatment no less favourable than they give their own domestic investors. Canada reserves the right to review direct acquisitions of Canadian firms by US-owned firms, but the threshold under which a review can be made was raised. Prior to the agreement, Canada could review and block an acquisition if the value of the company acquired was more than \$5 million—NAFTA raises that threshold to \$150 million. The review of indirect acquisitions, which occurs when a foreign firm purchases another foreign firm that has a Canadian subsidiary, will be phased out completely.

NAFTA parties are also prohibited from applying new conditions or performance requirements on firms from NAFTA countries. Specific measures that are prohibited include technology transfer requirements, export targets, job creation targets, and domestic content requirements. These types of performance requirements have been used by Canadian governments in the past to help maximize the benefits of foreign investment.

By grandparenting most existing restrictions and prohibiting only new ones, however, NAFTA is more restrictive towards the United States, which currently has almost no restrictions on foreign investment (except in telecommunications and maritime shipping) but might have considered imposing them in the future, given the recent increase in foreign investments into the country. In such an eventuality, Canadian investments would be exempt under the agreement. This is significant for Canada because in recent years its investments in the US have grown faster than the investments of US firms in Canada. Between 1982 and 1986, Canadian direct investment in the US grew by 56.4 per cent whereas US investment in Canada grew by only 15.3 per cent (Schott and Smith 1988: 135). Since then, Canadian direct investment in the US has jumped by 122 per cent while US investment in Canada rose by 77 per cent (Statistics Canada, 1997a: Table 25). In aggregate, however, cumulative Canadian investments in the US are still less than half the amount of US investment in Canada.

Government Procurement

The agreement opens federal purchases of goods and some services in all three countries to Canadian, Mexican, and American suppliers. NAFTA applies to all procurements over US$50,000 for goods and services and applies to government procurement of construction services in excess of US$6.5 million. But the provision excludes many government departments and agencies in all three countries and applies only to procurement at the federal level, leaving out the major expenditures of provincial, state, and local governments. Important exclusions also include procurement of defence, transport, and telecommunications goods at the federal level.

Dispute Settlement

One of Canada's most important objectives for entering into the negotiations was to gain security of access to the US market. This meant establishing an independent mechanism for adjudicating trade disputes and enforcing its rulings. The FTA and NAFTA made only minor improvements, if any, on the existing situation.

In the case of disputes over the use of anti-dumping or countervailing measures, each NAFTA country is entitled to appeal the other's decision to independent binational panels instead of the federal courts that used to be the appellate bodies. Each panel is comprised of five members, two nominated by each side in the dispute and the fifth chosen by consensus. Anti-dumping and countervailing duty panels are empowered only to determine whether measures taken by a party were a fair application of its domestic law. NAFTA, therefore, does not create a common set of trade laws governing anti-dumping measures and countervailing duties. A panel is required to issue its ruling within 315 days. The Canada-US FTA set a seven-year deadline for developing new rules governing anti-dumping and countervailing duties that would be mutually acceptable to both countries. However, NAFTA does not provide for any deadline. Consequently, the panels will continue to apply existing laws, and hence decisions are not likely to be substantially different from the judicial precedents (O'Brien, 1992). For critics of the deal, the dispute settlement mechanism is seen as inconsequential because it does not contain effective sanctions or guaranteed results. The US producers' ability to initiate actions on rather frivolous grounds will also continue as before. Perhaps the only beneficial impact of the dispute-resolving mechanism is the 10-month time limit for the resolution of disputes—in contrast to the several years this could once take (Davey, 1996).

The agreement provides for a separate mechanism for resolving general disputes related to the implementation of the agreement but excluding countervailing and anti-dumping measures. A dispute between NAFTA countries that cannot be resolved by mutual consultation is referred to the Free Trade Commission (FTC), a permanent body jointly established to oversee the implementation of the agreement. Should the FTC be unable to resolve the issue, then a NAFTA party may ask it to create a dispute resolution panel consisting of five persons. A panel must issue its initial report within 90 days of being formed and a final report must follow within 30 days. A defending party must comply with the ruling of the panel or the aggrieved party is authorized to retaliate by withdrawing 'equivalent benefits', which in trade parlance means erecting import barriers to the targeted country's exports. Any retaliation, however, can be reviewed by a panel if it is felt to be excessive.

NAFTA also contains an unprecedented system for the resolution of disputes between investors and governments of the three countries, giving investors the right to sue governments directly for breaching obligations under the investment provisions of the agreement. Traditionally, states have been the only actors capable of initiating international legal action in the case of such disputes. The investor-to-state dispute resolution process in NAFTA allows investors to seek monetary compensation from other NAFTA states if they feel they have lost profits or business opportunities because they have been discriminated against or not accorded most-favoured treatment.

One such legal action was launched against the government of Canada in 1997 when US-based Ethyl Corporation filed a $300 million claim. Ethyl is the sole producer of a manganese-based fuel additive, MMT, used to enhance automobile performance. Automobile manufacturers, however, say MMT damages emission control systems and thus contributes to the release of more pollutants into the air. As well, MMT is a neuro-toxin and its impact on animal and human health is not fully understood. Concerned about the environmental and health impacts of MMT, the Canadian government banned its use. Ethyl responded with a legal suit under the investor-to-state dispute resolution system in NAFTA, claiming the ban discriminated against it. For NAFTA critics, this case has highlighted the degree to which they claim Canadian political sovereignty has been sacrificed under free trade (Shrybman, 1993).

Cultural Industries

Canadian cultural industries are excluded from the agreement. Thus, the 'national treatment' provision for trade and investment does not extend to the cultural industries. Canada can discriminate against US firms in the cultural sector in the future, although doing so will trigger the US right to retaliate against Canadian exports in other sectors by imposing 'measures of equivalent commercial effect'. This means that Canada will have to compensate the United States (or Mexico) for any new measures taken to protect or promote Canada's cultural industries. This applies only to new measures, because all existing measures (such as the condition that all television and radio broadcasting should be fully Canadian-owned) are grandparented. While the existing Canadian control over its cultural industries may be protected, an increase in the level of control, while permitted, will have to be counterbalanced. For critics, this represents a fatal caveat in the cultural exemption (Macmillan, 1992).

Supplemental Agreements

Following the conclusion of NAFTA negotiations, the governments of Canada, the United States, and Mexico agreed to two 'side deals' or supplemental agreements to address public concern over the impact of free trade on the environment and labour.

The North American Agreement on Environmental Co-operation requires the NAFTA parties to enforce their own national environmental protection laws. The agreement also created the North American Commission for Environmental Co-operation (NACEC) based in Montreal. NACEC hears complaints from any person or non-governmental organization alleging the non-enforcement of environmental laws and regulations of a NAFTA party, but only governments can initiate actions to compel another party to abide by the agreement. As well, the agreement does not prevent any party from changing current laws to reduce environmental regulations (Johnson and Beaulieu, 1996).

The North American Agreement on Labour Co-operation was created to address concerns that free trade could lead to pressures for Canada and the United States to lower their labour standards in order to compete with the lower paid and less regulated Mexican labour force. The labour agreement does not require NAFTA parties to improve their labour standards or even to make their standards compatible. Instead, it simply calls on the three countries to promote, where possible, principles such as freedom of association, the right to strike, prohibition of forced labour, protection for children, equal pay for men and women, and compensation for occupational accidents and diseases. Like the environmental supplemental agreement, the side agreement on labour creates a body, the North American Commission for Labour Co-operation (NACLC), to report on labour and employment conditions in the NAFTA countries (Houseman and Orbuch, 1993).

Accession
Unlike the Canada-US FTA, which was strictly bilateral in nature, NAFTA was designed to be a *multilateral* framework document that could be expanded to include more parties. Consequently, the agreement provides that any country or groups of countries may join NAFTA subject to the terms agreed to by the new member and the FTC. The long-term goal of the current NAFTA signatories is to expand its coverage to include nations in Central and South America. In 1994, the heads of governments of 34 American countries (excluding Cuba) agreed to use NAFTA as a blueprint for constructing a Free Trade Agreement of the Americas no later than 2005 (Dobell and Neufeld, 1993). This arrangement would bring together in one gigantic, $10 trillion free trade area the existing NAFTA countries as well as those belonging to the Mercosur, Andean, Central American Common Market, Latin American Integration Association, and Caricom pacts in Central and South America and the Caribbean (Saborio, 1992).

Termination of the Agreement
Any nation can choose to withdraw from the agreement on six months' notice. The withdrawal of one party does not terminate NAFTA, which will remain in force with its remaining parties. While withdrawing appears simple enough, the decision will be anything but easy, especially for Canada, as Jean Chrétien's government found out during its first term in office, despite his earlier commitment to abrogate the

agreement. The adverse impact of the termination on firms that have adjusted to NAFTA or have been established to sell in the continental market would have to be taken into account. The decision will be relatively easy for the US, however, because a comparatively small percentage of its economy is dependent on trade with Canada and Mexico.

The Impact of Free Trade on Canada

Canadians may regard moderation and willingness to compromise as an integral part of their national character, but they have not displayed either quality in national debates on the pros and cons of free trade with the United States. That was true in the 1911 election campaign and it was true during the federal election in 1988, the two elections in which free trade was the key issue. Even the scholarly commentaries on the subject tend to exaggerate either the beneficial or the adverse effects of free trade. But all things considered, free trade with its neighbours is not likely to provide all the material benefits for Canada claimed by its supporters, nor is it likely to destroy Canada as alleged by its opponents (Whalley, 1993; Cadsby and Woodside, 1993).

Early studies on the likely impact of free trade with the United States predicted Canada benefiting by as much as a 10 per cent increase in GNP. These studies, conducted before the Canada-US FTA and NAFTA were signed, assumed the complete elimination of barriers to trade between the two nations, but the agreements reached provided for the continuation of many barriers. Consequently, later studies predicted much smaller benefits. The Economic Council of Canada (1988b: 18), in its prediction of the 'most likely outcome' for the Canada-US FTA, stated a real (that is, adjusted for inflation) increase of 2.5 per cent in GNP when the agreement is fully implemented in 1998. The federal Finance Department's study, using a totally different model, similarly predicted an increase of 2.5 per cent in real income in the long run (Canada, Department of Finance, 1988b: 108). The Economic Council's long-term forecasts also showed an increase of 1.8 per cent in employment, or a net gain of 251,000 in jobs, a 0.7 per cent increase in productivity, a 5 per cent increase in investment, and increases of 2.2 per cent in exports and 3.9 per cent in imports (Economic Council, 1988b: 18). Both studies indicated that the gains will be spread almost evenly across all regions in Canada (ibid., 24; Canada, Department of Finance, 1988b: 34).

These forecasts would seem to indicate that the expected gains of the FTA are rather small, hardly the stuff to get excited about. The expected increase of 2.5 per cent of the GNP over a 10-year period projected by the ECC and Finance Department is nothing when we realize that in each of the decades between 1951 and 1981 the country's real increase in GDP was well over 33 per cent (Canada, Department of Finance, 1988b: 7). No doubt, the 2.5 per cent increase will be in addition to the growth that would have taken place without the agreement, but still to call an average additional increase of only 0.25 per cent per year anything but small is an exaggeration. Between 1984 and 1987 alone, the average real GDP in Canada increased by 4.4 per cent (Canada, Department of Finance, 1988b). A close look at the figures for employment gains also casts doubt on the exuberance of FTA supporters.

Eight years into free trade with the United States, the accuracy of these predictions was mixed. Measured in constant dollars, Canada's GDP grew by 9.1 per cent in the eight-year period from 1988 to 1996. That only slightly outperformed the 8.5 per cent rate of growth during the *four-year* period between 1984 and 1988 (Statistics Canada, 1997b) prior to the FTA coming into force. The bulk of this growth has taken place since 1991 (8.9 per cent), after the recession of 1990–1 drove GDP down to within 0.2 per cent of its 1989 level. Trade has continued to play an increasingly important role in the Canadian economy, as exports grew from 33.8 per cent of GDP in 1992 to 38.4 per cent in 1996. Growth in imports followed a similar trend (Schwanen, 1997: 6). Following a historical pattern, much of this growth is the result of increased trade with the United States.

Whether or not this growth in trade can be directly attributed to the trade agreements, however, is somewhat questionable. A 1997 study commissioned by the C.D. Howe Institute found that exports to the United States in liberalized trade categories rose almost 40 per cent since the implementation of the agreements, whereas exports to other countries and in non-liberalized categories have risen by less than 15 per cent over the same period (Schwanen, 1997: 8). While the study notes that 'some of this growth clearly should be attributed to macroeconomic factors and long term industrial trends, trade liberalization seems to have an additional positive impact' (ibid., 9).

Table 18 charts the growth of Canada's industrial sectors from 1988 to 1996. As it illustrates, the 1988 predictions of both the Economic Council and the Department of Industry are in some cases close to being correct; in others they miss the mark completely. Overall, however, there has been no significant downturn in the economy, even in the manufacturing sector, as some critics predicted.

While the economy appears to have shown reasonable growth over the last eight years, there have been some striking changes in its structure, particularly in the area of employment. As Table 19 illustrates, job growth was generally

Table 18: GDP by Industry, 1988–1996 ($millions, constant)

	1988	1990	1992	1994	1996	% change 1988–96
Primary	33,954.5	34,357.9	33,799.7	37,458.2	39,727.7	8.5
Manufacturing	95,599.5	92,856.7	87,421.8	98,583.2	103,643.3	9.2
Construction	30,814.9	32,296.3	28,422.3	28,622.1	26,680.3	−15.5
Service	316,304.4	329,056.9	332,353.3	350,112.9	363,779.2	8.7

Source: Statistics Canada, *Provincial GDP by Industry, 1984–1996*, Cat. No. 15–203-XPB (Ottawa: Minister of Industry, 1997).

Table 19: Employment by Industry, 1986–1996 (thousands)

	1986	1988	1994	1996	% change 1988–96
Goods-producing	2,696.2	2,902.1	2,441.3	2,514.6	−13.3
Service	7,432.9	7,977.8	8,150.2	8,392.8	5.2
Industrial aggregate (total)	10,129.1	10,879.9	10,591.5	10,907.4	0.2

Source: Statistics Canada, Cat. No. 72F002.

stagnant between 1988 and 1996. Perhaps more important, however, is the shift in employment from the goods-producing sector to service industries.

Further details on shifts in employment are shown in Table 20, which reveals that between 1988 and 1996 more than 250,000 manufacturing jobs were lost.

As Table 21 shows, growth in the service industries more than compensated for the employment loss in manufacturing, yet service jobs paid on average 20 per cent less than their manufacturing counterparts in 1996.

In retrospect, then, the promise of 'jobs, jobs, jobs' made by many free trade proponents rings a little hollow. Shortly after the FTA came into force, Canada was plunged into its longest and most severe recession since the 1930s. Average real growth in the first six years of free trade with the United States was just 1.5 per cent per year, well below average rates of growth in the postwar period. Unemployment soared from 7.5 per cent in 1989 to nearly 12 per cent at the height of the recession. Even during the subsequent 'recovery', until 1999 unemployment rates continued to hover near 10 per cent, well above their levels prior to free trade. Overall, about 17 per cent of the total manufacturing jobs disappeared between 1988 and 1994 (Canadian Centre for Policy Alternatives, 1996: 8). Between 1989 and 1993, more than 200 manufacturing plants representing 43,000

Table 20: Manufacturing Employment, 1986–1996 (thousands)

	1986	1988 (FTA)	1994 (NAFTA)	1996	% change 1988–96
Food	190.1	207.7	181.0	188.5	−9.2
Clothing	120.6	120.8	83.8	85.0	−29.6
Wood	100.6	119.8	114.6	123.2	3.0
Primary metals	99.8	103.3	80.8	83.7	−18.9
Fabricated metals	163.2	174.3	143.5	154.0	−11.6
Transportation equipment	200.4	224.1	207.8	223.3	−0.3
Machinery and equipment	79.6	84.9	74.9	89.4	5.3
Paper	119.8	127.0	99.5	98.9	−22.1

Source: Statistics Canada, Cat. No. 72F002.

Table 21: Services Employment, 1988–1996 (thousands)

	1986	1988 (FTA)	1994 (NAFTA)	1996	% change 1988–96
Employment agencies	49.1	59.8	69.0	92.3	54.3
Computer and related services	40.3	44.9	62.5	82.7	84.2
Architects, engineers, and technical services	77.1	90.7	105.9	127.2	40.2
Educational services	748.3	803.1	894.7	890.6	10.9
Health and social services	990.5	1,086.2	1,169.0	1,199.4	10.4
Food and beverage services	532.9	580.3	588.8	627.3	8.0
Amusement and recreational services	146.7	165.7	169.7	193.7	16.9

Source: Statistics Canada, Cat. No. 72F002.

jobs left Canada for the United States and Mexico (Merret, 1996: 281–6). An analysis of 48 of Canada's largest corporations—ardent supporters of free trade—reveals that combined they eliminated more than 200,000 jobs between 1989 and 1997.

However, supporters of free trade point out that the serious economic downturn in the wake of free trade was not limited to Canada, but was global in nature. The severe recession of 1990–1, therefore, cannot be blamed on the free trade agreement with the US. Some proponents say that high unemployment and slow growth were primarily the result of high interest rates and tax increases. Other commentators note that the decline in manufacturing jobs began long before the FTA and NAFTA were implemented and is simply an extension of a longer-term trend away from the physical production of goods to the provision of various services associated with their production and consumption (Schwanen, 1997: 20). When these factors are weighed, supporters say, then only 15 per cent of job losses can be directly related to the FTA and NAFTA (Safarian, 1996: 34).

Another major concern surrounding the implementation of these trade agreements was whether or not Canada would remain an attractive site for investment. As trade barriers fell, there were two major questions. Would a flood of cheap imported products drive investment in import-competing industries out of Canada? Or, similarly, would large corporations that had maintained profitability by operating behind Canada's protective tariff barriers move their investments to places where the costs of production—such as wages and corporate taxes—were lower? Once again, it is difficult to provide conclusive answers. As Schwanen (1997: 15–16) notes, Canada's share of North American fixed private investment remained near record levels from 1988 to 1992, but then dropped sharply by more than 10 per cent from 1993 to 1996. Whether this is a product of new trade relationships or simply a cyclical response to the booming US economy is an open question.

US patterns of investment in Canada after NAFTA illustrate more decisive trends. In 1988, 56.9 per cent of American investment in Canada was direct investment, but by 1995 this share had fallen to just 24.6 per cent. The remainder, more than 75 per cent, was in the form of portfolio investment, or investment in stocks and bonds (Canadian Centre for Policy Alternatives, 1996: 13–15). While for some observers this shift in the pattern of investment signals a growing confidence in the strength of the Canadian economy, for others the easy liquidity of these investments signals a danger. Indeed, the financial chaos experienced by Mexico in late 1994 and 1995, as well as the Asian currency crisis of 1997, is often attributed to the whims of capricious portfolio managers searching for quick profits through the fast turnover of stocks and bonds.

For critics, the relaxation of investment rules in NAFTA has exacerbated the unemployment crisis that has followed in the wake of free trade. By banning performance requirements, NAFTA, it is claimed, makes it impossible for Canada to require that foreign investors locating here meet job creation targets, hire locally, or buy goods and services from local rather than offshore suppliers. According to one critic, the NAFTA provisions on investment mean that governments are 'greatly restricted from active industrial policies which regulate investment in order to influence where it is channeled and ensure that its citizens get a share of the employment and other benefits' (Campbell, 1993: 20).

Opponents of the FTA and NAFTA also offer a series of broader criticisms of free trade, ranging from the political and social impact to the effect of trade on the environment and Canadian sovereignty (for a comprehensive catalogue of these criticisms of free trade, see Cameron, 1988; Cameron and Watkins, 1993; Barlow, 1990; Merret, 1996). For instance, critics argue that Canada's cultural sovereignty is at risk. The cultural industries, they say, are not excluded from NAFTA because new measures against cultural imports and investments have to be counterbalanced. Under the agreement, the United States can take measures of 'equivalent commercial effect' in response to any Canadian cultural policy that discriminates against American imports. This flaw in the cultural exemption, critics contend, was made evident during the 1996 trade dispute over Country Music Television (CMT). That year, the Canadian Radio-television and Telecommunications Commission (CRTC), as was its policy, ordered the removal of US-owned CMT from cable packages in favour of the Canadian-owned New Country Network. CMT entered the Canadian market in 1984 with the understanding that it would eventually be replaced when a Canadian-owned country music network was formed. When the CRTC's decision was announced, however, trade officials in Washington pointed to the 'equivalent commercial effect' provisions of NAFTA and threatened to retaliate against Canadian exports of music recordings unless the CRTC reversed its decision. Fearing the matter could escalate further, Canadian officials offered a compromise whereby CMT would be allowed to purchase a major interest in New Country Network. Canadian officials also promised there would be no further de-listing of US cable channels in the future. For Canadian cultural nationalists, the incident simply highlighted the degree to which Canada's cultural policies have been put at risk by free trade.

Those opposed to NAFTA also say there is a hidden agenda behind the agreement. They charge that by signing the deal, Canada has committed itself to abandon the social welfare policies of the past in favour of the sort of *laissez-faire* liberalism practised in the United States (Grinspun and Kreklewich, 1994; Robinson, 1993). They fear that free trade is pressuring Canadian governments to reduce 'social wages' (for example, government expenditures on education, health care, and income support) to the lower US and Mexican standards so that Canadian producers will become competitive with their counterparts south of the border (Watkins, 1992; Hum, 1988). To support this claim, opponents of NAFTA point to recent changes made to Canada's unemployment insurance system, which have cut benefits and made it more difficult for the jobless to apply for assistance. Table 22 summarizes the changes made after the introduction of free trade with the United States.

Although Canada's unemployment insurance system may be converging with the US system, it is difficult to pin the blame for these changes solely on free trade. Domestic pressures and changes in the labour market that go beyond NAFTA have certainly been factors as well. Moreover, as proponents of NAFTA note, there are many more examples where Canada has not lowered its social wage. Health care, public pensions, and social assistance programs, despite recent changes and funding cuts, have not fallen to American or Mexican standards as critics warned they would. In fact, in many cases there has been a widening divergence between Canada and its NAFTA partners (Banting, 1996; Banting, Hoberg, and Simeon, 1997; Atkinson and Bierling, 1998).

Finally, critics worry that the competitive pressures of free trade will encourage companies to locate where environmental standards are weaker, thus putting pressure on all NAFTA parties to weaken protection. Environmentalists point to the lax enforcement of standards in Mexico's *maquilidora* region, the vast export-processing zone that stretches along the northern border with the United States.

Table 22: Changes to Unemployment Insurance in Canada, 1989–1995

	1989	1993	1994	1995	Most US States, 1994
% of unemployed eligible	87	64	49	40	33
Required period of insured employment	10–14 weeks	14–20 weeks	12–20 weeks	12–26 weeks	24 weeks
Maximum duration of benefits	40–50 weeks	35–50 weeks	14–50 weeks	45 weeks	26 weeks
Benefit levels as % of earnings	60	57	55–60	50–55	36

Source: Canadian Centre for Policy Alternatives, 1996: 18.

Such areas, they say, will become magnets for polluting companies unwilling to bear the cost of reducing their emission of pollutants. At a more fundamental level, environmentalists worry that the model of industrial development promoted by free trade will only heighten the current ecological crisis. Global warming, ozone depletion, water pollution, and the disappearance of old-growth forests will only worsen as corporations rush to make bigger profits with little or no regard for the natural environment (Swenarchuk, 1993; Shrybman, 1993).

To date, it is still difficult to determine the precise impact of free trade on Canada. Certainly, the country has undergone pronounced economic and social changes since the implementation of the FTA and NAFTA, but whether free trade is the primary cause of these changes is unclear. Uncertainties also abound in assessing whether free trade has benefited or harmed Canada. Free trade proponents hold up Canada's surging exports to the United States as proof that the principles of open markets and free competition implied in NAFTA are benefiting Canadians. On the other side, critics point out that unemployment rates remain stubbornly high and worry that Canada's political and cultural sovereignty is being eroded. One thing that both defenders and detractors can agree on, however, is that the Canadian economy has become increasingly integrated with the American economy (O'Brien, 1995).

Political Implications of National-International Integration

The aspect of Canada's position in the international political economy that is most significant for our purposes is the open nature of the Canadian economy. Canada is one of the most trade-dependent nations in the world, despite its numerous import barriers. This high degree of trade dependence, coupled with the economy's small size compared to some other nations, leaves Canada vulnerable to international political-economic factors (Katzenstein, 1985). The goods produced and the prices at which they are sold are often determined by international market forces, which diminishes Canada's capacity to control its political economy. As such, the international arena imposes an enduring constraint. The fluctuations and uncertainties endemic to the international economy further weaken Canadians' control over their own political-economic destiny.

Perhaps the most crucial feature of Canada's dependence on international trade is the importance of the United States as a destination for exports and a source of imports. The FTA and NAFTA are concrete acknowledgements of this dependence. In fact, Canada embarked on the road to continental free trade with the US as early as 1935. The pace was stepped up with membership in the US-sponsored GATT and has continued to accelerate since that time. By signing these agreements, Canada agreed to accept limitations on its policy options. It also agreed in principle to lower its trade barriers and not to subsidize its exports. And it agreed, for the most part, to accord 'national treatment' to imports. This limitation of options was extended with NAFTA and will likely also be the case with the planned expansion of that deal into a Free Trade Agreement of the Americas (Saborio, 1992). However, as the figures in Table 23 show, Canada's trade with Mexico and other Latin American countries is small and there is little possibility of dramatic economic restructuring in the immediate future as trade is expanded to other parts of Latin America.

The discussion in Chapter 5 showed that interregional, intersectoral, and interpersonal disparities in Canadians' incomes exist and that the operation of the Canadian political economy, on an aggregate national basis, has failed to result in an even distribution of benefits across different sections of the population. We know that certain groups have consistently benefited less than others from the operation of the existing domestic political economy. The significant question is why this has occurred, given the often-expressed belief that liberal market economies work to equalize wealth and opportunities across the population. The persistence of inequalities in Canada has not only caused theorists and members of the public to question the main tenets of classical liberal political economy but has also led to demands for government actions that have violated the principles of the dominant liberal political-economic theory.

The root cause of many of these inequities lies in the resource-export-dependent nature of the Canadian economy, but the governments' abilities to alter this situation are limited. Instead, to guarantee markets for its resource and resource-based exports, Canada relies on a liberalized international trading partner in areas such as automobiles and services. These international political-economic arrangements and institutions provide benefits to Canada but also greatly constrain the ability of Canadian governments to deal with the root causes of many of the country's pressing political-economic problems.

Table 23: Canadian Imports from and Exports to Latin America, 1993

Destination	Imports (% share)	Exports (% share)
Argentina	0.7	0.6
Bolivia	0.2	0.6
Brazil	1.2	2.6
Chile	0.6	1.8
Colombia	0.8	2.1
Ecuador	2.9	1.4
Mexico	5.6	1.0
Paraguay	n/a	0.2
Peru	2.5	1.5
Uruguay	0.7	1.7
Venezuela	1.6	3.5

Source: Randall, 1997: Tables 1, 2.

Chapter 7

The Structure and Organization of the State

Canada is among the oldest and most stable democratic polities in the world, and Canadian citizens are among the most satisfied in the world with their quality of life. Yet Canada is also a weak federation in which 'national unity' and related crises have dominated federal politics. There is a continual debate on the capacity of the Canadian state to steer an autonomous course from that of the United States, as well as a debate on the particular institutional or constitutional arrangements that could integrate and accommodate the distinct national and regional identities within the federation.

By the mid-1990s national unity politics had translated into two political crises. First, there is a wide gap between mass and élite goals and values with respect to issues of continental integration and the diminishing role of the state in the economy and society. It is clear that there is little popular support for the fiscal austerity, high levels of unemployment, and declining social role of the state that have accompanied the Canadian state's embrace of neo-liberalism and regional integration. In the global context governments are facing an expanded set of policy problems with less policy autonomy or state capacity than they enjoyed in previous times (Banting, 1996: 36–9; Banting, Hoberg, and Simeon, 1997: 3–5). Second, in Quebec federalist and sovereigntist political forces have fought to a deadlock that promises to fragment both Canadian and Quebec societies.

How did Canada arrive at this point? The first part of this chapter will examine Canada's historical trajectory of political development. The second section will examine each of the major state structures that have been produced by Canadian development. Here, one can more clearly differentiate the pattern of state-society relations at play—and more easily analyse and predict state intervention. This analysis does lead to general propositions—but they are limited to the particular category of institution or policy sector being analysed. This section, therefore, will give the reader a résumé of the major institutional dynamics—parliamentary democracy, federalism, and the Charter of Rights and Freedoms—that shape state intervention in the Canadian political economy.

Canada's Path of Development: From Colony to Modern State

State structures develop over time as mechanisms to bridge internal and external tensions. Canada's major structures have developed out of the legacy of the French and British empires, powerful pan-Canadian nation-building impulses, competing nationalisms and regionalisms within Canada, immigration, the mediation of class conflict, and a progressive North Americanization of the political economy. This legacy has left Canada united yet fragmented, developed, but partially dependent.

Imperial Wars, Conquest, Counter-Revolution, and Colonial Rebellions

The Canadian state derives its lineage from empire. Europeans began to colonize present-day Canada during the early seventeenth century and competed for control and possession of North America for the next two centuries. Much of what is Canada today traces its lineage to French colonization. After a prolonged seven years' war, the French lost New France and Acadia to the British. The decisive battle was the capture of the Citadel of Quebec in 1759. Popularly known as the Conquest—this solidification of British control over Atlantic North America is the first major formative event in Canada's political history. The war placed the French colonists in Acadia and New France in a precarious position. The Acadians were summarily expelled, thus beginning a long saga of exile, return, and struggle for cultural recognition and rights. Imperial authorities renamed their colony Nova Scotia and brought in colonists from New England to settle it. Approximately 7,000 colonists in New France did not share the Acadians' fate. Rather, they began an enduring struggle for cultural survival. The 'Canadian' colonists were cut off from the mother country in several senses. First, economic, political, and social ties were ruptured because the French and English continued armed conflict until the defeat of Napoleon Bonaparte in the early nineteenth century. One of the legacies of that European conflict was a continued antipathy between French and English colonialists in British North America. Second, the French Revolution propelled France itself into a path of development that in many ways rejected the ideas of politics embedded within the colony. There was a cultural abandonment of the French in America.

History and force of arms had brought the French and English together to share a common development within the confines of the British Empire, but settlement also involved dealing with Canada's original pre-colonial population. To ensure stability on the frontiers, imperial authorities decreed that Indian lands could not be bought or taken save by mutual agreement between the Crown and Aboriginal peoples. Subsequent constitutional development, however, was to institutionalize an authoritarian paternalism that did not award a constitutional recognition to Aboriginal peoples. The loss of political rights and recognition, as well as constitutional status, would last well into the twentieth century (Canada, Royal Commission on Aboriginal Peoples, 1996: 7–14).

The Royal Proclamation of 1763 also promised land and British institutions to English settlers who would move to Quebec. Imperial policy was to seek long-term peace by assimilating the French—an objective that was never realized. Faced with rebellion in the 13 colonies to the south, in 1774 the British authorities made strategic accommodations in the Quebec Act. The Act recognized French Canadians' rights to use the pre-revolutionary French civil code and legalized the right of the Roman Catholic Church to tithe the peasantry. These reforms made an alliance between Church and state that was more reminiscent of eighteenth-century Spain than post-revolutionary France. This close relation between Church and state would continue until the 1960s Quebec Quiet Revolution. Still, the majority French and Catholic population were excluded from positions of economic and political influence—beginning lasting schisms among concepts of nation, state, and economy among French Canadians. Survival of this small cultural nation became the central point of definition for French-Canadian politics and placed it clearly at odds with the imperial government.

Military victory gave the British control over entry into North America. The guns at the Citadel of Quebec controlled entry into the St Lawrence River and with it the water transportation system stretching from the foot of the Great Lakes to Quebec City. Donald Creighton (1957) termed this the '*empire of the St Lawrence*'. Montreal emerged as the centre of that empire, and the city's merchants strove to create the trade and commercial centre of the continent. Water transportation was constricted by rapids at Lachine outside of Montreal. Niagara Falls, which blocked water transportation between Lake Ontario and Lake Erie, became the western limit to water-based continental integration. The strategic position of the transportation corridor made control of the region essential to British hegemony. Though Montreal eventually lost its hegemony to New York after the construction of the Erie Canal, the 'empire of the St Lawrence' continued to lead Canadian development. Montreal continued to be Canada's leading city until it was surpassed by Toronto in the mid-twentieth century. The region contains the vast majority of the Canadian population and a more diverse industrial and manufacturing base than in the more resource-dependent economies of Atlantic and western Canada.

The Laurentian Shield insulated the British colonies from the territories west and north of the St Lawrence and Great Lakes areas. There, the Hudson's Bay Company gained a trade monopoly in furs over Rupert's Land, a vast territory that comprised much of what is now western and northern Canada. The Company was more than a trader, however. It governed the territories and its population of Aboriginal peoples in a paternalistic regime similar to that of a feudal power.

The hegemony of the British in North America ended with the 1776 American Declaration of Independence, revolutionary war, and the recognition of the sovereignty of the United States of America under the Treaty of Versailles in 1783. For the northern colonies the war posed strategic questions about choosing a path of development. The revolutionary colonies were the military and economic rivals of Nova Scotia and Quebec. Moreover, Quebec (as New France) had just finished a long war against the same American colonies. Joining a union of former enemies was an uncertain venture—especially since it would imply becoming a tiny French minority among approximately 2.5 million English colonists. The *realpolitik* was simply that prospects were better with the protection and association of empire than by joining forces with the Americans. Canadian colonies would continue to benefit from economic and military association with empire. This proved to be crucially important. Agricultural produce, fur, fish, timber, and ships were the primary staples exports. The provision of a *pax Britannia* on the seas ensured the security and stability of this trade.

It is important to note, however, that the American Revolutionary War was not just about territory, but was also about ideas of politics and the structure of the state. Canada became the centre of a 'counter-revolution' in counterpoint to the liberal 'revolution' in the US. British intellectual thinking was suspicious of democracy and rejected the excesses of the American and then French revolutions. Americans who fought for the Crown were expelled from the revolutionary colonies and resettled in Canada. Called Loyalists, these people were given land grants, special privileges, sometimes public office, and economic position. The influx of Loyalists completely reshaped the population structure and political composition of the colonies. They created a new province, New Brunswick, out of Nova Scotia and opened up the western land frontier (present-day Ontario). More importantly, having lost the war in the United States, they were determined to fashion the Canadian state in their image.

There has been a tendency among nationalist historians and social scientists to romanticize and homogenize the two founding cultural fragments and their societies around their collective projects—survival for the French Canadians and nation-building within a diverse society for Canadian nationalists. But as Fernand Ouellet reminds us, both French and English colonial societies were never homogeneous entities (Ouellet, 1991: 5–39). They were marked by social inequalities as well as cultural conflict. Merchants, both English and French, were the most powerful class in colonial society—particularly in Quebec where the significance of land and agriculture, foundations of power for the feudal seigniories, steadily weakened so that farming became a means of subsistence that had to be supplemented by wage labour in staples industries and, later, by migration. Undisguised attempts to assimilate French Canadians by fostering immigration and changing the land tenure system fostered distrust and resentment.

After the American Revolution, imperial authorities were reluctant to democratize colonial government. The Constitution Act of 1791 split Quebec into two colonies, Upper Canada and Lower Canada. Each colony was to retain British-style institutions—a governor, an appointed executive council, and an elected assembly. However, the legislative assemblies were without any effective power—leaving the exercise of power in the hands of the governor and his appointed executive. The constitution facilitated rule by an oligarchy of notables who controlled business, state, and Church. In Upper Canada they were called the 'Family Compact' and in Lower Canada, the 'Chateau Clique'.

In 1812 the Americans attempted to conquer the Canadian colonies. Although US forces were successful in controlling rivers and lakes—the natural transportation corridors of the political economy—they were not able to occupy Canadian lands. The stalemated war ended in 1814 with the British-American Treaty of Ghent. The treaty secured Canadian colonies from American aggression but it was a costly war. The colonies were devastated, and the British authorities were slow and reluctant to pay compensation. Defence-related infrastructure projects, such as the Rideau and Trent canal systems, were very expensive and without immediate economic benefit.

Immigration and land policies at this time proved to be very contentious. In Lower Canada British authorities still attempted to use immigration and land policies as means of curtailing or assimilating the French Canadians. In Upper Canada, the Family Compact adopted a policy of privatizing Crown and Church land reserves, turning them over to large land development companies such as the Canada Land Company. These companies would construct the roads and infrastructure needed to facilitate settlement. The sale of the land for settlement would pay the costs of the infrastructure. To succeed, this policy needed the land companies to supply large amounts of inexpensive land, a continual supply of immigrants with sufficient assets, and a vibrant agricultural economy. But this is not what history had in store (Teeple, 1972).

Land continued to be expensive and subject to speculation and market manipulation. The depressed colonial economies did not support a wage economy where immigrants could easily buy land. Moreover, the Church land reserves were dedicated to the state Church of England—even though the majority of the English colonists belonged to the growing Methodist and other smaller Protestant congregations. The Canadian colonies were the recipients of the poor of the Empire, and this role would only increase with the tragedy of the Irish potato famine. Indeed, prospective settlers with money left the United Kingdom for the more economically vibrant United States.

A state structure that concentrated power in the hands of a few while sanctioning social and political inequality was to court disaster. During 1837-8 there were two rebellions—one in Lower Canada led by Louis-Joseph Papineau, the Speaker of the Legislative Assembly, and one in Upper Canada led by William Lyon Mackenzie, a journalist, publisher, and politician. Though the rebellions were quelled by force of arms and the rebel leadership either jailed or exiled, it was clear the British colonies would not return to their old trajectory. In true parliamentary fashion, a commission of inquiry, headed by Lord Durham, was struck to look into the future of the colonies.

The United Provinces: Democratization, Assimilation, and Nationalism

The royal commission headed by Lord Durham advocated the liberalization of the colonial state and a unification of the two Canadian colonies—a crude attempt to assimilate the French-Canadian majority. The two policies were related. Durham distrusted the French majority in Lower Canada and argued that unifying the two provinces would put a check on their power. He also assumed that the French Canadians would place a check on the drive for democracy in Upper Canada. Hopefully, this unification would also lead to an integrated economic policy by diffusing the tension that had emerged between English merchants and the French members of the elected assembly. These became the operating principles of the Act of Union of 1840 that created the United Province of Canada East and Canada West.

Breaking up the Family Compact and Chateau Clique was a slow process that pitted several governors against legislative majorities. The major change was the implementation of conventions of parliamentary and responsible government— making the executive and council (now popularly termed Prime Minister and cabinet) responsible to elected officials. This is the essential principle of Parliamentary government, and endures today as one of Canada's primary constitutional conventions. Imperial authorities feared that responsible government would mean independence because the executive would no longer be responsible to the British government. Advocates of reform argued that responsible government could occur within the bounds of the Empire. Ten years after the rebellions, the imperial government abandoned its fight against responsible government.

Responsible government was attained earlier than anticipated by the British because parliamentary leaders of both the French and English communities were bound together in a common cause of reform. Durham also assumed that the French would be assimilated by the English. To avoid continued political struggle, the French and English worked out a unique system of parity and double majorities whereby major policies and legislation needed to gain approval from both English and French majorities. This worked well when the English were a minority. In time, however, the principle of assimilation embodied in the constitution was creating political deadlock because increasing immigration and economic development of Canada West (Ontario) placed the French-Canadian population in the minority. The growing population of Canada West demanded further democratization— 'representation by population', a political reform that would increasingly marginalize the French-Canadian minority. Clearly, the 1840 constitution had failed to assimilate the French Canadians, and the political conventions invented by both political communities to accommodate each other were strained. A new solution was needed.

The position of the United Canadas in the international political economy also changed. During the 1840s the British embraced a policy of international free trade, a strategic decision that threatened market security for Canadian staples producers. Until that point colonial producers had privileged access to the British market. New imperial policies of free trade and responsible government marked an end to the old order. The symbolic end of that older post-Conquest order occurred when rioters burned down the Parliament buildings in Montreal in 1849 after the legislature passed legislation to compensate those who sustained property damage during the 1837–8 rebellions (Cook, Saywell, and Ricker, 1963: 69).

In 1854, the British signed a Reciprocity Treaty with the United States that allowed for unrestricted trade in natural products between the Canadian colonies and the United States. The mid-century was a high mark for economic development. The Reciprocity Treaty provided the colonies a sound economic structure. The Maritime economy was engaged in a complex series of international trade relations and promised to be the first jurisdiction to begin heavy industrialization. British territories west of Lake Superior, however, were cut off from the other territories by the Laurentian Shield. The Hudson's Bay Company was still the major force structuring the internal economy and mediating relations between its internal empire and imperial authorities. Its internal form of governance was feudalistic, defined by the corporate hierarchy and the monopoly position of the company over Aboriginal hunters. Though there were pockets of subsistence agricultural settlements, First Nations and especially the Métis were the most populous and powerful western Peoples, but they were also excluded from representation and power within the corporate governance of their territories.

As the British colonies were outgrowing their constitutional structures, external economic and strategic pressures were pushing them into a reluctant union. The United States was becoming increasingly aggressive in its expansion and assertion of hegemony on the western frontiers. In the 1840s the British and Americans nearly went to war over ownership of the Oregon territory in the Pacific Northwest. Only its partition along the forty-ninth parallel in 1846 resolved the crisis. At this time, the popularization of *Manifest Destiny* and war with Mexico revealed that the Americans were not reluctant to take arms against European colonies in order to extend their territory. The threat of this aggression subsided during the American Civil War, but at the conclusion of the conflict the victorious North had the largest standing army in the Western world. The imperial government signalled the Canadian colonies that it would no longer be responsible for their military defence. Since the British government had informally allied itself with the South during the war, Canadians feared US retaliation, particularly from the Fenians, a group of anti-British Irish soldiers in the Union army. Also, at the end of the war the American government adopted a protectionist trade policy, which meant that they would not renew the Reciprocity Treaty. By 1865, therefore, the colonies had lost their traditional military and economic foundations (Ryerson, 1963, 1968).

Confederation and the National Policy

The changes within the political economy ensured that negotiations surrounding a union of British colonies in North America would reshape colonial political, economic, and military structures. In 1867 the Confederation of Canada, a Dominion within the British Empire, was established to deal with these exigencies. The process of constitution-building was that of *élite accommodation*, a negotiated settlement between imperial authorities and colonial political leadership. Sir John A. Macdonald and George-Étienne Cartier, the English and French leaders of the United Canadas, were the driving forces behind the Confederation project. The new constitutional structure, when passed by the British Parliament, was termed the British North America Act. The Maritime colonies were protected by the British navy and did not share the domestic political and economic crisis of the United Canadas. Understandably, they were more reluctant to join the Confederation settlement.

Constitutions embody underlying rules governing relations between state and society—what governments can and cannot do. Generally, there are three sorts of rules at play. Constitutional documents contain *formal laws and rules* that are subject to judicial review. The definition of Canada and its 10 provinces, as well as the rights and responsibilities of each, are broadly defined by such formal rules in the constitution. Second is *ordinary legislation* that has constitutional status. Legislation governing elections and political party finance, for example, has a constitutional status in that it regulates a complex web of private- and public-sector relations—as well as voting behaviour. Third are *conventions*, unwritten norms and practices that structure how politics and government are conducted (Archer, Gibbins, Knopff, and Pal, 1995: 30).

Confederation built on the 1840 Act of Union. For example, politics continued to be defined by conventions of British parliamentary government. Canadian provinces and the central or Dominion government had bicameral legislatures—parliaments containing both an upper and lower house. Ottawa's upper house, the Senate, an appointed chamber, contained equal representation from four regions (the Maritimes, Quebec, Ontario, and the West). The lower house, or House of Commons, was to be recruited by elections on the basis of representation by population.

The major innovation in the Confederation agreement was the adaptation of a form of *federalism* to resolve the political deadlock between French and English, to integrate the other British colonies into the union, and to create new provinces from newly acquired territories. The idea of federalism in Canada differed significantly from federalist thinking in the United States. For Canadians the idea was not merely shaped around the best way to manage a common polity, but also around older themes such as cultural identities and cultural survival. It pitted centralists, such as John A. Macdonald, who wanted a straightforward legislative union among British colonies, against radicals who sought only a minimum association—one that would allow the smaller provinces and French Canadians to maintain their particular identities (LaSelva, 1996: 31–48). Eventually, Macdonald and the moderate Cartier prevailed. French and English were to be the official languages of the laws, Parliament, and the judiciary. In an age when the differences between these groups were defined in terms of religion, the federal authority gained the responsibility for protecting minority denominational rights.

The central government gained all of the necessary powers for state- and nation-building while the provincial governments were oriented to matters of property and civil rights and other areas of a primarily local nature. The BNA Act established a highly centralized federalism—even though it was termed a 'confederation', nominally the name of more radically decentralized polity. Part of this centralization was a continuation of the colonial legacy whereby the Dominion received the powers normally assigned to imperial authorities, which would allow the central government to take a paternalistic role in provincial legislative assemblies. Also, however, the colonial élite attributed excessive decentralization as a principal cause of the American Civil War, and thus did not want to duplicate that experience (Smiley, 1987: 27–67).

The term 'Dominion' refers to a self-governing polity within the British Empire, not a fully sovereign nation-state. The imperial government still represented Canada in external affairs and highly influenced military matters. Generally, the appointed head of state, the Governor-General—and lieutenant-governors in the provinces—represented the mother country's interests. The British government continued to exercise great influence on domestic politics. The Judicial Committee of the Privy Council (JCPC), a subcommittee of the British House of Lords, was the highest court of appeal in the British Empire and as such provided the final word for the interpretation of the constitution until 1949. Also, the BNA Act did not include an explicit formula or method of amendment. Given that it was a piece of ordinary legislation it could be assumed that a resolution asking for amendment from the Canadian Parliament would be sufficient. But in fact there was a lack of agreement on the process by which a constitutional resolution would be made. Since there was no consensus among Canadian political élites on what a domestic amending formula ought to be, the continued quasi-colonial constitutional status papered over serious domestic political cleavages.

The development of the state and the economy within the framework of the National Policy was remarkable both for its successes and for its surprises. Often the term 'National Policy' refers to the protective tariffs and immigration policies adopted by Sir John A. Macdonald in 1878. For political economists such as Vernon Fowke (1949), however, the National Policy encompasses a wider field—from the elaboration of the new Confederation's constitutional structure to the policy framework needed for the establishment of a transcontinental state and economy. This entailed broad intervention on the part of the state—making treaties with Aboriginal peoples, securing possession of vast territories of land, the financing and construction of railways, supporting the development of export agriculture, and overseeing mass immigration. Steam and steel—the nineteenth-century technological revolution—made transcontinental transportation and communications possible and affordable (Tilly, 1984). Railway-building would allow what Hugh Aitken (1967) termed 'defensive expansionism'—integrating the British colonies together under a single polity as a means of defending them against American Manifest Destiny.

The economic and social development under the National Policy was a success. Slow to take off because of an international depression in the late nineteenth century, the investment boom in western Canada eventually saw the construction of competing transcontinental railways and other infrastructure, mass immigration, and the development of a viable wheat economy. By 1905, defensive expansionism had netted Canada Prince Edward Island, three prairie provinces, northern territories carved out of the former Rupert's Land, entry of the colony of British Columbia, as well as the Arctic Archipelago, a gift from the British government in 1880. In addition, Quebec and Ontario went through an intense period of industrialization—partially due to resource endowments and partially the result of the region's strategic location in relation to other North American markets. After the opening of the Panama Canal in 1914, Vancouver became a centre for the export of western staples. Canada found a unique position in the international triangle between Britain and the United States. It was the window for the British to the American market and a window for the Americans into the Empire or Commonwealth market. Canada's protective tariffs served not only to protect nascent industries, but also to induce foreign investment. The scope of the task appears unbelievable. Less than four million Canadians built a transcontinental state and economy in face of competition from an American republic with over 75 million people.

There were drawbacks. Canadian development continued to be uneven (Ryerson, 1968; McCallum, 1980). The economic position of the Maritimes declined, despite early high expectations. The reasons for this decline are complex, but among them is the fact that national transportation and finance policies discriminated against the region (Acheson, 1972). Similarly, although Quebec did undergo industrialization, particularly in the Montreal region, Quebec agriculture was in a structural crisis for much of the nineteenth century. Thus, while mass immigration arrived in Canada from Britain and Western Europe, there was mass emigration from the Maritimes and Quebec to New England.

Regional and class politics were not confined to the Maritimes and Quebec. The prairies were the centre of political struggles pitting Aboriginal peoples and then farmers against metropolitan powers. Despite the Royal Proclamation of 1763, mid-nineteenth-century nation-building was predicated on removing Aboriginal title to lands needed for agriculture and immigration. Louis Riel, the Métis founder of Manitoba, led a revolt that stopped the Dominion government from taking over Rupert's Land without ensuring Métis political and land rights. Though Riel was successful in negotiating the entry of the first 'Métis government' into the Confederation in Manitoba in 1870, the Dominion authorities ensured that he would never lead it, nor would the terms of the settlement between Métis and Ottawa be fully implemented. Fearful that challenges to Ottawa's sovereignty in the West might incite American annexationist sentiments, the Dominion authorities crushed a second rebellion in Saskatchewan a decade later. Unlike Louis-Joseph Papineau and William Lyon Mackenzie, Louis Riel went to the gallows in Regina in 1885.

Riel was a symbol of both French and Catholic power in the West. His execution rekindled profound English-French cleavages and destroyed the governing Conservative coalition. It marked the end of Cartier's dream of making Canada's West a space for both founding peoples. In fact, the public and social space of the prairies was reshaped by non-Anglophone immigration. In the end the new prairie provinces turned to unilingualism and assimilation as means to integrate diverse ethnicities. Even the Minister of Immigration (and owner of *Winnipeg Free Press*), Clifford Sifton, quipped that they were going to 'teach the Ukrainians that they won the battle of Trafalgar'. Quebec became the centre of French Canada. Outside of Quebec, French minorities were reduced to one of many ethnic groups and even lost the language rights ostensibly guaranteed by the BNA Act. French-English relations hit a nadir when the Union coalition government decided to implement a policy of conscription during World War I. In Quebec the conflict was considered more Britain's than Canada's war. However, the predominant British non-French majority did not make a major distinction between the defence of Canada and Britain. As Canada headed into the 1920s it was still very much an English and British federation where the national anthem, 'The Maple Leaf Forever', celebrated the 1759 Conquest.

By 1930 Canada was much different from what had been envisaged by the framers of the constitution. The Confederation leadership thought they had established a centralized federation where provinces were important but minor players in national policy and economic development, but the reverse had occurred as a series of decisions by the JCPC on constitutional matters resulted in Canada emerging as highly decentralized. In its decisions, the JCPC interpreted the BNA Act as a flawed document, reasoning that if the Dominion government exercised the full scope of its authority as defined in the constitution, then there would be little left for the provinces. Consequently, the British lords embarked on a judicial campaign that defended and expanded provincial jurisdiction beyond the intent and even the letter of the Act (Cairns, 1971; Olmstead, 1954).

Underneath this judicial redefinition of Canadian federalism, however, lay several profound social and political realities. The union envisaged by Macdonald was much too centralized for the far-flung heterogeneous political community bound together by the BNA Act. Provincial governments jealously guarded their powers. Provincial rights became the critical avenue of accommodation between French and English—and increasingly so as the French did not share in the expansion of western Canada.

Depression, War, and the Construction of Modern Canada

Depression during the 1930s followed by the European and Pacific wars in the 1940s set in place forces that would completely reshape Canadian state structures and the trajectory of Canada's development with the global political economy. The period begins with Canada still an integral part of the British Empire and ends with a debate on the political significance of Canada's integration in the continental economy and the influence of American interests within domestic political life. Issues of regionalism and conflict over the linguistic duality of the country permeated the period, although other conflicts over issues such as religion faded, to be replaced by a new set of issue-areas related to class and the economy. From 1960 to the 1980s new structures of accommodation, such as executive federalism, a reordering of the country's symbolic order, and then the Charter of Rights and Freedoms were established to mediate these tensions.

First, the exigencies of the Great Depression and war realigned Canada's international position, the role of the state in markets, and practices of federalism. The Depression destroyed the momentum of the National Policy and exposed the inadequacy of the inherited structures of economic and fiscal policy to deal with the crisis. Protectionism was the first response of Western nation-states to the Depression. The failure of protectionism to rekindle viable international trade led to Canadian efforts to lower trade barriers between members of the Commonwealth (former British colonies) and between Canada and the United States. New ideas emerged from a monumental study by the Royal Commission on Dominion-Provincial Economic Relations (the Rowell-Sirois Commission), as well as from later postwar planning centred on defining a new, more centralized state where the federal power would take greater responsibility for orchestrating social and economic policy. The role of the state would change from that of taking direct responsibility for the infrastructure of economic development to that of macroeconomic planning. Although the provinces would not agree to any wholesale centralization of power, the exigencies of the war effort provided a window of opportunity for the centralization of authority in Ottawa. With little political resistance, wartime federal governments restructured the fiscal system, took responsibility for war-related industrialization, and ushered in a postwar era of federally led social policy development. The Keynesian state was born out of the pain of the Depression, the ashes of war and dreams of what might be.

Throughout the 1950s the first contours of modern Canada were established. Trade, fiscal, and economic policy focused on Canada taking the position of a middle power in multilateral institutions, such as the GATT and the United Nations. Foreign direct investment, primarily from the United States, fed a booming manufacturing and resource sector. The United States had replaced the United Kingdom as Canada's primary market and source of capital by the 1920s, and now this American dominance in the Canadian economy was solidified. Both governments embarked on common large-scale infrastructure projects such as the St Lawrence Seaway and the Columbia River Treaty. The Canadian economy was supplying new industrial staples, such as various minerals, iron, petroleum, and natural gas, to a booming American economy (Eden and Molot, 1993).

Modern Canada no longer defined itself in relation to Britain or its colonial roots—nor with the old agenda of gaining sovereignty. The 1931 Statute of Westminster had formally recognized Canada's international sovereignty. The Supreme Court of Canada replaced the JCPC as the final court of appeal in 1949, thus promising a more stable and legitimate judicial interpretation of the constitution. And, the same year, Newfoundland and Labrador—caught in a similar process of realignment—joined Confederation.

After a decade of open economic doors, by 1960 about one-half of Canadian manufacturing and resource assets were in foreign, primarily American hands.

Pan-Canadian nationalism then focused on economic affairs, seeking to limit the power of foreign capital and to negotiate fair terms of continental integration. Responding to public pressure, Ottawa took a few reluctant steps to regulate continentalism. Some examples of the new state structures were: the National Energy Board, the Canadian Radio-television and Telecommunications Commission, the Canadian Transport Commission, the Canadian Development Corporation, the Foreign Investment Review Agency, and the Auto Pact (Clark-Jones, 1987).

Provincial economic development strategies also centred on attracting foreign capital and finding market niches in the continental economy (Jenson, 1989). For example, the establishment of a petroleum and natural gas industry in western Canada during the postwar period redefined western interests from wheat and export agriculture to industrial staples. The 'New West' was defined by international oil tied to Canadian regional and continental US markets—and closely nurtured and regulated by provincial governments. Indeed, federal initiatives to redistribute oil revenues and regulate the national market during the 1970s OPEC oil crisis were met with intense regional opposition (Richards and Pratt, 1979.

Not all parts of the federation benefited from the modernization of the economy. The spatial definition of Canada began to include terms such as 'have' and 'have-not' provinces, which were placed on top of the older geographical definitions of region. During World War II Ottawa's centralization of the tax system had brought a redistribution of the fiscal capacity of provincial governments. As the war experience faded into the past the wealthier provinces began to reassert their constitutional authority in the most lucrative tax fields. The federal government emerged as the central tax collector for all governments except Quebec. Tax revenues are then shared between governments according to the formulae worked out in five-year agreements. To compensate for the unevenness in the tax yield between provinces, the federal government committed to a policy of *equalization* whereby the fiscal capacity of provincial governments were brought up to a representative standard. To facilitate structural adjustment, the federal government began a program of regional economic development, targeting large segments of have-not provinces. Comprehensive and controversial, these programs focused on labour market adjustment, job creation, infrastructure, and influencing the location decisions of investors (Bickerton, 1990; Savoie, 1992, 1995).

Modern Canada was also defined by the implementation of a welfare state—but in a curious fashion. Wartime centralization allowed the federal power to take the lead in orchestrating its implementation. During the postwar period, however, normal constitutional practice prevailed. The BNA Act ensured that much social policy was left in the hands of the provincial governments, but because of the complex jurisdictional interdependencies, single provinces could not develop welfare state policies without finding some means of pooling the costs. The solution, therefore, was to turn to series of 'cost-shared' and 'conditional' grants whereby the central power awarded cash to provinces in return for

implementing particular programs. The provinces, in a sense, 'rented' their jurisdictions to the central power. These sorts of agreements escaped constitutional
review by the courts and obviated the need to embark on implausible projects of
constitutional reform. Ottawa's 'power of the purse' became an effective tool to
formulate national policy throughout the federation. Support for transportation
infrastructure, post-secondary education, health insurance, hospital services,
and income assistance took this pattern. For the most expensive commitments to
income support, such as unemployment insurance (1940) and pensions (1966),
the provinces agreed to arrangements that would give the field to Ottawa.
Quebec, however, resisted most of these early federal modernization initiatives
(Banting, 1987).

In Quebec modernization took place under the umbrella of the early 1960s
Quiet Revolution. The legacy of Quebec's traditional Church-state alliance had
been the institutionalization of an authoritarian conservative nationalism that
portrayed Quebec society as a Catholic, French, and chiefly rural oasis in a
secular, materialist, urban, and largely English-speaking North America. Society,
particularly social policy, was led by the Church and dedicated to celebrating the
rural and messianic survival mission of Quebec society. By the 1950s, however,
it was apparent that Quebec was an urban and industrial society where the
majority spoke French, yet the language of the workplace, business, technology,
and the professions was English and non-Francophone élites owned and
controlled the majority of the province's economic assets. The Quiet Revolution
centred on using the provincial level of state as a means to modernize Quebec
society—to reorder the imbalances of power between language groups within
the province and to diversify and expand the economy within North America
(McRoberts, 1993; Coleman, 1984). The revolution's original broad-based coalition of a new middle class, business, and labour soon split on different decisions
in the modernization path that spanned two decades (Gagnon and Montcalm,
1990). Nevertheless, its secular, social, and economic goals differed completely
from those of the former conservative nationalist regime. Its intellectual
antecedents derived more from post-colonial national liberation movements and
the US civil rights movement than from anything indigenous to Canadian politics.

The Quiet Revolution threatened the federal regime by forcing the reordering
of Canada into apparently competing and incompatible pan-Canadian and
Quebec national projects. As the identity of the majority population of Quebec
was being redefined from that of being French Canadian to that of being
Québécois, the Canadian federal government was implicated in the tolerance of
the old order. Federal state structures were condemned as embodying a unilin-
gual English and monocultural polity with British colonial trappings.

Quebec political parties formed a consensus on the goals of the Quiet
Revolution, but not on the means of achieving them. A heterogeneous indepen-
dence movement emerged. One infamous group, the Front de Liberation de
Québec (FLQ), worked outside the democratic parameters, modelling itself after
North African, Asian, and Latin American revolutionary movements. A bombing
campaign in Montreal ended with the October 1970 kidnapping of the British

Trade Commissioner and the Quebec Minister of Labour. The former was released after negotiations, but the latter was murdered. The shock of this incident and the use of the War Measures Act and army on the part of the federal government to root out the FLQ solidified public opinion in a rejection of political violence and towards support for the democratic parameters of the social revolution. In the 1970s the Parti Québécois, led by René Lévesque, defined an alternative constitutional program characterized by *sovereignty-association*—political independence matched by an economic and political association between Canada and Quebec as equal partners.

For federalists and Canadians, the message was clear: accommodate the Quiet Revolution or face the breakup of Canada. Like the reformers working under the 1840 Act of Union, they sought to remake the federal state so that it could be a home for French Canadians, now defined as Francophones, and English Canadians, defined as Anglophones. The federal response, particularly under Prime Ministers Lester Pearson and Pierre Trudeau, was first to recognize and redefine the Quiet Revolution as a problem of Canadian unity, language, civil rights, and citizenship.

The Official Languages Act (1969) gave legal status to the French language in government operations and ensured that all federal government services would be available in both official languages. Francophones were recruited into the federal administration. The symbolic order of the federal state changed. For example, the older imperial lineage and colonial structures were replaced by Canadian symbols that resonated within both linguistic groups. For example, Trans-Canada Airlines became Air Canada, the Royal Canadian Post Office became Canada Post, and the Royal Canadian Navy and Royal Canadian Air Force became part of the Canadian Armed Forces. A new flag replaced the British Ensign, and a new national anthem celebrated Canada—as opposed to the Imperial Conquest of New France—though the reader ought to be aware that there are substantially different meanings to its lyrics in French and English. The federal government also accommodated the Quiet Revolution's statism by allowing Quebec to 'opt out' of key federally funded social programs and use the federal moneys to construct alternatives, as long at it met federal objectives.

Though precipitated by events in Quebec, the symbolic redefinition of Canada did not confine itself to a federation exclusively defined by the encounter between French and English. Clearly, large numbers of immigrants who were non-British and non-French in origin had identities that could not be accommodated within such a formulation. Accordingly, the federal government adopted a *multicultural policy* to recognize the contribution of these peoples to Canada and to facilitate their integration into Canadian society. At first Canadian governments gave no such recognition towards Aboriginal peoples and, indeed, wanted to remove all traditional treaties and other distinctions that made Aboriginal citizens of Canada different from others. The assimilation policy that had accompanied the BNA Act was extended by incorporating Aboriginal peoples in the pan-Canadian welfare state and through resource industrialization in northern peripheries. By the late 1960s, however, the assimilation strategy had reached its limits. Aboriginal political leadership was in a position to veto any federal attempts to nullify treaties, and when Ottawa proposed in 1969 to abolish the Indian Act this leadership held fast to maintain the special, though marginalized, status the Act had provided since its first enactment in 1876. They insisted that federal authorities recognize the failure of the assimilation strategy and seek a redefinition of the relationship of the state to Aboriginal peoples. By the mid-1970s jurisprudence had finally begun to recognize Aboriginal land rights and to check the arbitrary exercise of federal power over Aboriginal peoples (Weaver, 1981; Ponting and Gibbins, 1980; Ponting, 1986; Little Bear, Boldt, and Long, 1984).

During this period, too, mechanisms of political integration turned towards a quasi-diplomatic process of intergovernmental relations among provinces and the federal government. First ministers' conferences, ministerial conferences for various portfolios, annual premiers' meetings, regional meetings, and even Canada-United States regional conferences became the means of policy determination and co-ordination. These were mirrored at the level of senior officials, with provincial bureaucracies expanding to match their federal counterpart. Termed 'executive federalism', this represented an *interstate* as opposed to an *intrastate* federalism. Regional and provincial interests were represented by governments, not by representation within federal institutions. From taxation and energy prices to health care and the constitution—executive federalism became the method to make policy (Smiley, 1987; Watts, 1989).

Canada's complex system of interstate federalism can be understood as a solution to the limitations of the constitution as it had been elaborated a century earlier in the National Policy. One of the key policy lessons to be drawn from the JCPC experience was that enduring solutions occurred when governments negotiated rather than litigated (Tuohy, 1992). These negotiations took an intergovernmental form because there were no suitable openings, such as an effective Senate, within federal institutions to accomplish that task.

The modernization of federal and provincial institutions during the 1960s and 1970s precipitated a debate on alternative strategies for structuring the federation. There had been long-term agreement on the need for an amending formula and to 'patriate' the constitution from the United Kingdom. During the period of conservative nationalism the idea was to make an amending formula that discouraged change; during the modernization phase the idea was to make an amending formula that facilitated change. The big question, however, was what the substantive changes ought to be. The Progressive Conservatives and New Democrats flirted with the idea of giving Quebec a *special status* in Canada. Though relatively undefined, the idea was to recognize that Quebec was not a province *comme les autres* and to constitutionalize greater autonomy for the Quebec government within Canada. Those supporting special status were expressing a form of support for the continuation of the pattern of interstate federalism under which Canadian modernization had occurred.

The path chosen by Pierre Elliott Trudeau, as Liberal Party leader and Prime Minister, went in the opposite direction. For Trudeau such initiatives would simply spell the end of Canada because they would formally bestow on the government of Quebec the heavy burden of ensuring cultural survival. There would be little justification for continued association with Canada—and general resentment on the part of other Canadians for the limited participation of Quebec in the federation. For Trudeau, special status was redolent of the traditional formulae that justified the power and actions of a reactionary and backward nationalism (Trudeau, 1968).

Prime Minister Trudeau's idea was to add a Charter of Rights to the constitution that would be binding on all governments. In that way, the Francophone population inside and outside of Quebec would look to Canadian institutions to protect their linguistic rights, and no government could trample on anyone's civil rights for nationalist purposes. Stated another way, the idea was to redefine Canada as a community of rights-bearing individuals. The source and protection of those rights would emanate from Canadian state structures, not from provincialism or Quebec nationalism. Trudeau was unable to gain support for this idea from the government of Quebec, and given the convention that major constitutional change could only occur with the unanimous support of the provinces, the issue faded. In 1976, however, the election of the separatist Parti Québécois in Quebec brought the problems of Canadian unity to a head.

The Parti Québécois made two major constitutional initiatives. The first act of its first session, Bill 101, The Quebec Language Charter, made French the official language of Quebec, but at the same time preserved important minority rights. Second, the PQ held a referendum seeking a mandate to negotiate sovereignty-association. In May 1980 a decisive 60–40 'Non' vote killed that option for the time being. The Trudeau government seized the moment to pursue its constitutional program—and in doing so stretched the limits of constitutional convention. Since the majority of provincial leaders now opposed the establishment of a Charter that would discipline prerogatives of their legislatures, Trudeau could not pursue reform under the existing rules. Consequently, the federal government resorted to unilateral action by threatening to introduce a direct resolution to the British Parliament. The threatened constitutional *coup d'état* sparked a political crisis that saw eight of the 10 provinces in a common alliance against the federal constitutional initiative and the parliamentary opposition leave the Commons. The opposition returned when the federal proposals, known as the 'people's package', were subjected to parliamentary review. After the Supreme Court ruled that the federal initiative was legal but broke constitutional convention, one last First Ministers' Meeting was held. During that meeting the parties struck a deal—but one that the government of Quebec refused to join.

The 1982 constitutional reforms reshaped the dynamics of politics in Canada but were not able to put closure on the idea of constitutional reform. What did it accomplish? First, the constitution was patriated, with a formal amending formula to replace the lowest-common-denominator bargaining that accompanied the convention of unanimity.[1] Second, there were small changes to the division of powers, clauses to formalize provincial control over natural resources (to address western and Quebec concerns), and clauses committing Canada to a support equalization payments (to address the fiscal concerns of have-not provinces). Third, Trudeau's Charter strategy prevailed. The Canadian Charter of Rights and Freedoms contained a mixture of individual and collective rights that would limit the power of administrators and legislatures throughout the country and enhance the constitutional role of Canadian courts as the enforcers of the new rights regime.

The 1982 Constitution Act did not bring closure to the project of constitutional change in the first instance because the package was not supported by the Quebec government or by any political party in the Quebec National Assembly. Why not? None of the 1982 changes recognized Quebec as the centre of French Canada, nor did they give Quebec responsibilities commensurate with its position as the only jurisdiction in North America with a Francophone majority. In this sense they were a blow to Quebec's post-Quiet Revolution constitutional objectives. The late-night agreement among English-speaking provincial leaders symbolized the marginalization of Quebec in constitutional politics—and, in fact, was popularly termed 'the night of the long knives' in that province, a reference to an infamous purge of political opponents carried out by the government of Nazi Germany. Nor was it supported by Aboriginal political leadership. The Act, however, acknowledged the importance of a wider constitutional agenda, particularly as it pertained to Aboriginal peoples. Aboriginal rights were recognized in the Charter but they were not defined. That definition—including a model of self-governance—was to be developed in a further round of negotiations, which ultimately proved to be dishearteningly fruitless for the Aboriginal community.

The 1982 constitution also facilitated the restructuring of Canada's traditional national and regional political identities to that of a community of rights-bearing individuals. Here, collectivities and identities, such as women, ethnic minorities, labour, the disabled, and Aboriginal peoples, poorly represented by established representative institutions, worked to develop new sources of political power within the Charter and the legal system. Alan Cairns (1992) termed this increasingly powerful and heterogeneous category 'Charter Canadians'. Above all else, Charter Canadians would emerge as the defenders of the 1982 constitution.

In sum, Canada was reshaped during the 1930–82 period. International conditions helped facilitate the development of pan-Canadian nationalism. The central power was instrumental in defining modern Canada. Important steps were made to implement a modern welfare state and fiscal system within the parameters of federalism, to facilitate and regulate continental integration, to mediate, ameliorate, and accommodate various regionalisms, to restructure the symbolic order of the federation, and to compete with and accommodate, within the confines of the constitution, Quebec's Quiet Revolution.

Redefining Canada: Globalization and Community

The Canadian state entered into yet another period of change in the mid-1980s, a process that continues today. This was due to seven interrelated trends that undermined the old order. First, and most significantly, the internationalization of the world economy in the post-1945 period has turned into a functional integration—what was termed 'globalization' in the previous chapter. In the Canadian case, Glen Williams argues that this really just extends the path of continental integration started during the postwar period (Williams, 1995; Clement and Williams, 1997). However, the state structures regulating that integration have changed dramatically. Nation-states, especially those with open economies, cannot manage their economies by themselves. In response, national governments have invested efforts in establishing new regional and multilateral institutions, such as the European Union, NAFTA, and the World Trade Organization, to manage and regulate globalization. This has both strengthened and weakened state sovereignty (Risse-Kappen, 1995; Gummett, 1996).

Through NAFTA, North America has become one of several global trading blocs. Canada is now a North American state and the federal and provincial governments have to respect the terms of a common North American economic regime (Anderson et al., 1998). Globalization presupposes a paradigmatic shift in state intervention. The new international regimes prohibit forms of intervention that interfere in the workings of traditional markets and induce the formation and stabilization of new global or regional markets, protect capital flows, secure property (including intellectual property) rights, and establish dispute resolution mechanisms (Gummett, 1996).

At first glance one might conclude that these new organizations have replaced much of the role of national governments—and prohibit time-honoured patterns of seeking to use rules for national advantage. But closer examination reveals a different game. John Ikenberry (1986), for example, studied the response of the US, Japan, and West Germany, three powerful and import-dependent nations, to the 1970s oil crisis. He concluded that the irony of state strength is that a state's effective power or capacity is no longer simply measured by its ability to undertake political projects or regulate national markets by itself. Rather, state strength is measured by the capacity to have other states play by the same rules of international trade. There is no doubt that the FTA, NAFTA, the European Union, and the expanded GATT and World Trade Organization were successfully established because they met the interests of the United States and other G–7 leaders. Ironically, it is in the Canadian interest to enlarge the membership of global trading blocs and to participate in as many as possible. This ensures that a common regime is binding on all governments and that the United States does not create a set of hierarchical 'hub and spoke' relationships between itself and other North American states (Wonnacott, 1991).

The division of labour between federal and provincial governments is less clear in a period in which Ottawa's central role in economic and social policy has been diminished. During the modernization period the federal government was the summit of a clearly hierarchical federation and used its power of the purse to grease and power its initiatives. Over the past decades, however, all governments in the federation have moved to downsize their role and reduce their expenditures. In the case of the federal government, this has meant offloading many responsibilities and expenditures to provincial governments.

Failures to Renew Federalism:
Aboriginal, Quebec, and Canada Rounds

There were three failed attempts under the term in office of the Conservative government of Brian Mulroney to address the legacy of the 1982 constitutional package and to modify the constitution so that it would more easily adapt to the challenges of globalization. First, from 1983 to 1987 the first ministers, in three constitutional conferences, were not able to agree with Aboriginal political leadership on the definition of Aboriginal rights or how self-government would be included in the constitution. Second, during the period 1987–90, an attempt fell apart to bring Quebec into the 1982 constitution under the terms of the Meech Lake Accord, which had been agreed to by all provincial leaders and the federal government, because the Manitoba and Newfoundland legislatures failed to ratify the agreement within the allotted time period. Third, in the years 1990–2 a hurried attempt to make a general agreement that would address Quebec, Aboriginal, regional, and federal needs in the wake of the Meech Lake failure was put together as the Charlottetown Accord—an agreement that was rejected by the majority of the Canadian electorate inside and outside of Quebec in an October 1992 national referendum (Russell, 1995; Watts, 1996).

Throughout this process the constitutional agenda grew to unmanageable proportions. During the Aboriginal round, it became apparent that a minority interest could not force first ministers to agree to changes that limited their power or influence. The idea of Aboriginal self-government, particularly of recognizing an inherent right to self-government, implied a constitutional status and power not enjoyed by others in the federation—and particularly not by French-speaking Québécois (Cairns, 1995). In the post-1982 period the Parti Québécois government began a process of withdrawal from the intergovernmental machinery of executive federalism. First ministers' conferences, as the pinnacle of executive federalism and élite accommodation, were boycotted. Although the conferences were able to make one small amendment, to entrench land claims agreements in the Canadian constitution, it was evident that Aboriginal issues would not be resolved until settlement of the Quebec issue.

What would be the terms of Quebec's ratification of the constitution? During the 1982–5 period it was not really possible for the governments of Pierre Trudeau and René Lévesque to come to an agreement, for each blamed the other for the constitutional crisis. When Prime Minister Brian Mulroney and Premier Robert Bourassa replaced Trudeau and Lévesque, the two leaders moved quickly to attempt a constitutional *rapprochement*. Bourassa and the Quebec Liberal Party had distilled the post-Quiet Revolution constitutional agenda into five points:

1. entrench a constitutional recognition of Quebec as a distinct society;
2. strengthen the government of Quebec's role in immigration;
3. create a role for the government of Quebec in selecting three Quebec justices of the Supreme Court;

4. allow the government of Quebec to opt out of federal spending programs in areas of exclusive provincial jurisdiction without suffering a fiscal penalty;
5. regain Quebec's veto on constitutional amendments on matters affecting provincial interests. (Russell, 1995: 133–4)

As the leaders moved into negotiation the *rapprochement* resembled a textbook case of élite accommodation. The annual summer premiers' conference had endorsed the idea of making a constitutional settlement with Quebec as a first priority. The interests of the government of Canada were clear—to reintegrate Quebec into the Canadian constitutional family. The interests of Quebec were clear. The interests of the other provinces were equally clear—to get exactly what Quebec got. The simplicity of Meech Lake was that all of these interests coalesced. During the bargaining, the only difficult point was a clause that gave recognition to Quebec as a distinct society within Canada. From this came the special role of the Quebec government in preserving and promoting its culture and language, while the role of the federal Parliament and the provincial legislatures was to preserve the fundamental characteristics of Canada. It should be noted that the distinct society clause did not change the division of powers within the federation. Rather, it was to be an interpretive clause to guide the judicial interpretation of the Canadian Charter of Rights and Freedoms.

The substantive terms of the Accord constituted a symbolic decentralization of the federation, restoring an effective veto over constitutional change to Quebec and the rest of the provinces. Provinces were to have key but not exclusive roles in selecting senators and Supreme Court justices and in exercising control over the federal power of the purse. The latter was to be constitutionalized, but subject to the 7/10 rule of the 1982 amending formula, whereby agreement from the Parliament of Canada and seven out of 10 provincial legislatures comprising at least 50 per cent of the population is sufficient for most constitutional change.

As in the modernization period, Quebec and any other province—under Meech Lake—could opt out of federal transfer programs with full compensation (providing they implemented similar programs that met national objectives). The only particular element that spoke directly to a globalization agenda was that Quebec had negotiated a separate agreement on immigration reflecting its wish to encourage French-speaking immigrants to settle in Quebec. Increasingly, Quebec and Canada would rely on immigration to compensate for a decline in population growth. Immigration, like language, economic, and social policy, thus became an integral part of the post-Quiet Revolution agenda.

Meech Lake raised political opposition to its substantive clauses and process. Substantive arguments against the Accord tended to fall into two categories. First, the use of a distinct society clause as an interpretive clause in the Charter raised a multitude of issues on how one ranks rights and whether the clause set up two categories of rights in Canada—one pertaining to Quebec and one to the rest of the country. Clearly, the new 'Charter Canadians'—English-Canadian feminists, the disabled, ethnic minorities, Native peoples—and their political allies opposed it. Second, critiques of the Accord focused on issues left off the agenda—and alleged that it foreclosed the constitutional objectives of others. For example, Meech Lake did not deal with the constitutional definitions of Aboriginal rights and self-government. Nor did it address institutions, particularly Senate reform, an issue important to the western provinces. The Accord also required that the entry of new provinces into Confederation had to be unanimously approved by the federal and provincial legislatures, thus threatening the constitutional aspirations of the political leadership of the northern territories. Symbolically, Meech focused on the Quebec agenda and thus prioritized a dualist interpretation of the constitution. Those who saw this definition as too narrow then concentrated on the construction of a 'Canada clause' that would include a much more inclusive definition of the political community (Manitoba, 1989).

The procedural arguments against the Meech Lake Accord also revealed a wider rejection of the conventions of constitutional reform. As the Accord moved towards ratification, there was little real choice given to interested or affected publics. The process of élite accommodation had produced a 'seamless web' of balanced interests and compromises. Legislatures and the public had no real chance of shaping its terms. Stated in other terms, it represented the 'democracy deficit' associated with older conventions of executive federalism and élite accommodation. During the 1980s, as Neil Nevitte (1996) reminds us, Canadians became more politicized and pressed for meaningful participation in political life. One of the popular interpretations of the rejection of the Accord centres on the rejection of conventions of élite accommodation, an argument that discredits the legitimacy of the 'deal' negotiated by 'ten white men' (Simeon and Willis, 1997).

The democracy deficit argument, particularly around the Meech Lake Accord, makes sense when one realizes that the politicization of the constitutional issue occurred during and after a divisive national debate on free trade. The debate forced Canadians to define the nation in relation to the United States, exposed the apparent weakness and fragility of the federation, and also highlighted the differences between popular vote and political power, since a majority of Canadians in the 1988 federal election voted against the party supporting the Canada-US Free Trade Agreement but the election gave the Conservatives a majority government.

As the Meech Lake Accord headed into its final stages two provinces, Manitoba and New Brunswick, had not ratified the resolution. Also, the government of Newfoundland, in a bizarre twist, both ratified it under Premier Peckford and then withdrew ratification under Premier Wells. The federal government established a parliamentary committee, chaired by Jean Charest, to see how the agreement could be saved by means of a parallel accord addressing opposition concerns. The strategy almost worked. In the longest (but unofficial) first ministers' meeting in Canadian history this 'parallel accord' was hammered out. It attempted to include the agenda of all the critics of Meech Lake:

- the establishment of a parliamentary committee to create a 'Canada clause' defining the essential characteristics of Canada;

- the establishment of a commission to develop proposals for a reformed Senate;
- the resumption of constitutional meetings with Aboriginal peoples;
- the government of Quebec's agreement to give up its veto on Senate reform if an agreement was not reached in three years;
- the commitment to draft new constitutional provisions to strengthen gender equality in the Charter, protect minority language rights, and deal with the future of Yukon and the Northwest Territories;
- a review of the amending formula

Though the recalcitrant provinces agreed to bring Meech to a vote, only the New Brunswick government met the deadline (Russell, 1995: 147–53).

In Québec, the June 1990 death of the Meech Lake Accord was a watershed. A good part of the province's political élite and by far the majority popular opinion firmly interpreted the fate of Meech as a rejection of Quebec by the rest of Canada. In Quebec, analysis turned to ways of establishing a viable small nation-state or radically decentralized federation given the new global economic and political realities. These alternatives were developed by means of an intense process of public hearings within the framework of a bipartisan commission (Bélanger and Campeau, 1991). The Quebec Liberal Party also entertained the option of a radically decentralized federation (Allaire, 1991). The final policy response was a commitment to hold another referendum on sovereignty within two years. In addition, the government of Quebec was to boycott all processes of executive federalism—to begin a symbolic withdrawal from the federation.

In Canada outside of Quebec, the globalization analysis took other forms. One key priority was to address the democracy deficit by creating a mechanism for public participation in the constitutional question. A second substantive issue was to come up with a new set of proposals that would incorporate the essence of Meech within the wider constitutional agenda identified by the parallel accord. Joe Clark, a former Prime Minister and Minister of External Affairs, was given the task of shepherding the negotiations for the Charlottetown Accord.

The play of interests in the so-called 'Canada round' of negotiations was much more complex than had been the case in the Aboriginal and Quebec rounds—and the resulting agreement was much more ambitious and ambiguous. Take, for example, the powers over the economy. The Canadian government entered into the negotiations with a new and distinct set of objectives regarding the further development of the Canadian common market, wanting to open up the domestic market so that it could function along GATT-like patterns. The government proposed a new institution comprised of federal and provincial authorities to exercise these new powers over the management of the common market. Taking a leaf from the European social democrats, the NDP government of Ontario then proposed that those powers should be accompanied by a new social charter that defined a common set of social and labour rights in the new market. Fearful of losing historical prerogatives, provincial governments sought exemptions for particular sectors and services. The result was agreement on a new set of powers, but no new institution to do the task, a set of exceptions so significant that it was a moot point whether market integration would be improved or weakened, and a symbolic new social charter, the terms of which could not be enforced by the judiciary. The whole document suffered from similar ambiguities in its commitments to decentralization, Senate and parliamentary reform, Aboriginal self-government, and recognition of Quebec as a distinct society.

A generous summary to make of the Charlottetown Accord was that it was a noble and transitional attempt. It was noble in that it attempted to work on an expanded agenda and placed a novel package on the table, one that included the older Quebec agenda, the federal globalization agenda, and the aspirations of those outside centres of power. Aboriginal self-government, the social charter, and the reformed Senate were all new 'non-Quebec' constitutional objectives. It was transitional because it attempted to break conventions of executive federalism and élite accommodation, but it offered no firm model of how that could be done. Its process, therefore, was more ad hoc than predictable and consistent. Even the decision to take the agreement before the public in a referendum was done at the last minute, and was clearly to the disadvantage of those trying to sell it. One critical flaw was that it did not really integrate the Quebec agenda into the package. Partially, this came from the fact that the government of Quebec came to the negotiations only after a consensus had been reached among the other participants. At that point is was too late to reshape the agreement. The final Quebec add-ons—such as a guarantee of a 25 per cent share of seats in the House of Commons in perpetuity in exchange for an agreement on Senate reform—were awkward. The agreement was rejected by majorities in both Canada and Quebec. It had delayed the promised sovereignty referendum but had not replaced the apparent need to have one.

Failed Unilateral Declaration of Independence: The Sovereignty-Partnership Referendum

In September 1994 the Parti Québécois came to power under Jacques Parizeau. A former provincial finance minister under Lévesque and a long-time separatist, Parizeau was a hard-liner on the sovereignty issue. He realized that a platform of sovereignty-association gave the so-called partners in the proposed association (Quebec and the rest of Canada) the power to say no—thus destroying the strategy. For Parizeau the best way to deal with the question was simply to declare independence unilaterally, thereby forcing others to bargain on the PQ's terms. The mid-1990s appeared to be the most opportune time for Quebec to issue such a declaration because the failure of both Meech Lake and Charlottetown had thoroughly discredited federalist forces. The Mulroney Conservatives had disintegrated during the 1993 federal elections and been reduced to two seats in Parliament. Many Québécois had voted for Lucien Bouchard, Mulroney's former Quebec lieutenant and now the leader of the *souverainiste* Bloc Québécois formed at the federal level in the wake of the Meech Lake failure. Jean Chrétien, as Trudeau's Justice Minister the architect of the 1982 'night of the long knives' agreement, was the Canadian Prime Minister.

The PQ acted quickly by passing a January 1995 draft declaration of independence that would be enacted following its completion and ratification in a referendum to be held within one year. That declaration of independence held that Quebecers could still be Canadian citizens and use Canadian dollars after independence. The Quebec government then engaged popular participation by setting up regional sovereignty commissions to define the new Quebec nationality. The Quebec Liberal Party, however, decided not to participate in the process. By late spring it was apparent that the PQ strategy was failing to capture support beyond the party's traditional constituency. As a way of breaking out of the partisan definition of independence to gain support of 'soft separatists' in the Quebec electorate, the PQ signed an all-party agreement with both the Bloc Québécois and the Parti Action Démocratique (a *souverainiste* splinter from the provincial Liberal Party after the failure of the Charlottetown Accord). The 12 June agreement changed the *souverainiste* strategy. Instead of a straightforward vote on the declaration of independence (the Parizeau strategy), the idea was to open a discussion at the same time with Canadian authorities on the negotiation of a new 'partnership' between the sovereign Quebec and English Canada.

What was the difference between the sovereignty-partnership and the failed sovereignty-association strategy? Generally, the ambiguity of the terms 'partnership' and 'association' would link the two concepts. Now, however, the PQ government would only offer the possibility of a new partnership with Canada; it would not directly link one with the other. The Parizeau government would resort to the unilateral declaration of independence if a satisfactory partnership agreement could not be negotiated within one year of the referendum. The great difference between the 1980 and 1995 referenda, then, was that the idea of association or partnership had become an option, not a necessity to attain sovereignty. According to the *souverainistes*, the economic and international underpinnings of the new state would be secured by its entry into international regimes such as NAFTA. Linking the referendum vote with future negotiations also had the appeal of strengthening the bargaining position of Quebec within Confederation as well as declaring sovereignty. The ambiguous strategy induced support from disenchanted federalists as well as from *souverainistes*.[2]

Federalists won by less than 1 per cent of the popular vote—a plurality that was smaller than the number of spoiled ballots. The *souverainiste* forces had a clear moral victory and the very closeness of the vote ensured that the issue was not closed. Another referendum would be in the works.

Neverendum-Referendum Canada: Between Plan A and Plan B

The closeness of the referendum vote sent political shock waves throughout the federation. It led the federal government to work on two new constitutional initiatives—the so-called Plan A and Plan B. Plan A refers to those policy initiatives that would give the federalists a more convincing case when facing the Quebec electorate in the next referendum. Plan B seeks to discipline the referendum process by which the separatists are pursuing their objectives and also to establish the process under which a province can leave the federation.

One way to think of the objective of Plan A, in the words of Samuel LaSelva (1996), is to 'overcome the Trudeau-Lévesque debate'. Quebec is certainly not a province *comme les autres* and yet it is not so distinct that its long-term interests cannot be fulfilled by continued participation within the Canadian community. The principal elements of Plan A are federal legislation to fulfil referendum promises, a general decentralization of the federation, the recruitment of more Québécois leadership into the federal government, and a provincially defined framework for the next round of constitutional bargaining.

Following the referendum the federal government enacted legislation to recognize the distinctness of Quebec in Canada and to restrict the federal government's autonomy in constitutional change. The former is symbolic recognition and follows Chrétien's referendum promise. The latter, although an ordinary statute, has important constitutional implications. The government of Canada has disciplined its use of a constitutional resolution to the extent that federal support will only be given to a resolution if it has support from the legislatures of the majority of provinces in Atlantic Canada, the province of Quebec, Ontario, the majority of the Prairie provinces, and (after some insistence) British Columbia. The net effect of the legislation has been to restrict severely the autonomy of the federal government in constitutional affairs and to confine it to a cultural and regional definition of political community (Cairns, 1997).

As the reader will discover in subsequent chapters, much of the federal agenda since 1993 has been driven by its fiscal policy and goal of deficit elimination. Ottawa has signalled an intention to withdraw funding and policy-making in several fields, marking a major shift in federal-provincial relations. The pragmatic and fiscally driven decentralization has opened the doors for a more general province-centred shift in policy-making, which is more in keeping with the letter of the constitution. In this era the government of Quebec and the other more powerful provinces can make common cause for policy autonomy.

Finally, all Canadian provinces save Quebec signed a 'Calgary Declaration' in September 1997 outlining the contours of the next round of constitutional negotiations.[3] The declaration melds together three systems of thought—that of the Charter stressing the equality of individuals, that of the Charlottetown Accord stressing a limited recognition of Quebec's 'uniqueness', and that of the Reform Party of Canada stressing the equality of provinces. The political strategy is to address the democracy deficit that accompanied the Meech Lake process by submitting the principles of the declaration to different forms of democratic consultation in each province before the start of negotiations. Although predictably rejected by the PQ as too late and too little, the declaration stands as the starting point for the next round of constitutional bargaining.

Plan B stems from concern and frustration on the part of federalists that the Canadian government has been unprepared for a sovereignty victory and that the *souverainistes* are setting the rules of the game (Gibson, 1994; Monahan and Bryant, 1996; Rose, 1995). Accordingly, the 'plan' is really an assemblage of initiatives by different parties that seeks to impose discipline on the referendum and secession process. Under the PQ referenda, the fate of Canada resided with the ability of one provincial government to enact a unilateral declaration of independence (UDI) when the yes side attains 50 per cent plus one of the popular vote. Federal concerns are numerous. First, the referendum campaigns are not based on full knowledge of the implications of the vote. The PQ resolution outlining Quebec's UDI, for example, indicated that Quebecers would keep the Canadian dollar, the Canadian common market, and Canadian citizenship—all items that would be the subject of negotiation, not assumption. Within the PQ strategy is also the assumption that one can separate (gain sovereignty) in order to reintegrate (gain a partnership) on better terms. For federalists, another referendum campaign has to be conducted with more forthright and honest information concerning what is being voted for (sovereignty or a new partnership) and its implications. Second, the question has to be clear and unambiguous. The 1980 referendum resembled a collective bargaining vote where the 'mandate to negotiate' translates into strengthening the bargaining position of negotiators rather than legitimating an end. Similarly, the 1995 referendum's 43-word question was a brilliant exercise in ambiguity designed to capture a majority of different constituencies. Third, federalists are concerned about the use of a simple majority to legitimate the declaration of independence.

The federal government also took the extraordinary step to submit questions to the Supreme Court in what is termed a reference case. The case queried the right of a province to make a unilateral declaration of independence.[4] The federal government did not argue that secession is illegal, just that exit must be negotiated with other partners in the federation. The August 1998 judgement ruled that a province does not have the right to make a unilateral declaration of independence. However, it also ruled that if a clear majority of the electorate voted in a clear question to secede from Canada, the rest of the federation would be obligated to negotiate. On face value the Supreme Court gave a partial victory to both sides. In reality, it is helping to define a process by which such an issue can be determined.

Governance: The Organization and Operation of State Institutions

Five distinct sets of state structures have emerged over the course of Canada's historical development. Each has its own set of dynamics and political effects.

1. International regimes help to define the sovereignty and effective autonomy of the Canadian state, from the statutes that defined Canada's place

within Empire to the treaties and military alliances that outline its status as a middle power within the international state system and regional North American state within NAFTA. These were discussed above and in the previous chapter.

2. Various structures and conventions define Canada's particular form of *parliamentary democracy*. They include the conventions of parliamentary supremacy, the *electoral system*, and the *party system*. Parliamentary democracy presupposes an independent and neutral *public administration*. This comprises an extensive range of institutions, from those that help cabinets formulate and evaluate policy, as well as control, co-ordinate, and direct governments, to 'line departments' that deliver services, various regulatory bodies, and state-owned firms.

3. Canada relies upon federalism to accommodate and mediate profound regional and cultural cleavages. Accordingly, the *federal system* constitutes a wide range of structures, from the constitutional division of powers that defines the distinct and shared jurisdiction of two levels of government, to negotiated interdependent policy regimes in fiscal and social policy, to the quasi-diplomatic process and machinery of inter-governmental relations.

4. Still other state structures have defined and managed national, cultural, and religious differences, from constitutionally guaranteed linguistic and denominational rights, the Official Languages Act, and the Quebec Language Charter to treaties, land claims settlements, and the Indian Act.

5. The Charter of Rights and Freedoms and related parts of the judiciary define Canadian society as a community of rights-bearing individuals. To a large extent the Charter has absorbed the fourth category of structures, so the two will be discussed together.

Parliamentary Democracy

Though the reader will not find the words 'Prime Minister' or 'Leader of the Official Opposition' in any of the Constitution Acts, the conventions of parliamentary democracy are a fundamental pillar of Canadian political life. Developed over a thousand years in Britain, the parliamentary form of government is characterized by the existence of a central representative institution or Parliament, which controls the raising and spending of revenues (Jennings, 1952; Dicey, 1908; Bagehot, 1920). In the United Kingdom, Parliament is traditionally comprised of the monarch, House of Lords (seat of the hereditary and appointed power), and House of Commons (seat of democratic power). In the Canadian case, Parliament is comprised of the representative of the monarch (Governor-General) and two chambers, the House of Commons (seat of democratic power) and the Senate (appointed power). As in the United Kingdom, power is centred in the House of Commons. The provincial institutional structures are slightly different. The lieutenant-governor is the representative of the monarch. Provincial parliaments are comprised of one legislative assembly, named differently throughout the federation: Parliament, Legislative or Provincial Assembly, and, in Quebec, National Assembly.

Parliamentary systems are quite different from congressional republican systems, in which a representative legislative body has the exclusive ability to make laws (Landes, 1997). Congressional or republican systems, like those of the United States and many developing countries, were created to replace a monarchy or dictatorship with a form of representative government. Power is deliberately fragmented between the President and the legislature. Sovereignty, in these systems, lies with 'the people'.

Parliamentary systems, on the other hand, developed with the intention not of replacing the lawmaking power of the Crown but of ensuring that the Crown's power would not be abused. The eventual result of the 1837–8 rebellions, for example, was to ensure that the cabinet or political executive was responsible to Parliament—and not to the imperial government. Sovereignty in these systems lies with Parliament, which can make laws on any matter it chooses: the power of *parliamentary supremacy*. After the rise of mass political parties, the net effect of 'responsible government' has been to concentrate political power in the hands of elected parliamentary leadership. A great deal of lawmaking power rests with the government or cabinet, and to a very great extent the deliberations of Parliament are intended to publicize and monitor the government's activities.[5] The political power of the cabinet to organize and control government is tremendous. Many important positions in the Canadian political structure are effectively appointed by the Prime Minister, including cabinet ministers, the Governor-General and provincial lieutenant-governors, court justices, regulatory commission members, military leadership, and top civil servants. This power of appointment even stretches to the members of the Senate.

The government consists of a cabinet composed of the Premier or Prime Minister and other ministers of the Crown. Cabinet government is group government. Ministers practice conventions of *individual and collective responsibility*—that is, they are responsible for their own conduct and, as well, take a collective responsibility for the affairs of the government as a whole. Ministers, therefore, express their policy disagreements within cabinet and never publicly criticize the government. Cabinets are served by an extensive network of central agencies, although the exact nature of organization depends on the wishes of the first minister. Legally, the Prime Minister and cabinets are appointed by the Governor-General (or lieutenant-governor in a province) under the convention that they must enjoy the confidence of the House of Commons or provincial legislature.

The growth in the size and complexity of government administration in recent years has called into question the ability of parliaments and legislatures to control government expenditures, challenged the ability of cabinets to control the decisions and regulations issued by administrators, and undermined the links between the administration, cabinet, and legislatures maintained through the parliamentary convention of *ministerial responsibility* (Kernaghan, 1979,

1985; Dwivedi, 1982). As a result, critics have proposed a variety of reforms to bolster political control over the administration, including dramatically reducing the size and scope of government expenditures and regulatory activities through privatization, deregulation, hiring freezes, and tax reform (Kamerman and Kahn, 1989). Some of these proposals have been put into place. Other proposals have involved bolstering ministerial responsibility through the creation of larger ministerial staffs and staff agencies, strengthening parliamentary surveillance by allocating more resources and powers to parliamentary committees, and allowing individual citizens greater control over administrative activities through enhanced Freedom of Information legislation, judicial review, and the creation of human rights commissions and ombudsman offices (Kernaghan, 1979). Despite these changes, administrative accountability remains a major issue at all levels of the Canadian state.

Partisanship is a critical organizing principle for parliamentary democracy. The Prime Minister is the leader of the majority party in the House and chooses the cabinet from among other members of his/her party in the legislature. Constitutionally, governments have to face the electorate at least every five years, although convention tends towards a four-year term. Another convention is that the Prime Minister decides when to call the election within that five-year period. There are exceptions. Should the government lose the confidence of the House, the Governor-General or lieutenant-governor would expect an immediate resignation. Losing confidence means failing to win a vote on a critical piece of legislation (i.e., the budget or other legislation affecting the government's spending power) or being defeated in a 'non-confidence' motion presented by the Leader of the Official Opposition. In these cases, there may be new elections or opposition parties may be asked to form a government.

During the globalization period there has been pressure to change parliamentary governance. First, the Canadian Senate stands as a sort of institutional fossil. It was intended to reflect nineteenth-century suspicion of democracy—to provide 'sober second thought' to the Commons—as well as to represent money and regional interests in central decision-making. Legally, it has more power than the British House of Lords. However, the Canadian Senate lacks the legitimacy to use it. For most of the life of the federation, governments were content to bury the Senate by filling it with the Prime Minister's partisan followers and allowing it to take other roles—from investigative committees to legislative fine-tuning. Over the past 10 years, Senate reform has become a constitutional objective. There are many sources for this goal. For pan-Canadian nationalists such institutional reform is a means of political integration because conflict is managed within central institutions as opposed to the more centrifugal processes of intergovernmental relations. Support for Senate reform has also become integral to the doctrine of equality of the provinces now embedded in regional constitutional strategies. As well, it has gained support from those concerned with executive federalism's democracy deficit. This set of ideas is most powerfully embedded in western Canada, where the Reform Party campaigned to have a Triple E (elected, equal, and effective) Senate. A new Senate was part of the ill-fated Charlottetown Accord and will most likely be added to the next set of constitutional negotiations.

A second pressure for change is what Herbert Kitschelt (1993a) terms the liberalization of organized democracy—making democratic institutions more responsive to forms of popular participation. Traditionally, sovereignty resided in Parliament, not the people, and parliamentarians were elected to use their discretion in deciding on issues. The centralization of political and executive power within cabinet is supposed to let governments take a long-range view of policy-making—to insulate them from popular pressures. In the 1990s, however, these old conventions are being altered. Limitations on the autonomy of parliamentarians are legion—beginning with the need to follow the party line and the consequences for disagreeing with cabinet or Prime Minister. Cabinets, Herman Bakvis and David MacDonald (1993) argue, are schizophrenic, exhibiting autonomous power and long-term horizons in one or two areas, yet weakened by regional and distributional concerns in others.

To counter these tendencies there is more pressure to give parliamentarians free votes in the Commons and to supplement traditional parliamentary scrutiny of cabinet with new forms of institutional and democratic control. For example, the federal government is also scrutinized by Freedom of Information legislation, a Privacy Commission, a Human Rights Commission, and an Auditor-General. The cabinet even has an 'ethics adviser'. Also, there are more avenues for public participation in policy-making—a pluralism of the policy process (Simeon and Willis, 1997). Fundamental issues such as constitution-making are not settled by Parliaments alone, as the resort to referenda indicates. There are also initiatives to discipline parliamentary democracy, including legislation that forbids governments to run deficits in Alberta, New Brunswick, and Manitoba. In British Columbia recall legislation, the power to unseat elected officials, has become an integral part of partisan politics.

The Electoral System

The electoral system is composed of the rules governing who can hold office, who can vote, and how that vote is translated into political representation. These concern how elections are run and the definition of electoral boundaries. At the outset one can define our electoral system as a single-vote, simple-preference, and single-constituency system. While there are numerous different types of electoral systems in place in different countries around the world, most parliamentary systems have a system of *territorial constituencies* from which representatives are chosen according to the *plurality principle*—that is, the winning candidate is the one who gets the most votes regardless of the margin of victory or the proportion of total votes received. This is the case with all federal and provincial elections in Canada. These rules have changed significantly since Confederation, and have had an important impact on political life in Canada.

During the National Policy period, the Canadian electoral system reflected the nineteenth-century suspicion of democracy, as well as the class, gender, and ethnic conventions of the day. Until the passage of the Dominion Elections Act in

1920, national elections were carried out according to a mixture of federal and provincial regulations, which meant that considerable variance in the franchise existed from province to province.[6] Usually only male Caucasian British subjects with a certain level of property holdings were enfranchised. This greatly restricted the number of individuals actually casting ballots in elections, as did several provincial statutes insisting that prospective voters pass literacy tests.

The first major extension of the franchise occurred in 1918 when women obtained the vote. Although not all women were originally given the vote, universal adult female suffrage was instituted shortly afterwards in federal elections. In many provincial elections, however, women remained disenfranchised. In Quebec women did not receive the right to vote in provincial elections until 1940. Along with gender discrimination, ethnic and racial discrimination also continued to exist at both the federal and provincial levels. In British Columbia, persons of an 'oriental or Hindu' background were disenfranchised until 1945, while at the federal level status Indians and Inuit remained without the vote until 1960–1. Although the property qualification was gradually reduced and the literacy tests were eliminated in most provinces, significant elements of the populace remained disenfranchised until recently. It was only in the 1970s that the provision allowing British subjects to vote was dropped and the franchise limited to Canadian citizens. At the same time, the voting age was lowered to 18 from 21.

These limitations on the vote were of great significance in the first 50 years of Confederation when the system of adult male propertied suffrage existed. Although technically a democracy in that its legislature—and, in effect, government—was determined by means of ballots cast at periodic elections, in practice the composition of the legislature reflected the concerns of only a restricted section of the populace and not the entire public. Even the drawing of electoral boundaries for each constituency was done by the government in power with its partisan advantage in mind. It should not be surprising, therefore, that many of the actions of government in this early period should have been biased towards established power, sectional, and propertied interests.

During the modernization period, the Canadian electoral franchise was gradually extended to the point where Canada now has a universal franchise—every Canadian citizen over the age of 18 has the right to cast a single ballot in elections held in the constituency where that person lives. The right to vote is one of the democratic rights now protected by the Canadian Charter of Rights and Freedoms, reflecting the fact that suffrage is now considered a democratic right for all, not a privilege to be entrusted among the few. Also, since the 1960s the federal electoral boundaries have been drawn by independent commissions and, since 1982, subject to judicial scrutiny. There are still great discrepancies between the relative weight of a single vote in each part of the country, reflecting the geographical distribution of the population. This leads to territory-population trade-offs. For example, rural constituencies have about half as many votes as their urban counterparts, and some jurisdictions, such as Yukon Territory and Prince Edward Island, have fewer votes per constituency than the rest.

An electoral system is part of a complex of policies that structures and regulates democratic life. No system is benign—and the Canadian system displays a set of political biases that has become the subject of the contemporary reform agenda. First, this *simple plurality system* favours stability over direct representation of popular vote. Even in contests between two parties the system will normally boost the representation of the winner at the expense of the second party. Ostensibly, this bias helps to form majority, i.e., stable, governments. But the cost is to make Parliament and legislatures less representative of the popular vote. In Canada it is not uncommon to have majority governments formed with less than 50 per cent of the popular vote—and sometimes when the elected majority government received almost the same or even fewer votes than the leading opposition party.

Second, the territorially based electoral system rewards geographic concentrations of power. Perhaps this would not be a great problem if Canada were regionally or culturally homogeneous. But when the profound regional articulation of the Canadian political economy is tied to an electoral system that rewards geographic concentrations of voter support, the result is a political system that exacerbates national unity problems by cultivating regionalism (Johnston, 1980). One can now effectively argue that national elections are in fact a series of regional contests, each with separate issues and patterns of competition. Indeed, the last two federal elections returned regional parties to Ottawa as the Official Opposition—the Bloc Québécois in 1993 and the western-based Reform Party in 1997. Moreover, there is an effective 'confederalization' of party systems, which means that provincial and federal parties and electoral competition are each organizationally autonomous (Smiley, 1987; Dyck, 1996).

Third, there are tensions between territorial and non-territorial representation. The constituency-based system does not include non-territorial representation and underrepresents non-territorial groups, such as women, the poor, and Aboriginal peoples. The emergence of new parties to contest elections has intensified in the twentieth century, and in recent years, and has made much more obvious the territorial and representative biases present in the electoral system. Parties with diffuse national support are penalized under a constituency-based system while parties with concentrated territorial support are rewarded. A party that achieves, for example, 25 per cent of the total vote but obtains this by winning 25 per cent of the vote in each riding will not win very many seats. On the other hand, parties that can muster 25 per cent of the total vote but do so by winning 50 to 60 per cent of the vote in each constituency in a specific region of the country or a province can win a large number of seats (Cairns, 1968; Lovink, 1970).

One idea for changing the system is to implement some form of proportional representation. The German polity, for example, mixes both plurality and proportional representation. The Australians have a more complex system of multiple-preference voting. The French have vacillated between single-plurality single constituencies and proportional representation and have always had 'run-off' elections for the top two candidates. Having a mixed system would also allow political parties to select women and minority lists. As well, Senate representation could be in part, at least, non-territorial, including Aboriginal constituencies as in New Zealand or gender representation as proposed by the National Action Committee on the Status of Women. The Canadian government rejected any substantial changes to the electoral system in 1992, and at present there is no great movement to improve the ability of institutions to represent social identities—or to extend democratization to the economy or public bureaucracy (Seidle, 1996). However, this could easily change.

The Party System

Political parties are an integral and contested part of parliamentary democracy. Parties select the political leadership and candidates, structure voters' political choice, form and organize governments. Depending on one's political perspective they also have a brokerage function, to integrate the cultural and social diversity of the federation, as well as a class function, to use the state to mediate social inequality.

Like other political structures, parties change over time—but very slowly (Archer, Gibbins, Knopff, and Pal 1995). During the National Policy period, they were groups of notables or cadre parties contesting for power and using patronage to grease the wheels of democracy and governance. From the late 1920s to the late 1950s they were *ministerialist* and *brokerage* machines where powerful ministers also had regional portfolios. During the 1920s and 1930s several class-based and regional political parties, the Progressives, the Co-operative Commonwealth Federation (CCF), and Social Credit, unsuccessfully attempted to change the dominant brokerage model of Canadian politics. In the end, brokerage prevailed, although powerful third parties remained. For these reasons Canada's party system was sometimes termed a 'two-party plus' or a 'three-party' system— terms that endured until the fragmentation following the 1993 election.

During the height of the modernization period political parties changed to become *personalized* and *electronic*. Attention focused on leadership and communication strategies, particularly evening news bites, and political polls reflected the rise of executive federalism and the particular structure of power during the period. Parties defined themselves in a pan-Canadian context. After 1942 there were two major parties, the Liberals and the Progressive Conservatives.[7] Social Credit remained a force, especially in provincial politics in BC, Alberta, and Quebec. Also, the New Democratic Party, a British Labour Party type of social democratic party, formed in 1961 as a successor to the CCF. The Liberals, under Prime Ministers William Lyon Mackenzie King, Louis St Laurent, Lester B. Pearson, and Pierre Elliott Trudeau, dominated the modernization period—largely because they monopolized the Quebec vote until 1984. The federal Liberals' long period of dominance witnessed a fusion between party and state, a set of relationships that Reg Whitaker (1977) summed up with the term 'the government party'. The NDP rose to have some influence during a 1974 Liberal minority government but never came within reach of forming a government. The Progressive Conservatives governed under Prime Minister John Diefenbaker, 1957–62, and during most of 1979 under a minority government headed by Prime Minister Joe Clark.

During the period of globalization the party system began to change (Smith, 1996). First, under Prime Minister Brian Mulroney, 1984–93, the era of 'the government party' vanished. The Conservatives gained national majorities in both elections and built support in Quebec from a diverse set of forces in opposition to the long incumbency of the Liberal Party. But the Mulroney Conservatives were unable to hold any of their key majority constituencies. In 1993 the party system fractured along regional and national lines. The Liberal Party, under Jean Chrétien, formed a majority government with representation from all regions— including all of the seats in Ontario. The *souverainiste* Bloc Québécois under Lucien Bouchard, a former Mulroney cabinet minister, took the majority of seats in Quebec to become the Official Opposition in the Canadian Parliament. The western Canada-based Reform Party, led by Preston Manning, the son of a former Alberta Social Credit Premier, closely followed the Bloc. The Conservatives, with a share of the popular vote equal to Reform, were reduced to two seats! The NDP was also reduced to a small rump. Since both the Conservatives and NDP failed to gain 12 seats they lost their official party status—and the level of official recognition and resources that goes with party status in the House of Commons.

The fragmentation and regionalization of the party system were confirmed by the 1997 election. Only the numbers changed. The Liberal majority was less comfortable. Reform replaced the Bloc as the Official Opposition. The Progressive Conservatives, under Jean Charest, bounced back, though not to a position to overtake Reform, and the NDP regained 'party status' in the House. Also of interest is the large number of small parties attempting to break into federal politics, including the Greens, the National Party, and several religiously affiliated parties.

Both Reform and the Bloc trace their origins to the Mulroney period. Ideologically, the Bloc is a centre-left party and would make a natural ally to either the NDP or Liberals, save that its fundamental goal is to pave the way for the sovereignty of Quebec. Reform, a right-wing conservative party, provides both a political and economic critique of what it calls 'old-time parties'. In many ways Reformers also reject the political and constitutional conventions of the modernization period. Like many others, the party rejects the conventions of executive federalism and élite accommodation. As well, the Reform's strict focus on individual equality has attracted those who reject collective conventions that define the political community, such as multiculturalism and bilingualism. The party stresses more of a populist participatory ideology where representatives are 'delegates' of the popular will. Economically, Reform is more neo-conservative than any other party, stressing the virtues of fiscal responsibility, low taxes, small government, and individual responsibility. Not surprisingly, the Bloc has no representation or support in the other nine provinces, and Reform has no representation east of the Manitoba border and no significant support in Quebec.

Governments regulate campaign expenditures to ensure that political competition does not simply reflect the existing social and economic inequality. There are limits to campaign contributions and the amount of money each candidate can spend. Particularly contentious after the 1988 'free trade' election was legislation regulating the activities of public interest groups during elections—during that election pro-FTA business alliances spent great sums of money on public advertisement for the agreement, which indirectly amounted to extra campaign funding for the Mulroney Conservatives. Governments also subsidize research and communication activities of parties, as well as campaign advertising. The legislation that regulates elections has unintended consequences. Federal political parties, for example, do not gain subsidies unless they fielded at least 50 candidates in the last campaign and gained at least 12 seats in the House of Commons. This makes it difficult for the vast number of new parties to break into national politics. Ironically, it also contributed to the fall of the Progressive Conservative Party after 1993. The Tories were reduced to a rump of two MPs— and thus lost official party status—even though their share of the popular vote was approximately the same as that of the Reform Party.

The contemporary political landscape, therefore, is composed of political parties with substantially different ideas of state-society relations. Both Reform and the Bloc are, in a sense, anti-establishment parties. Both would like to reshape the federation according to their interests. The Liberals are more pragmatic, although they are often accused of 'campaigning from the left and governing from the right'. Their attention to attaining fiscal goals, for example, is very similar to that proposed by Reform and other conservative thinking. What separates the Liberals from the rest is that they are the most committed to the constitutional and political conventions of modern Canada, which they, of course, largely created.

The result of the combined workings of the Canadian parliamentary, electoral, and party systems, then, has been to continue the regionalization of Canadian politics—and for the business agenda to prevail in contemporary political discourse. Changes in the electoral system and party finance legislation could mediate but would not resolve these issues. Barring exceptional events, there is unlikely to be a change in governing party until the two competing parties of the right—the Tories and Reform—end their political competition. Alternatively, it is unlikely the NDP or any other social democratic grouping could take power without significant restructuring. A constitutional settlement or state fragmentation would change the equation. For the time being, however, the Liberal Party is 'stuck in power'.

The combined operation of the parliamentary, electoral, and party systems serves to limit the extent to which non-territorial issues will come to prominence in political deliberations. Non-territorial representation and the non-territorial political agenda will most likely continue to be addressed by the recruitment and policies of existing regionally based political parties, and by the existence of a strong set of special interest associations. Political choice is somewhat wider at the provincial level, where the NDP took power in three provinces, Ontario, Saskatchewan, and British Columbia, during the globalization period. Also, in Quebec, the PQ mixes its focus on sovereignty and language with social democratic ideology.

Public Administration

The boundaries between politics and administration are never tidy or clear. Administrations do not simply carry out the wishes of the government of the day, they are also very much involved in policy-making at all levels. As a result, many criteria can be used to study and evaluate administrations. Classically, one looks at mechanisms of *administrative accountability*, making sure that the administration follows practices and policies approved by the political government and thus ensuring the rule of democracy. As well, one may look at performance criteria, such as how effective administrations are in carrying out their tasks.

Each political economy has a distinct set of political-administrative structures that directly affect it. For example, Canada is a parliamentary democracy— meaning that the political executive (cabinet) controls the agenda and timetable of Parliament and can in most circumstances guarantee passage of its legislation in the form in which it is introduced. The administration, therefore, is relatively powerful and operates without significant checks from legislatures. Ostensibly, the administration is a neutral organization that can serve any party that forms the government. Much political debate in parliamentary systems, therefore, occurs outside the legislature in the process of formulating policy proposals rather than in the debates on the proposed legislation (Pross, 1986). Civil servants play an important role in this process of policy formulation, which raises questions about the extent to which the administration is responding to its own desires and needs rather than to the elected politicians.

Canada's public service is composed of four types of administrative agencies at three levels of government: federal, provincial, and local. These are *central agencies*, which help cabinets direct the government as a whole; the traditional *departmental* form of organization; government-owned enterprises or *Crown corporations*; and *independent regulatory commissions* (Kernaghan and Siegal, 1987; Adie and Thomas, 1987). Each of these agencies has a different structure and a different relationship to the political government, and each has experienced growth in recent years at all three levels of government.

Canadian parliamentary democracy is formally led by a cabinet that combines political and administrative leadership. At the élite level, therefore, several central agencies formally bridge the neutral and independent public service to the political executive. On the administrative side, the cabinet is served by a Privy Council Office (PCO), the tip of the career civil service. In addition, the Prime Minister's Office (PMO) serves as a political central agency for the Prime Minister. The elaboration and ranking of other central agencies depends on the political agenda, the organizational structure of cabinet, and the leadership style of the Prime Minister. During the modernization period, for example, the Trudeau governments elaborated a complex web of 'horizontal' central agencies in broad policy fields, which gave financial and policy evaluation to each ministerial proposal. Ministers had to gain support for their initiatives from the Treasury Board and then from their respective policy secretariat. The difficulty, of course, was that the system was so cumbersome that the tendency was to try to get around it.

Globalization has brought a new agenda—to reduce the cost and size of government. The Canadian federal government ran successive deficits from 1974 until 1997. During the 1980s fiscal control became one of the key cornerstones of governance. As a result, the Treasury Board Secretariat (which oversees public spending) and the Department of Finance became especially prominent. The Mulroney government, however, pursued contradictory fiscal and monetary policies—a combination that did not reach its intended objectives. Nevertheless, newer neo-liberal policy initiatives from the Prime Minister's Office—on free trade, deregulation, and privatization—began to reshape the Canadian state. Without an elaborate set of horizontal central agencies, power is contested between the Department of Finance, reflecting fiscal priorities, and Foreign Affairs and International Trade, reflecting the internationalization of public policy (Doern, Pal, and Tomlin, 1996). Finance, in particular, has co-ordinated the massive fiscal cuts that produced the first federal budgetary surplus in nearly a quarter of a century in 1997–8.

The traditional departmental form of organization is the most important for influencing policy formulation. This type of hierarchically structured organization, with large numbers of public servants, is funded by legislative appropriation and carries out duties assigned by legislation or statute. Each department is headed by a senior official or deputy minister and is responsible to a senior politician or cabinet minister for its activities. Although the number and size of departments vary considerably, depending on jurisdiction and the responsibilities assigned to the department by a legislature, collectively departments make up the backbone of the Canadian administrative system and have always been the primary device that governments use to carry out their wishes (Hodgetts, 1973). Some are line departments—i.e., they fulfil an identifiable function (such as transport)—and some are horizontal in nature—such as Finance, which affects the operation of government in general. In the globalization period departmental organization has changed to reflect the broader definition of policy. For example, a Ministry of Human Resources Development now takes care of all social policy matters at the federal level.

Government enterprises or Crown corporations are what Paul Thomas and Orest W. Zajcew (1993), following J.E. Hodgetts, refer to as 'structural heretics'—part government department and part private firm. Crown corporations have historically been important instruments of public policy, serving as tools for industrial development, creating national markets where none previously existed, and providing essential infrastructure, particularly for 'natural monopolies' such as hydroelectricity, nuclear energy, and transportation (railways, air travel). They even provide an organizational mechanism to run institutions such as museums. Crown corporations operate as private-sector businesses, with the exception that their shares are held by governments. Parliament and provincial legislatures also guarantee corporate debt. Governments thereby control appointments to their boards of directors and are in a position to influence general policies if not their day-to-day activities. Part of the organizational structure insulates the corporation from the government, and part of it ties the corporation to the minister of the day. One important economic significance of state enterprises is that they can invest at a lower cost than private firms—thus they can produce more at lower prices. They have been used, therefore, to reduce costs of infrastructure, energy, and services such as automobile insurance. Although Canadian governments at all levels have used this form of administration, public ownership grew dramatically during wartime at the federal level and after 1960 at the provincial level (Prichard, 1983). The largest Crown corporations, especially provincially owned utility corporations such as BC Hydro, Hydro-Québec, and Ontario Hydro, are among the largest corporations of any kind in the country.

During the globalization period many of these Crown corporations have been privatized or deregulated. Large publicly owned transportation companies, such as Air Canada, Petro-Canada, Canadian National Railways, and Northern Transportation have been privatized, as have most major airports and harbours. At a provincial level all Crown-owned utilities have undergone regulatory restructuring whereby they no longer have natural market monopolies over the production of energy in their jurisdictions. In the case of the Canadian government, reforms have also placed Crown corporations under more direct control of ministers and strengthened the government's overall financial control of them.

Why the change from historical patterns? Trade and fiscal issues are important determinants. Economic competition and fiscal stringency have been accompanied by a cost-control method of governance. Governments want their enterprises either to be financially viable or to return money to the public treasury. Both the FTA and NAFTA have circumscribed the activities of state firms, particularly when they are in competitive positions with private capital. Also, financially squeezed governments sometimes have not been able to fulfil the capital needs of large state enterprises. Private-sector status may also place firms on a better footing to respond to large-scale market and technology changes. As well, privatization has been a standard policy of neo-conservative governments eager to gain political support from the business community.

Finally, independent regulatory commissions are similar 'structural heretics' (Thomas and Zajcew, 1993). Based on the model of the US Interstate Commerce Commission established in the late nineteenth century, independent regulatory commissions are created to monitor and control the activities of private-sector industries to ensure compliance with government objectives and avoidance of partisan political manipulation. They have also been used in the Canadian case to foster the orderly growth of an economic sector and to fulfil other social or economic policies. They have broad powers to investigate and modify private-sector behaviour using a quasi-judicial process that examines evidence and makes binding regulatory decisions, subject only to cabinet modification. The details and mandates of these agencies differ substantially according to the activity regulated, who can participate in the hearings, and the jurisdiction granting regulatory authority. In Canada they are accountable primarily to cabinet, while in the United States they are accountable to Congress.

The number of agencies and the areas of economic activity they regulate have been growing at both the federal and provincial levels throughout this century (Economic Council of Canada, 1979; Baggaley, 1981). During the modernization period many regulatory agencies facilitated the orderly development of national industries in the process of continental integration. During the 1970s this emphasis turned to redistributive issues as it appeared that many agencies were 'captured' by the corporations they were intended to regulate. Throughout the 1980s regulatory commissions were important to a 'legalization' of the policy process—what George Hoberg has termed (in the US context) 'pluralism by design' (Simeon and Willis, 1997; Hoberg, 1992). During the period of globalization, corporations have sought the deregulation of industrial sectors—or a switch from 'process-based' to 'performance-based' regulation. This structural change gives corporations much more autonomy from government intervention in their affairs, and as a result is very controversial. Recently, for example, some of the largest Canadian chartered banks started a merger process arguing that merger is necessary for global competition. Other banks deny this necessity. Consumer and industry watchdogs are also wary of limiting competition and the long-term effects of such concentrations of power. The federal government has temporarily blocked the initiative.

Common property resources—water, air, the high-altitude ozone layer, fisheries, and, to a certain extent, forests—provide the most difficult regulatory problems because there is no obvious incentive for any one economic agent to pursue a conservation strategy. These problems have been compounded in recent years as it has become apparent that new international regimes are needed to preserve the sustainability of these resources. Simply put, global ecological systems do not respect national boundaries. The new regulatory concerns are often at odds with corporate objectives for deregulation or performance-based regulation, particularly when corporations are engaged in volatile international markets. Globalization is similarly inducing national governments to form international regimes to deal with other issues—from the content of the Internet to bringing alleged war criminals to justice.

The Federal System

Federalism has been one of the enduring innovations of the 1867 constitution. Federalism presupposes the existence of at least two orders of government. Each government is allotted responsibility for different classifications of state activities, or jurisdictions, and each is sovereign in its own right. Parliamentary sovereignty, therefore, is limited by the division of powers between orders of government. This is the principle of *divided sovereignty*. Jurisdictional conflicts between governments are settled by a Supreme Court that rules whether or not any one government's activities are *intra* or *ultra vires* (within or outside its sphere of jurisdiction). Not everyone believes that such systems of divided jurisdiction are workable. The nineteenth-century Maritime opponents to Confederation did not adhere to the principle. Contemporary Quebec *souverainistes* believe it is an impediment to their national development.

To date this system of federalism has provided a tremendous flexibility and plasticity to a formally written constitution. To understand why this is the case, it is instructive to look at federalism through democratic theory. Federalism creates two sets of majority power. The broader community is governed by a national majority. But smaller communities can also constitute a majority on many important issues to make their own particular preferences translate into public policy. In this sense smaller communities are protected from the tyranny of the national majority because social and economic policies can match regional preferences, and regional majorities can also take political responsibility for them.

Federalism is significant for political-economic analysis for a number of reasons. First, it means that the state in a federal system is actually a number of states, each with its own procedural nuances and institutional arrangements. Second, it means that considerable attention must be paid to the specific areas over which the different levels of government have jurisdiction. In a federal system, for example, it makes a great deal of difference whether the central government or the state governments control important areas such as banking, social insurance, and labour law; this control will help determine which interests and actors are involved in the policy process, how these interests and actors are structured internally, and how they interact with each other in the allocation of goods and services in society.

The effect of federalism on political life, therefore, depends a great deal on the degree of centralization or decentralization of power. This cannot be determined from a formal reading of constitutional documents. The definition of contemporary state intervention departs considerably from nineteenth-century political thought. As a result a constitutionally defined division of powers is subject to judicial interpretation, the necessity of gaining political acceptance, and future contingencies. Thus, the working division of powers between the two orders of government takes on a life of its own over time.[8]

Fiscal relations are another significant element of federalism. In Canada, both levels of government have the authority to tax business and personal incomes. But Canada's economic and population structure has resulted in vastly different tax yields among the provinces. The federal government has slightly greater powers of taxation. However, no provinces, as owners of natural resources, are the sole recipients of most natural resource revenues. Until the 1930s provinces were highly reliant on an ad hoc set of federal subsidies as well as their own revenue-raising capacity, a system that virtually collapsed during the Depression when municipalities and prairie provinces were unable to finance relief expenditures on their own. During World War II the federal government assumed the role of the general tax collector for the federation and then distributed per capita grants in a *tax rental* scheme. The wealthier provinces realized that this would amount to a form of regional redistribution. As a result the federal government then implemented a system of *tax-sharing* (whereby it gave out shares of the income tax yield to each province) accompanied by a set of *equalization* transfers that brought the fiscal revenues of provinces up to a national average or acceptable benchmark. As a result, the more decentralized the fiscal system becomes, the more difficult it becomes for Ottawa to fund interregional redistribution.

Presently, provinces are taking a greater lead in social, fiscal, and economic policy (Atkinson and Bierling, 1998). This is accompanied by demands for greater decentralization, formally (as in the Charlottetown Accord) or by convention, as with the current policy thrust of the federal government. It has also induced provincial administrations to look for ways to cut costs and establish greater economies in public administration. These processes are sometimes termed 'disentanglement' or 'cutting duplication'. Presently, Ottawa and the provinces are negotiating the implementation of a social charter that would recognize provincial priority in social policy and, at the same time, discipline Ottawa's power of the purse (Richards, 1997; Lazar, 1997). It would be inaccurate to infer that the federation is undergoing a straightforward decentralization. For example, the federal government has a great deal of autonomy in areas where it has exclusive jurisdiction and is able to impel other jurisdictions to follow its policy priorities. Hence, the federal Parliament has exclusive jurisdiction over monetary policy and the leading levers of public financial policy, despite having a minority share of taxes or expenditures.

Finally, federalism also reflects a policy process. During the modernization period, attention turned to building the administration of a welfare state and, given constitutional complications, this was produced through the process of executive federalism, discussed above (Smiley, 1987). Executive federalism, in conjunction with the centralization of authority in parliamentary democracy, produced a highly systematic and purposeful set of federal-provincial relations in comparison with the complicated mesh of relationships embedded within the American federal-congressional system (Watts, 1989).

Premiers have used executive federalism to define and solidify provincial constituencies. For example, the Premier of Alberta may take policy positions that reflect the close working relationship between the petroleum industry and the provincial government. Ontario may take positions more consistent with manufacturing and financial interests. In this way sectoral economic conflicts can be played out within executive federalism. Sometimes, the operating assumption is that the federal government cannot represent regional interests or that concurrent federal and provincial majorities are needed to implement 'national' policies throughout the federation. Executive federalism is also a means for making agendas and cementing consensus on broad issues. There are annual meetings of particular ministers, such as Finance and Education, and extensive meetings among senior departmental bureaucrats. More and more policy has become the product of negotiation between different sets of élites—so much so that the process of executive federalism has become embedded as one of the operating conventions of Canadian politics.

The process is mirrored at a regional level, with annual premiers' conferences, regional meetings such as that of the Atlantic Premiers Council and the Western Premiers Conference, and mechanisms of regional integration, as with the three Maritime provinces. As well, there are broader international regional conferences, such as that between New England governors and Atlantic premiers and Cascadia in the Pacific Northwest (Washington, Oregon, Alberta, and British Columbia).

In Canada federalism has helped to ensure the survival of a French-speaking majority in Quebec and to protect the autonomy of regional political communities outside central Canada. One of the reasons for a pattern of successful integration has been cross-cutting cleavages. Political alliances are rarely fixed across policy and provincial lines. For example, Quebec and the western provinces can make common positions on such things as a new social charter governing social policy and Ottawa's power of the purse—or to ward off apparent federal ambitions to 'encroach' on provincial jurisdiction. Though political parties may reject 'old-style federalists' or seek, as the PQ does, a new 'partnership', what they are saying, in effect, is that they want to change the form of the Canadian federal system, not reject federalism.

Federalism is spreading globally. It is growing as a mechanism for uniting formally autonomous national units or (as in the Canadian case) for resolving disputes between cultural communities. For example, in Europe, Germany and Switzerland have long had federal systems. Also, Belgium is federating as a means of settling political tensions. Spain has created a form of federalism to accommodate its linguistic national minorities, and the United Kingdom has looked to a form of federalism to settle long-standing tensions between England and the Celtic fringe of Wales, Scotland, and Northern Ireland. In North America, Canada, the United States, Mexico, and Brazil are among the large political communities organized as federations.

Federalism is also influencing the development of the European Union. There are now European elections, a common European passport and consular services, common European social, human, and political rights available to all persons, regardless of citizen status, throughout the Union, and large policy areas that are the exclusive responsibility of the central administration in Brussels. The division of powers within the EU is guided by the *subsidiary* principle—i.e., that policy be undertaken by the lowest level of jurisdiction capable of undertaking the task. Ostensibly, this is a check on creeping centralization and a protection of local democracy. In North America integration has conformed to an intergovernmental model that reinforces national sovereignty as opposed to inducing pan-North American federalism.

The Charter

If we return to examining politics through democratic theory we can see that federalism was one way to protect against the tyranny of the majority—to allow smaller collectivities to flourish within the greater body politic. But, as Alan

Cairns reminds us, 'federalism is not enough' (Cairns, 1995). There have always been legislation and ad hoc constitutional provisions to protect minorities, even from smaller territorial majorities.[9] However, the protections that secured linguistic duality and protected other collectivities against majority rule would never be secure if they depended on majority rule to implement them. The federal government's fiduciary relationship to Aboriginal peoples was highly contested—and eventually corrupted because Aboriginal peoples were denied political rights and power to hold the federal government accountable for its actions. The responsibility for denominational rights did not stop the highly contested policy of assimilation towards French Catholic minorities outside of Quebec. More recently, immigration has produced multicultural urban societies—political environments in which neither British parliamentary institutions nor federalism has been considered appropriate for securing collective rights or protecting minorities (Cairns, 1995).

The federal response to these problems, as discussed above, was the embedding of a Charter of Rights and Freedoms in the 1982 Constitution Act. The Charter defined a series of fundamental freedoms, democratic, mobility, and legal rights, entrenched the Official Languages Act, and defined minority-language educational rights. The judiciary was given the responsibility for enforcing the Charter, and the federal government even established a legal fund to aid those wishing to pursue Charter cases. Ostensibly, the nationalizing effects of the Charter would institutionalize a common set of state-society relations across the federation—applicable to all regardless of regional or national identity and enforceable on both orders of government. The 1982 Constitution Act also entrenched existing (but undefined) Aboriginal rights and land claims settlements, and ensured that they apply equally to male and female persons. The problem with the Aboriginal rights provisions, however, was that the subsequent constitutional conferences intended to define them—including the rights of self-government—failed.

The Charter added a completely new structural dimension to Canadian politics because it further conditioned parliamentary sovereignty and federalism with judicial review. In this sense it has reshaped Canadian political life. The one exception rests with a controversial provision of the Charter—the 'notwithstanding' clause—that allows any legislature or Parliament to pass legislation that is not subject to Charter provisions for renewable five-year periods.[10]

The most notable effect of the Charter and the new role of the judiciary have been, as intended, to discipline Parliament, provincial legislatures, and administrations to conform to provisions of the Charter (Russell, 1994). Governments that seek to use the notwithstanding clause to minimize the financial or policy implication of rights infringement pay high political costs and often have to backtrack. The Charter, of course, is driven by litigation. Here, the most notable effect has been the use of the Charter as a vehicle to represent what Alan Cairns (1992) terms 'Charter Canadians' or what Jane Jenson (1995) refers to as non-territorial identities, particularly those who have been ill-served by political parties: women, Aboriginals, other minorities often mobilized as amorphous social movements. In this sense the Charter has risen to complement the weaknesses of other instruments of representation within Canadian politics.

The Political-Economic Significance of Canadian State Structures

'The state', Charles Tilly reminds us, 'does not equal society' (Tilly, 1992). There is no better way to summarize the significance of Canadian state structures on the political economy of Canada during a period of change. Looking at the structures themselves, we see historical development has left a residue of powerful and integrated institutions: centralized, stable parliamentary government focusing authority in the hands of democratic and administrative élites, and a constitutional federation that has unified and integrated jurisdictions comprising half a continent. The combination of these two is a system of executive federalism or policy-making between political executives of different orders of government. To check powers of élites, the constitution provides a Charter that protects minorities from large and small majorities, and defines a common set of fundamental, legal, democratic rights and mobility rights throughout the country. Moreover, the use of referenda to settle major constitutional issues is now a matter of course. Still, one of the key weaknesses of the state structure centres on the democracy deficit—the way in which the machinery and process of federalism and intergovernmental relations, in the context of parliamentary democracy, can effectively disenfranchise large segments of the population from taking part in key political decisions.

When we add some basic characteristics of the social and economic structure, however, a different picture emerges. First, there are profound limitations on the centralized cabinet governance. Cabinets have to be representative—and they have to deliver the goods to major constituencies. The failure of the Mulroney government to gain popular acceptance of its constitutional proposals and the necessity of using a federal election as a form of referendum vividly illustrate that cabinet dominance is bounded by an informal set of political constraints. Breaking them—as in the case of the Progressive Conservative government's constitutional and tax initiatives or even in the 'social contract' of Bob Rae's Ontario NDP government—may lead to political disintegration. Generally, globalization has brought an increasing gap between élite and mass priorities, plus a population that is more politically informed, more critical of élites, and more demanding of political participation than ever before (Banting, 1996; Nevitte, 1996).

The significance of the political control of élite accommodation is that private interests can no longer simply head for the top—to influence cabinet and senior administrative officials. Rather, they also have to sell their message to others. Recent bank merger initiatives, for example, have been accompanied by a federal task force that has sought input from the broader community. Banks have started their political offensive with advertisement campaigns highlighting their role in personal and economic development (Canada, Task Force, 1997).

The Canadian federal system is more than a means to deal with an abundance of geography. Federalism has been a means of forging a unity among different nations and regions. Alan Cairns (1995), for example, cites four competing nationalisms in Canada. The dominant political nationalism is pan-Canadian— that which seeks a unity among Anglophone and Francophone, centre and periphery, Aboriginal and non-Aboriginal. Pan-Canadian nationalism was fashioned during the modernization period, and for different reasons has had difficulty absorbing other national collectivities. Second, Aboriginal peoples were never significantly incorporated within pan-Canadian nationalism. Most contemporary Aboriginal nationalisms, therefore, seek to build on historical political status deriving from the Royal Proclamation, treaties, and Aboriginal rights to forge a new space within the constitutional structure. Third, the Quiet Revolution transformed Quebec nationalism into a movement split between gaining constitutional recognition and autonomy within the Canadian federation and gaining full sovereignty matched by a working 'partnership' with the feder- ation. Finally, the ascendancy of the *souverainiste* project has helped define parameters of a rest of Canada (ROC) nationalism. Though understandably undefined, it will build on the institutional framework of modern Canada. Clearly, the bilingual and dual definition of the federation disappears in the ROC nationalism. Following the logic of interests within the Charlottetown Accord, the ROC national project would most likely deal directly with regionalism, more likely than not by incorporating various forms of intrastate federalism among legally equal provinces.

Federalism is also a key to mediating the regional articulation of Canada—and has several lasting consequences for the political economy. For example, the resource specialization of economies outside of the centre directly affects the autonomy of provincial governments. What is good for petroleum, for example, has to be good for Alberta. This ties the representation of the Alberta govern- ment in intergovernmental relations to that of the oil patch, a relationship that makes the province less autonomous than that of jurisdictions with a more diversified economic structure. Regions vary not only according to their economic specialization, but also according to their relative economic strength. As a result, regional politics are also redistributional politics. This territorial definition of redistribution even surfaces within the Canadian constitution, in its commitment to the principle of equalization and its qualification of mobility rights. Finally, different regions also have distinct economic linkages—Quebec and the Maritimes, for example, with New England, and British Columbia with Japan and the Pacific Northwest. What this means is that regionalism is part and parcel of trade, economic, and environmental policy.

The effects of federalism, regionalism, and nationalisms together produce a state structure that is fragmented and much weaker and perhaps less efficient or effective than that of a small and homogeneous state. The competitive nature of this federalism can also work in the favour of citizens, as competing élites seek political support for their ideas. It also works to the benefit of capital because the system induces interregional competition for investment. On the other hand, it does not directly work to the benefit of labour because provincial control over professions and labour markets and industrial relations rewards a regionalization—not a nationalization—of wage rates, work, and occupational safety standards. For the most part, however, cross-cutting cleavages and the habit of negotiation, balance, and compromise obviate political crises. Moreover, because of the federation's ability to internalize a great deal of diversity, the net policy result is more efficient than if all provinces were simply left on their own. Still, there is mounting pressure for regime change. Contemporary ideas include a restatement of Meech (constitutional recognition of Quebec as a distinct society that would legitimize the autonomy of the Quebec government in linguistic and cultural affairs), the idea of a binational partnership between sovereign equals, and a broad reform agenda that would bind together a federation of equal provinces with a reformed Senate and further decentralization of powers.

Notes

1. The 1982 constitutional revision provides a multi-tiered amendment formula. Most constitutional changes, including those that affect the division of powers, can be made according to a 7/10 50 per cent rule, that is, if there is agreement among the Parliament of Canada and the legislatures of seven out of 10 provinces that represent 50 per cent of the Canadian population. Still, a provincial legislature that does not support a constitutional resolution that changes its powers can opt out of these changes, thus allowing multiple constitutional regimes under the umbrella of one constitution. Further, the Parliament and provincial legislatures can unilaterally amend certain parts of their constitutions, but unanimus agreement is needed for changes that affect all governments.
2. The ambiguity of the PQ strategy is captured in the October 1995 referendum question. 'Do you agree that Québec should become sovereign, after having made a formal offer to Canada for a new Economic and Political Partnership, within the scope of the Bill respecting the future of Québec and of the agreement signed on June 12, 1995?'
3. The Calgary Declaration reads as follows:
   • All Canadians are equal and have rights protected by law.
   • All provinces, while diverse in their characteristics, have equality of status.
   • Canada is graced by a diversity, tolerance, compassion and equality of opportunity that is without rival in the world.
   • Canada's gift of diversity includes aboriginal peoples and cultures, the vitality of the English and French languages and a multicultural citizenry drawn from all parts of the world.

- In Canada's federal system, where respect for diversity and equality underlies unity, the unique character of Quebec society, including its French-speaking majority, its culture and its tradition of civil law, is fundamental to the well-being of Canada. Consequently, the legislature and Government of Quebec have a role to protect and develop the unique character of Quebec society within Canada.
- If any future constitutional amendment confers powers on one province, these powers must be available to all provinces.
- Canada is a federal system where federal, provincial and territorial governments work in partnership while respecting each other's jurisdictions. Canadians want their governments to work co-operatively and with flexibility to ensure the efficiency . . . of the federation. Canadians want their governments to work together particularly in the delivery of social programs. Provinces and territories renew their commitment to work in partnership with the government of Canada to best serve the needs of Canadians.

4. The government of Canada referred three questions to the Supreme Court:

   Question 1: Under the Constitution of Canada, can the National Assembly, legislature or government of Quebec effect the secession of Quebec from Canada unilaterally?

   Question 2: Does international law give the National Assembly, legislature or government of Quebec the right to effect the secession of Quebec from Canada unilaterally? In this regard, is there a right of self-determination under international law that would give the National Assembly, legislature or government of Quebec the right to effect the secession of Quebec from Canada unilaterally?

   Question 3: In the event of a conflict between domestic and international law on the right of the National Assembly, legislature or government of Quebec to effect the secession of Quebec from Canada unilaterally, which would take precedence in Canada?

5. Although modelled on British institutions, the Canadian state does not maintain a set of parliamentary institutions identical to those found in the United Kingdom. In both, Parliament is a bicameral body. In Britain Parliament is composed of an appointed House of Lords and an elected House of Commons. In Canada, because of the federal nature of the country, two sets of parliaments exist. Although most were originally bicameral, at the provincial level the appointed second chambers of legislative councils were eliminated within the first hundred years of Confederation, leaving the present *unicameral* elected provincial legislatures or legislative assemblies. At the federal level, Parliament remains bicameral with an appointed Senate and an elected House of Commons. The Senate continues to exist at the federal level partly to ensure regional representation and it is structured to ensure more or less equal representation of the eastern and western regions of the country and Quebec and Ontario.

6. At Confederation the power to control elections was vested in the federal government with the provision that existing provincial rules would remain in effect until the federal Parliament specifically overrode them. This did not occur until 1920, when the Dominion Elections Act was passed.

7. In 1942, when the Conservative Party sought Progressive Manitoba Premier John Bracken as its leader, he accepted on the condition that 'Progressive' be added to the party name. After this, the Progressives disappeared from the political scene.

8. For example, the American central government has less power in its constitution than the Canadian federal government, but the Congress became the central player in American politics after the Civil War. Conversely, as we have seen, the Canadian constitution provided for a strong centre and weak provinces—just the opposite of what has occurred.

9. For example, the 1867 constitution gave the Anglophone minority in Quebec certain constitutional protections from the Francophone majority, and the federal government undertook a paternalistic fiduciary role for Aboriginal peoples. In response to the Quebec Quiet Revolution the federal government institutionalized policies of official bilingualism and multiculturalism.

10. The initial response of René Lévesque's PQ government was to exempt all legislation from the Charter, a process that only stopped with the return to power of Robert Bourassa, the architect of the Meech Lake Accord. The provision was also used by the government of Quebec to insulate it from judicial attack on its French-only business advertising laws.

Chapter 8

The Structure and Organization of Canadian Labour

Introduction

For sociologists, 'labour' can be the broad collection of classes engaged in the activity of social reproduction within the household (domestic sphere) and market. For economists it refers to those actively working, training, or seeking work in the labour market. Feminists point out that what occurs at home to prepare people for the market or to nurture workers is largely ignored in the calculation and distribution of wages, making any definition of the labour force highly contested (Fox, 1980; Luxton, 1980). Politically, 'organized labour' refers to workers who belong to trade unions, the main vehicle through which workers express their interest as a group in politics and the workplace. 'Industrial relations' involves the laws, customs, and structures that regulate the ongoing co-operation and conflict between 'labour' and 'capital' (i.e., between union and management), as well as the regulation of relations between employees and employers in non-organized workplaces. 'Labour movement' refers to the ensemble of organizations, including political parties affiliated with or sympathetic to trade unions, committed to furthering workers' interests.

Labour shapes and reflects the social and political dynamics of the context within which it exists. In Canada these dynamics vary with the international, regional, and federal articulation of the political community. There is a wide variation in the articulation of industrial relations across provinces and fundamental differences between the Quebec and English-Canadian labour movements. Similarly, the dynamics of the labour market for Aboriginal peoples differs significantly from the Canadian norm. Hence, although we speak of 'labour', one should keep in mind that there is no single entity called Labour within the political community. The 'labour' we speak of is fragmented and complex—and its particular identity and interests change over time.

Politics, Labour, and Collective Organization in Capitalist Society

The term 'labour' has several different political connotations, making it a value-charged term. At stake are different ways in which the legal equality of liberal democracy is reconciled with the economic inequality of the capitalist market-place. Under capitalism, individual labourers—because of their dependence on continued employment for day-to-day sustenance—are in a weak position to influence the operation of the labour market and at a severe disadvantage when it comes to bargaining with capital for better terms. Collectively, labourers can deprive capital of a workforce through strikes or work stoppages, thus greatly increasing their ability to gain concessions through collective bargaining from the owners of the means of production (Taylor, 1987).

Successful collective organization or unionization of labour is no simple task because capital can single out and penalize individual workers for advocating and promoting such activities. For unionization to occur, workers must be willing to risk individual penalties for future collective benefits. Conversely, union strength stems from the collective withholding of labour from capital, but such action encourages capitalists to pay more for scarce labour, which in turn provides an increased incentive for individual workers to break ranks and return to work. The power to withhold labour also diminishes in strength with turns in the business cycle and the rise of unemployment. This leads to a paradox whereby the economic and political strength of labour reaches its zenith during times of full employment and plunges to its nadir during economic slowdowns and changes, just when it is needed the most. Once again, successful organization means workers must place their collective interests ahead of their individual interests or, at least, place long-term prospects ahead of short-term gains.

The collective organization of labour, particularly by means of unions, then forces employers to deal with labour as one, thus greatly increasing the market power of each worker. To be sure, employers use all sorts of means to resist such attempts to change market power and even workers find it difficult to stay united for collective gains. Indeed, for a long period union activity was considered a form of untoward manipulative activity—verging on illegal conspiracy—discouraged and at times forcefully suppressed by the state.

Alternatively, unionization and collective organization can be abetted by the state, which can use its authority to facilitate union organization, legitimize collective bargaining, and even prohibit employers from engaging in vindictive activities against workers and their leaders. In most modern nation-states, a more tolerant policy towards unions accompanied democratization and the extension of the franchise because of attempts by political parties to gain the electoral support of workers. This has resulted in the existence of a complex system of labour or industrial relations in which the state regulates the relationship between labour and capital.

For the labour movement to pursue policy objectives beyond issues of industrial relations it needs to gain greater organizational power. Individual unions have to amalgamate and then combine into central labour organizations. These larger organizations, theoretically, then have the capacity to influence government decision-making in areas of social life that affect workers' interests. They can work, for instance, at influencing the redistribution of income through the tax system or at otherwise altering the market advantages enjoyed by the owners of the means of production.

In Europe, the emergence of trade unions and their centrals was intertwined with the development of labour and social democratic political parties. Thus the labour movement was comprised of both trade unions and an organized political party competing for parliamentary power in a formal or informal alliance with a union movement. Unions, in this model, were instrumental agents pushing for the extension of the franchise and other forms of democratization—such as industrial and economic democracy—and could achieve a greater role in the management of the work, in corporate-level decisions, and in ownership of assets.

In actual fact, there is a great diversity within the organization of labour in Western Europe. The high levels of union density and highly centralized industrial unionism in Sweden contrasts with the fragmented craft unionism in the United Kingdom and the low density and high fragmentation of French organized labour. In much of the postwar period, the northern European social democratic model, represented in large part by Sweden, was associated with highly centralized corporatist processes of representation and decision-making in labour policy and collective bargaining, making it a model for many other labour movements to emulate. The message appeared clear. The centralization and unification of labour leads to political strength and progressive labour relations and social policy, as well as efficient capitalism. Yet, comparative analysis indicates that much more than the centralization of labour unions was at play in the shaping of northern European social democracy. In France, for example, the union density is low and the labour movement has been fragmented by ideological and partisan cleavages. Nevertheless, under the French regime of industrial relations, about 90 per cent of the workforce is covered by collective agreements (see Figure 1). The critical issue for the study of the labour movement, therefore, is not simply how it is organized but also how it is able to influence the political context of its relationship with capital.

There are large differences between European and North American patterns. In Canada, and to even a greater extent the United States, democratization and capitalist development preceded the development of trade unions, which provided for a different complexion to the politics of organized labour. By mid-century North American unions had developed a hybrid organizational structure that combined craft and industrial unionism (Pontusson, 1992). Since that time the Canadian and American labour movements have diverged, with Canada becoming more of a cross between European and American models. Canada's industrial relations regime, however, remains more liberal than corporatist or social democratic.

Figure 1: Union Density and Collective Bargaining Coverage, Selected Industrialized Countries, 1990*

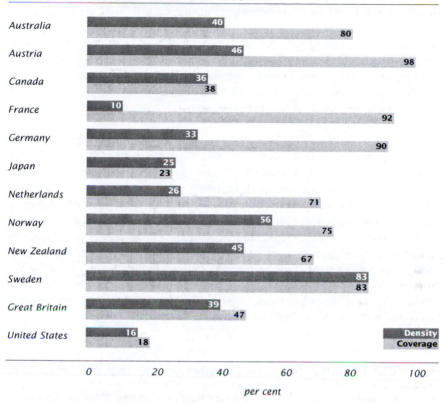

*Union density refers to the number of trade union members as a percentage of wage and salary earners. Collective bargaining coverage rate refers to the number of workers covered by collective agreements negotiated by unions as a percentage of wage and salary earners. methodological differences in how countries collect these data make direct comparability difficult.

Source: OECD, 1994, *Employment Outlook July 1994.*

Four broad sets of ideas have worked to shape the Canadian labour movement. First, Canadian unions' operating strategy has been what is referred to as *business unionism*, which is the tendency to view unions primarily as a means to redistribute income and bring stability to the work process. Second, *social unionism*—the desire to use unions as a key agent seeking broad labour goals in extending democracy, eliminating social and gender inequalities, and sometimes establishing a form of socialism—has been an integral and an increasingly important part of Canadian labour politics. Third, *confessional unionism* in Quebec was organized originally by the Roman Catholic Church and shared with social unionism a collective view of workers under capitalism. However, it departed from radical thought by advocating ideas of establishing harmony and co-operation between management and labour. Fourth, *classical liberalism* and *neo-liberalism* view unions as actors of questionable democratic legitimacy that distort markets and impede economic growth. Nineteenth-century liberalism was suspicious of the formation and recognition of unions; contemporary neo-liberalism seeks to reduce the autonomy of union leadership by increasing their accountability to their membership, the public, and the state—a political strategy that could weaken the bargaining power of labour within the political economy.

The ability of key actors within the political economy to shape the labour movement and industrial relations policies, or labour regime, according to their ideas has always been a political process. At the micro level, the conflict between labour and capital is often termed a 'struggle', for it is a conflict that until relatively recently had few rules and an umpire of questionable impartiality. At the macro level, the issue has always been how organized labour and the mass labour constituency can influence public policy and/or participate in governance through a political party, be it agrarian in the early parts of the century or a social democratic party in the latter parts. For capital, the issue has been similar, though somewhat narrower in focus: how to conduct labour relations that pursue labour peace, secure management rights, and contribute to corporate profitability and economic efficiency.

Colonial Canada: Staples, Immigration, and Paternalism

When the British Empire consolidated its hold over North America during the mid-eighteenth century its society was undergoing a slow transition to capitalist wage markets, particularly in agriculture (Dobb, 1964; Weber, [1904] 1958). Canada was tied to the changing British economy by means of its staples industries (fish, fur, agriculture, timber) and the mercantilist trade policy that structured relations between colony and empire. Those within Great Britain who were displaced by the process of transformation and industrialization often emigrated to colonies in North America, then to Australia and New Zealand.

Curiously, the British wage system was not simply extended to Canada. According to one of Canada's foremost labour historians, Bryan Palmer (1992), the development of a broad wage market would wait another century. What emerged was a labour force fragmented by different experiences but united by *paternalistic* economic and political structures and grounded on an agricultural base.

This colonial economy was dominated by merchant capital engaged in staples trade. In the cases of fur and fish, colonial authorities discouraged either permanent settlement or the development of capitalist wage relations. Thus fishers, voyageurs, and Aboriginal peoples were not incorporated within broad wage markets and did not emerge as an industrial workforce. Instead, a unique form of *independent commodity production* dominated the labour market development until the middle of the nineteenth century. The majority of original settlers were either military conscripts or indentured servants, a system that predominated until the first decade of the nineteenth century (Pentland, 1981; 1991). The original labour system included the institution of slavery of both African and Aboriginal peoples until 1800.

The powerful colonial staples merchants seeded the development of a permanent labour force by establishing linked economic activities: from the fur trade came hat manufacturers, from the timber trade came a powerful shipbuilding industry, and from grain merchants and governments came canals and other large infrastructure projects that necessitated large workforces. As the population increased, so did small manufactories based on the home market that employed a handful of employees, often as apprentices. Aboriginal peoples by and large were not drawn into these processes for a complex of reasons, not the least of which was their marginalization by the three centuries of European contact that preceded the development of a permanent labour force.

Immigration, agriculture, and the closure of the land frontier worked to provide the final bases for the formation of the labour force. The Canadian colonies received different waves of immigration. From the United States came the loyalists after the War of Independence and then the 'second-wave' loyalists after the War of 1812–14. From the United Kingdom came craft workers, small farmers, and peasants displaced by industrialization and the transformation to capitalist wage markets in agriculture. These immigrants, particularly the Irish, were destined to be pioneer farmers. Ironically, immigration patterns changed during the tragedy popularly known as the Irish potato famine (Houston and Smyth, 1990). Increasingly, famine victims went to the United States, where western expansion and emerging urban labour markets could absorb large increases. In the British North American colonies, the land frontier was closed and urban and industrial labour markets were not strong enough to absorb large increases. Still, the Canadian population grew from about two million in the late 1840s to about 3.2 million in 1861 (Lower, 1946; Palmer, 1992; Buckley and Urquhart, 1965) as a result of this immigration.

New immigration flowed to all the principal urban centres as well as the agricultural frontier. Farming then provided the last and greatest source of wage labour. This was so simply because the land frontier was closed to immigrants until the mid-nineteenth century. In Quebec, the existing feudal organization of agriculture meant that most land had already been allocated. In Upper Canada, lands had been parcelled out under the Family Compact. High land costs and continued immigration induced many to seek subsistence livelihood as tenant farmers or agricultural labourers. This pool of labour was then absorbed into urban services and manufacturing oriented towards the home market. The governing oligarchies of Upper and Lower Canada, as discussed in the previous chapter, wanted to induce the emergence of a labouring class as opposed to a class of independent farmers.

Paternal authority oversaw social, religious, and political as well economic affairs. It reflected an established social hierarchy based not simply on wealth and landownership, but also on religion and ethnicity. There was a world of difference, for example, between the congregations and social thought of the nineteenth-century state Church of England and that of the Methodism (and other dissenter religions) of many immigrant communities and the Catholicism of the French-Canadian majority. Paternalism also included patriarchal relations of power and the subjection of women. Though the family was the basic unit of production, men had legal power over the labour of their wives and children (Cohen, 1988). Women, therefore, though they contributed equally to the subsistence livelihood of pioneer and tenant farm families, had no direct rights to participate in decisions about the distribution of family property.

Over time the paternal bond between patron and immigrant labour crumbled. Colonial paternalism was challenged in the 1837–8 rebellions but not immediately removed. By mid-century, paternalism had given way to the establishment of a broad labour market. Worker efforts to improve wages and working conditions took the form of local and site-specific strikes and work stoppages. Landless immigrants employed on large-scale canal projects on the Ottawa and St Lawrence river systems organized the first large-scale collective labour resistance to capital. The workers, mainly Irish immigrants, protested appallingly poor working and living conditions, and their work stoppages and strike activities rapidly spilled over into other areas of economic activity, including the timber trade, which employed large numbers of Irish and Québécois workers (Cross, 1973; Pentland, 1981).

Despite the strides in economic development taken during the century after consolidation of British rule, economic life remained precarious. For example, when economic fortunes failed both before and shortly after Confederation, workers simply emigrated to the United States to find better conditions. In fact, this emigration throughout the latter half of the nineteenth century consistently undermined Canadian government efforts to increase the labour force through immigration (Porter, 1965). This would only be changed with the development of the National Policy.

Liberal Unionism Under the National Policy

After Confederation, the labour force, the labour movement, and industrial relations policies changed significantly. A mobile labour force responded to urban and resource industrialization, the rise of mass manufacturing, and the merger and concentration of industry into large corporate entities. A growing and dynamic labour movement now was dominated by craft unions. However, union density remained thin and the labour movement maintained many inequities of the earlier system of labour relations and authority patterns. The pattern of organized labour formed in Canada reflected a complicated set of cleavages that had developed between capital and labour and within the continental and national labour movement itself. In addition, the labour movement and system of industrial relations reflected the national and regional institutional cleavages within the broader political community. As a whole, the movement remained fragmented, decentralized, and dominated by international (that is, American-based) craft unions. Accordingly, the system of industrial relations adopted in Canada replaced the subordination of labour under paternalism by a liberal and business-oriented system that tolerated but did not advance collective bargaining.

Craft Unions and Liberal Industrial Relations

At Confederation official labour policy discouraged labour organization and legislation rendered many workers' collectives illegal as the common-law tradition regarded unions as a form of conspiracy in restraint of trade. By 1872, however, federal legislation had decriminalized labour organization.

Labour unrest in the period led to a royal commission and the creation of a Department of Labour, whose deputy minister was the future long-serving Prime Minister, William Lyon Mackenzie King, an internationally recognized expert in industrial relations. The department's intent was to get both sides in an industrial conflict into a process of independent arbitration where strikes and walkouts would be suspended until an independent investigation could be completed and non-binding recommendations made. This was a voluntary—not a mandatory—policy whereby the Dominion government responded to requests for assistance from capital or labour. For unions, this offered both the prospect of recognition and the enforceability of contracts gained through collective bargaining. For business, it represented a means to avoid the costs of strikes and sympathy strikes—to reduce risk and uncertainty in labour relations. In the 1907 Industrial Disputes Investigations Act, this policy was authoritatively extended to key sectors of the economy, a move that established the prototype of the contemporary industrial relations system (Kealey, 1973; Palmer, 1992). The IDIA legalized strike activity, but only after a compulsory investigation by a conciliation board of the reasons behind the dispute. This legislation was to provide a relatively stable system of industrial relations throughout the economic expansion of the 1910s and 1920s, while the poor economic conditions of the 1930s served to 'discipline' workers through the threat of unemployment.

The industrial relations system reflected the contemporary political boundaries of business, labour, and government. Ostensibly, government policy was to serve as umpire—to regulate conflict in order to establish a form of fair play in industrial disputes. Clearly, however, the state was not an impartial referee. Governments were concerned with the effects of strikes on essential services and the overall effect of strikes and labour unrest on key parts of the economy—not in extending unionization. For these reasons, the IDIA responded more to the needs of capital than of labour. Certainly, unions gained the ability to enforce hard-won contracts. But the cost was to lose control over the ability to time strikes and other job actions strategically and to ally with other unions in common cause, costs that focused industrial relations on the specific workplace and significantly reduced union powers in industrial conflict. So the industrial relations system induced labour and management to work together but within very circumscribed limits. The major objectives of the labour movement during the National Policy, therefore, were simply to organize workers and get employers to sign contracts with them.

The TLC and Hegemony of International Craft Unions

Several ideas competed as to how best to organize workers. The dominant but not exclusive stream of ideas came from the *business unionism* of craft unions. Trade unions based on the craft apprenticeship principle had been formed in Canada by weavers, printers, cigar-makers, dock workers, bakers, and other skilled workers before Confederation. Craft unions wanted to maintain their monopoly over employment in particular crafts—sometimes called 'professions'—and to exercise control over the work process in the face of management's attempts to break skilled craft processes into unskilled mass manufacturing jobs. In the earlier years of Confederation, struggles between employers and employees over such items as the 12-hour and nine-hour day were successfully led by indigenous skilled labour organizations, including, especially, the unions in Ontario affiliated with the Toronto Trades Assembly. These groups were able to create monopolies or near-monopolies in specific skilled activities. They could discipline strikebreakers by removing their credentials or certifications, and they governed admittance to the trades through apprenticeship requirements. As a result these unions were able to compel owners to improve wages and working conditions in specific sectors. The great majority of workers, however, possessed few skills and were employed in activities requiring even fewer. The craft-based labour organizations saw little advantage for their members in organizing other, less-skilled workers, who tended to be left to their own devices.

Beginning in the years immediately before Confederation, many of the craft unions began to affiliate with larger craft unions based in the United States. Although motivated to some degree by international solidarity, the unions were also responding to the poor economic circumstances in Canada, since membership in US unions allowed Canadian craft workers access to jobs south of the border (Logan, 1928, 1948; Lipton, 1967). By 1886 the Canadian craft unions had formed the Trades and Labour Congress (TLC), a national central of craft unions closely affiliated with the American Federation of Labor (AFL), the head of the large US craft-based union movement. During the 1902–12 period, the TLC model was adopted on a provincial level in Ontario, British Columbia, and Alberta.

Affiliation between the two centrals gave the TLC unions greater organizational resources. But there was a price to be paid. AFL leadership feared that Canada would become a haven for cheap labour that would undercut the wages of US craft workers. Accordingly, in 1902 when the Canadian TLC became the central for the affiliates of US international craft unions, it was then forced to 'shut out' independent Canadian unions. The TLC assumed the status of a state-level US organization within the powerful AFL, splitting the Canadian labour movement between independents (as in the powerful railway workers craft unions) and the TLC international unions.

Regional organization in Quebec did not follow the English-Canadian TLC model, although craft unions were influential in the provincial labour movement. In most of English Canada after 1886 the Knights of Labor began to wane and after 1902 their locals were legally absorbed by the TLC. The Quebec locals, however, did not disband or affiliate. Eventually a *confessional unionism* took over the Quebec labour movement. According to Palmer (1992: 191–2), the switch from community to Church-based organization and the refusal to be absorbed within the TLC -AFL alliance reflected two unique features of Quebec labour politics: nationalism and religious conservatism. The Roman Catholic Church leadership took an active organizational role in the province around the time of World War I. By 1921 the Church had organized 96 *syndicats* and formed the Confederation of Catholic Workers of Canada (Confédération des Travailleurs Catholiques du Canada).

The Catholic Church's goals differed from those of international craft unions. The Church was concerned that it was losing the support of the working poor, and thus the new confessional unions assumed that the clergy, throughout the Catholic world, would play a central role in mediating conflicts and tensions between labour and capital. To be sure, the Church view of capitalism stressed harmony and co-operation and, like most craft and business unionism, rejected socialism, class conflict, and revolution (Latham, 1930). On the other hand, the *syndicats* did not have the restricted social interests of the TLC craft unions. As a result, they were more open and, over time, tended to include more of the unskilled and general industrial workers from such sectors as the pulp and paper industry and asbestos mining into their ranks. As a whole, the success of the confessional trade union movement in Quebec reflected the power of the conservative nationalism of Church and intellectuals that prioritized national survival—the messianic mission of Church, state, and nation.

Elsewhere in Canada *social unionism* that linked labour organization to a broad program of social and economic change surfaced primarily in the industrial and resource sector and, after the turn of the century, became increasingly influenced by currents of socialist thinking. Early working-class struggles laid the groundwork for *community-based organization* carried out by the Canadian branches of the US-based Knights of Labor in the early years of Confederation (Palmer, 1992; Palmer and Kealey, 1982). The Knights sought to bring a broad labour agenda to politics and developed an extensive network in Ontario and Quebec. Initially, they had some successes organizing strikes in Ontario manufacturing industries and lumber towns, but they were unable to prevent employers from offering higher wages and better conditions to strikebreakers. The Knights did not have the workplace focus, the membership solidarity, or the financial resources necessary to conduct prolonged job actions. By the turn of the century the organization had disappeared from the English-Canadian labour scene.

In the resource industries, workers had long resorted to strikes and work stoppages to press their demands for better wages and working conditions (Hamelin, Larocque, and Rouillard, 1970). But they began to form separate trade unions only after 1900. Disdained by craft unions for their unskilled membership and in turn disdaining craft unions for their 'aristocratic' pretensions, in western Canada workers in the resource sector began to form unions with a decidedly militant, socialist, and internationalist flavour, such as the mass-based Industrial Workers of the World (IWW) and the One Big Union (OBU), which led strikes among resource workers in both western and central Canada before and immediately after World War I (Logan, 1948; Lembcke and Tattam, 1984). In the resource sector by the mid-1920s the various industrial unions in English Canada united to form a national, industrial central, the All-Canadian Congress of Labour (ACCL) (Lipton, 1967; Palmer, 1992). This organization competed with the TLC and Catholic trade unions for the allegiance of the country's workers, but in the end it stood as a minority voice in a labour movement still dominated by craft unions. These industrial unions clashed repeatedly with both employers and craft unions. The craft unions were much more moderate in their approach to collective bargaining and tended to side with employers on many key issues.

Much production also continued to remain outside of any form of labour organization, most notably the work of owner-operated family farms or independent commodity producers in the agricultural sector. Owner-operators, or farmers, tended to organize not into trade unions, which are institutions created to improve the market conditions of wage labour *vis-à-vis* employers, but into co-operative organizations created to challenge the unequal market advantage enjoyed by refiners, grain handlers, and transportation companies. Broad-based farmers' movements mobilized along particular economic and political agendas. Although there were instances of farmer-labour alliances, for the most part they took different patterns of organization.

Labour and agricultural politics in the West, especially, took on a particular regional hue. On the prairies, most labour derived from the exigencies of the export wheat economy. Within the primarily family farm unit, women's and men's labour and income depended on successfully growing and selling one cash crop, which resulted in a much more volatile set of conditions for independent producers and fewer opportunities for women. Not surprisingly, this was the origin of much social (reform-oriented) feminism and novel forms of labour organization. Most farmers eventually organized into social movements that rejected alliances with organized labour and much of the political focus of the early farmers' movement concerned the political inequality of staples trade— opposing railway monopolies, private grain exchanges, and financial and other 'big' interests that shaped staples trade in their favour (Laycock, 1990). Given the concentration of insecure western producers in the prairies while central Canada maintained the powerful industrial, political, and financial interests, it is not surprisingly that the farmers' movement became intertwined both with regionalism and with a critique of conventional politics. Over time, and especially after the Winnipeg General Strike of 1919, the rift widened between farmers and organized labour.

Throughout this formative period the connections between politics and unions were very poor. Influence on the electoral process is often achieved through the use of labour parties, which exist in many countries under a variety of names. In Canada, early political alliances between workers and farmers enjoyed successes in Ontario and the prairie provinces, although these coalitions—in parties such as the United Farmers of Alberta, the United Farmers of Manitoba, and the United Farmers of Ontario—were dominated by farmers. The same was true of the Progressive Party, which contested elections at the federal level after 1920. As the significance of farmers declined with the industrialization of Canada, so, too, did the fortunes of these parties. Various early labour parties and candidates were limited by the same liberal world-view that bounded the industrial relations system. Other, more radical views did not receive meaningful political support.

In summary, then, National Policy industrialization was not a period of labour triumph. Though the labour movement had grown and responded to significant shifts in the political economy, labour density was still low and the industrial relations system still discouraged collective organization and bargaining except when they met business interests. Crucial labour defeats occurred after World War I, particularly with the ill-fated Winnipeg General Strike. Politically, labour remained weak and isolated.

Modern Canada: Fordism and Industrial Legality

During the 1930s the labour movement, through a series of internal conflicts, began responding to changes in industrial production that occurred in this era. The Depression experience also challenged the neoclassical liberal orthodoxy that had historically permeated state intervention by introducing new sets of ideas on the role of the state in managing capitalism (Hall, 1989). By the 1940s a new *industrial unionism* had redefined the labour market and pressed for what Palmer (1992) terms 'industrial legality'—the compulsory recognition of unions and enforceability of negotiated contracts. New Keynesian ideas, wartime exigencies, full employment, competition for the labour vote, and acquiescence from US capital all worked to provide the conditions under which different forms of industrial legality were eventually institutionalized across Canada. During the next decade the model was extended throughout the established industrial sectors of the Canadian economy and accompanied the articulation of the modern Canadian welfare state. As in the case of the earlier ascension of craft unionism, Canadian industrial unionism outside Quebec was led by the US labour movement. The dominance of the US model of industrial unionism continued throughout the Cold War period.

There were also great continuities. Initial drives to organize the female-dominated retail sales sector failed. As a result, labour markets, trade unions, and industrial relations policies all tended to reinforce historically entrenched segmentation, patriarchy, and gender inequalities, despite the increasing participation rates of women in the labour force. The labour movement was still marked by important regional and national differences. Despite its new organizational face, Canadian organized labour was still following patterns set in the United States, and its centrals were dominated by international affiliates. The conflict between social and business unionism, therefore, took the shape of a conflict between the established internationals and the more radical national and independent unions.

By the 1960s, however, the stability of the established model was in question. Quebec's Quiet Revolution would set new standards as the modernization of its labour movement and industrial relations system occurred outside of the Depression–World War II–Cold War context. In addition, those left out of the industrial model—women, white-collar workers, immigrants, and the public sector—wanted to gain the benefits of unionization and the protection of legalized industrial relations. These new forces were distinctly nationalist in orientation, supported by a form of Canadian 'new left' and would seed the formation of a more uniquely Canadian labour movement.

Déja Vu: The Ascendancy of International Industrial Unionism and Industrial Legality

The 1930s brought massive deflation as well as unemployment. Some sectors, such as mass manufacturing, were hit worse than others, such as mining and pulp and paper. Export agriculture, based primarily in the prairie provinces, was hit by both drought and a loss of traditional markets. Under the inherited industrial relations regime employers were compelled neither to recognize unions nor to negotiate contracts. In the Depression environment union strength began to deteriorate seriously. Moreover, labour's problems could not be tackled within the framework of craft unionism.

In the United States, a Committee for Industrial Organization, representing the industrial unions, formed within the AFL. Organizing all employees within an industrial sector would greatly increase labour's bargaining strength, but it also threatened the privileged position of the craft unions. The CIO and its affiliates, after being expelled from the AFL, formed an independent central, the Congress of Industrial Organizations (CIO). The CIO platform became intertwined with the Democratic Party and US President Franklin Roosevelt's New Deal legislation. In particular, legislation protecting union members from intimidation and unjust dismissal led to the passage of the Wagner Act, designed to facilitate the move towards the recognition of industrial unions. In Canada, the domination of AFL affiliates in the TLC meant that the transition to industrial unionism would also manifest itself as a conflict within the labour movement. Canadian industrial unions attempted to make alliances and draw organizational resources from the

CIO during the 1930s. However, CIO-affiliated unions were eventually expelled from the TLC in 1939, which led them to ally with the older ACCL to form a new central for industrial unions, the Canadian Congress of Labour (CCL) (Palmer, 1992; Heron, 1996).

Political conditions in Canada during the 1930s also worked against industrial organization. First, the federal government's leading role in industrial relations policy ended during the 1920s when judicial review made industrial relations a provincial field of jurisdiction. In 1925 the Judicial Committee of the Privy Council ruled in the case of *Sniderman vs the Toronto Board of Electric Commissioners* that labour-management relations were contractual relations that, with the exception of federal employees, fell within provincial jurisdiction. From 1925 to 1939 the provinces, led by Ontario and British Columbia, began to implement their own systems of industrial relations. The importance of jurisdiction should not be overstated: the federal government retained authority over its own employees and those in federally owned or regulated industries. The conventions of the IDIA model of industrial relations prevailed. Some provinces even kept federal regulation.

In 1934 the Quebec government intervened in labour markets to establish a long-lived decree system in which the government was empowered to extend collective agreements to unorganized sectors and to set wage scales for whole sectors (Boivin and Déom, 1995). Since many of the pioneer activists in the industrial unionization movement had ties with the Communist Party or with the new CCF, they became targets for and perhaps excuses for conservative provincial politicians to clamp down on unions and to enforce the fairly docile Catholic labour relations system that had characterized the Depression (Heron, 1996; Palmer, 1992).

During the 1939–45 war political and economic contours changed. Economically, the war effort vastly increased the pace of recovery and the pace of industrialization. Wartime and war-related industrialization necessitated full co-operation and personal and social sacrifice from key sectors of the political economy. Under the War Measures Act, the terms of the IDIA were extended over much of the economy and the federal government even controlled labour mobility. Nevertheless, Canadian business still kept to its traditional non-recognition policy towards unions and would not let unionists sit on joint industry-government management boards. As a result the unions then refused to abide by a 'no strike' policy during the war (Heron, 1996; Palmer, 1992).

Wartime full employment brought important changes: increased participation of women in war industries, and a changed social psychology of expectations that, as the war dragged on, took the form of planning for a better postwar order. One of the political manifestations of these changes in Canada was a new labour militancy, which escalated by 1943 to a record number of strikes and job actions and a revival of fortunes for the CCF. Clearly, the old liberal labour relations policy was neither economically nor politically effective. In order to buy labour peace, facilitate the industrial war effort, and avoid alienating labour from the

Liberal Party fold, Prime Minister Mackenzie King's war cabinet passed an Order in Council, PC 1003, that effectively restructured the industrial relations system without legislation or great debate. In characteristically ambiguous terms, PC 1003 obliged companies to recognize unions and negotiate binding contracts with employees' representatives. The ambiguity of this wartime decision had several pointed implications. The decision was tentative, so the Canadian government had an avenue of escape should conditions change in the postwar period. As well, it provided an avenue for corporations to institutionalize company unions and their own human resources policies as alternatives to the new federal union recognition labour policy (Palmer, 1992).

PC 1003 opened the floodgates for restructuring both the labour movement and the system of industrial relations. (See Figure 2 for statistics on Canadian union membership during the twentieth century.) Essentially, the official embrace of industrial unionism supplied needed political resources to the fledgling CIO and independent industrial unions. As is often the case in labour relations, the critical defining point was a strike, in this case the prolonged 1945 strike at the Ford Motor Company in Windsor, Ontario. Ford had maintained an 'open shop',

Figure 2: Union Membership in Canada, 1911–1996

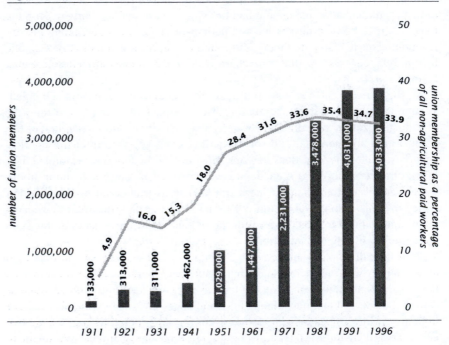

Source: Reproduced with the permission of the Minister of Public Works and Government Services Canada, 1997; from Krahn and Lowe, 1998: 332.

meaning that it employed both unionized and non-unionized employees, a labour policy that seriously undercut the union bargaining position. Following intervention the issue was resolved by the formula that transformed the open shop into the union shop. A union was recognized to be the official bargaining representative for the workforce if it had been democratically and legally certified by the government as having support from a majority in the workplace. The reasoning of the *Rand Formula*, named after Supreme Court Justice Ivan Rand, who arbitrated the case, was that no single employee could be forced to join a union. However, that employee would benefit from union bargaining activity. Accordingly, companies were obliged to recognize unions as bargaining agents for all employees and to deduct dues from payroll income on behalf of unions. PC 1003 and the Rand Formula then became the conventions in industrial relations legislation passed by the federal Parliament and provinces. In 1948 the federal Industrial Relations and Disputes Investigations Act (IRDIA) confirmed both the conventions of the industrial relations regime that had developed during the war and also the importance of provincial regulation (Jenson and Mahon, 1993).

The Cold War, nevertheless, helped to turn industrial unionism into a conservative business unionism. During the previous two decades the CCF and the Communist Party of Canada (CPC) competed for positions of leadership within the labour movement. The CCF had been more entrenched within the TLC-AFL unions and the CPC, weak as an electoral force, had concentrated on the growing industrial unions. The Soviet-Allied alliance during World War II had given the CPC a temporary status of respectability, though the CPC's open support for the ruling Liberals in the pursuit of the war effort solidified the enmity of its social democratic rivals. The tables turned the following decade. Communist enemies were now threatening international war and domestic subversion. Inordinate CCF energy was spent on factionalism and expelling Communists from the union movement. Anticommunism was a goal and ideology that brought together the interests of the CCF, domestic and international business, the US industrial unions that dominated the Canadian labour movement, the older TLC affiliates, and provincial and federal governments. The movement to industrial legality was uneven across the federation because provincial jurisdictions used the pretext of anticommunism to weaken unions and labour demands. The 1949 Quebec Asbestos strike, for example, revealed that the regime of Premier Maurice Duplessis would not allow any significant change from the old industrial relations regime—and provided one of the pivotal events that propelled the Quiet Revolution.

As a measure of continuing Canadian dependency, final TLC-CCF unity would await moves to settle the AFL-CIO split in the United States. By 1956, however, when the US rift had been settled, the Canadian craft and industrial centrals, as well as several notable independents, united to form the Canadian Labour Congress (CLC). Throughout the 1950s unionism had spread as the structure of the Canadian economy changed to reflect massive foreign direct investment in the manufacturing and resource sectors and as the industrial workplaces themselves adopted technologies and processes of mass production, sometimes referred to as Fordism. As a result, Canadian locals of US international unions comprised over 70 per cent of affiliates within the CLC. In the same year Quebec industrial unions joined to form a large central in the province, the Quebec Federation of Labour (QFL), a rival organization to the renamed Catholic central, the Confederation of National Trade Unions (CNTU).

Forces for Change: Public-Sector Unions, the National Questions, and Youth

As the generation that fought for, institutionalized, and led the new labour regime reached the 1960s, it may have comfortably felt that a real historical plateau had been attained. Labour had achieved industrial legality, economic growth, and an unfolding welfare state. The lacklustre CCF was being transformed into the New Democratic Party, with more direct links to the industrial unions that became the backbone of the new union movement. The future did not continue to arrive as expected.

The labour movement had been transformed, at least in its organizational form, into an established force with conservative business unionism ideology. In part, formalism and union bureaucratization were the price to be paid for industrial legality. In addition, union density had levelled off and had not gone beyond the obvious highly organizable workplaces. Large progressive corporations had also learned that the best way to offset labour problems was to work with unions and establish their own human resources capacity. This sort of formalism and legalism did not speak directly to the 1960s youth movement, and as the decade produced increased labour militancy, wildcat strikes, and labour demands it was clear that the business unionism espoused by the leadership did not meet the social and political aspirations of large segments of the workforce.

The most challenging workplaces still existed outside of the organized labour movement. Public-sector workers, in particular, lobbied to gain collective bargaining rights. With some exceptions, the convention governing civil servants was that their employment security, benefits, and easy workloads (in comparison to the private sector) provided a justification for low wages. By the 1960s, however, it was clear that none of these old myths held true. Private-sector employment had more security and benefits, and there was all-party agreement that low civil servant salaries should not be used to balance budgets (Morton, 1990). Quebec civil servants gained the right to strike in 1964 and Canadian public-sector employees were provided a similar model in the 1967 federal Public Service Staff Relations Act (PSSRA). The PSSRA model, which gives unions a choice between binding arbitration and collective bargaining, was eventually adopted by other Canadian jurisdictions. The new labour regime provided an impetus to organize and unify public-sector employee associations. In 1961 there were only 15 public-sector unions. By 1981 there were 71, and total membership in those unions had risen from 183,000 to 1.5 million. As a proportion of unionized workers, public-sector members in 1961 accounted for only 12.5 per cent of union members; by 1981 the figure was close to 40 per cent. Teachers and hospital workers also joined union ranks in the mid-1970s, and the affiliation of public-sector workers to trade unions was responsible for most of the general growth of unionization throughout this period. By the end of the decade unions of government workers had become some of the largest in Canada (Kumar, 1986). By 1981 the three largest public-sector unions at the local, provincial, and federal levels, the Canadian Union of Public Employees (CUPE), the Public Service Alliance of Canada (PSAC), and the National Union of Provincial Government Employees (NUPGE), had 267,000, 210,000, and 155,000 members respectively. This growth had a significant impact on the balance of power within the labour movement.

The emergence of public-sector unions rekindled some aspects of the old social unionism within a predominantly business-oriented labour movement. They also became one of the most important entry points for women into the labour movement. During the 1960s and 1970s the pattern of women's participation in the labour force changed dramatically. Women had entered the workforce on a permanent or part-time basis during all stages of life—and with the growing practice of family planning they were more and more likely to be part of the permanent full-time workforce. However, women were entering a fairly segmented labour market where particular white-collar service occupations became 'pink-collar' concentrations. In these circumstances, the old family wage system, under which men bargained for a wage to support a family, turned into an ideological convention used to justify wage gaps between men (primary earners) and women (secondary or supplemental income-earners). Public-sector unionism, therefore, became a means to address historical gender segmentation and stratification, to reduce wage gaps in public service occupations, and to bring a wider range of issues to labour politics. From 1961 to 1991 the percentage of women in unions increased from 16 to 40 per cent (Krahn and Lowe, 1998: 166–73, 346–51).

In Quebec, the Quiet Revolution ensured that the province's labour movement shed its confessional ideology. The CCTC had been transformed by the early 1960s into a secular union, the Confederation of National Trade Unions (CNTU). Eventually, the CNTU began to support fairly radical non-parliamentary social action—a manifestation of the complex relationship of labour, the left, and nationalism in Quebec. The language of industry, management, and technology for most of the century had been English, which meant that the French-speaking labour force was disadvantaged not only in pan-Canadian labour markets but also within the province. Non-Francophone élites controlled the majority of the province's economic assets and there were significant wage differentials between Francophones and Anglophones. Quebec labour's support of the Quiet Revolution, therefore, was also a means to ensure that Francophone working people had a future working in their own language. Without a historical legacy of social democracy within the province (until the arrival of the Parti Québécois in the late 1970s) the CNTU and newly organized teachers and public-sector workers became central actors pursuing a social democratic vision within the nationalist movement (Hebert, 1993).

Nationalism was also significant outside Quebec but took on a more complex and diffuse form as the Canadian and American labour movements developed different organizational and political characteristics. Since the public service in the United States did not enjoy collective bargaining rights and the new industrialization in the American sunbelt took place within open shop or 'right-to-work' environments, organized labour in the US faced insecurity and declining growth. In Canada, consequently, older national unions, the new public-sector unions, and newer industrial unions began to question the orthodoxy of Canadian unions' international branch-plant status. Palmer (1992: 317–20) indicates that by 1978 national unions independent of the CLC comprised fully 20 per cent of organized workers in Canada. At the time a new rival union central organization, the Confederation of Canadian Unions (CCU), emerged, attempting to become a national alternative to the internationalist CLC. The CLC, for its part, developed a set of minimum guidelines for the autonomy of Canadian affiliates of US internationals.

Finally, the security of industrial legality was shattered during the 1970s when inflation and then stagflation induced governments to suspend free collective bargaining for different forms of wage and price controls—generally, and then selectively for the public sector. Forms of wage controls were supported across the board, from the ruling Liberal Party in Ottawa to the new NDP governments in British Columbia and Manitoba, to the PQ (after the 1980 referendum).

Globalization

By the early 1980s it was clear that the international conditions that had propelled the Canadian political economy into three decades of economic growth had changed. Instead, new realities shaping the contours of state intervention were dramatically affecting the labour market, the labour movement, and industrial relations (Bradford, 1998b). First, the internationalization of investment, trade, and finance after 1945 had produced, by the late 1980s, a complex global economy marked by increasing regional integration and competition. The regulation of this more competitive environment by means of new regional economic and trade regimes—such as the FTA, NAFTA, the European Union, and APEC—changed the geographic space in which economic policy is conducted (Anderson et al., 1998). Canada became more a part of a North American bloc dominated by the United States than was the case earlier.

Labour, Training, and Competitiveness

Labour markets have changed significantly (Banting and Beach, 1992; Krahn and Lowe, 1998). Some of the significant characteristics include: a rise in structural unemployment from technological displacement; a decline in full-time employment, particularly in the manufacturing and industrial sectors; the rise of part-time employment in a secondary labour market; an increasing participation rate of women (in relation to men) in the labour force; declining personal incomes; an increasing polarization of wage incomes; and a persistent problem of youth unemployment (Schenk and Anderson, 1995).

The position of labour in the postwar economy was buttressed by the institutionalization of the welfare state and other forms of market intervention ostensibly promoting equality. By 1980, however, public-sector deficits invited an attack on public spending. The ensuing fiscal orthodoxy and pressures to maintain international competitiveness produced a constricting climate for labour. Regional integration under NAFTA was followed by severe recession in which 300,000 manufacturing jobs, many unionized, disappeared. Unemployment and economic insecurity made for a hostile environment for labour and partly account for low union membership and the prevailing labour peace during this time (Kumar, 1993; Lipsig-Mummé, 1995).

Industrial relations policies have reflected both the relative position of labour and new government priorities. In the United States, the rise of right-to-work legislation—meaning that employees do not have to join, pay dues to, or be represented by unions—has changed the fundamental characteristic of the labour regime. Certainly, the application of the Charter of Rights and Freedoms to collective agreements in Canada has highlighted the rights of individuals within unions and collective agreements and that public-sector institutions in particular must respect the Charter's collective as well as individual rights. The Charter was used to challenge the Rand Formula and thus effectively change Canadian union shops into open shops. The attempt failed, however, when the Supreme Court of Canada ruled that the Rand Formula conformed to the Charter of Rights and Freedoms and that social unionism did not contradict dissenting individuals rights (Carter, 1991). Change came from other quarters.

The changing gender composition of the workforce and labour movement has also resulted in attempts to organize in gender-segmented sectors and seek gender-related social policy objectives—a reflection of the 'feminization of labour' (Krahn and Lowe, 1998; CLC, 1997; Briskin and McDermott, 1993; Creese, 1995). Key objectives have been to address employment conditions and pay equity for women. Employment equity is the 'strategy to eliminate the effects of discrimination and to fully open the competition for job opportunities for those who have been excluded historically' (Krahn and Lowe, 1998: 190).

Drawing on the work of a 1984 Royal Commission on Equality of Employment (Abella, 1984), the federal government passed the 1986 Employment Equity Act (EEA) with the intent to improve working conditions for four categories of people: Aboriginal peoples, persons with disabilities, visible minorities, and women. For women, this has meant gaining access to non-traditional occupations as well as breaking into positions of organizational leadership. The EEA requires governments to recognize and remove barriers for these groups, to take measures so that they will become more representative within the workforce, and to take appropriate special measures to accomplish this task. Such policies are controversial because they go beyond conventional employment policies to target unintended systemic discrimination, such as rules and standards that happen to be exclusionary. In a very tangible way employment equity touches on key issues relating to individual and collective equality—not only in the workplace but also in public schools and universities (Cockburn, 1991; Fekete, 1994; Richer and Weir, 1995; Marchak, 1996)

Pay equity refers not simply to *equal pay for equal work*, but *equal pay for comparable work*. The key issue has been how to judge and decide scales of comparability, decisions that, given the lingering wage gap between men's and women's incomes, can entail the redistribution of billions of dollars (Weiner and Gunderson, 1990; Quaid, 1993; Fudge and McDermott, 1991). Like the issue of gender equity, the focus of policy has been on the public sector. Provincial human rights legislation is the primary means of addressing private-sector gender discrimination. Addressing the wage gap through changing pay scales has been highly controversial. For example, both the federal government and the Public Service Alliance have agreed with the principle of pay equity. However, in the late 1990s the two disagreed on a formula that would compensate for comparable worth. They are billions of dollars apart in their valuation of compensation. Inevitably, the issue of compensation for discrimination is bound to politics. Thus, for example, the NDP government in Ontario extended pay equity to the private sector, a move that was subsequently terminated by the succeeding Conservative government of Mike Harris.

The persistent budget deficits of governments throughout the 1980s provided the pretext for replacing collective bargaining with a series of legislated contracts and wage increases. Leo Panitch and Donald Swartz (1993) term the new public-sector labour regime 'permanent exceptionalism'. The inherited system of industrial legality within the private sector has also been changed at the margins, reflecting the ideology and policy intent of the governments in power (Russell, 1990, 1997a). Social democratic governments have tended to strengthen the position of unions within collective bargaining and to facilitate the unionization process, whereas Conservative and Liberal governments have tended to do the opposite.

Tensions between the exigencies of governance and the exigencies of organized labour have produced some serious rifts between the NDP and organized labour. At various times from 1981 to 1998, NDP governments in Manitoba, British Columbia, Saskatchewan, and Ontario largely maintained the general pattern of being tough on public-sector unions while strengthening the position of labour in the private sector. The NDP government of Bob Rae in Ontario provided the most notorious example. The Rae government came to power at the height of the post-FTA recession when the provincial economy lost over 200,000 permanent jobs. Initial labour legislation strengthened the position of organized labour by banning the use of replacement workers during strikes, a policy innovation first introduced by the Parti Québécois in 1977. Later, as the provincial government's burgeoning deficit called for austerity, the NDP looked to cutting the public-sector wage expenditures as an integral part of its fiscal strategy. Under the banner of 'social contract', the Ontario government altered existing collective agreements to freeze the public-sector wage bill for three years in return for a promise to further entrench public-sector collective bargaining in the future. Not surprisingly, the 'social contract' soured relations between labour and social democrats (McBride, 1996).

NAFTA, Labour, and Nationalisms

The treaties that define the current pattern of North American economic integration do not establish common standards for wages and working conditions, thus leaving labour costs as a key determinant of economic competitiveness among NAFTA members. While goods, investment, and some services are permitted complete mobility, people are not free to seek employment throughout North America, as is the case for citizens of the European Union. As a result, wage-earners are dependent on national labour markets, which has led to an overwhelmingly nationalist response to trade and investment liberalization on the part of the Quebec and Canadian labour movements.

The CLC, reflecting its American linkages, had been a key supporter of integration and continentalization of the economy until the recession of the early 1980s and its failed efforts to seek the support of Canadian business and the state for a new industrial strategy based on resource-based mega-projects (Smith, 1992). This failure led the CLC to defend the national markets for the purposes of protecting jobs. The CLC then became a major organizer of the anti-free trade forces—a policy that saw labour united with a variety of new social movements. In contrast, Canadian business, which traditionally had been split between an internationalist staples sector and a defensive manufacturing sector, dropped the historical preoccupation with the home market and trade protection to become a principal agent pushing for free trade.

The commitment of Canadian labour to nationalism was strengthened by the differential strategy taken by US labour during the 1980s. American organized labour practised concessionary bargaining that allowed companies to claw back wages and/or benefits in order to improve their competitive position, which in turn led to the withering of the US labour movement (Rogers, 1993; Kumar, 1993). The Canadian labour movement took the opposite stance of 'no concessions' bargaining within the industrial sector. Beginning with the celebrated breakaway of the Canadian Auto Workers (CAW) from the United Auto Workers, the Canadianization of the labour movement proceeded along the path of a well-publicized and successful 'no concessions' strategy (Yates, 1993). By the late 1980s, about 75 per cent of organized labour was affiliated with national unions. However, the meaning and success of 'no concessions' are difficult to pinpoint, as is discussed below. As well, the politicization of labour during this period caused further fragmentation of the union movement because the CLC's social unionism was not accepted by all. In particular, Canadian construction trades left the CLC to form a small Canadian Federation of Labour (CFL), constitutionally tied to a non-partisan business unionism.

Quebec labour's response to globalization has been to bury its radical social unionism for a more co-operative bargaining posture, sometimes termed 'defensive accommodation' (Lipsig-Mummé, 1993), to reinforce its position with the *souverainiste* political forces and to gain institutional autonomy from the pan-Canadian labour movement (Tanguay, 1993; Boivin and Déom, 1995). In many ways, therefore, the Quebec and Canadian movements have found themselves engaged in different and conflicting political projects. *Souverainistes* hold that the new international trade regimes represent a mechanism in which an independent Quebec can secure its international economic position outside of the Canadian common market. The importance of this internationalization to the independence movement is therefore more politically important than its costs to organized labour. The Parizeau government attempted, and almost succeeded, in selling this sovereignty as a form of social democratic nationalism in contrast to the allegedly cold and harsh neo-liberalism that was reshaping Canada (Gagnon and Lachapelle, 1996).

Redressing the Balance in Collective Bargaining: Organizational Changes

Collective agreements are the product of different and conflicting goals, constraints, and resources and of the relative strength of those bargaining. The postwar labour relations regime centred on the certification of unions at the workplace and induced the proliferation of small unions and locals. Table 24 illustrates the result. The structure of bargaining in Canada is fragmented and decentralized. Most bargaining occurs between a single union and a single employer in which union centrals can play only a small role. Each union does much of its own research, communications, and strategy work, activities that are paralleled by the central. Sectoral bargaining involving employers and a dominant union does occur, particularly in provincial public sectors such as health and education. Cases of negotiation between multiple employers and multiple unions are rare and tend to be reserved for sectors with a history of industrial relations problems. In an era of corporate restructuring, the decentralized and fragmented system places labour at a disadvantage in dealing, for example, with issues of employment security and labour adjustment.

This small-scale bargaining structure of Canadian industrial relations contrasts with the situation in many other countries where bargaining takes place on an industry-wide or even country-wide level, so that less time is devoted to local organizations and the necessities of multiple contract bargaining and more time is spent on issues related to the general health of the union movement and the promotion of labour's interests in policy formation (Esping-Andersen and Korpi, 1984; Hibbs, 1987b). Canadian union density peaked near 40 per cent during the mid-1980s and declined slightly to 37 per cent by the late 1990s. Workers in the resource and manufacturing sectors had reached levels of over 70 per cent unionization by 1965, while workers in the public sector had reached over 90 per cent unionization by 1981. In the service sector, only about 30 per cent of workers were unionized (Kumar, 1993). Unionization in Canada has not been a uniform process. Figure 3 indicates significant regional variations in union density.

Although union growth has been more rapid than the growth of the civilian labour force, some two-thirds of Canadian workers remain unorganized. Not surprisingly, this tends to limit the ability of unions to influence markets in a way that would offset the advantages enjoyed by capital. The importance of the difference between those in and out of unions becomes even more important when one examines the breadth of collective bargaining as well as union density. France, it will be recalled, has a union density that hovers around 10 per

Table 24: Common Bargaining Structures in Canadian Industrial Relations

Employer	Establishment	Union	Example	Classification
Single	Single	Single	single establishment or a policy of plant-by-plant negotiations	most decentralized very common pattern
Single	Multiple	Single	companies with an integrated set of operations, such as food chains, utilities, telecommunications	decentralized, common pattern
Single	Single	Multi	company bargains with a partnership of unions in the same establishment, e.g., newspapers	very rare situation
Single	Multi	Multi	few large employers bargaining with a coalition of craft unions, e.g., railways	rare situation
Multi	Multi	Single	coalition of employers bargaining with a dominant industrial or occupational union, e.g., health care, garment-making, forestry, transportation	centralized, used for specialized sectors
Multi	Multi	Multi	coalition of employers bargains with a coalition of unions; used after history of labour problems as in construction trades in Quebec; used in British Columbia for post-secondary education, construction sectors	most centralized, traditional social democratic ideal

Source: Adapted from Richard P. Chaykowski, 'The Structure and Process of Collective Bargaining', in Gunderson and Ponek, 1995: 231–3.

cent and yet collective bargaining sets the terms of employment for 90 per cent of the workforce. In Canada, the 1990 rate of 36 per cent density was matched by a 38 per cent coverage (Figure 1). These figures also hide the fact that public-sector unions, the largest component of the labour movement, have not fully exercised collective bargaining rights since 1975. What emerges, therefore, is the picture of a labour force divided between primary and secondary markets and, within the primary labour market, between more powerful private and more controlled public-sector unions.

Given shrinking employment in the high-density older industries, Canadian unions have responded by intensifying organizational efforts in non-traditional settings. The CAW, for example, became involved in fishing and other non-auto-manufacturing activities. Several attempts have been made to organize the service sector, such as banks and retail trades. Maintaining an effective presence in industries characterized by a high turnover is very difficult, however, and may well be impossible without changes in the labour regime. Industrial unions have also re-examined their traditional attitudes towards women and work by taking bargaining positions that reflect gender and pay equity as well as items that reflect the feminization of the workplace. These policies have been matched by the recruitment of women to trade union leadership positions (Kumar, 1993). Figure 4 indicates that much has to be done to close gender gaps and organize the retail and sevice sectors.

Changes have also been made within the internal politics of unions, which have always been caught between the tensions of maintaining external solidarity and internal pluralism. Part of the new policy is to encourage internal democracy

Figure 3: Unionization Rates by Province, 1994

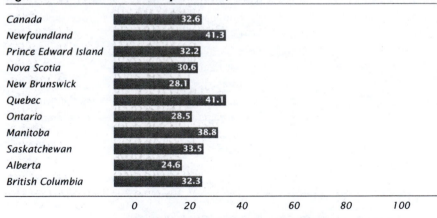

*percentage of wage and salary earners belonging to unions**

*Currently employed only; unemployed and self-employed excluded.

Source: Statistics Canada, 'Unionization Rates by Province, Canada, 1994', from *General Social Survey, 1994,* cat. no. 11–612.

and participation. Another aspect is to use new methods of communication, such as polling and focus groups, to maintain closer links between leadership and members, particularly in large unions undergoing change. Lastly, information campaigns for members and the general public have been an important part of the effort to maintain general public support for unions.

There have been organizational changes within the labour movement as well. Union mergers have been a common way to respond to economic restructuring. CLC thinking holds that merger gives an affiliated local more resources for organizing and delivering member services, solidifying membership and strengthening bargaining power, counterbalancing corporate mergers, acquisitions, and

Figure 4: Unionization Rates by Industrial Sector and Gender, 1994

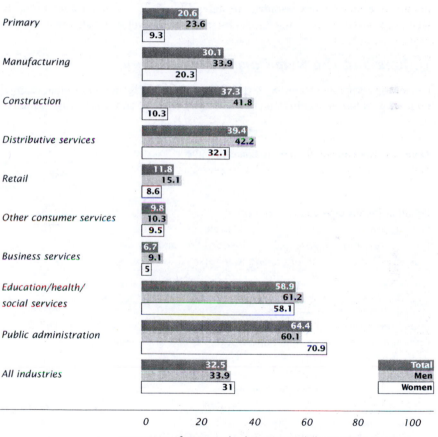

percentage of wage and salary earners belonging to unions*

*Currently employed only; unemployed and self-employed excluded.

Source: Statistics Canada, 'Unionization Rates by Industrial Sector and Gender, Canada, 1994'. from *General Social Survey, 1994*, cat. No. 11–612.

takeovers, and undertaking broader political campaigns (CLC, 1992; Kumar, 1993: 57–8). Some of the new giants are: the Canadian Auto Workers, the Communications, Energy and Paperworkers' Union (CEP), the United Steel Workers of America (USWA), and the Canadian Union of Public Employees (see Table 25). Some of these, like the CEP, have recruited from diverse settings, making them more general or omnibus unions than occupational or sectoral representatives. Again, this means that this form of union will bring greater resources and political strategy to single-firm/single-union bargaining. The development of general unions will also add pressure to change the existing conventions governing centrals and their union affiliates because the new general unions are also performing some of the same roles as a union central. Anderson (1995) projects that in the future unions may be distinguished as much by their programmatic differences as by their occupational representation. Mergers and general unions give locals more resources to defend against concession bargaining, to shape pattern bargaining, and to operate in a wider sectoral and strategic context.

Unions and the New Corporate Strategy

One of the corporate responses to the new economic exigencies has been to draw on their workforces to help them become more efficient and competitive. Much of

Table 25: The Largest Unions in Canada, 1996

Union	Membership (000s) in 1996
Canadian Union of Public Employees	455.8
National Union of Public and General Employees	310.6
National Automobile, Aerospace, Transportation and General Workers Union of Canada (Canadian Auto Workers, or CAW)	205.0
United Food and Commercial Workers International Union	185.0
United Steelworkers of America	170.0
Public Service Alliance of Canada	167.8
Communications, Energy and Paperworkers Union of Canada	165.2
Fédération des affaires sociales inc. (Quebec)	97.0
International Brotherhood of Teamsters	95.0
Service Employees International Union	80.0
Total union membership	4,033.0
Membership of ten largest unions	1,931.4
Percentage of total membership in ten largest unions	47.9%

Source: Human Resources Development Canada, Workplace Information Directorate, *Directory of Labour Organizations in Canada 1996* (Ottawa: Canada Communications Groups, 1996), xiv, xvii.

the new human relations strategy is oriented towards breaking down management-worker dichotomies within the workplace and to tie interests together by use of new pay policies such as bonus systems and profit-sharing. There are different alternatives, some of which simply can be added onto existing corporate organization, such as the Japanese-style 'quality circles', whereas others require radical departures from the hierarchical chain of command and institutionalization of work teams, such as participation in 'total quality control' management programs. These changes have become highly institutionalized within the United States and slightly less so in Canada (Wells, 1993; Verma, 1995).

There are several implications of these changes in corporate strategies (Russell, 1997a). Their primary objective is increasing labour productivity and competitiveness, and they make little effort to include labour objectives such as employment security (Murphy and Olthius, 1995; Roberts, 1995). New organizational structures, for example, may necessitate abandoning and/or modifying the elaborate seniority and job classification systems—pillars of defining employment security and labour-management relations in the postwar Fordist industrial workplace. Another issue for unions that represent wage-earners in multiple plants is that new systems can institutionalize competition among plants. Locals are induced, therefore, to compete against each other as opposed to forming a solidarity of interests when facing management.

Union responses have taken one of two broad stances. The CAW rejected these programs, reasoning, with some justification, that participation within the new management techniques had contributed to the decline of US union density and power within the auto sector (Yates, 1993). Moreover, the Canadian plants that stayed outside of the process had very efficient ratings (Wells, 1993). Other unions, however, are more receptive to the idea of employee participation, particularly if it is tied to labour training and other means to ensure that employees, giving current job security, are equipped with marketable skills (Gannagé, 1995). Inevitably, labour's response to firm-level changes in the work process are linked to broader considerations of the politics of labour and globalization.

Conclusions

Labour within the Canadian political economy has shaped and been shaped by common labour regimes, the fragmented *paternalism* of the colonial period, a centralized *liberal* labour regime during the period of industrialization under the National Policy, and diverse *industrial legality* under modern Fordism. In the period of globalization, the industrial legalism has only been modified on the margins for the private sector, but substantially changed for the public sector.

Labour has also always been a weak force in national politics and the labour regimes reflect this weakness. During the pre-Confederation period, the revolts of 1837–8 failed to displace the entrenched paternalism that constrained labour, and emigration provided the only escape for many. During the National Policy period, trade movement activities were decriminalized, but organized labour was not able to reach its long-standing goal of industrial legalism. Led by craft unions, it was ideologically and organizationally dominated by forms of American business unionism and Catholic confessionalism that could not reshape the state in labour's interest. That is not to say there were not real struggles, mixes of radical social unionism, and even direct actions, as in the Winnipeg confrontations of 1919, to challenge the existing order. The organization of the labour movement, however, made it difficult to take broad sectoral or class perspectives on the political economy.

Industrial legalism was built on a combination of several unique factors, beginning with structural shifts in the domestic and international political economy. Initially, it continued the model of lagged development that might be expected in dependency. The US hybrid model of a mixed craft-industrial union labour movement (AFL-CIO) was matched in Canada with the TLC-CCL compromise that became the CLC, which was still dominated by US affiliates. However, the American and Canadian regimes begin to diverge at that point. The Quiet Revolution, the advent of public-sector unionism, and the rise of Canadian nationalism tied to a dependency reading of Canadian-American relations became some of the unique forces that began to shape the Canadian labour movement.

In recent years the Canadian labour movement has reflected the federal and multinational nature of the federation, with substantial pan-Canadian and Quebec dynamics. It has, as well, been coloured by a social unionism that has consistently opposed the rise of neo-conservatism and neo-liberal globalization.

The union movement's ability to change labour regimes at provincial, national, and international levels is conditioned by another set of factors relating to the cohesiveness and organizational capacity of the movement as a whole. Especially significant are two factors: the ability of labour to cohere into powerful central organizations that can directly influence the nature of state policy-making; and the ability of labour to influence directly the composition of the government itself through the democratic electoral process.

Unlike the situation in many European countries, dominant political parties in Canada at both levels of government have historically been able to use their positions in government to disarm both agrarian and labour protest. Through the passage of 'progressive' legislation and the expenditure of state funds on social programs, Conservatives and, especially, the Liberal Party successfully attracted many former members of agrarian and labour protest movements into their ranks. During the modernization period this left only a hard-core 15 to 20 per cent of electoral support for the NDP (Young, 1969; Morton, 1974).

Why the failure of alternatives? One body of literature emanating from the 'new left' argues that the NDP did poorly because the party itself was trapped by its ties to business unionism and unable to add a discourse of class to the established politics of national unity. In other words, the social democrats were unable to shake off the aphorism that they were just 'liberals in a hurry' (Brodie and Jenson, 1988; Jenson, 1990). When the time came for Canadian social democracy to adapt to a changing paradigm of state-society relations, it had little to offer as an alternative to the prevailing neo-liberalism and was then overtaken by events such as the emergence of continental free trade (Bradford, 1998; Netherton, 1991). This critical perspective has to be balanced with a recognition of the strategic barriers and opportunities facing the NDP in electoral competition (Kitschelt, 1994). From this perspective the disappointing performance of the NDP in national politics is attributable to the strategic electoral position of the Liberals. The NDP can only make a great difference if and when the dominant centre-left Liberal Party falters.

Given the importance of provincial jurisdiction over industrial relations, it is important to address the rise of social democratic movements in provincial politics. Here the results are strikingly different from the federal scene. During the 1990s social democratic parties have formed governments in Quebec, Ontario, Saskatchewan, Yukon, and British Columbia—as well as formed the official opposition in Nova Scotia and Manitoba. During the same period, neo-conservative/neo-liberal political parties have enacted more restrictive labour regimes in Ontario, Manitoba, and Alberta. This points to a growing polarization of provincial politics.

Thus, while workers in Canada have obtained a greater state presence in activities that benefit them, this presence has been accomplished not so much through the creation of specific workers' parties as through more diffuse electoral activity. Voting, clearly, has been significant in influencing Canadian governments to address workers' interests, and partisan political activity has been much less so, save at the increasingly important provincial level.

Canadian workers have also failed to develop unified labour centrals capable of directly influencing government decision-making. As in the US and the UK, the initial influence of craft unions and the elaboration of hybrid models of organization foreclosed the possibility of labour movements dominated by large industrial unions and a single, cohesive, and unified labour central. In short, Canada is not Sweden. Yet, the critical issue is not fragmentation in the conventional sense—either by jurisdictions or by competing centrals. The critical fragmentation for Canadian labour is produced by an industrial relations regime that focuses on the bottom level. There is no incentive for labour and capital to take wider and longer views at labour relations—and, indeed, they are limited in their ability to do so. Similarly, collective agreements could be extended along sectoral lines and thus become a more formal bridge between organized and unorganized wage-earners. The lack of central direction, therefore, is dependent both on conventions of federalism, internationalism, and factionalism within the labour movement and on the model of industrial relations that has framed the whole labour regime.

The Canadian labour movement has used diverse strategies to deal with fragmentation. In the postwar period the political strategy was to concentrate on organizing industrial and public-sector workers and establishing strong centrals and a special relationship within the political economy. This was done by means of a natural political ally such as the NDP (Russell, 1997a). The political strategy, as we have seen, was not entirely successful. What, then, propelled the movement? The most significant political tool left to labour in Canada has been neither the political party nor the central labour organization but, befitting its fragmented and decentralized nature, the grassroots protest. The pattern of industrial strife erupting periodically over wages and working conditions throughout the country, though necessarily in a somewhat crude and inarticulate manner, has been the best demonstration of labour's interests in resource allocation and distribution (Hibbs, 1976, 1978; Lacroix, 1986).

In the period of globalization, the political strategy has again changed. Labour movements are seeking allies with other popular movements that also want to stop or change the terms of global integration (Russell, 1997a). This new political agenda has also exacerbated the nationalist divisions between the Quebec and Canadian labour movements. In Canada, the CLC formed alliances with the environmental and feminist movements and was a central actor shaping the FTA and NAFTA debates. The labour movement's *social unionism* has been matched by a rekindled deep-rooted nationalism. In Quebec, the union movement has practised defensive accomodation as a result of restructuring imperatives and has subordinated its particular trade-related economic objectives to those of the larger *souverainiste* movement. Throughout the federation, the level of industrial conflict has diminished but not disappeared. Indeed, the arrival of a 'jobless recovery' indicates that traditional distributive politics remain critically important.

Chapter 9

The Structure and Organization of Canadian Capital

Introduction

Capital, as the following discussion indicates, is central to our understanding of Canadian development. The role of Canadian capital is subject to debate because of the large part that foreign capital has played in Canadian development and the ambiguity of the role the domestic market plays in the accumulation strategies of business. The relationships that exist among foreign, national, and regional capital in Canada are central to assessments of the position of the country within the international political economy—and specifically the characterization of Canada's relationship to the United States and the North American Free Trade area.

Academic and public policy debate since the 1970s has centred on different assessments of Canada's position in the world. Some have viewed Canada as a *rich dependency* in which domestic and foreign capital has worked to block autonomous national development. Others have examined the same evidence and arrived at the converse conclusion, seeing Canada as a wealthy First World nation that merely is located on the periphery of the international centre. This debate emerged during the modernization period. It permeates contemporary understandings of Canada's role in the world and colours the different interpretations made of the effects of globalization on Canadian capital.

Understanding the role played by capital in Canadian society is also integral to our understanding of how social and political power is created and exercised. For socialists this power is relational to that of other classes, particularly labour. Capitalist power is seen as inherently illegitimate since it is derived from the exploitation of labour. However, capital, like labour, is also usually seen not as a timeless monolithic entity, but as a fragmented one with a time-bound identity. Hence, capital can sometimes be a hegemonic force, while on other occasions and instances it is much less powerful and can be curbed by governments or labour, or by other social actors. Most analysts attribute fragmentation to spatial and organizational issues such as scale (large or small), industrial structure (competitive or monopolistic), and geopolitics (especially differences that exist at the international, national, and regional levels). However, as we shall see below, such spatial classifications are sometimes awkward.

For liberals, on the other hand, capital is seen as a much more benign entity. The fact that major decisions regarding society are made by a relatively small group is seen as inevitable. The only questions are whether or not these decisions result in an efficient allocation and production of goods and services, and, to some extent, whether the activities of the capitalist class or élite are considered to be acceptable, or legitimate, by the remainder of society. Thus, the study of élites becomes a means of measuring the fairness of the rules that condition the struggle to the top and the distribution of power within society (Porter, 1965). The key questions are the extent to which the social composition of élites reflects the mosaic of culture, gender, and nations that make up a community such as Canada and the extent to which power is distributed or concentrated at the top. The overall objective is not to overturn the capitalist order but to remove barriers and make fair rules for competition.

The Role of Capital in a Capitalist Economy

One of the key features of the capitalist political economy is the institutional differentiation between the economic and the political. The exact boundaries between the private and public can vary over time, but business always seeks to guard its autonomy. Socialists define capital as a class of people that owns the means of production. This economic power, it is argued, translates into tremendous social and political power—so much so that governments, or the state, are considered at best to be only relatively autonomous from capital.

Similarly, for liberal political theorists such as Charles Lindblom (1977) the extraordinary power of business relative to other groups in society stems from the privatization of key decisions about our social and economic lives. Simply stated, decisions made in private boardrooms have broad social implications. Corporations determine where and when investment will take place, what sorts of technologies will be used, and what goods and services are produced in society. With these decisions, policies that determine when, where, and at what price labour will be used in production are also adopted. Equally important, particularly in resource industries, is that corporate decisions structure the relationship of the economy to the environment.

Certainly, governments also play an important role in these decisions, but government involvement is often indirect or regulatory. Even when governments become very active in developing economic strategies, the long-term idea is to stimulate a self-reproducing private sector, not to take over its functions. Hence, capital takes centre stage and there is long-standing debate on exactly how autonomous governments are, relative to capital.

At the macro level, an assessment of the power of capital also provides a measure of a state's position within the international political economy. In part this is a spatial definition: for example, whether the focus of the Canadian state is Canada, the United States, or North America. In part it also concerns the ranking of Canada within the international division of wealth, such as rich or poor, developed or developing. Often, assessments of a society's position within the international division of wealth are also couched in historical terms of the strategic trajectory of Canada in relation to other states. In Canada's case, for example, it has been a significant factor of capitalist development that industrialization first took place within the British Empire and then became closely allied with US capital, technology, and markets.

For socialist political economy, as noted above, power is relational. Therefore, the strategic advantage of capital centres on its continual ability to expropriate surplus value from labour. Labour can offset some of this advantage by collective organization and through parliamentary politics. Unions can use collective influence and resort to strikes, while other social movements can engage in confrontations to alter particular decisions or policies made by corporate actors. To change significantly its power or role in capitalism from that of negation to that of creation, however, labour has to participate within the process of decision-making, a process called 'co-determination' or industrial democracy. Alternatively, in the Swedish model, unions could become major shareholders in firms, a process called economic democracy (Esping-Andersen, 1985; Kitschelt, 1995).

Politically, wage-earners always form the majority of the population and, at least theoretically, can exercise the franchise as a means of persuading governments to enhance their market position. Labour cannot always achieve in practice what is possible in theory, however. Even a unified and cohesive labour organization capable of obtaining some redress in the marketplace through state action is not able to overcome all of the advantages that capital enjoys in a capitalist economy. Capital's additional advantages directly influence the state's ability to alter market relations and offset labour's democratic electoral advantages (Przeworski, 1990).

First, capitalist productive activities directly affect the fiscal health of the state, which, in a capitalist system, must rely for its revenues on taxes paid by corporations and individuals. Any decrease in capitalist productive activity, all other things being equal, reduces the state's ability to obtain revenues through taxation of individual incomes or corporate profits. Although states have other means of obtaining revenues—for example, through royalties, licence fees, inheritance taxes, and customs duties—in the modern era all nation-states rely heavily on income and sales taxes for their revenue needs. To make sure they don't 'kill the golden goose' that provides them with a ready source of income, states must be extremely cautious about regulating or otherwise restricting capitalist decision-making.

Second, capitalist profits are highly mobile and not confined by national boundaries. Various mechanisms exist for taking profits from one country and investing them in another, and business can respond to any unwanted state intervention in the market by removing its capital to another location. While this theoretical mobility is limited by a variety of factors—including possible restrictions on investment opportunities in other countries or jurisdictions—the potential loss of employment and revenues is a threat that both labour and the state must contend with in making decisions. Any attempt by the state to limit or remove this mobility, for example, through a ban on expatriation of profits, can have adverse consequences for investment in the domestic economy by non-resident capitalists. Because of the negative consequences this entails for state revenues, capitalists—both domestic and foreign—have the ability to 'punish' the state for any actions it takes that meet with their disapproval. During the period of globalization the economy has become even more open as the flexibility of capital has been enhanced. This openness has often been associated with diminishing corporate taxation despite record levels of profit-taking, as states attempt to induce capital to remain within national boundaries.

As Western economies have turned from producing goods to creating and exporting services, capital in developed states has demanded new forms of protection against mercantilism. The proposal for the creation of a Multilateral Agreement on Investment (MAI), promoted by the Organization for Economic Co-operation and Development, represents an attempt by international capital to secure capital mobility and intellectual property rights throughout the global economy (Clarke and Barlow, 1997). Of interest in this agreement is the proposal that corporations will be able to use the treaty to sue governments in jurisdictions that do not follow its terms. Until the MAI, firms always have had to work through domestic governments. Now it is proposed that they become political actors in their own right. Conversely, proposals such as the 'Tobin tax'—a small charge levied on all international capital movements in order to discourage speculation—attempt to counteract this power by taxing short-term capital flows that cross national borders.

Third, capitalist profits can be and are used as an important source of funding for modern political parties, greatly outweighing the funding available to labour parties through union dues. In many countries, including Canada, the attachment of workers to labour parties is tenuous, and there are many other countervailing influences on workers' voting behaviour. Even social democratic political parties may not expose a political discourse that is substantially different from that of business parties (Brodie and Jenson, 1988). In many countries modern elections often turn on relatively short-term issues or personalities, and parties require large budgets to influence voters through extensive media advertising campaigns. Although labour parties may be able to turn out large numbers of campaign workers, they often lack the financial wherewithal required to conduct media-extensive campaigning. Parties funded out of capitalist profits have precisely the opposite advantages and disadvantages, and in many countries they have successfully used these techniques to neutralize, if not overpower, labour's numerical advantage at the polls.

Finally, capitalist profits can be used to legitimize the unequal distribution of political and economic power enjoyed by capital—to present the existing order not only as the 'natural' outcome of the historical development of modern societies but also as the 'optimum' outcome. Profits are used to fund research institutes and individual researchers and to publicize findings, results, or prescriptions for government action that favour the continuation or extension of the society's mix of state-market relations, that is, that favour the continuing dominance of capital in society. In the present period, for example, neo-liberal economic strategies emanate from a highly concentrated print media.

Like the other political-economic actors, capital must also be organized, united, and cohesive if it is to use these various advantages successfully to shape state activity in its favour and/or offset labour's advantages in the electoral system. If capital is not well organized, or if it is divided in its aims and ambitions, it will only be able to exercise its capabilities partially or unsystematically. In such circumstances capital may well be overcome by state or labour-based political or economic activities, although this, too, depends on the organization and cohesiveness of those other two political-economic actors.

And like the organization of labour and the state, the organization of capital is a significant determinant of the pattern of state-market relations in any country. In many countries capital exercises political and economic power not only through the actions of individual businesses but also through the activities of large and united business associations that undertake a variety of political activities to promote the interests of capital as a whole. Determining the nature of these capitalist firms and associations, then, becomes a key element of political-economic analysis.

The Development of Capital

The Colonial Period

The singularity of Canadian as opposed to European development, as Harold Innis and succeeding generations of political economists pointed out, is that European development progressed from stages of agriculture, trade, and manufacturing to finance. Canada, on the other hand, began its process of integration into the world economy through the production and trade of staples. A staples relationship, it will be recalled, is where raw materials or resources are extracted from one *region* for export to *metropolitan* markets. Within this relationship the primary agent is external demand, and it is difficult to establish domestic linkages to reap the rewards of staples. Capital is directed towards overcoming geography with technology, transportation, and finance. The difficulties of the staples economy intertwine the interests and activities of state and capital.

Staples capital dominated early Canadian development. Staples production preceded settlement in North America's northern half, which was first exploited for its fish and fur resources by great trading and fishing monopolies established by the British and French and operating under the mercantilist system. At first these companies actively prevented permanent settlement of the areas under their control, although in most cases they were unable to stem the tide of immigration and permanent settlement for more than 50 years.

In Newfoundland, rich fishing grounds had been harvested by Basque fishermen in the thirteenth and fourteenth centuries and later by a variety of French, English, and Spanish fishing fleets until the British gained control of the island and the Labrador coast in the eighteenth century. Almost immediately the British extended a monopoly over the fishery to a group of Kentish fishing interests. The monopoly proved difficult to enforce in practice but remained in law until the mid-nineteenth century (Hiller and Neary, 1980).

In New France, a monopoly over the fur trade was granted to the Company of New France or the 'One Hundred Associates' in 1627. Although that charter was taken over by the Compagnie des Habitants in 1645, it remained in effect under the Compagnie du Canada and the Compagnie d'Occident until 1742 (Lower, [1946] 1977). The monopoly was challenged by the English through the East India Company in 1664 and most significantly through the creation of the Hudson's Bay Company in 1670 (Rich, 1960).

All of these companies viewed permanent settlement as a threat to their exclusive access to New World resources. In New France the French Crown changed the charter of the fur trade monopolies to allow for agricultural settlement, primarily for military purposes. In Newfoundland the offshore fishing interests could not prevent permanent colonization of the island and Labrador coasts. In the Hudson's Bay Company territories the Arctic or subarctic lands immediately surrounding the Bay forts were unfit for cultivation, while settlement of the southern limits of company lands awaited the push into the area by rival fur traders of the Montreal-based North West Company in the early nineteenth century. The lack of large permanent settlements in early Canada was significant since, in the absence of a domestic market, business was limited to activities aimed at export.

It was only with the development of the lumber industry after 1806—when British North America was supplying masts and spars for the British navy after the imposition of Napoleon's continental blockade (Albion, 1926; Lower, 1938, 1967, 1973)—that the agricultural frontier was extended throughout the Maritime provinces, Quebec, and Ontario, bringing in permanent settlers and creating the conditions for the development of domestic businesses to serve the needs of local populations (Lower, 1936; Wynn, 1981). The timber trade not only cleared land for later agricultural settlement but also provided early settlers with a ready source of capital and a wintertime occupation. Loggers and river rafters also provided the first domestic markets for agricultural goods, allowing many farming settlements to survive and thrive in a precarious climate (Minville, 1944; Cross, 1960).

The timber trade, then, played a major role both in the process of domestic capital accumulation and in the establishment of permanent agricultural settlements in the colonies of British North America. These agricultural settlements in turn provided the basis for future large-scale food exports, especially of wheat and other grains, which accompanied the settlement of first western Ontario and later the prairie provinces in the second half of the nineteenth century and the first quarter of the twentieth (Fowke, 1978).

From the very beginning of settlement in Canada, significant capital was invested in the resource and agricultural sectors with the intention of promoting exports in international markets. In the resource sectors, business was dominated by large foreign capital until the growth of the timber trade, which provided an avenue for small domestic operators to enter into the business world. Although many enterprises were small, part-time affairs, large concerns quickly emerged. Some of these, in different form, still exist today.

The accumulation of capital by domestic interests and the establishment of permanent large-scale communities had two further effects. First, the retention of some profits within British North America led to the development of a rudimentary banking and financial industry; second, the creation of permanent communities led to a demand for manufactured consumer and capital goods.

The first permanent domestic banks, established in Canada at the beginning of the nineteenth century, were intimately involved in the timber trade. They included the Bank of Montreal (1817), which followed other efforts to establish domestic banks beginning in 1792 (Hammond, 1957; Shortt, 1896). The growth of these banks was aided by the influx of funds required to sustain the British war effort during the War of 1812–14. The war, like the timber trade, also served to provide a domestic market for Canadian agricultural production. The banks were originally founded by rival merchant groups in cities such as Halifax, Montreal, Kingston, and York (now Toronto) to help finance the export trade, and they were generally opposed by the agrarian interests, which faced the burden of mortgage and interest payments. Although these agricultural interests continued to press for the establishment of 'free banking' along US lines, the colonial governments generally refused the requests and instead established a pattern of chartered banking that continues in Canada to the present day.

The result has been, not surprisingly, the creation of only a few very large banks in this country, which service local communities through branches controlled by head offices located in one of the larger cities. At various points in Canadian history, including during the rebellions of 1837–8 and the farmers' reform movement of the 1920s and 1930s, the size and power of the Canadian banks have aroused discord. Many proposals for their reform have been enunciated, although few have been put into practice.

The development of manufacturing activities in Canada was a slow process, encumbered first by British colonial practices that attempted to preserve the British North American market for British goods and later by the competition that domestic producers faced from US imports. Manufacturers in Canada enjoyed some comparative cost advantages over British goods, primarily because of the costs of transportation between Britain and North America. High tariffs raised by the British against US goods to protect the Canadian market for their own exports also allowed indigenous manufacturers the same protection (Forster, 1986). Even so, Canadian producers could not compete with either mass-produced and well-financed British goods or cheap US products. They could only survive in businesses that required small capital investments and where manufacturing relied on abundant Canadian resources. These fields included tanning and shoemaking, as well as furniture and other woodworking activities, all based on the flourishing agricultural and resource industries.

National Policy Industrialization

The transformation of the Canadian economy during the National Policy period has left an important legacy of debate (Laxer, 1989a: 25–6). For left-nationalists, the roots of Canadian dependency were seeded during this period, although analyses differ. The problem starts with the relationship among staples, industrialization, protective tariffs, and foreign investment. Staples capital was allegedly risk-adverse and blocked the expansion of indigenous manufacturing by means of protective tariffs—a hypothesis first developed by Tom Naylor (1975) and then modified by Wallace Clement (1977). For left-nationalists the result has been a blocking of what would be an otherwise autonomous pattern of national development. For Gordon Laxer, the whole development model was faulty. Canada's promising beginning as a leading late industrializer failed largely because the capitalist class and its economic strategy were not effectively challenged by subordinate classes (Laxer, 1989a).

For Harold Innis and later new staples political economists such as Hugh Aitken, much the opposite occurs. Canada displays a remarkable economic development. Yet the dominant position of staples in the economy points to the fragility of that development and to Canada's continuing need for US technology and markets in order to continue its course of economic development. For Glen Williams (1986), Canadian development reflects the weaknesses of import substitution: technological dependence and a preoccupation on the part of manufacturers with the home as opposed to export markets. For William Carroll (1986), Canadian development and the increasing penetration of US capital into the Canadian economy reflect a healthy, autonomous, and expansive national finance capital.

When the British began dismantling their protective tariff system in the 1840s to provide cheaper raw materials for their own manufacturing industries, Canadian manufacturing interests wanted to replace the British tariffs with Canadian tariffs in an effort to keep out US goods. The much more powerful resource sector was also threatened by the loss of British markets and wanted to replace those lost markets with new buyers in the United States. The result was the establishment of the free trade Reciprocity Treaty with the United States from 1854 to 1866.

The dependency school interprets this as part of the pattern of sacrificing the interests of manufacturing to the needs of resource capital (Naylor, 1972, 1975b). In fact, the treaty dealt primarily with natural resources. Canadian tariff protection did occur, which provided needed revenues (in an age before income taxes), matched US levels of protection, and protected threatened industries. Still, early commercial policy pointed to differential treatment between domestic manufacturing capital and internationally oriented resource capital.

The emerging Canadian pattern of development crystallized as the National Policy in 1878 when it was formalized to respond to an economic recession (Forster, 1986). The outlines of the policy were clear from Confederation:

- the territorial expansion of the Canadian state to include the colony of British Columbia, the Hudson's Bay Company's lands, and the Arctic Archipelago, or all lands and waters north of the forty-ninth parallel west of Ontario;
- the provision of government financial aid and traffic monopolies to private companies involved in the extension of a transportation infrastructure into new territories (this included, most notably, the Canadian Pacific Railway) and connecting the existing colonies (especially the Grand Trunk Railway linking Quebec and Ontario and the Intercolonial Railway linking central Canada and the Maritime provinces);
- the rescue of existing financial institutions through the takeover of provincial debts by the federal government (many of these debts were railway connected);
- the creation of tariff walls to protect Canadian manufacturing industries from both US and British imports (Fowke, 1952);
- the establishment of a common market and monetary union by means of Confederation (Chapter 7);
- the stimulation of export agriculture by means of integrated immigration, transportation, research, and land policies.

This policy pattern is also referred to as *defensive expansionism*. It points to the high involvement of the Dominion government in protecting manufacturing and in stimulating the development of export agriculture on prairie lands. The National Policy did succeed in fostering industrialization and large-scale export agriculture. Yet, several aspects of the structure of capital under the National Policy warrant attention, particularly since they relate to later discussion concerning the national question.

- Economic growth was regionally uneven, leaving regional concentrations of capital with particular structures and interests and a legacy of regional tensions.
- Resource and manufacturing capital worked under different policy frameworks.
- Capital became highly concentrated, with the older financial or staples capital maintaining an important lead in Canadian development.
- US capital and technology took a large role in Canadian manufacturing and resources.

Uneven Regional Development
The regional differentiation of capital under the National Policy stems from the diverse geopolitics of the Canadian economy. On the prairies, for example,

Winnipeg became the regional centre of the emerging West where activities such as foundries, railway yards, metal works, grain and food processing, abattoirs, construction, merchandising, and even needle trades fuelled the imperial visions of Winnipeg business. For the most part, however, the health of the prairie economy depended on immigration, capital flows, and the health of export agriculture and was subject to all of the vicissitudes of the international staples trade.

Turn-of-the-century industrialization in Ontario and Quebec was not as dependent on linkages to prairie export agriculture. Important linkages were intraregional, based on resources and domestic and contiguous US markets (McCallum, 1980; Pomfret, 1981). There are two versions of this process—one that links this industrialization to continuing dependency (staples versus manufacturing) and the other that links it to successful continental integration. Most economic historians do not substantiate the 'staples triumph over manufacturing' hypothesis during this period. Pointing to the active state role in support of manufacturing, H.V. Nelles (1974) has shown that the creation of Ontario Hydro, for example, entailed an intervention by the provincial government against older financial capital, which had been involved in railway construction and expansion, and in support of a nascent manufacturing class wanting 'power at cost' to aid in their competitive struggle with American manufactures. Although the provincial government intervened on behalf of manufacturers in hydro, timber, and mining, Nelles does not conclude that the pattern of development was substantially altered. In a similar vein, John Dales's (1957) study of hydro and industrialization in Quebec reveals that staples capital did become involved directly in stimulating manufacturing as a by-product of the search for secure markets for abundant hydroelectricity. Conversely, utility monopolies could block or retard industrialization if this rewarded their market position.

The National Policy was also related to the collapse of the regional Maritime business class. Maritime manufacturing and financial interests had heavily committed to produce for the national market, only to find themselves disadvantaged by national railway and financial policies and weakened by a prolonged late nineteenth-century downturn in the business cycle. By the 1920s financial collapse and deindustrialization had been accompanied by mergers and regional consolidation (Acheson, 1972).

Continuing Corporate Concentration

National Policy industrialization was, as the Maritime experience indicates, also associated with an increasing concentration of industry, especially in the manufacturing sector. Capitalist firms and a capitalist market economy were well established in Canada before 1880 and received a boost with Macdonald's National Policy, which dedicated state activity to the perpetuation and intensification of these activities. Since 1880 capitalist development in Canada has been characterized by two phenomena, one characteristic of all capitalist political economies and the other more particular to Canadian circumstances. Characteristic of capitalist political economies has been the increasing concentration of capital as individual firms merge with each other and fewer firms come to control more and more of a nation's corporate assets. More particular to Canadian circumstances has been the development of extensive foreign ownership of corporate assets, in this case the increasing US ownership of corporations operating in the country. Both phenomena have led to the development of further cleavages within an already fractured Canadian business community, and these cleavages have had an important influence on the formation of business associations in this country.

Concentration of production facilities increased in Canada in most sectors, especially the manufacturing sector, since the turn of the century. In 1890, 2,879 plants accounted for 63 per cent of manufacturing output in the country. By 1922, 936 plants accounted for 66 per cent of manufacturing output (Rosenbluth, 1957: 94ff.). Although this tendency towards increasing plant size continued until 1930, it declined in many industries during the 1930s and 1940s, a phenomenon explained by the tendency of companies first to adopt labour-saving technologies in the period 1900–30, resulting in the establishment of plants of increasingly larger scale, and then to adopt capital-saving technologies in the period 1930–50 to offset this tendency (Rosenbluth, 1957: 102).

Plant size is only one method of measuring industrial concentration. Although informative, it tells us little about the financial concentration of industry, that is, about the concentration of ownership and economic power into the hands of fewer and fewer companies and individuals. In this sense, concentration also refers to the extent of vertical or horizontal integration present in an industry and across industrial sectors.

Vertical integration refers to the extent to which individual firms in an industry control other firms producing inputs to or controlling outputs from production activities. For example, in the steel industry a company might produce steel and also control companies providing iron ore for steel production and selling steel products in the marketplace. It might also control companies shipping raw materials and finished goods to markets. *Horizontal integration* refers to the ownership of different companies involved in the same productive activity. Thus, for example, one steelmaker might own shares in or control other steelmaking companies. These relationships are not apparent in statistics on plant and enterprise dominance. As a result, we must consider not only the concentration of plants and employment but also the concentration of corporate assets in the economy.

Merger and acquisitions, in the context of the international turbulence of the early National Policy boom, began to define the structure of Canadian capital. By the turn of the century, notwithstanding the importance of foreign investment, Canadian business was dominated by the railways and banks. By 1930, economic power was focused on the three major chartered banks. Canadian finance and manufacturing became increasingly linked (Carroll, 1986).

There were several waves of mergers. During the 1920s domestic manufacturing and resource enterprises began to consolidate. The predominance of horizontal mergers reflects attempts by firms to control markets in the face of turbulent competition and business cycles (Weldon, 1966). By 1933, as Table 26 indicates, a wave of mergers produced a highly concentrated industrial structure.

Small firms and workers in Canada have consistently objected to this increasing concentration of control over production decisions in the hands of fewer and fewer individuals. Both groups have been concerned with the development of *oligopolies*—where a few large firms control the market—or *monopolies*—where one firm controls the market. Such developments bolster the market advantages already enjoyed by capital *vis-à-vis* labour and simultaneously allow large firms to exclude small firms from the market through the use of collusive pricing techniques. Not surprisingly, this development has led to repeated demands by these groups for state action to curb the process of financial concentration.

Canada's first legislation opposing business combinations in restraint of trade was passed in 1889, one year before the Sherman Anti-Trust Act in the United States. The Canadian Act remained in force until 1910, when it was replaced by the Combines Investigations Act (Gorecki and Stanbury, 1984), which itself was only replaced by new legislation in 1988. The 1889 legislation was passed following a report the previous year from the Select Committee of the House of Commons to Investigate Alleged Combines in Manufacture, Trade, and Insurance in Canada. The Act was designed to be enforced by provincial attorneys-general and was intended to protect consumers, especially farmers, from price-fixing by manufacturers and financial institutions. It was also meant to protect small producers from the predatory pricing practices of larger producers and cartels (Bliss, 1973).

The first (1889) anti-combines legislation, the Act for the Prevention and Suppression of Combinations Formed in Restraint of Trade, like similar legislation passed at other times in Canadian history, did not oppose the concentration of capital or attempt to keep markets open for small capital. Rather, it simply attempted to protect consumers and producers from the excesses of monopoly behaviour in the marketplace. The courts upheld the power of the legislatures to prevent the abuse of market power by monopolies or oligopolies and steadily convicted price-fixers when their schemes were uncovered and prosecuted under the various acts. However, the courts did not uphold any vestigial

Table 26: Net Assets of 100 Largest Non-Financial Companies by Size, 1933

Company Size by Net Assets ($000,000s)	Total Net Assets ($000s)
Greater than 100	5,093,580
75.0 to 99.9	77,016
50.0 to 74.9	512,398
25.0 to 49.9	782,086
10.0 to 24.9	762,542

Source: Canada, *Concentration in the Manufacturing Industries of Canada* (Ottawa: Consumer and Corporate Affairs, 1971), 41.

anti-concentration elements that remained in the acts, refusing to label mergers and business takeovers as actions in restraint of trade if that was not their sole object. Only five convictions were obtained under the first Act between 1889 and 1910, and the second Act of 1910 created a Combines Investigation Branch to replace provincial governments as prosecutors in future cases (Gorecki and Stanbury, 1984: 20). This act was ruled unconstitutional by the Judical Committee of the Privy Council in 1921.

In 1923 a new Combines Investigation Act was passed. It was modified during the Depression when farmers and consumers again complained of the predatory practices of both manufacturing and finance capital. These complaints received detailed investigation by the federal Royal Commission on Price Spreads in 1935. By that time, the commission had already found a significant concentration of Canadian industrial assets in a few large companies.

Foreign Investment

The initial investments made in export industries were largely foreign—especially British—in origin. Foreign investment usually took the form of *portfolio investment*, i.e., share equity in firms or the financial underwriting for large undertakings such as railways and utilities. While much of the initial investment in Canadian manufacturing came from domestic sources, by the turn of the century a great deal of it was foreign and involved direct foreign ownership of firms producing for the Canadian market. Indeed, according to Kenneth Buckley's calculations, British and American capital boosted gross domestic investment by about 10 per cent of gross national product during the 1906–15 boom years—and only became insignificant during the economic downturn of the early 1920s (Buckley, 1967).

US investment in Canadian industries had begun in the lumber trade, and many prominent people engaged in that trade—including Henry Franklin Bronson, D.D. Calvin, E.B. Eddy, and Henry Rathbun—were immigrants from the United States. However, US involvement in resource development was limited by rules restricting ownership of lands to British subjects. In the minerals sector, for example, Nova Scotia's coal resources were exploited by British capital, although Americans were involved in gold, copper, and manganese extraction, frequently extending mining activities begun on the US side of the border to follow seams across the international boundary (Marshall, Southard, and Taylor, 1936).

In the manufacturing sectors, British and European capital was often involved in early industrial projects, including the construction of steelmaking facilities in Nova Scotia and the establishment of pulp and paper plants in Quebec and Newfoundland. Investments in these areas were soon taken over by US interests. At first US investment was made by emigrants from the United States to Canada, people who became, in effect, domestic Canadian capitalists. By the 1870s and 1880s US companies began to establish branch plants in Canada. These were wholly owned subsidiaries of US parent companies producing for the Canadian market in competition with domestic capital.

Significantly, 50 of these US-owned or US-controlled firms were located in Ontario and 25 in Quebec; only six were established in the Maritimes and one in western Canada. This development was interpreted favourably at the time, as confirmed by an 1885 inquiry into manufacturing industries that noted with great satisfaction the influx of US capital into central Canada (Canada, 1885).

Canadian manufacturing activity accelerated after 1878 in both the primary and secondary sectors, and foreign (primarily US) direct investment grew with it. Table 27 illustrates the comparative growth of manufacturing production for the period 1870–1938 and demonstrates that Canada's pattern of development compares more readily to other 'late-follower countries' than to other, even more recently industrialized countries. Table 28 indicates that US investment became an integral part of key non-financial industrial sectors—particularly manufacturing, mining and smelting, and utilities—a trend that would continue throughout the century. The table also shows that, by 1932, American involvement was largely associated with large firms—those with capitalization over $1 million, or the 19 per cent of total firms that accounted for 79 per cent of national production. American investment was negligible among the smaller firms.

If one considers the period as a whole, the Naylor-Clement thesis does not look very rewarding. With close to 25 per cent of Canadian GDP derived from manufacturing in the 1920s, one has to agree with Gordon Laxer (1989a) that the 'staples versus manufacturing' hypothesis does not fit the actual pattern of

Table 27: Income from Manufactured Production in Millions of International Units, Selected Countries, 1870–1938

	1870–4	*1905–9*	*1925–9*	*1935–8*
*Selected late-follower countries**				
Italy	146	735	1,395	1,503
Japan	—	343	1,533	2,835
Sweden	45	356	570	948
Median of all late-follower countries		489	768	1,226
Canada	70	334	1,090	1,218
*British Dominions***				
Argentina	—	—	360	479
Australia	—	150	433	475
New Zealand	—	63	127	172

*'Late-follower' refers to those countries that began industrialization in the late nineteenth century, as opposed to the first group of industrializers (such as Great Britain, Germany, France, and the United States). The full group also includes Czechoslovakia, the Netherlands, and Russia.
** 'British Dominions', sometimes referred to as the 'White Dominions', refers to those countries that industrialized after the late-followers.
Source: Colin Clark, *The Conditions of Economic Progress*, 3rd edn (New York: Macmillan, 1960), Table VII. Adapted from Laxer, 1989a: 41, Table 1.1.

Table 28: US-Controlled and US-Affiliated Companies in Canadian Production, 1932 (percentages)

	Capital under $50,000	Capital $50,000– $199,000	Capital $200,000– $499,000	Capital $500,000– $999,000	Capital $1,000,000 +
Manufacturing	1	3	6	8	14
Mining	1	1	1	3	47
Utilities	1	1	1	1	56
Merchandising	1	3	4	4	18
Miscellaneous	1	2	8	14	21
Total all sectors	1	2	3	5	19

Source: Marshall, Southard, and Taylor, 1936: 27.

Canadian national industrialization. Still, the new industrialization, the new north-south trade axes, and the rising importation of US capital, technology, and industrial organization all point to an important reshaping of the political economy that is not captured by the term 'defensive expansionism'.

Had Canadians lost control of the economy by the end of the National Policy period? Gordon Laxer's analysis of Canada as a 'failed late follower' provides a more general critique of the Canadian development model (1989a, 1991a). Laxer asks why a small country like Sweden can undertake a path of autonomous development within the European context, while Canada's development features such markedly increasing reliance on the United States. He argues that Canada once led the group of late industrializing countries, but Canadian business and state actors then engaged in a highly inefficient process of development that avoided innovation and risk-taking and inevitably led to a reliance on foreign direct investment to provide the motor for the Canadian economy. In elaborating his argument Laxer dismisses some old explanations, such as protective tariffs and proximity to the United States, as central explanations for the rise of foreign investment. Some of the usual suspects are maintained, such as self-interested railways and commercial banking and the delay of settlement of the Prairies. Some new culprits are added, however, such as the lack of investment in military technology. What is most striking about Laxer's analysis, however, is that he attempts to explain the nature of Canadian development not by the conservative character of the capitalist class but by the failure of subordinate classes (weak and fragmented agrarian and working-class politics) to press for reforms to the development model. The absence of class-based challenges to Canadian capital, unlike in Europe and elsewhere, led, in his view, to the abandonment of an autonomous path of development.

Also in contrast to the idea that staples capital either blocked indigenous manufacturing or allied with foreign interests as a risk-avoidance strategy,

William Carroll (1986) argues that during the National Policy period successful indigenous financial capital developed that was fully capable of autonomously financing and merging with industrial capital. The argument is illustrated by the early twentieth-century case when the financial house, Nesbitt Thomson, established a holding company, Power Corporation, to direct its large holdings in Canadian hydroelectric utilities. What is of interest is the conclusion that foreign capital invested in conjunction, as opposed to in alliance, with the growth of Canadian capital. According to Carroll, US capital, management services, and technology were important for Canadian industrialization, but were not a dominant force within Canadian capital. Whether Canada could or should have become a North American version of Sweden, or more precisely, if subordinate classes could have pressured Canadian capital and the state to undertake a more autonomous model of development, presents questions that engage one's historical imagination (Mahon, 1989).

Modernization and Fordism

Regardless of the reason for it, during the 1940s the Canadian economy resumed the pattern of development established during the earlier period: staples industrialization and the establishment of standard-product mass manufacturing. Economic policy during this time was geared towards institutionalizing a particular form of the Keynesian welfare state and to the multilateral liberalization of international trade. As postwar reconstruction took off, the Canadian economy experienced close to three decades of economic expansion. Several features of that expansion led to significant debate about the structure of Canadian capital and the national question. These included:

- massive infusion of foreign direct investment in resource and manufacturing sectors;
- continued weaknesses of import substitution industrialization (ISI) in manufacturing (technological dependence and reliance on the home market);
- increasing reliance on continental markets for manufacturing imports and resource exports;
- continued corporate concentration;
- substantial interregional tensions within Canadian capital.

Foreign Direct Investment and the Structure of Canadian Capital

The real centre of the debate on whether Canada emerged from the modernization period as a 'rich dependency' or an autonomous political economy stems from the rise of the multinational enterprise (MNE) and the change in the structure of foreign investment from portfolio equity and financial participation in domestic firms to *foreign direct investment* (FDI)—the acquisition of plants or companies in a host country by a company based in another jurisdiction. FDI occurred either through the takeover of existing Canadian firms or through new investment producing a wholly owned subsidiary of a foreign-owned firm operating in the Canadian market.

Much of the FDI streaming into Canada in the postwar period was directed to the manufacturing and resource sectors, and the home country of the majority of the MNEs was the United States. Table 29 reveals that by 1970 these sectors were half American-owned. Such investments were not motivated by cost-cutting motives, but were rather strategic investments for rent-seeking resource extractors and processors interested in industrial staples. Strategic market access investments within the auto sector, for example, produced Canadian branch plants that were miniature replicas of home-country companies. They produced a full range for a sheltered (tariff-protected) host market, usually in much smaller and less efficient production runs than in home countries (Clement, 1977; Clark-Jones, 1987; Eden, 1993). The postwar boom in FDI led to the articulation of the Canadian economy in what Jane Jenson (1989) terms a configuration of 'permeable Fordism' in which each region in the country competed to find niches in the emerging continental economy. The United States became the most important source of FDI and the most important export market for Canadian goods and services.

FDI incorporated Canadian firms within an international value chain that also contained a hierarchy of authority and technology, with resource extractors at the bottom and leading high-technology enterprises at the top. Miniature replica investments, such as predominated in Canada, used the second highest levels of technology—higher than resource investments focused on selling a single bulk commodity product on the global market, but lower than state-of-the-art, large-scale, world-class manufacturing facilities. Generally, multinational firms enjoyed a competitive advantage over domestic competitors (Eden, 1993; Dunning, 1993). For these reasons, after 1960 a general and popular response to the rearticulation of the Canadian economy and a politicized debate on the effects of FDI on national economic sovereignty emerged in Canada.

The consolidation of Canadian capital during the modernization period had been aided by the Canadian government in recognition that FDI branch plants

Table 29: Percentage of US Control of Canadian Non-Financial Industries, 1926–1970

Sector	1926	1930	1939	1948	1954a*	1954b*	1960	1965	1970
Manufacturing	30	31	32	39	45	41	44	46	47
Petroleum and gas	—	—	—	—	—	67	64	58	61
Mining and smelting	32	42	38	37	54	49	53	52	59
Railways	3	3	3	3	2	2	2	2	2
Other utilities	20	29	26	24	11	7	4	4	4

* Petroleum and natural gas included in manufacturing and mining and smelting before 1954.
Source: Clement, 1977: 91, Table 3.

had strategic advantages over domestic firms. The government had provided changes in the tax structure and allowed the privatization of Crown corporations that had been instruments of wartime industrialization. In part, public support for these efforts in the immediate postwar period had come from the fact that the national/foreign capital cleavage cut across the divisions already existing in the country between large and small capital and between resource-financial and manufacturing capital. Canadian subsidiaries of foreign companies had access to foreign capital and technology, which allowed them to establish and retain large domestic market shares (Khemani, 1980).

The logic of continental integration was an essential part of Canadian economic policy throughout the whole modernization period. However, beginning in the 1950s, the Canadian government began to promote enhanced domestic participation in many resource and manufacturing activities either for regional or for national development purposes. Similar activities were undertaken by provincial governments. To aid these activities, the federal government began to institute restrictions on foreign ownership of Canadian firms. This became an issue in Canada in the late 1950s and early 1960s when the full impact of US investment in the post-World War II period became apparent (Safarian, 1966). The Royal Commission on Canada's Economic Prospects (the Gordon Commission) pointed out the possible divided loyalties of branch-plant managers, who would work to defeat any Canadian government schemes to develop the national economy (Canada, 1957), while in the mid-1960s the impact of US ownership of key sectors of the economy became a *cause célèbre* when Liberal Finance Minister Walter Gordon attempted to restrict foreign investment in his 1963 federal budget (Rugman, 1980: 125). In 1968 a Privy Council task force on the structure of Canadian industry (the Watkins Task Force) looked into the issue, as did a 1970 parliamentary standing committee (Watkins, 1968; Levitt, 1970). In 1972 yet another task force investigated the situation, resulting in the creation of the Foreign Investment Review Agency (FIRA) in 1974 (Canada, 1972; Rugman, 1977).

FIRA remained in operation for only 10 years. Foreign investors objected to the restraints placed on their activities by the Canadian government and appeared to withhold investment from Canada in protest. Following the recession of 1981–2, FIRA was replaced in 1984–5 by a new and less powerful review agency, Investment Canada. Finally, in 1989, the Canada-US Free Trade Agreement raised the limits on reviewable investments to $150 million, effectively exempting all but the largest takeovers from government surveillance (Laxer, 1989a).

The net effect of postwar changes was much different from what had been foreseen by nationalists. Canadian capitalists regrouped, diversified, and consolidated in the face of pressures from foreign investment and new business opportunities. As in the pre-war period, Canadian capital was dominated by chartered banks organized around highly distinct networks. Significantly, by 1976 foreign firms lost leading positions in those networks, which meant that the large foreign and Canadian-owned sectors of the economy operated in different organizational contexts (Carroll, 1986: 128–57). The 'silent surrender' was somewhat exaggerated. Carroll attributes this growth to a number of factors. The spectacular rise of US investment was not accomplished by the purchase of large Canadian firms but by buying out small Canadian firms in a competitive process with large domestic firms. Canadian firms reclaimed lost market shares and also diversified into new, more dynamic sectors. Large-scale indigenous investment firms emerged with the power to pursue new investment strategies. Important to reducing the power of foreign firms in key networks was the gradual repatriation of control of older foreign firms through stock purchase. The 1970s also witnessed ambitious repatriation programs, sometimes by means of public ownership. As well, there was an increased concentration of the domestically owned parts of the Canadian economy (Carroll, 1986: 158–69). Foreign firms, on the other hand, did not consolidate in the same manner during the postwar period. The changing national control of Canadian capital is illustrated in Table 30.

Concentration and International Competition

The consolidation of Canadian capital during the postwar years featured increasing economic concentration. Table 31 indicates the pattern changed from horizontal to vertical merger and acquisitions—reflecting the drive by large firms to integrate backward and forward. In the pulp and paper industry, for example, vertical acquisitions reflected the tendency of large corporations to buy new sources of supply—small pulp and paper operations and their various rights to resources. Increasing corporate concentration also reflected the growing export orientation of the resource and manufacturing sectors. The large scale of the economic structures in both sectors produced effective barriers to entry for small firms (Bain, 1968).

Activity undertaken on the part of the federal government to prevent mergers and acquisitions was inconsequential and failed in any way to stop the process of concentration. Although several elements of its anti-combines program failed because of federal-provincial wrangling, the commitment of the federal government to the policy was never more than half-hearted. Between 1910 and 1960 the federal government prosecuted only four merger cases, all unsuccessfully (Brecher, 1981: 5). The net result was an economy dominated by a small set of big firms, a shrunken 'middle' range of intermediate-size firms, and a large group of small firms, as illustrated in Table 32.

The attitude of the federal government towards concentration was most consistently illustrated by the findings of the federal Royal Commission on Corporate Concentration (the Bryce Commission) in the mid-1970s. Discontent with the existing policy was voiced once again by small business and labour when the country's two largest conglomerates—Argus Corporation of Toronto and Power Corporation of Montreal—proposed a merger. The commission made the most eloquent statement of the government's position in favour of the development of large pools of capital in Canada, stating that these corporations were

Table 30: Percentage Distributions of Canadian and Foreign-Controlled Corporate Assets by Industry, 1970, 1976, and 1982

Sector	Year	All Corporations with Assets of $25 million and over			All Corporations		
		Canada	Foreign Control	Total	Canada	Foreign Control	Total
Mining	1970	24.08	75.92	100	30.60	69.40	100
	1976	43.09	56.91	100	44.79	55.21	100
	1982	64.49	35.51	100	65.87	34.13	100
Manufacturing	1970	33.91	66.09	100	40.37	59.63	100
	1976	38.83	61.17	100	45.49	54.51	100
	1982	49.24	50.76	100	54.54	45.41	100
Utilities	1970	93.71	6.29	100	92.14	7.86	100
	1976	93.36	6.64	100	92.53	7.47	100
	1982	96.34	3.66	100	95.28	4.72	100
Wholesale	1970	66.98	33.03	100	72.75	27.25	100
Retail	1976	65.37	34.63	100	75.81	24.19	100
Trade	1982	72.48	27.52	100	80.81	19.19	100
Total industrial	1970	60.09	39.91	100	62.10	37.90	100
and commercial	1976	63.34	36.66	100	67.68	32.32	100
capital	1982	70.54	29.46	100	74.65	25.35	100

Note: Mining includes petroleum and natural gas unless the company is integrated into the manufacture of petroleum. Utilities include transportation, communications, storage, and public utilities. Total industrial and commercial capital includes the major sectors listed in detail plus the construction and services sectors. Very small corporations (with assets of less than $250,000 and sales of less than $500,000) are excluded, as are non-profit organizations; most Crown corporations are included.
Source: Carroll, 1986: 162.

required if Canadians were to compete in international markets. It reaffirmed the need only to ensure that domestic consumers were not unjustly penalized by monopolistic behaviour on the part of the large firms (Canada, 1978). Although criticized vigorously by proponents of a more competitive marketplace, the commission's findings and recommendations were consistent with both historical and current government practices (Gorecki and Stanbury, 1979). The narrowness of the federal government's policy towards corporate concentration, as Wallace

Table 31: Percentage of Mergers by Type, 1900–1973

	Horizontal	Vertical	Conglomerate	Total
1900–9	90	4	6	100
1910–19	85	10	5	100
1920–9	85	11	4	100
1930–9	88	7	5	100
1940–8	73	19	8	100
1945–61	64	23	13	100
1960–8	63	19	18	100
1968–73	57	18	25	100

Source: Lecraw and Thompson, 1978: 64.

Clement (1983: 107–33) points out, would subsequently weaken its ability to deal with politically sensitive and complex issues—such as media concentration and its effects on the quality of democratic life in Canada.

The final shape of Canadian capital is best illustrated in Table 33. It indicates that the decline in foreign ownership, while significant, is still relative. Increasing levels of corporate concentration, a large, but declining publicly owned corporate sector, and significant levels of foreign ownership characterize the structure of capital in Canada.

Mercantilism, Regionalism, and Nationalism

The consolidation and organization of Canadian capital in the modern period has been shaped not only by questions of foreign investment but also by mercantilism and regionalism. The weaknesses of Canada's tariff-sheltered manufacturing sector were not resolved by miniature replica FDI. Rather, the sector continued to display weak export performance and low research and development. Debate during the 1970s centred on the necessity for making the transi-

Table 32: Corporate Concentration of Assets, 1965–1973

Asset Size ($000,000)	Number of Companies		Assets (%)	
	1965	1973	1965	1973
Over 1,000	11	29	25.5	35.1
Over 500 to 1,000	13	40	6.1	8.3
Over 100 to 500	135	297	18.7	17.1
Over 1 to 100	9,462	18,909	35.5	29.5
Under 1	155,638	239,226	14.2	10

Source: Marfels, 1977: 42.

Table 33: Percentage Distributions and Concentration of Assets in Leading Non-Financial Enterprises, 1975–1982

Enterprise Rank	Year	Canadian Capitalists	Canadian State	Foreign	Total	Concentration Ratio
25 leading						
enterprises	1975	34.33	46.89	18.53	100	29.2
	1977	29.56	51.64	18.80	100	29.4
	1979	31.72	49.18	19.11	100	30.3
	1981	51.43	30.79	17.78	100	32.1
	1982	48.67	35.01	16.32	100	34.1
100 leading						
enterprises	1975	35.84	33.06	31.10	100	46.5
	1977	33.50	36.19	30.31	100	47.5
	1979	35.16	35.90	28.94	100	48.5
	1981	47.15	27.54	25.31	100	49.8
	1982	48.39	28.45	23.16	100	52.1
500 leading						
enterprises	1975	36.35	25.92	37.73	100	64.6
	1977	34.60	29.31	36.09	100	65.2
	1979	37.03	28.86	34.11	100	65.3
	1981	47.65	22.19	30.15	100	65.6
	1982	49.06	22.73	28.21	100	67.2
All						
enterprises*	1975	47.86	18.37	33.78	100	95.7
	1977	47.88	20.47	31.65	100	95.9
	1979	50.36	20.11	29.54	100	96.5
	1981	58.64	15.08	26.27	100	97.0
	1982	58.90	15.75	25.35	100	97.1

* Excludes small companies not classified by the Corporations and Labour Unions Returns Act, e.g., 147,993 firms in 1975, accounting for 4.3 per cent of all non-financial assets; 235,800 firms in 1981, accounting for 3.0 per cent of all non-financial assets.
Source: Carroll, 1986: 163.

tion from a resource-based to a technology-based economy. It was thought that Canada's comparative advantage in resources would diminish over time and that successful political economies were based on manufacturing and value-added technological economies. There were two ideas for carrying out this task. One was a fairly *dirigiste* and mercantilist strategy of picking winner firms and then supporting their efforts to gain a high-technology export threshold. The other was a more straightforward resort to market determination—to drop all tariff protection and then let the market decide (Williams, 1986). The former would be more politically driven while the latter would play into the hands of existing concentrations of economic power.

Similarly, the influx of foreign direct investment during the postwar period exacerbated Canada's uneven economic development and heightened regional tensions. Branch-plant head offices were centred largely in Montreal and then in Toronto. Increasing international competition made it more and more difficult to induce regional economic development in peripheral provinces despite both federal and provincial government support. Foreign investment, therefore, became one of the best means of securing economic growth. Alberta, British Columbia, and to a lesser extent Saskatchewan benefited from international resource development, particularly in petroleum during the 1970s escalation in oil prices. Understandably, provinces used their significant constitutional authority and administrative capacity to cultivate MNEs, secure rents, and foster local economic development. Regional capital, therefore, became tied to the mercantilist policies of increasingly powerful provinces (Richards and Pratt, 1979; Niosi, 1983).

In the early 1980s, the federal government attempted a series of nationalist mercantilist policies geared towards fostering a Canadianization of the resource sector, reclamation of national control over the energy sector, and the disciplining of regionalism and provincialism. The corporate reaction to this mercantilism was to reject economic nationalism and instead support a market solution that would discipline government's ability to resort to mercantilist intervention (Duquette, 1993). Eventually this commitment would be reflected in the FTA and NAFTA. Although many, following the dependency logic, thought the FTA presented a real threat to Canadian capitalism, it is probably more accurate to follow Williams's (1995) reasoning that the agreement simply marked the further entrenchment of Canadian firms within the continental economy and, as such, extended the processes of integration already in place.

Globalization

Regionalization, with the establishment of new transnational trade regimes, has been one of the major responses to the functional integration of the international economy often termed 'globalization' (Chodos et al., 1993; Anderson et al., 1998). The FTA and NAFTA have defined a new economic space, so that it is now perhaps best to think of Canada as a region within the greater North American economy and North America as a region within the global economy (Williams, 1989; Jenson and Mahon, 1993). How has capital responded to the new rules, markets, and identity? Though this is an ongoing process fraught with political conflict and uncertainty, it is worthwhile to identify key trends. These include the new focus on the international competitiveness of capital, concomitant processes of an increased North Americanization of the Canadian market and an internationalization of capital, and, lastly, issues stemming from corporate mergers and restructuring. Each of these is addressed below.

Global Regionalism and Competitiveness

By the mid-1990s the world economy had been articulated around the 'triad' of the EU, NAFTA (dominated by the United States), and the Pacific Rim (dominated by Japan). Though some like to point to the convergence within leading triad countries of levels of technology, incomes, and consumption patterns, the fact of the matter is that each region is characterized by substantially different motives and terms of integration (Milner, 1998; Higgott, 1998; Stubbs, 1998). Moreover, despite the rhetoric of globalization, there are uneven trading relations among triad countries. Canada is the greatest trading partner of the US within NAFTA, and increasingly so. The links between North American and East Asian economies are so great that in many ways they are part of the same economic region. However, this is not a balanced trade. North American firms have not fully penetrated the Japanese consumer market. In contrast, EU countries have developed a more diversified internal trade, although there is competition between Eastern and Southern European peripheries for investment and market access to the more lucrative Central European markets. East Asian-EU trade and investment linkages are not well developed (Donnelly, 1994; Kearns, 1994; Knubley, Legault, and Rao, 1994; Padoan, 1994). The new trade and investment relationships are summarized in Figure 5.

Figure 5: Geographic Distribution of Canadian Trade and Direct Investment Stock, 1991 (% of total)

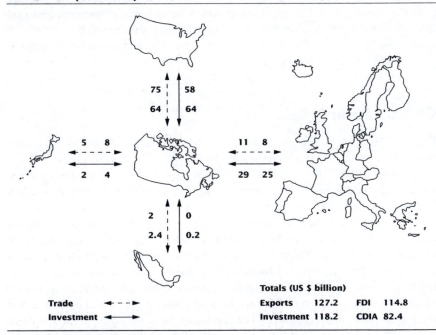

Totals (US $ billion)

Trade		Exports	127.2	FDI	114.8
Investment		Investment	118.2	CDIA	82.4

Source: Knubley, Legault, and Rao, 1994: 152.

MNE investment strategies have moved away from the strategic resource and market access investments to *cost-cutting* (Eden, 1993). In part this has been driven by the exportation of Fordism to less developed countries (LDCs) where cheap labour can be combined with high technology and strategic market access. In this context the international position of Canadian business has changed. Regionalization and globalization have reopened questions of the importance of national competitiveness, the role of FDI, Canadian direct investment abroad (CDIA), and the future of miniature replica investment within the industrial structure. In the globalization context, therefore, one assesses the structure of Canadian capital in relation to its regional competitors and trading partners.

The new competitive position of Canadian capital is illustrated by a recent study of the top 1,008 North American firms (in value of sales) during the 1985–91 period (Knubley, Legault, and Rao, 1994). The sample of 823 American, 158 Canadian, and 27 Mexican firms roughly represents each country's share in the North American economy. For the United States, these firms represented 50 per cent of total gross output and 25 per cent of employment. The comparable figures for Canada were 52 per cent of output and 19 per cent of employment, suggesting that leading firms in Canada do not have as high an employment performance as do those of the United States. In the Mexican sample the top firms comprised 19 per cent of output yet only 2 per cent of employment, suggesting a much less concentrated economy. The majority of top US firms were MNEs, while none of the top Mexican firms were multinationals. When the sample was reduced to a comparison of the 20 leading firms of each country, similar trends appeared. The top US firms were extremely large in comparison to those of the other two countries and showed better employment performance.

Close to one-third of the top Canadian firms were classified as mining or resource-intensive manufacturing enterprises, while the relative share of the similar sector for the United States was 16 per cent. Over 40 per cent of Mexican firms were in the mining and resource-intensive manufacturing categories. On the other hand, more than 23 per cent of US firms were classified as technology-intensive manufacturing, as opposed to under 11 per cent for the Canadian sample. There was a slightly higher percentage of Canadian than American firms in the services category, although the specializations of each country were different. Top US service corporations were in communications, while top Canadian service corporations were in transportation and finance. The results are summarized in Table 34.

The specialization of Canadian capital, however, is not fully reflected without accounting for foreign ownership. Table 35 summarizes the breakdown of top firms by country of control. It indicates that half of Canada's top mining firms are foreign subsidiaries, as are the majority of the technology-intensive manufacturing firms. For these reasons it is hard to measure those firms as part of Canada's comparative advantage because corporate policies are highly influenced by parent resources and strategy. Moreover, the historical inefficiency of the miniature replica FDI investments indicates that much of the manufacturing sector is vul-

Table 34: Industrial Distribution of the Top US, Canadian, and Mexican Firms (% of total)

Industry	United States				Canada				Mexico			
	No. of Firms	Assets	Sales	Employees	No. of Firms	Assets	Sales	Employees	No. of Firms	Assets	Sales	Employees
Agriculture and Fishing	3	0.07	0.21	0.27	0				0			
Mining	25	4.06	8.52	2.07	20	5.05	10.55	6.17	1	2.42	1.40	3.63
Construction	9	0.32	0.76	0.58	2	0.10	0.56	0.50	1	1.75	2.04	
Labour-intensive manufacturing	44	1.18	2.23	2.35	7	1.39	3.15	5.20	0			
Resource-intensive manufacturing	109	5.95	13.09	8.96	31	7.07	14.78	18.34	10	53.85	53.50	35.13
Technology-intensive manufacturing	193	17.55	28.45	24.21	17	3.08	14.71	10.89	7	12.88	16.22	35.86
Transportation	23	1.59	2.81	3.07	9	3.27	5.88	10.45	1	0.91	1.58	2.32
Communications	19	4.30	5.19	4.34	5	4.18	4.95	6.55	2	10.97	9.86	12.22
Utilities	86	6.81	6.00	2.89	12	8.71	5.54	3.42	0			
Trade	119	4.76	15.41	41.18	30	3.46	16.51	24.86	3	3.17	6.92	6.57
Finance	145	51.99	15.00	6.94	25	63.69	23.37	13.61	2	14.04	8.48	4.27
Services	48	1.42	2.32	3.15	0				0			
Total*	823	7,806	3,874	27,329	158	1,241	457	2,382	27	125	62	520

Note: Sales and assets are denominated in US$ billion and employment in thousands.
Source: Knubley, Legault, and Rao, 1994: 169.

nerable to reorganization and rationalization, a point we will return to later in the discussion. There is no such ownership fragmentation in the top US firms.

Three different measures of revealed comparative advantage indicate that Canada had comparative advantage relative to the United States in resources, resource-intensive manufacturing, and financial services. The US comparative advantage was in technology-intensive manufacturing, trade, and services (Knubley, Legault, and Rao, 1994: 170–2).

Do these figures reveal that Canada is heading for deindustrialization? A pessimistic reading of the situation is supported by figures indicating that Canada's overall comparative advantage has declined over the past 20 years (Bryan, 1994: 91), that top Canadian firms did not grow as much as their US counterparts during the 1985–91 period, and that there are serious concerns about the level of Canadian productivity (Porter and Monitor Company, 1991; Bryan, 1994: 205–43). Knubley, Legault, and Rao's (1994) survey indicated the greatest difference in labour productivity varied with sector and country of control, revealing, among other things, that domestic and foreign firms have different methods of innovation. On the other hand, the 100 fastest growing firms in the Canadian economy during the same period were small to medium-sized technology-intensive firms,

Table 35: Industrial Distribution of Domestic and Foreign-Controlled Canadian Firms (% of total)

Industry	Domestic				Foreign-Controlled			
	No. of Firms	Assets	Sales	Employees	No. of Firms	Assets	Sales	Employees
Mining	10	2.42	6.00	5.15	10	41.83	23.38	8.51
Construction	2	0.10	0.66	0.59	0			
Labour-intensive manufacturing	7	1.43	3.69	6.05	0			
Resource-intensive manufacturing	26	10.79	26.25	27.78	5	5.04	4.33	4.53
Technology-intensive manufacturing	4	1.19	3.44	5.30	13	29.75	50.69	30.83
Transportation	8	3.25	6.47	12.08	1	1.69	1.52	0.35
Communications	5	4.29	5.79	7.63	0			
Utilities	11	8.77	6.13	3.81	1	2.71	1.30	0.73
Trade	22	2.32	14.50	15.82	8	18.57	17.77	54.81
Finance	24	65.44	27.08	15.79	1	0.41	1.00	0.24
Total	119	100.00	100.00	100.00	39	100.00	100.00	100.00

Source: Knubley, Legault, and Rao, 1994: 171.

indicating that Canadian capital is restructuring, not simply playing on declining strengths (Gera and Mang, 1998).

Restructuring

Regionalization and globalization have induced economic and corporate restructuring. Restructuring is often associated with a downsizing and focusing of firm's operations to gain competitive position within NAFTA. The integrated market has allowed firms to restructure operations at every stage of production, from sourcing of materials and primary production to more finished stages of production, management services, and research and development. In these terms, Eden (1994a) suggests that Mexico has an advantage in resource extraction and primary production, Canada in middle levels of production, and the United States in final stages of production and services. Firms will eventually reorganize so that they can locate plants in a value chain that takes advantage of specific comparative advantages and that maximizes the overall efficiency of operations. This form of restructuring depends not only on sectoral and corporate variables but also on broad national and regional variables that affect long-term corporate efficiency and profitability.

In fact, the restructuring is somewhat more complex, reflecting the fact that capital now has new organizational alternatives (Eden, 1993). Formerly, MNEs maintained a vertically integrated structure where FDI, having wholly owned subsidiaries, was the dominant means of investment. Declining institutional barriers and new information technologies have changed internal corporate relations by making it easier for parent companies to centralize and co-ordinate operations and thus effectively to manage distant subsidiaries and thereby eliminate layers of middle management. The same variables have allowed MNEs to change form—to downsize into a more flexible and less structured form. For example, the organizations of new MNEs resemble networks where units that tie together the value change are fairly autonomous. A smaller corporate core can be linked to several competing source companies and a range of other corporate entities that contribute to the production chain or supply research and development or financial services. This allows the MNE to develop new forms of efficiency based on agglomeration (Eaton, Lipsey, and Safarian, 1994).

Traditionally, FDI engendered conflicts between host governments and foreign capital. Currently, the use of wholly owned branch plants, or FDI, is also only one of a series of options open to MNE global investment. Other options, such as contractual links and minority investments, can accomplish the task with greater efficiency and a broader distribution of risks and greater potential gains for host countries. MNE investment, therefore, becomes a more attractive goal for host economic development. It is no coincidence that this form of organizational change has been associated with a dramatic rise in foreign investment in the global economy.

The definitive answer on restructuring is, of course, yet to come. Restructuring initially targeted the weakness of Canada's postwar miniature replica manufacturing branch plants concentrated in Quebec and Ontario (Eden, 1994a; MacLachlan, 1996). NAFTA has also changed investment incentives, inducing strategic MNE investment into resources and other sectors of the Mexican economy previously closed to foreign investment. Similarly, NAFTA encourages US-based multinationals to centralize support and research and development activities within parent companies where they can take advantage of the agglomerations—the geographic concentrations of high technology and service expertise in the US Northeast and Southwest. Nevertheless, the continued growth in investment in sectors such as automobile parts and production reaffirms that NAFTA restructuring plays on existing strengths.

Initially, the government of Canada's monetary policy made readjustment difficult for Canadian manufacturing. As interest rates declined in the mid-1990s this situation improved, allowing Canadian firms to use their greater organizational flexibility to address their structural weaknesses. Here the golden triangle in central Canada and the resource centres such as Calgary and Vancouver in western Canada provide the geographic bases of Canadian agglomeration.

Given the significant employment effects of manufacturing, restructuring will likely continue to be highly controversial. The restructuring of large firms often leads to a smaller, more tightly focused core. Small businesses also emerge from restructuring as suppliers and supports for larger companies. These firms, in fact, are becoming the largest source of employment in Canada. This form of restructuring poses a number of issues that are poorly understood, ranging from labour market policy, industrial relations, and industrial strategy to competition policy (Ray, 1996).

The traditional pillars of Canadian capital, financial services, resource extraction, transportation, telecommunications, and utilities continue to have major comparative advantages and are fairly well placed to benefit from increased regionalization. These sectors display two trends, a tendency towards internationalization through Canadian direct investment abroad and a trend towards merger and conglomeration.

International capital flows have changed. During postwar modernization, the United States was the source of the majority of Canadian and world FDI. During the 1980s, however, the United States turned into a major FDI host. During the 1985–90 period FDI in North America increased an average 34 per cent per year (Knubley, Legault, and Rao, 1994), making North America, and the United States in particular, a major magnet for international investment. Also, more recent foreign investment in Canada has taken the form of portfolio investments.

Both Canadian capital and American capital have invested abroad. Proportionally more Canadian than American firms have engaged in foreign direct investment. The greater outward focus is revealed by the increase in Canadian direct investment abroad over FDI in Canada. The destination of capital flows is outside of North America, meaning that there is less mutual investment between the US and Canada. It also suggests that these investments are oriented towards improving competitive position within NAFTA. For Canadian high-tech manufacturing the focus is on seeking technological alliances with the EU firms. For Canadian resources, the motivation has been to make strategic market and resource access investments. As a whole, Canadian direct investment abroad has been profitable. Nevertheless, some of these investments have been problematic, as the case of MacMillan Bloedel illustrates, because ecological and management expertise is not necessarily transferable between resource bases and Canadian resource multinationals often do not have the financial strength to weather the pitfalls of starting long-term investment projects (Vertinsky and Raizada, 1994).

Mergers and Concentration

Globalization has induced further economic concentration and solidified the essentially ologopolistic structure of the Canadian economy. By 1990, for example, in 90 per cent of all economic sectors four or fewer firms had 60 per cent of the market share (Khemani, 1991). Motives for merger generally follow from restructuring initiatives. In the forest and pulp and paper industries, for example, the traditional motive of seeking resources and new sources of supply has changed to consolidation of operations and market position, that is, to have fewer and more efficient mills. Such rationalization raises profound issues of sustainability and regional economic development.

In 1986 the Canadian government changed its antiquated and ineffective competition policy to encourage restructuring in the face of globalization. In part, this was done by adopting new objectives, such as encouraging efficiency-enhancing restructuring, providing opportunities for Canadian firms in world markets and for small and medium-size business, and seeking to enhance consumer protection. Legal and administrative changes in the definition of competition moved away from took a traditional and restrictive criminal law framework, thus allowing the Canadian government to implement and co-ordinate initiatives more effectively and to pursue its policy mandate in NAFTA negotiations and other international forums (Doern, 1995). Much international business studies literature argues that such mergers and concentration are a profitable, healthy, and logical consequence of global restructuring (Daniels, 1991; Kudrle, 1994). However, the real problem for a small, open political economy, such as that of Canada, is how to deal with conflicts between goals seeking greater efficiency through global merger and restructuring and that of protecting national consumer interests. Resolving this issue defines the limit of the merger movement. Two key examples illustrate the point.

First, globalization has presented new opportunities for the domestic banking and financial services industries. Recognizing this, the government of Canada established a task force to examine the issue—ostensibly to make policy recommendation to the Minister of Finance. Before that task force could report, however, the leading chartered banks attempted to force the government's hand by declaring their intention to merge. The rationalization was that these mergers were essential to meet global competition and that consumer protection in Canada is ensured by the wide range of competition in global markets. Thus, mergers within an already centralized banking system would not threaten consumers. This form of argument has not been supported by productivity experts (Porter and Monitor Company, 1991) or majority political parties. Given that Canadian banks have provided record dividends to their shareholders in recent years, the case that restructuring was needed to meet the global competition lacked credibility. Indeed, it was easier to make the case that the mergers presented means of cutting costs and reducing the availability of traditional services—particularly when one of the major banks distanced itself from the initiatives. In the end, the government of Canada said no—for the time being.

A second example is found in Canada's so-called cultural industries. Globalization and economic concentration present significant problems for Canadian cultural and media industries. The traditional assumption for the regulation of media concentration was that competition ensured political pluralism. Protection, as it evolved, was directed towards securing Canadian industry's place in the face of the dominance of US media even within the Canadian market. The Canadian Radio-Television and Telecommunications Commission (CRTC) became the major regulatory instrument to accomplish the task. Cultural industries were apparently protected under the terms of the FTA. Then, as discussed in Chapter Five, the emergence of NAFTA and the WTO left these sheltered sectors increasingly vulnerable. For cultural industries the problem is that producing primarly for the Canadian market, in the context of NAFTA's integrated market, leaves a firm at a market disadvantage. And when governments act to protect those industries, they are in violation of emerging international trade law.

Part of the difficulty is the global hegemony of the US cultural industry, thus making it difficult to define a 'national' cultural industry or product. During the late 1980s the export value of US cultural industries doubled to $7 billion. In contrast, the export value of all Canadian cultural industries was less than 0.5 per cent of the value of US exports. Canadian cultural industries will have to both renew their sheltered status within the North American market and grow or merge with stronger North American partners in order to survive. Both Canadian and American cultural industries, over the past few years, have entered into a merger maze to gain market position in new media technologies. What has emerged is a series of large conglomerates. In that process most traditional conventions that have regulated corporate ownership and structure have been changed or abandoned.

During the last decade merger activity has accelerated. According to James P. Winter, from 1988 to 1994 media assets grew by 225 per cent, largely by merger and acquisition. Cable-related media companies experienced the fastest growth. Newspapers have nearly doubled their level of concentration. By 1998, one newspaper group in Canada, headed by Conrad Black, controlled approximately 60 per cent of daily newspapers. In some provinces, such as Saskatchewan, New Brunswick, and Newfoundland, one company owned all dailies, and in New Brunswick, through cross-media ownership, the Irving family owned all the major newspapers and television stations.

This level of concentration raises the traditional concerns. For the left, concentration ties the media into established power and thus robs it of its ability to criticize power (Winter, 1997). In addition, conglomerates, it is claimed, produce a mass package that does not adequately cover local news. For the right, the question is a matter of professionalism, economic efficiency, and political prerogative. Black's newspaper editorial staffs, for example, are beginning to reflect the owner's conservative ideology. The logical and yet unanswered question that this raises is how political pluralism can be protected when media pursue a singular political agenda, when competition is muted, and when the barriers to entry are so high as to be prohibitive.

The Growth of Business Associations

The divisions among Canadian capital are often overcome at the board level, the site of extensive corporate directorship interlocks (Ornstein, 1989). But in terms of political organization, these divisions are manifested in the associations that represent the interests of capital to governments.

Sectoral Organization and Activities of Business Associations

Before Confederation, business associations in Canada were linked with particular industries, but they tended to represent general business interests at the local level. During this era municipal boards of trade, such as those located in Montreal, Quebec, Saint John, Halifax, Kingston, and Toronto, were especially important (Coleman, 1988: 19). Other associations existed on a regional basis during times of crisis in an industry and attempted to regulate supply or entry into the field, but they usually ceased to exist once market conditions improved (Forster, 1986: 110). Still other associations emerged in response to unionization in an effort to keep wages down in a particular industry; these included the Lumbermen's Association of St John and the iron founders' associations in Quebec and Ontario (ibid.: 111). By the time of Confederation, according to W.D. Coleman (1988), the number of 'nationally relevant' business associations was under 15. This number increased rapidly after Confederation, and an additional 55 such organizations existed by 1900. Between 1900 and 1980 the number grew to over 700; the major periods of growth were 1915–19 and 1940–5 (Coleman, 1985a, 1988).

Several of the most significant national business interest associations were formed before 1900, including the Canadian Manufacturers' Association, which grew out of the Ontario Manufacturers' Association to become an independent agency between 1879 and 1899, and the Canadian Bankers' Association, established in 1891. In the transportation sector, the dominance of the Canadian Pacific

Railway obviated the need for a separate business association until the emergence of highway and air transportation in the 1930s and 1940s. In the agricultural sector, the numerous associations that existed among producers of different products at the provincial level eventually merged to form the Canadian Council of Agriculture in 1910. In the resource sector, permanent organizations did not emerge until the 1920s and 1930s and then only at the provincial level, reflecting the dominance of provincial governments in resource regulation. National associations operating on a federal principle emerged in some resource industries, such as the Canadian Pulp and Paper Association (1917) and the Mining Association of Canada (1935). In others they were not formed until much later— the Canadian Petroleum Association (1952) and the Canadian Forest Industries Council (1984), for example. In many resource sectors dominant provincial associations, such as the Council of Forest Industries of British Columbia, often acted as national representatives in liaison with the federal government.

Much of the growth immediately after World War I and during World War II can be attributed to government encouragement of industry organization. During both world wars the federal government took over price and supply regulation of most major industries and demanded that industrial producers choose between government regulation and self-regulation. Many industries, of course, preferred self-regulation and formed industry associations to interact with government officials and monitor industrial performance (Coleman, 1988: 24–6; Traves, 1979).

By 1980, about 500 national business associations and 125 farmers' organizations were active in Canada. Associations representing manufacturing firms accounted for about 40 per cent of national business associations. Significantly, 480 of the associations represented firms engaged in only one sector or subsector of the economy. About 45 per cent of these associations were organized on a federal basis, that is, with the national association acting as the collective voice of provincial organizations.

National Organizations and Activities

Most national associations have weak links with each other and tend to look after only the affairs of their own sector rather than promoting the interests of capital as a whole. However, several groups do attempt to enunciate national positions for business. While not divided sectorally, none the less they are divided along other lines, principally between large and small capital. Given the nature of Canadian corporate ownership, this first division also involves a division between domestic and export orientation and differences in foreign and domestic ownership. These associations include the Canadian Chamber of Commerce, the Canadian Federation of Independent Business, and the Business Council on National Issues.

The Canadian Chamber of Commerce is a relatively small organization established as the federal voice of multiple local, regional, and provincial chambers. Although the Chamber represents both small and large businesses, it is dominated by its provincial wings and serves primarily as a spokesperson for small business interests at that level. At the national level, those interests are represented by the Canadian Federation of Independent Business, an association that grew out of small business protests against the proposed federal tax reforms of the 1970s.

Until 1976 large capital tended to be represented by major sectoral associations at the federal level (especially the Canadian Manufacturers' Association). At that time, the Business Council on National Issues was formed, partially in response to the imposition of federal wage and price controls in 1975. The Business Council unites large corporations in the resource, financial, and US-controlled manufacturing sectors and represents the interests of the internationally oriented business community to government decision-makers (Coleman, 1988: 81–99).

Business organization has remained fairly stable during the globalization period and fairly closely aligned behind various forms of neo-liberalism, particularly fiscal austerity and tax relief. Questions of nationalism and federalism, however, still reveal important political splits among Canadian capitalists. For example, during the early 1990s, there were indications that major Quebec business organizations, following the failure of Meech Lake and Charlottetown, were becoming more openly supportive of sovereignty objectives. The same could not be said for Canadian business. The issue was then put to the test in the 1995 sovereignty-partnership referendum, where large and globally active business allied with federalists and Canadian capital to oppose the PQ's attempted unilateral declaration of independence, significantly increasing the antipathy between business and the PQ on the national question. The implementation of a post-referendum neo-liberal fiscal policy has subsequently diffused these tensions.

Conclusions: Cohesion, Fragmentation, and Competitiveness

For a long time studies of Canadian capital have been placed within a polarized debate that emerged from the response to postwar continental integration and the widespread Americanization that accompanied massive capital flows into the manufacturing and resource sectors. The question, in different forms, was whether Canadian financial capital had aligned itself with US multinationals and therefore blocked what would have been autonomous Canadian development. In challenging that hypothesis, studies have revealed a much different organization and structure.

Canadian capital is highly concentrated in areas of competitive advantage and able to respond to changed market and historical circumstances. Foreign direct investment has always been an integral part of Canadian capital but, in contrast to myth, is somewhat of an 'outsider' rather than an 'insider'. FDI, because of its association with MNEs, does have competitive advantages over domestic firms. In Canada the division between domestic and foreign firms is often measured by levels of technology (Britton and Gilmour, 1978; Britton, 1996).

During the modernization period the Canadian government established the policy framework that would integrate the Canadian and American economies. At the same time it attempted to offset MNE advantage by a number of mercantilist policies centred on disciplining FDI and subsidizing or sheltering selected domestic industries. Provincial governments have also competed for FDI and have established mercantilist strategies to gain rents and economic linkages. In the end the inconstancies of this policy framework spilled over into several regional conflicts. Capital rejected economic nationalism and favoured a straightforward market integration with the United States. The FTA and NAFTA, in this sense, are products of the business agenda.

Globalization has engendered a period of restructuring for Canadian capital. Part of that response has been to internationalize Canadian capital. Part, too, has been to increase the concentration of the capital. Hardest hit has been the miniature replica manufacturing sector. Compared to US competitors, Canadian companies were slow to respond to new market conditions and Canada's comparative advantage declined.

Globalization has favoured the rise of corporate power and the corporate agenda in public policy. In many ways, globalization is the day of the multinational or transnational enterprise. But that power should not be exaggerated. Canadian business, at an organizational level, displays all of the fragmentation of other actors within the Canadian community. Canadian business associations reflect the divisions in the structure of the economy and the structure of trade and ownership of Canadian firms. Most associations are sectoral or subsectoral in nature, and the few national multisectoral associations tend to reflect divisions between large and small or domestic and foreign capital. In addition, the federal nature of the country has also contributed to the promotion of two levels of interest associations, with many national associations existing as weak voices for powerful provincial groups.

Globalization has also made small business the country's greatest employer and opened up a series of policy questions on how the needs of this sector can be best met. If one puts this in context, the Canadian state faces powerful but fragmented capital and a weak and fragmented labour movement. Mediating their interests and developing policy take place on an international or continental scale. In the future, capital (and labour) will have to develop the appropriate organizational capacity to be effective. In other countries this situation has resulted in states promoting their own interests, however politically defined, aimed at shaping the society's mix of state-market relations. In Canada this does not occur because of the fragmentation of the state itself. Instead, the Canadian state pursues ad hoc, incremental interventions into the market that reflect the conjunctural strengths and weaknesses of different actors at different times and in different areas of economic activity. These interventions often lead to the establishment of contradictory policies at the different levels of government and, in most instances, to the failure of state policies aimed at managing the micro- and macro-political economies.

Chapter 10

The Macro-Political Economy: Monetary and Fiscal Management

Although states and markets are intertwined there are distinct differences in the types of state-market relations that exist at the micro level and macro level of a nation's political economy. At the micro level, extensive state-market interactions have an effect on the specific production and distribution decisions made by individual producers. While in capitalist countries the market is the primary mechanism for making these decisions, the state is also actively involved in the process, most often through the use of subsidies or the manipulation of tax systems. The state can also regulate individual producers and, in some cases, directly provide goods and services through public enterprises. But these sorts of activities do not exhaust the potential of state actions to influence the market behaviour of individual producers and consumers. State actions at the macro level also work to determine the behaviour of individual producers and consumers by altering the cost of credit in the domestic economy and by changing the value of a nation's currency in international markets.

The Instruments and Ends

The Rationales for Fiscal and Monetary Management

States are concerned at the macro level with altering the basic framework of market decision-making by controlling the value of the currency, the supply of money circulating in the society, and the ease of access of investors to investment funds. The general aim is to control the aggregate rate of growth of domestic production, but attainment of this goal is subject to many constraints. One constraint is constant international pressure on the terms of trade of a nation's exports. Others are questions about political stability (which can alter foreign and international investment behaviour) or about the propensity of producers to produce and consumers to consume different amounts of different products at different prices. As a result, the effectiveness of the state's efforts to manipulate the market is never certain. Nevertheless, all modern nation-states do make these efforts and a vast array of domestic and international institutions, rules, and instruments exists to guide and make them (Cohen, 1983).

Governments in Canada have always followed some sort of fiscal and monetary policy, but until the post-World War II era the notion of fiscal and monetary management was absent from government deliberations. Traditionally, government fiscal policy was simple and completely determined by the notion of balancing the government budget: to ensure that government revenues from all sources matched government expenditures and that government budgets were balanced on an annual basis. The logic behind this approach was to treat government spending just like any other economic 'enterprise' and to avoid debt payments wherever possible. Any debts forced on governments by unexpectedly high expenditures or lower revenues than anticipated were retired immediately; taxes were either raised or expenditures cut to ensure that the problem did not repeat itself in the following year (Mundell, 1993).

This kind of fiscal policy held sway in Canadian governments for the first 70 years of Confederation, until governments realized that their expenditures and tax policies had a major impact on the general functioning of the economy and could, at least in theory, be manipulated or managed in a fashion that would spur economic activity or decrease it. This realization, codified in Keynesian economic theory, led to a continuing debate between advocates of the pre-Keynesian balanced budget orthodoxy and advocates of Keynesian fiscal management techniques—a debate that has continued to characterize Canadian fiscal policy to the present day.

At the same time there was a similar evolution of thinking about monetary policy and monetary management efforts involving most of the same participants (Granatstein, 1982). Before World War II, monetary policy in Canada was restricted to government efforts to control inflation by controlling the issuance of credit and the printing of bank notes and by protecting the value of the Canadian dollar on international exchange markets.

Governments initially encountered difficulties in these policies because credit control and the issuing of bank notes were in the hands of private banks. Ostensibly as part of its effort to ensure public confidence in the banking system, in the early years of the twentieth century the federal government began to take over responsibility for regulating the money supply, although it did not consider actually manipulating the money supply to help expand or contract the economy until much later. Similarly, Canadian governments were always involved in efforts to ensure stability of the domestic currency in foreign exchange markets, but they did so for the first 70 years of Confederation through adherence to fixed exchange rates for the Canadian dollar against international gold and silver, or 'specie', standards.

These monetary orthodoxies also succumbed to problems encountered in the Depression as governments failed in their attempts to maintain fixed exchange rates against gold and silver and began to embrace the idea embodied in Keynesian economic theory that the supply of money and credit in the economy could be manipulated to boost or restrain economic activity. As in the case of fiscal policy, however, adherents to the pre-Keynesian orthodoxy contested the efficacy of government monetary management efforts, arguing that these efforts were ineffective or inflationary, or both. Debates between adherents of the two views continue to the present day.

Contemporary Canadian debates in both fiscal and monetary policy take place within the dominant liberal political-economic discourse centring on the question of market failures and the effectiveness of government activity designed to correct those failures. Many Keynesians and post-Keynesians argue that government intervention in markets is required to promote full employment, iron out temporary fluctuations in the economy, and offset the adverse consequences of international pressures on the Canadian economy (Chorney, 1989). Adherents to the neoclassical orthodoxy, including contemporary neo-conservatives, on the other hand, argue that markets should be given priority and that government fiscal and monetary management efforts should eschew attempts to manipulate them. Instead, they maintain that governments should only 'manage' their expenditures to ensure that they are matched by revenues and, in this sense, remain 'neutral' in their effect on private-sector production. Concerning monetary policy, the monetarist wing of this group argues that, again, governments should avoid attempts to manipulate the economy and simply limit their management efforts to combating inflation by linking the growth in the money supply to growth in national production or GNP (Buchanan and Wagner, 1979; Friedman, 1968).

Techniques of Monetary and Fiscal Management

The devices or tools that states can use in macroeconomic management can be classified into two groups: *monetary* and *fiscal*. Techniques of monetary management include manipulation of the value of the domestic currency on international markets, of domestic interest rates, and of the amount of domestic currency in circulation. Techniques of fiscal management include the manipulation of government revenues and of expenditures (Binhammer, 1977).

Fiscal management efforts are the most straightforward, at least in theory. Governments have the ability to raise and lower taxes or increase and decrease their expenditures, and they can do so in a way that will increase or decrease the amount of funds available to market actors for investment in productive activities. The primary tool used for this is the annual government *budgetary process*. The expansion of government expenditures and/or the lessening of taxes paid by market actors serves to increase the funds available to the market for investment and, at least theoretically, can spur these actors into expanding their productive activities. The reverse effect is possible through contracting government expenditures and/or increasing the proportion of incomes and profits that market actors pay to the government in taxes. These actions can reduce the amount of funds available for investment and hence decrease or restrict productive activity within the country. In fact, even if the state wishes to have no effect on the market, it must carefully manage its fiscal resources to ensure that expansions and contractions do not occur accidentally as a result of state expenditure and taxation measures.

Monetary management efforts are more complex and theoretically sophisticated, although they have essentially the same goals as techniques of fiscal management. Monetary management efforts involve the manipulation of the money supply, foreign exchange rates, and domestic interest rates, all aimed at encouraging or discouraging market investment behaviour. The state's primary instrument for modern monetary management is the *central bank*. Through several specific activities, central banking institutions can alter, within limits, interest and exchange rates and the total monetary supply. Central bankers can use a variety of specific techniques in their monetary management efforts. Three of these have historically been significant in Canada: manipulation of *reserve requirements* or *reserve ratios*, manipulation of the *bank rate*, and a variety of so-called *open market transactions*.

To manipulate reserve requirements, the government either increases or decreases the percentage of total deposits that commercial banks must keep 'on hand' to guarantee those deposits. Commercial banks operate by accepting deposits from their customers, paying these depositors interest on their accounts, and lending the deposited funds out to other customers, who pay the bank a somewhat higher rate of interest, thus generating a profit for the bank on each transaction. When the depositors wish to obtain their original funds, the banks must repay those funds within a short period of time, if not on demand. To meet this eventuality commercial banks have always been required by law to retain a certain percentage of their deposits on hand—the reserve requirement.

One effect of this reserve requirement is to remove certain amounts of cash from circulation. Manipulation of the reserve requirement, then, provides a tool governments can use to inject or withdraw cash from the entire economy. A higher reserve requirement forces commercial banks to withdraw additional cash; lowering the reserve requirement injects new cash into the economy. In effect, changing the total amount of money circulating in the economy, or the money supply, can also change the behaviour of potential borrowers as they find more cash available for investment, or less, as the case may be. When cash is withdrawn, assuming a constant demand, borrowers can be forced to pay more for the scarce funds—as commercial banks adjust interest rates to the new market situation. The borrowers will tend to invest only in projects promising to return profits higher than the new rate, leading to the cancellation of projects expected to be unprofitable at the new rate and a general decrease in productive activity.

Manipulation of the bank rate by central banks has the same effect. In the modern era banks keep their reserves on deposit with the central bank, which acts as a kind of 'bankers' bank'. The central bank can lend or advance these deposited funds back to the commercial banks whenever the commercial banks require new funds to lend to borrowers or discover a shortfall in the funds required to meet legal reserve requirements. When these advances are made, the central bank charges a commercial bank interest at the bank rate. Like the commercial banks' interest rates, the central bank's bank rate has an impact on market behaviour. A high bank rate discourages commercial banks from borrowing additional funds and a low rate has the opposite effect. When the banks do borrow funds, this money becomes available to investors desiring to increase their productive activities and has the effect of increasing the money supply and the general level of economic activity in society. The manipulation of the bank rate, therefore, like the manipulation of reserve requirements, can have either a negative or a positive effect on economic activity and market behaviour, as the government-controlled central bank sees fit.

Bank rates can be set in different ways. The simplest mechanism, and one that gives a government a great deal of discretion in establishing rates, is to establish a rate by statute. A more complex instrument, which delivers some control over rate establishment to commercial banks, involves a competitive bidding process for the auction of government securities, or treasury bills. Both of these mechanisms have drawbacks in terms of the length of time required to alter rates. The use of legal means to establish rates, for example, means that changing the rate can be difficult and time-consuming. It may take months, if not years, for rates to change. Treasury bill auctions can occur more frequently but usually take place only once or twice a month. As a result, in an age of electronic commerce in which billions of dollars can be transferred around the globe in milliseconds, central banks have looked for a more flexible instrument that allows adjustments to bank rates to be made on a much more frequent basis. The current system in place in Canada since February 1996, for example, sets the bank rate at the upper limit of a narrow band at which the Bank of Canada lends funds to the 'overnight market' or the market at which banks with a temporary surplus or shortage of funds are able to lend or borrow until the start of the next business day (Lundrigan and Toll, 1997–8). If the Bank allows overnight rates to fall below longer-term money market rates, it signals the Bank's desire to see money rates fall and aids this process by injecting additional funds into the economy. If it sets overnight rates higher than money market rates, the opposite situation and effects prevail (Laidler and Robson, 1993).

Open-market transactions are of two types. First, to manipulate foreign exchange rates central banks maintain stocks of domestic and foreign currencies and use those funds to intervene in foreign currency markets to increase or reduce the supply of the domestic currency in circulation and thereby help to regulate its price or value. Central banks purchase foreign currency with domestic funds whenever they wish to increase the amount of the domestic currency in circulation in international markets and hence reduce its price. Similarly, they can purchase domestic currency with foreign funds whenever they wish to decrease the amount of the domestic currency in circulation and increase its price or value.

Central banks make these transactions to regulate the amount of money flowing in and out of the country—the balance of payments—and to regulate the amount of goods flowing in and out of the country—the balance of trade. A domestic currency with low value on international markets helps exports by making them cheaper in international markets; this can boost export activity. A cheap domestic currency, however, also makes imports more costly and makes repayment of debts denominated in foreign currencies more expensive. A relatively highly valued domestic currency can have the opposite effect, reducing exports, increasing imports, and easing repayment of foreign debt. Governments usually seek to increase the amount of funds flowing into the country and to reduce their balance-of-payments deficits, if any, and to a certain extent they can manipulate the exchange rate through central bank transactions to accomplish these goals.

The second type of open-market transaction is more directly related to the domestic money supply and works in much the same fashion as do manipulations of reserve requirements and bank rates. Commercial bank deposits with central banks are usually not retained as cash but invested in government securities—sometimes long-term bonds, but more often short-term treasury bills. The central bank can purchase additional securities from commercial banks or sell these securities to them in exchange for cash. When the central bank sells securities to the commercial banks, the banks deposit additional cash with the central bank in payment. This has the effect of withdrawing cash from the economy and reducing the money supply, with all the attendant effects on investor and borrower behaviour. Similarly, the central bank can itself repurchase these securities from the commercial banks, thereby injecting additional cash into the system, increasing the money supply, and encouraging productive activity.

Through the use of these and other macro-level fiscal and monetary management techniques, governments are capable of altering some aspects of the performance of the market. The tools, however, influence only the general decisions made by market actors about whether or not to invest in additional productive capacity at a particular time; they don't determine the actual content of those decisions, which the state can manipulate through micro-level activity. Although the two types of decisions, and corresponding government activities, are clearly linked, they can be usefully disaggregated for analytical purposes.

Whether or not, to what extent, and how successfully a state participates in this type of macro-level activity is a significant question for political-economic analysis. A survey of how these techniques have been used in Canada reveals a great deal about this question and the operation of the Canadian political economy.

The History of Fiscal and Monetary Management

Like everything else in Canada, the state's macro-level activity is influenced by Canada's federal system of government. Under the Constitution Act of 1867, the federal government received exclusive jurisdiction over important areas of monetary policy, such as the issuance of currency and the regulation of banks and interest. In addition, in the field of fiscal policy the federal government received the right to raise funds on the 'public credit' and by 'any mode or system of taxation' (Sections 91[3], [4], [14–16], and [18–20] of the Constitution Act, 1867). Provincial governments, on the other hand, have no influence over monetary policy. Their fiscal powers are restricted to raising funds on 'the sole credit of the province' and raising revenues only through 'direct taxation within the province'[1] (LaForest, 1981) and to whatever revenues accrue to them from natural resources and landownership (Sections 92[2], [3], [5], and [109] of the Constitution Act, 1867).

The jurisdictional situation makes monetary policy relatively straightforward, since it is strictly a matter of federal policy-making. Fiscal policy is more complex (Courchene, 1986: 49–100) because provincial governments have limited revenue-raising capabilities but at the same time they have jurisdiction over major expenditure areas, such as health, education, and social welfare (Sections 92[7], [13], and [93] of the Constitution Act, 1867). The oft-resulting 'fiscal gap' has been addressed by a variety of means:

- first through statutory payments to provincial governments, culminated in the present-day, constitutionally entrenched equalization process;
- later through the extension of conditional federal government financing to provincial programs; and
- more recently, through systems of unconditional grants or block transfers. (Maxwell, 1937; Lynn, 1967; Smiley, 1963; Canada, Parliamentary Task Force on Federal-Provincial Fiscal Arrangements, 1981)

Provincial expenditures, tax rates, and debt loads can have a major impact on federal expenditures. Combined, they all influence the country's general fiscal situation. Unlike monetary policy, then, which is highly centralized, fiscal policy is decentralized in Canada. But jurisdictional disputes over monetary and fiscal policy were not a great concern of Canadian governments until the post-World War II period, when major efforts were made to integrate fiscal and monetary policy in a program of macroeconomic stabilization fashioned along Keynesian lines. Since that time, federal-provincial collaboration on macroeconomic regulation has been essential, though rarely forthcoming. The reasons for this lack of co-operation can be traced to the different structures of the regional and central Canadian economies and the very different impact that stabilization policies have on the regions and on their particular configuration of political and economic interests.

Fiscal and Monetary Policy before World War I

In 1964, writing for the Royal Commission on Banking and Finance, Grant Reuber suggested that the aims of monetary policy were to promote full employment, stable prices, and economic growth. In this sense, Canada has only had a 'monetary policy' in recent times—essentially since World War II. This is not to say, though, that Canada did not have a policy for money and banking before World War II.

Canada has had a private banking system since the early years of the nineteenth century when groups of large merchants joined forces to create the first chartered banks. Before then, barter transactions between local merchants and settlers had prevailed under both the French and the British regimes, with larger merchants in cities extending their own credit to local merchants (Shortt, 1986). These bills of exchange formed the basis of most commerce, and a variety of coinages, including Spanish, Dutch, Portuguese, and those of other countries involved in the West Indian trade, circulated freely in the country. Throughout the eighteenth century the British government restricted itself to establishing correct exchange values for these currencies, using sterling, and to limiting the issuance of paper money by colonial authorities (Shortt, 1986).

Following the creation of the chartered banks, bank notes issued by these institutions became the norm. Those notes remained as valid currency until the Bank of Canada took over the issuance of currency in 1934. Both the British and colonial governments quickly became involved in the regulation of bank activities, including note issue, however, to ensure the integrity of the entire banking system against the dual threats of bank failure and monetary inflation. Restrictions were placed on the amount of money the banks had to reserve against note issues, and such restrictions remain to this day in successive bank legislation.

For a brief period in the 1850s the colonial governments experimented with US-style 'free banking' in which charters were issued to any individuals who deposited appropriate securities with colonial officials. This plan, along with another to establish a uniform system of colonial coinage, was disliked by British officials, who argued that such rights were reserved for the monarchy. Free banking was abandoned after the fall of the Hincks-Morin administration in 1854, and the colonial currency legislation was disallowed by the imperial government. The colonial governments also attempted to wrest control over note issue from the banks from 1860 onwards, but succeeded only in instituting the issue of Dominion of Canada notes alongside bank notes (Shortt, 1986).

Following Confederation, under the terms of the British North America Act, banking became an area of federal government jurisdiction and the ties with Britain were cut. The federal government passed the Bank Act of 1871, which, with regular revisions every 10 years, continues to govern Canadian banking practices. Until World War I, the federal government's monetary strategy had two components.

First, the government was concerned with maintaining its control over the financial levers of monetary policy—that is, interest rates and bank charters—and virulently defended its jurisdiction against provincial efforts to expand credit for regional development. Numerous provincial government bills were reserved and disallowed by the federal government. The federal government also won several important cases at the Judicial Committee of the Privy Council, which backed its claims (LaForest, 1955; Olmsted, 1954; Howlett, 1986). Second, the government continued to press for control over note issue, still encountering resistance from the chartered banks. Along with its own note issues, the government was only able to institute various sorts of insurance schemes designed to protect holders of bank notes from loss in the event of the failure of the issuing bank (Breckenridge, 1910).

Fiscal policy was another matter altogether and was never considered conjointly with monetary policy. Governments in Canada were concerned with balancing their budgets, and given the overinvestment of many provincial governments in railway, canal, and other infrastructural undertakings, the federal government became involved in programs of provincial debt relief. The chief mechanism used for this purpose was the federal statutory subsidy. This involved cash grants to the provincial governments, made for a number of reasons, including maintenance of the provincial legislatures as well as debt relief (Canada, Royal Commission, 1940).

Although provincial revenue sources in natural resources and direct taxation were expected to be adequate to meet provincial expenditure needs at the time of Confederation, JCPC decisions restricting federal government powers and expanding those of the provincial governments produced a fiscal imbalance, with the provinces in a deficit position. This led to constant demands by provincial governments for 'better terms' and the renegotiation of the statutory subsidies on several occasions. In 1905 the subsidies were permanently linked to increases in provincial populations (Maxwell, 1937).

More significant, however, was the fact that many expenditures associated with continued industrial development fell into provincial jurisdiction and increased the need of the provincial governments for additional revenues. This was true of many matters related to agriculture and immigration and, especially, education, highway transportation, and unemployment relief. The growth of expenditure programs in these areas exacerbated the fiscal deficit position of the provincial governments and resulted in the establishment of a new instrument for federal funding of provincial programs: *the conditional grant* (Gettys, 1938).

These grants involved federal transfers to the provincial governments, usually on some sort of shared-cost basis, providing that provincial governments used the funds for the intended purposes, which were set out as conditions attached to the grant. The grants began to be used extensively immediately before World War I, and their use accelerated thereafter, although their constitutionality has always been in question. The use of this federal spending power to influence provincial governments in their approach to legislation within their areas of constitutional jurisdiction has always been resented by the provinces (Smiley, 1963), but it has never actually been challenged in the courts.

The hallmark of this period of monetary and fiscal policy in Canada is the division into separate areas of policy. Monetary policy existed as an effort to preserve the integrity of the Canadian currency and banking system from multiple threats: the threat of simple currency inflation caused by printing excess bank notes; the more complex threat resulting from fragmented, provincially led, easy credit legislation; the threat of a loss of confidence caused by bank failures or a loss of trust in the banking system as a whole by depositors. The government fully realized the need to maintain a stable currency to protect domestic savings and investment from inflation as well as to preserve the value of the currency on international exchanges and, thus, the value of Canadian exports in international markets.

Fiscal policy, on the other hand, was oriented almost exclusively towards retaining the solvency and favourable credit position of both levels of Canadian government. Although by the first decades of the twentieth century the federal government had begun to use fiscal transfers as a device for correcting what had come to be perceived as a structural problem of fiscal federalism—that is, a long-term, and growing, provincial fiscal deficit—these transfers and government expenditures in general were not seen as linked in any manner to the general performance of the economy or the relative strength or weakness of the nation's currency. Hence, observers such as R.C. McIvor (1958) could argue, many years afterwards, that Canada had continued to lack a long-term monetary and fiscal policy during the pre-World War I era.

Fiscal and Monetary Policy, 1914–1945

That all changed during World War I, when the government undertook massive borrowing to fund the war effort. It was forced in 1917 to implement a comprehensive system of personal income taxation to offset war-related expenditures (Perry, 1955). Under the strains of attempting to maintain and equip a large army, the federal government was forced to intervene in the economy not only to develop a massive armaments industry but also to manage both fiscal and monetary policy in an integrated manner (Gillespie, 1991).

The Canadian currency was removed from the gold standard in 1914 and its exchange value regulated, while strict controls were placed on prices and supplies of goods, as well as on banks and the issuance of credit. Savings were attracted through Canadian War Savings Bonds, while government expenditures on non-war-related activities were curtailed (Deutsch, 1940). Nevertheless, these efforts were devoted simply to ensuring that Canadian production would be directed towards the war and the maintenance of the military overseas. Although monetary and fiscal policies were united for the first time, this union took place because of the emergency, without any long-term commitment. After the war monetary and fiscal policies were redivided and most government wartime regulatory arrangements undone. Questions of monetary theory and policy did become a focal point for liberal economic theory after the war: both A.C. Pigou and John Maynard Keynes wrote major works reflecting on the success of British wartime fiscal and monetary arrangements in overcoming the otherwise apparently endemic employment and credit problems of modern capitalist economies. But in Canada permanent changes did not occur until the events of the 1930s brought home the problems of an unregulated *laissez-faire* approach to government and the economy (Brecher, 1957).

After the war Canada attempted to go back onto the gold standard for international exchange and to return in other ways to pre-war arrangements. Throughout the 1920s, however, the major concern of the federal government was with inflation and its control. The control of inflation had always been a key target of Canadian monetary policy, and the severe price inflation that followed the end of World War I caused great consternation and a rethinking of the traditional mechanisms for controlling prices and the value of Canadian currency.

The problem was quickly perceived as involving the failure of traditional banking regulations to control the issuance of credit. By that time most business in the country was carried on through the use of chequing accounts in banks, a system that had replaced specie payments and the exchange of cash or notes. Without proper reserve requirements for those new accounts, banks were able to create huge amounts of credit, which had the effect of driving up prices for goods and services in the marketplace. In 1923 a new Finance Act attempted to give the federal Department of Finance control over the extension of credit by restricting total bank loans to a percentage of the Dominion notes held by the bank. The reconversion to the gold standard in 1926 represented an effort in the same direction. But the mere increase in the volume of international trade after the war made the move back to gold impractical. Canada was quickly forced off the standard by the events of the early 1930s and the threat of the flight of large amounts of gold out of the country (Plumptre, 1934; Curtis, 1931, 1932; Knox, 1939). By the early 1930s many people realized that some new mechanism was required to control credit and foreign exchange regulation. In 1934, spurred on by western provincial governments and federal opposition Progressive members who blamed much of the damage of the post-1929 Depression on 'eastern' bankers, the R.B. Bennett government, following a brief and perfunctory royal commission investigation into the subject, created the Bank of Canada to perform these functions (Canada, Royal Commission, 1933; Neufeld, 1958; Watts, 1972).

Meanwhile, government fiscal policy in the years immediately after World War I had also given support to those who wished to see monetary and fiscal policy integrated in a way that would moderate swings in the economy. Having created new revenue sources capable of raising large amounts of funds, the government moved quickly to increase taxes so it could pay off the huge war debts it had amassed. This dampened the postwar boom resulting from the increase in domestic demand for goods and services and had some salutary effects on countering inflation.

After most of the wartime debt had been paid off by the mid-1920s, tax rates were reduced, and this reduction, in conjunction with easy credit, caused a major expansionary boom. This boom lasted until 1929, when poor agricultural conditions and an oversupply of manufactured goods resulted in a sudden depression and a massive demand for governments to provide social relief (Brecher, 1957). Faced with these additional demands for funds, the federal government again responded in an orthodox manner by raising taxes, only exacerbating the slide towards worsening economic circumstances.

The degree to which government fiscal arrangements sometimes benefited and sometimes worsened economic upturns and downturns in the 1920s was not lost on the economists and politicians who had become sensitive to the effects of government spending on economic performance after reading the work of Keynes and others in Europe and the United States (Granatstein, 1982). Some of these individuals, both in the federal administration and Parliament, pressed for the adoption of a more coherent and unified monetary and fiscal policy that could control swings in the economy, depressing expansions and expanding depressions. The monetary tools were available through the new central bank, and all that was required was a change in government thinking supportive of the adoption of countercyclical spending and taxation measures. Such a change in fiscal policy involved more than simply a decision to adopt enhanced policy tools; it therefore arrived more slowly than the decision to create the Bank of Canada.

Proposals that the government adopt just such a policy emerged from the 1937 and 1938 report of the National Employment Commission and the recommendations of the 1940 Royal Commission on Dominion-Provincial Relations. The National Employment Commission recommended that the federal government maintain a series of programs in such areas as housing and public works and tailor its use of these spending programs to economic conditions—promoting the economy when necessary and demoting it when required. The Rowell-Sirois Commission devoted a large part of its analysis to devising mechanisms by which provincial fiscal deficits could be eliminated and federal and provincial constitutional responsibilities and spending plans could be better harmonized.

Although the government of William Lyon Mackenzie King moved to strengthen the powers of the Bank of Canada and rescued the three prairie provinces from bankruptcy, it did little in the 1930s to follow up on the proposals for a more integrated monetary and fiscal policy. The Liberals faced opposition from the provinces to such a policy, but in any case they only half-heartedly accepted the need for a move that would clearly involve greater government intervention in the economy than they were willing to countenance. As a result, little was accomplished in this direction until after World War II (Neatby, 1969).

Fiscal and Monetary Policy, 1945–1975

Until recently, judging from the utterances of Canadian politicians in the post-World War II era, it was assumed that Canada had consciously adopted a Keynesian monetary and fiscal policy in 1945 and that this policy remained in place until the mid-1970s when it crumbled under the new phenomenon of 'stagflation' (the combined and simultaneous presence of high rates of inflation and unemployment) (Samuelson and Scott, 1971; Wolfe, 1984; Perry, 1989). Indeed, Canadian politicians and administrators did espouse Keynesian objectives (Reuber, 1964; Will, 1966; Gordon, 1966). But a close study of the actual performance of the federal government during this period casts doubt on whether this rhetoric was matched in reality (Campbell, 1987; Gillespie, 1979).

The federal government formally stated its acceptance of Keynesian principles of fiscal and monetary policy in its 1945 White Paper on employment and income (Canada, Department of Reconstruction, 1945; Mackintosh, 1966). In this document the government expressed its intention to engage in countercyclical budgeting and to follow a taxation and interest rate policy designed to encourage investment in times of need and to discourage it in times of expansion (Perry, 1989).

Virtually from its inception doubts were raised about the efficacy of such a policy. Many economists pointed out that the federal government in the immediate postwar period was faced with paying off a large wartime debt and as a result had to keep interest rates low to minimize repayment costs. These actions were certainly not Keynesian and as often as not exacerbated business cycles rather than offsetting them (Barber, 1957; McIvor and Panabaker, 1954; Brewis, 1968). Commentators also noted that in the Canadian context, with an economy reliant on international trade, trade flows and trade cycles can have an enormous impact on the domestic economy and are largely outside of the government's control. If a government in such a situation attempted to follow a strict Keynesian regime, it would have to react constantly to changes in trade balances with monetary and fiscal measures that would in themselves create a very uncertain climate for business and discourage long-term investment. Therefore, it was argued, Keynesian demand-management techniques were inappropriate for a small, open economy (Brewis, 1968). Although finance ministers continued to pay lip service to Keynesian ideals in their annual budget speeches (Perry, 1989), the record of fiscal and monetary policy initiatives displays a distinctly non-Keynesian approach (Campbell, 1987).

In fact, rather than attempt to regulate the domestic economy by using domestic tools alone, successive Liberal governments sought to ensure that international conditions would not unduly harm the performance of the Canadian economy. Canadian governments not only wholeheartedly supported the negotiation and implementation of the GATT in 1947, but they had also already enthusiastically accepted other US-sponsored proposals to stabilize the international banking and currency markets through the 1944 Bretton Woods agreement (Ikenberry, 1993). This agreement established major international financial institutions such as the International Bank for Reconstruction and Development (the World Bank) and the International Monetary Fund and finally replaced the gold standard for international exchange with a standard based on fixed convertibility against the US dollar. Canadian officials, and especially Bank of Canada officials, were very active in the negotiation and implementation of this postwar international financial system (Watts, 1973a; Plumptre, 1977: 17–60).

Once again, however, Canada was unable to maintain a fixed exchange rate against the US dollar, as US investment poured into the country's resource industries after World War II and drove up the value of the Canadian dollar. To abate the pressure the federal government had to purchase large amounts of foreign exchange to be held in reserve. In 1950, as the cost continued to mount, the government was forced to float the Canadian dollar, allowing its value to rise and fall against the US dollar as economic changes occurred (Watts, 1974). This decision eliminated the possibly of a strictly domestic monetary policy, because any actions of the government in the area of interest rates could now easily be negated by flows of capital in and out of the country (Caves and Reuber, 1969; Mundell, 1964).

In addition, during this period the federal government greatly accelerated its use of conditional grants and especially tax transfers to the provincial governments to provide funding for major program expenditures in areas such as education, health, and welfare (Banting, 1982; Guest, 1980; Taylor, 1987). The net effect of these programs and techniques was to lock the federal government into major long-term expenditure commitments and to reduce even further its ability to use fiscal measures for short-term stabilization purposes (Perry, 1982).

By the time the Progressive Conservative government of John Diefenbaker was elected in 1957, even the lip service paid to Keynesian ideals by federal finance ministers had disappeared, to be replaced by a policy of national economic expansion based on the increased extraction and processing of Canada's resource wealth (Canada, 1957). Under the Conservatives the federal government abandoned any pretence at countercyclical budgeting and pursued an expansionary program—at least until fears of rising inflation drove it back to a balanced budget orthodoxy (Will, 1966). This more or less ad hoc and reactive approach to fiscal and monetary policy would continue under the successive Liberal minority governments of the 1960s, with monetary policy reacting to international events and circumstances and fiscal policy to domestic needs (Purvis and Smith, 1986).

Throughout the 1960s and early 1970s, the government was faced with rapidly rising real inflation rates. Although unsure of the origins of this inflation, government ministers began to argue that the problem was not cyclical but structural in nature, that the root of the problem lay in monetary and government expenditure increases that had not been matched by increases in productivity (Perry, 1989). To deal with the problem, the government argued in its 1968 White Paper, *Policies for Price Stability*, that new policy tools were required, especially wage controls to combat inflation. In 1969 the government established the Prices and Incomes Commission to review wage and price increases (Haythorne, 1973). Although the imposition of mandatory controls was delayed by the 1972 election of a minority Liberal federal government that required NDP backing to remain in power, a new Liberal majority government after 1974 quickly moved to implement wage and price controls.

Fiscal and Monetary Policy after 1975

By the early 1970s the international situation had deteriorated. The US government had abandoned the Bretton Woods dollar standard and allowed its own currency to float under the inflationary pressures brought about by the expansion of the Vietnam War. The 'new economic policy' adopted by President Richard Nixon in 1971 not only altered the nature of the international financial system but also imposed wage and price controls in the United States as well as a global 10 per cent surcharge on imports (Plumptre, 1977).

Although Canada was able, eventually, to negotiate an exemption from the import surcharge and avoid major economic disruption, its economy appeared to be more and more vulnerable to international developments, especially given the major changes that followed the increases in oil prices announced by the Organization of Petroleum Exporting Countries (OPEC) in 1973–4. These increases exacerbated inflationary problems in Canada and reinforced the federal government's desire to undertake a major and permanent shift in monetary and fiscal policy to combat inflation (Perry, 1989; Courchene, 1976a, 1976b).

The new policy adopted by the government in 1975 was motivated by the desire to manage macroeconomic policy in accordance with the general growth in the national economy. It replaced the little-observed Keynesian doctrine based on the manipulation of monetary and fiscal tools to boost or cool down the economy with fiscal restraint and monetary gradualism (Courchene, 1976b; Sparks, 1986; Howitt, 1986). In both cases the object of policy became the restriction of monetary and expenditure growth to the same rate of growth as GNP in order to avoid government activities in these areas that might fuel inflation.

One part of the government's strategy was to create the Anti-Inflation Board (AIB), an arm's-length government regulatory agency with powers to review and overturn wage or price increases if it felt these were inflationary. The AIB operated without the consent of organized labour, which mounted a large-scale campaign against the use of mandatory controls and in favour of retaining the collective bargaining process for establishing wage rates. This protest culminated in a one-day national general strike led by the Canadian Labour Congress in February 1976. The imposition of price controls also upset organized business. The Business Council on National Issues was set up primarily to ensure that the views of the business sector would be taken into consideration by governments in the future.

Although the AIB was eventually disbanded and wage and price controls removed from the private sector, the federal government and several provincial governments retained self-imposed controls on public-sector expenditures throughout the 1970s and 1980s. Proposals to restrict the growth of government spending to the level of the GNP were made at the 1978 Federal-Provincial Conference on the Economy (British Columbia, 1978a, 1978b), and controls were put into place by most governments in the early 1980s, although not without considerable opposition from public-sector unions and provincial governments opposed to cuts or limits placed on federal transfer payments. The most publicized restraint program was in British Columbia (Magnusson, Doyle, et al., 1984), but other provinces and the federal government acted in similar ways (Perry, 1989; Wilson and Dungan, 1993).

Although the Progressive Conservative victory of 1984 brought with it a renewed emphasis on fiscal management, and especially on balanced budgeting, the record of federal governments throughout the 1980s was of increased expenditures and deficit financing (Wolfe, 1985; Bruce and Purvis, 1984). This was largely because of the long-term, committed nature of federal expenditures, which, despite Conservative efforts to find programs to cut, proved intractable (Canada, Department of Finance, 1985). This situation was exacerbated by tax cuts implemented in the first term of the Conservative era (Coté, 1993). Cuts to areas such as capital gains did not affect the situation of most taxpayers but did reduce the amount of taxes paid by wealthy Canadians and contributed to the creation of a large fiscal deficit (Vermaeten, Gillespie, and Vermaeten, 1995; Richardson and Moore, 1995; Osberg and Fortin, 1996).

The diverse path of political discourse and political activity only changed in 1989 when the federal budget attempted to match expenditures not with program cuts but with tax increases, using a new Goods and Services Tax (GST) for this purpose (Perry, 1990; Gillespie, 1991). Resistance to the new tax on the part of many sectors of Canadian society, however, meant that the amount that could be raised through the GST was limited. As a result, federal deficits continued to mount until 1998 when program cuts undertaken by the Liberal government caught up to increased revenues provided by a surging economy and produced the first surplus federal budget in 30 years (Robson and Scarth, 1994).

A major part of the federal deficit-cutting measures introduced after the Liberal victory in 1993 involved cuts in transfer payments made to the provinces. Although the government had tried to restructure several of its own major expenditure programs in areas such as health and social welfare, it proved much simpler to reduce the amounts given to the provinces in the form of block transfers. The new Canada Health and Social Transfer (CHST) developed in 1994–5 eliminated some federal transfer programs and, overall, cut transfers by up to 30 per cent in some areas (Leslie, 1997; Snodden, 1998). The cuts forced provincial governments to alter their own tax and revenue structures and led to significant political protests in several provinces. However, the provinces were able to absorb the transfers with little change to their overall fiscal position, and most provinces produced surplus budgets by the mid- to late 1990s (Robson, 1994; Harris, 1993).

On the monetary side, after 1975 the federal government was also forced to abandon its efforts to target monetary growth and link that growth with growth of the economy as a whole. This failure occurred as the government found itself in the position of having to accept the international rate of inflation, because international inflation kept international interest and exchange rates at levels over which the Bank of Canada had no control (Courchene, 1981, 1982). By early 1981 the inflation rate in Canada was over 10 per cent and interest rates stood at close to 20 per cent as the Bank of Canada attempted to retain the value of the dollar against high interest rates offered in the United States. The US government was also attempting to control inflation via monetarism and to attract foreign capital at the same time in an effort to spark economic growth. This situation forced the Bank of Canada to abandon the policy of monetary gradualism in 1982 and replace it with a strategy of more or less slavishly following US interest rates while adding a premium to both attract capital to Canada and help control inflation (Courchene, 1983; Crow, 1988).

This approach proved successful in combating inflation, although at the cost of plunging the entire economy into a serious recession (Dungan and Wilson, 1985; Boessenkool, Laidler, and Robson, 1996). This led to the re-emergence of political concerns with the degree of legitimacy and accountability of the central bank for its actions and calls for reform of the mechanisms linking the bank to parliamentary oversight (Laidler and Robson, 1993; Clark, 1996). Later, interest rates were allowed to fall both in the United States and in Canada in an effort to reinvigorate the economy. Eventually, bank officials began to rationalize this new approach, calling it 'adaptive monetary control'. This strategy accepted that medium-term fluctuations in money supply will occur within a broadly conceived goal of long-term supply (Howitt, 1986, 1990). Some evidence exists to indicate that this policy has successfully dealt with inflationary pressures without artificially disinflating the economy (Johnson, 1997) and it remains the principal monetary policy followed by the Bank of Canada at the turn of the century (Thiessen, 1996).

Constraints on Macroeconomic Management

Some of the reasons for the failure of Canadian governments to establish a unified fiscal and monetary policy with twin goals of low inflation and full employment are international in origin and intimately linked to Canada's role as a small open economy in the international political economy (Katzenstein, 1985; Macdonald Commission, 1985). The Canadian economy is open to investment flows and must retain a competitive interest rate if capital is not to flow elsewhere. Raising Canadian rates above international limits may cause additional funds to flow to Canada, but it dampens the domestic demand for money. Lowering Canadian rates below the international standard, on the other hand, might increase the domestic demand for funds, but it makes Canadian investments less attractive to both national and international lenders. In either case, the expected Keynesian result of contraction or expansion may not necessarily result (Crow, 1993).

Unlike major economic nations, which may exercise some control over their international environment (Iida, 1993), Canada, with a small, open economy, is susceptible to balance-of-payments problems that alter the value of the Canadian dollar and are largely beyond Canada's control, originating as they do in fluctuations in the terms of trade and the changing international demand for Canadian dollars (Crow, 1993). Again, a very important aspect of monetary supply is subject to fluctuations beyond the government's control, since interventions by the Bank of Canada to sell or purchase Canadian dollars to stabilize international exchange also substantially change the amount of currency in domestic circulation. Thus, regardless of the government's monetary aims, it is forced to alter them in the course of pursuing a stable exchange rate for the Canadian dollar.

Keynesian fiscal mechanisms, on the other hand, tend to be constrained by domestic circumstances, although these are not without their international aspects. In the first place, the amount governments spend is only mildly discretionary; many expenditures have been promised and guaranteed over the long term, and powerful constituencies are opposed to the removal of benefits. It is difficult to manage these types of expenditures in any meaningful countercyclical manner.

Second, governments are constrained in the amount of revenues they can command. Although the actual crisis point varies by country, at some point additional taxes will inevitably result in electoral difficulties for the government that imposes them, either from taxpayer resistance or from capital flight (Przeworski, 1991; Della Sala, 1994; Steinmo, 1994). In addition, governments can only borrow so much from external or internal sources without risking repayment difficulties if interest rates rise or revenue sources disappear. The use of public-sector restraint techniques is also politically problematic. Public-sector unions, which are large, well organized, and resourceful, not only have the ability to resist restraint programs through work actions, but in many jurisdictions they are also large enough to create severe electoral problems for a government that institutes such measures (Howlett and Brownsey, 1988; Chorney and Hanson, 1985).

The current Canadian macroeconomic policy, then, is a highly reactive, uncoordinated, and non-interventionist strategy that aims at the same two goals—foreign exchange stability and low inflation—that have traditionally characterized Canadian monetary and fiscal policy (Curtis, 1997; Thiessen, 1996; Leslie, 1997). After international constraints are taken into account, the only device that remains in government hands for influencing the general direction of the economy is high interest rates. But high interest rates can only deflate an economy and have very serious consequences for government finances. Any increase in interest rates also results in an increase in government domestic debt charges, which can seriously restrict its fiscal manoeuvrability. This is especially important in Canada because a large percentage of government debt is held in Canada savings bonds (CSBs), which are easily converted to cash or other investments if CSB rates are allowed to fall below market norms.

Similarly, domestic constraints greatly limit the use of government spending and other fiscal instruments to influence economic activity in the country. Resistance from taxpayers reduces the possibility of stimulating a depressed economy by raising new revenues and spending them on public works projects. According to current macroeconomic thinking, such an economy should be left to correct itself through the traditional market technique of having increased unemployment stimulate reductions in production costs through wage cuts. Resistance from labour, on the other hand, as well as from taxpayers concerned about their entitlements, reduces the possibility of using fiscal restraint to deflate an overheated economy.

State macro-level activity is not a simple technical exercise in economic planning and efficiency, nor is it in any manner a purely automatic process (Helleiner, 1996; Willett, 1988). Rather, macro-level activity thoroughly combines economics and politics. It has significant political dimensions in which key political actors pursue their own interests, and in so doing they can either seriously constrain state actions or force the state to make trade-offs between the different interests involved. At the same time, the state must operate within an international economy, which can also serve to constrain its actions or force difficult choices to be made in the policy process. In attempting to formulate macroeconomic policy, Canadian federal governments have thus been constrained by an array of changing international, institutional, and partisan forces.

Notes

1. The distinction between 'direct' and 'indirect' taxation is ambiguous. In practice the terms have been interpreted by the courts as referring to whether a tax is paid directly by the consumer or passed on by some middle agent to a final taxpayer, who thus pays it 'indirectly'. Examples of direct taxes are personal and corporate income taxes. Indirect taxes include most customs and excise taxes. Sales taxes are the taxes that provincial governments turn into direct taxes by appointing merchants as government collection agents.

Chapter 11

The Micro-Political Economy: Industrial Development

Since the last century Canada has been among the most industrialized nations in the world (Laxer, 1989a). Yet some analysts describe it as an 'underdeveloped' nation, referring to the natural-resource orientation of the economy, which is not unlike the economies of many Third World nations. Others oppose this description, and the ensuing controversy has generated some of the liveliest debates in Canadian political economy—debates not confined to scholars but involving politicians, bureaucrats, and business and labour leaders. The controversy concerns the state's role in strengthening Canada's manufacturing sector. Some view the state as critical in promoting manufacturing industries. Others believe that state intervention is unlikely to enhance Canada's competitiveness in manufacturing or that, if it does, the gains are likely to be at an excessive cost to the economy as a whole.

Although this theoretical controversy remains unresolved, in practice the Canadian state has intervened extensively in the market to promote industrial development for more than a century. The character and extent of the interventions have varied over the years and many have been carried out in a highly incoherent, even contradictory, fashion. Nevertheless, the effects of these interventions have not been inconsequential.

The Instruments and Ends

Industrial policy is almost impossible to define comprehensively in a precise or meaningful sense. There is a danger of being either too specific to capture the numerous elements of such a policy or too general to be of much analytical use. We prefer the rather narrow definition proposed by D.G. McFetridge (1985: 1–2), who says industrial policies are 'those government policies which are intended to have a direct effect on a particular industry or firm'. They represent an effort by the state 'to encourage particular types of industrial activity'. The policies can involve encouraging the use of certain inputs, such as plastics instead of steel, the production of certain goods or services, such as computers or high-price consumer items, or the adoption of certain organizational forms, such as larger firms or Canadian ownership. But government does not necessarily have to take particular action before it can be described as having an industrial policy. Even the decision not to have an industrial policy is itself a policy—of leaving the course of industrial development in the hands of the market.

The concept of *industrial strategy* is broader than that of industrial policy. Industrial policy describes individual policy measures aimed at altering industrial activity in a country. Industrial strategy, on the other hand, describes a collection of interrelated policies directed at industrial development. It is more than the sum of individual policies, for it requires the various policies to form an integral whole and be complementary to each other. The emphasis is on coherence and co-ordination among policies. A lack of cohesiveness among different industrial policies, no matter how effective they are individually, will make for a poor industrial strategy. Indeed, it can be more harmful than not having any policy at all.

Rationales for Industrial Policy

The rationales behind the need for industrial policy can be classified loosely into two broad categories. The first is the approach of mainstream liberal Keynesian-welfare political economists; using the terms of welfare economics, they see policy as involving the adoption of measures necessary to correct market failures. The second is the approach of social democratic political economists, who are inspired by economic nationalism and develop policies that tend to promote indigenous industrial development, especially manufacturing.

The first group has economic efficiency as a goal and tends to use technical arguments to justify particular policy choices. The second group makes use of a variety of arguments, including many borrowed from the first group, to justify its preferences. Both have a huge corpus of literature to back them, and both enjoy sizeable support among scholars and the general populace. There are, of course, analysts who have other ideas, especially those of the neo-conservative variety, who tend not to see any role at all for the government in industrial development.

The most commonly cited rationale for government action in this area relates to the public goods character of many industrial inputs. It is argued that the nature of scientific and managerial information, technology, or labour inputs is such that their producers cannot restrict their usage to those paying for them. Others—so-called 'free riders'—can benefit without incurring any costs for their usage, which eliminates the profit incentive for creating them. While society as a whole clearly benefits from the production of public goods, in a capitalist economy work will not be undertaken unless producers are compensated. This is often cited as the main reason why governments should, for example, provide subsidies for industrial research and development (R&D), and labour training.

Another market-failure rationale relates to infant industries. It is argued that the initial costs, and the corresponding risks, to firms in new industries are sometimes so high that companies are deterred from getting started, even though it is in society's interest to see them established. Similarly, new industries may not be able to compete in the short run with imports. In such circumstances, it is argued, governments can provide subsidies to facilitate the establishment of socially desirable industries. Just about every country, to various degrees, has supported industries on these grounds. The protection of infant industries, for example, was one of the professed goals of the nineteenth-century National Policy tariffs (Eden and Molot, 1993).

Yet another argument in support of industrial policy is that the government can improve the efficient operation of market forces by easing the economy's adjustment to changing circumstances. This is called *positive adjustment policy*. When an industry is faced with increased competition from imports or a decline in consumption of its products, business and labour in that industry often seek government protection from change. However, the result of increased protection is often economic inefficiency and a reduction in the wealth of society as a whole. In such circumstances, it is argued, it will be to society's benefit for government to compensate the victims of change, encouraging them to leave the industry to invest or seek employment in more competitive sectors.

There are numerous other rationales for industrial policy, but the ones cited here should convey their general thrust—that industrial policies ought to be employed only to correct market failures (Watson, 1983). Neoclassical and neo-conservative liberal political economists, while broadly agreeing that there can be instances of market failures that might be corrected through state intervention, remain suspicious about the need or efficacy of such interventions. They insist that before intervention is undertaken, the government must ascertain, first, whether the market has indeed failed and, second, whether the state is genuinely more capable than the market of correcting the failure (Wolf, 1987).

In the case of government support for industrial R&D, for instance, neo-conservatives argue that it must be demonstrated—and not just assumed—that the existing level of R&D is indeed lower than socially desirable. Next, it must be ascertained whether the lower R&D is caused by lack of demand or lack of supply, because if it is a lack of demand then government subsidies for undertaking R&D would not solve the problem. Even after the case for intervention has been established, the government's capacity to intervene effectively must be questioned. How will the government know which R&D activity to target? How will it implement its decisions unhindered by political pressures from other industries also competing for subsidies? Neo-conservatives have similar misgivings about the infant industry rationale. They wonder how an industry that grows up in a protected environment will survive when protection is removed and the industry is exposed to open competition. In fact, such industries might become dependent on protection and be unable to survive without it. Positive adjustment measures, especially those directed at labour adjustment, find more widespread support among liberal political economists of all stripes and colours.

The economic nationalist rationale put forward by social democrats favours a state-led industrial policy to promote the nation's interests, and especially the interests of the working class. Underlying this rationale is the belief that international market forces do not deliver equal benefits to all nations and tend to favour the strong, which necessitates state intervention to correct the imbalances. Manufacturing is of special interest to economic nationalists because of the positive spin-offs they argue it generates and the national autonomy they believe it promotes. They see a healthy manufacturing industry as essential for national well-being, an argument largely rejected by most liberal economists, who subscribe to the notion of comparative advantage. Most social democrats propose that the government, at a minimum, should nurture indigenous manufacturing industries through protection from imports and subsidies of various kinds until these industries become internationally competitive. In subsequent economic downturns, they usually favour continued support and even nationalization of an industry rather than see it collapse or disappear.

Another rationale for supporting domestic industries is to correct the problem of the low level of research and development undertaken in many countries. While this argument is essentially the same as the public goods argument, it is not usually expressed in the same formal language by social democrats. The most commonly cited social democratic argument in favour of industrial policy in Canada, for example, is that it is needed to offset the adverse affects of extensive foreign, mainly US, ownership of Canadian manufacturing. Social democrats argue that foreign-owned subsidiaries do not undertake sufficient R&D, do not make adequate efforts to export, and maintain small plants engaged in small-scale production of a wide variety of products—thus lacking the economies of scale required to be internationally competitive. In addition, in recent years many economic nationalists have been concerned with the increasing liberalization of trade, and especially the adoption of the FTA and NAFTA, which they suggest have resulted in foreign branch plants being wound down and the Canadian market supplied from offshore plants in low-wage countries or from excess capacity in US facilities. They propose that the government try to increase Canadian ownership in manufacturing and, in addition, pressure foreign-owned firms to serve Canada's interests.

Techniques of Industrial Strategy

Industrial strategies have come in many guises and colours in different countries. These have included *forced industrialization*, in which states have nationalized entire sectors of the economy and funnelled enormous resources into them in the effort to increase production, and the less state-reliant strategy of *import substitution industrialization* in which states have targeted specific industries on which they have relied for imports and provided a variety of subsidies and incentives aimed at fostering growth in the domestic production of these goods. In the nineteenth century, Canadian governments tended to follow an import-substitution strategy, with mixed results. The mainstream debate on the direction of contemporary Canadian industrial strategy has displayed elements of three different visions: (1) a strategy of *non-intervention*; (2) a strategy of *positive adjustment*; and (3) a strategy of *targeting*. Neo-conservative political economists tend to support the first strategy, welfare Keynesians the second, and social democrats and post-Keynesians the third. The differences among these relate to the extent to which each requires state involvement in market processes.

Non-intervention is the traditional liberal strategy that postulates that the market is the most efficient means of allocating society's economic resources and must be left alone to work out the course of industrial development based on the principle of comparative advantage. It follows that the state should keep its hands off industrial development and must pursue the strategy of having no strategy. This is, of course, an extreme position, and only a few Canadian economists and politicians have actually proposed or attempted to follow such a strategy. Most people associated with this school of thought are content with minor state interventions to correct market failures and will support ad hoc efforts by the state to protect industries from major fluctuations in market conditions. In addition, they support the use of macro-level fiscal and monetary policies to combat inflation, balance the effects of government spending on private-sector behaviour, and maintain a stable exchange rate for the Canadian dollar. They also support the negotiation of major international trade treaties in order to secure access to foreign markets for Canadian goods and offset the advantages larger economic players have in manipulating the international political economy.

The strategy of *positive adjustment* begins from the same premise, assuming that the market is the most appropriate mechanism for determining the course of industrial development. What distinguishes this strategy from the non-interventionist strategy is that it recognizes the existence of rigidities in the market or society that impede the withdrawal of labour and capital resources from declining industries and their deployment in growth industries. Advocates of this position consider that government activities to remove these rigidities are legitimate as long as the goal of economic efficiency is pursued. In other words, they call for positive adjustment strategies to neutralize or eliminate the sources of resistance to change in order to enhance 'the flexibility and resilience of markets in the face of change' (OECD, 1983). Firms and workers faced with the prospect of a decline in their industries, for example, are often reluctant to leave and seek employment in growth industries, and this reluctance introduces inefficiencies into the economy. The government can help the adjustment process along by subsidizing the retraining and mobility costs of the workers involved. This mode of reasoning is typical of welfare-Keynesian approaches to industrial policy, which are concerned with government intervention to increase the efficiency of the market.

There is, however, a general scepticism about subsidizing the adjustment costs borne by capital. David Richardson (1985: 177) summarizes the reasons for opposition to subsidies for capital adjustment: 'Capital markets are national and international; labour markets are local. Risktaking owners of capital are presumably better informed than workers about prospects for international change, and also about finding more lucrative employment of their resources by moving to other industries. They therefore have more opportunities to diversify than workers.' The strategy of positive adjustment, especially for workers, has few opponents in Canada, and Canadian governments have attempted to follow this strategy in many labour training and transition programs.

The industrial strategy of *targeting* suggests that the government ought to aid industrial development not generally but in a focused way, aiding only certain industries singled out for their growth potential. As elaborated by social democrats and post-Keynesians in the current situation, this approach focuses on developing winning industries in the high-growth, high-technology sectors, which are currently generating above-average returns and spin-offs to other industries. This strategy is based on the assumption that comparative advantage is not entirely dependent on the existing endowment of natural resources, labour, and capital (which is what the traditional theory of comparative advantage assumes) but can be 'engineered' with the assistance of the government.

The theoretical underpinning of this strategy is the familiar argument related to the public goods character of technology that discourages private risk-taking, a problem that can be corrected through government intervention. It is assumed that without government support for high-growth, high-technology industries, the established industries and industries in countries that receive such support will dominate the market. The proponents of this strategy cite Japan and South Korea, and also France and Sweden to some extent, as having engineered comparative advantage through targeting. In addition to adjustment policies for workers to help them leave declining industries, the proponents of targeting are not averse to subsidies and protection for declining firms to preserve employment in communities while the firms are undergoing restructuring. This strategy is only distantly related to welfare economics, because it does not justify state intervention necessarily in terms of market failure.

The more orthodox neoclassical and neo-conservative liberal political economists disagree with this strategy entirely, on both theoretical and practical grounds. Mainstream welfare Keynesians, while agreeing that it is theoretically possible to engineer comparative advantage in certain industries, remain unconvinced about the government's capacity to 'pick winners'. They doubt that the state is better equipped than the market to predict the future and target its efforts accordingly.

The strategy a government chooses to follow in practice, of course, is never simply a question of theoretical elegance. Rather, the types of activities a state considers and implements are determined by the nature of the constraints and opportunities it faces in the national and international political economy. Especially significant is the organization of state and societal actors, a variable that is extremely important in determining whether governments will be able to develop and enunciate a consistent and coherent industrial strategy. In Canada the fragmentation of state and societal actors has prevented the state from articulating any general industrial strategy and has resulted instead in an ad hoc and incremental response to the problems faced by industry. Although this can look like a conscious decision to adopt a neo-conservative non-intervention strategy, in fact, as the discussion below will illustrate, it is inspired much less by ideology than by structural problems and constraints facing the Canadian political economy, problems that have led to the failure of attempts to develop and implement more activist policies and strategies.

The History of State Intervention in Industrial Development

Manufacturing in Canada is as old as the earliest European settlements. It accounted for 18 per cent of GNP as early as 1851 and grew rapidly in the subsequent decades (Pomfret, 1981: 122). In fact, by the 1890s the share of the GNP accounted for by manufacturing (21 per cent) was not much lower than it is today. However, the scale of production remained small until the turn of the century. In 1870, for example, the average plant size was 4.7 employees and the value added per employee was only $2,414 (Blackbourn and Putnam, 1984). Manufacturing grew rapidly between 1870 and 1929. By 1920 Canadian manufacturing had shed much of its artisan character, and the average size of capital invested in manufacturing firms had increased dramatically. This was reflected in the reduction of the workforce by one-third between 1870 and 1929, even though the value added in Canadian manufacturing had increased eightfold (ibid., 24). After a period of stagnation due to the Depression, growth resumed with the outbreak of World War II and was rapid immediately after the war.

The comparative advantage arising from the local availability of natural resources and the adverse transportation costs for foreign exporters wishing to sell in Canada were to a large extent responsible for the establishment of an indigenous manufacturing capacity. However, the role of the Canadian state was by no means insignificant. Lord Durham, in his *Report on the Affairs of British North America* in 1839, remarked that whereas in Europe the main role of the state was national defence, in North America it was active engagement in the construction of public works, mostly canals, highways, and railroads (Aitken, 1967). Immediately before Confederation, for example, the government of the United Province of Canada was directly involved in the construction of canals on the St Lawrence River, such as the Welland, Cornwall, Williamsburg, Beauharnois, and Lachine systems.

The support for canals pales in comparison to the government's subsidization of railroad construction. Under the Guarantee Act of 1849, $33 million was disbursed to the Grand Trunk Railway alone (Pomfret, 1981). Similarly, under a contract reached with the Canadian Pacific Railway in 1880, the government provided the company with $25 million in cash, 25 million acres of land, existing rail lines worth $38 million, and many other indirect subsidies. The actual value of the subsidy to CPR in 1885 has been estimated at between $121 million and $146 million. In following decades other private railroad companies, including the Canadian Northern and Grand Trunk Pacific, received similar substantial subsidies for building lines north of CPR lines.

Whether the railway subsidies were a success or failure depends on the criteria used to evaluate them. At a minimum, it can be argued that as a result of the subsidies the railways were built much earlier than would have otherwise been the case. They provided the infrastructure required for the settlement of the prairies and movement of goods, all of which had a beneficial impact on the growth of Canadian manufacturing. But if the size of the subsidies is compared to the actual returns to government revenues resulting from them, the evaluation must be negative. The subsidies were undoubtedly excessive, and more often than not they were used to line the pockets of powerful politicians and railroad barons—often the same people. Moreover, most of the subsidized railways eventually went bankrupt—many of them ultimately being merged and taken over by the federal government in 1919, becoming the Canadian National Railway (CNR).

Another instrument the government used to assist manufacturing was the tariff on imports under the National Policy of 1879. The Cayley-Galt tariffs of 1858–9 had been the first Canadian use of tariffs as a means of not only generating revenue but also protecting Canadian manufacturing from imports. This was reflected in the differential level of tariff protection levied on goods depending on their level of processing: the average tariff on primary products was in fact reduced from 2.3 per cent to 0.13 per cent, that on intermediate goods was increased marginally from 5.24 per cent to 7.18 per cent, and that on manufactured products was increased by a much larger margin, from 12.81 per cent to 19.62 per cent. A concerted effort to promote manufacturing through differential tariffs began with the National Policy, which represented a substantial increase in most existing tariffs. The spread between tariffs on inputs, now subject to between 10 to 20 per cent tariffs, and on finished manufactured goods, subject to a 30 per cent duty, was especially increased, clearly indicating the desire on the part of the federal government to encourage domestic production of manufactured goods by discouraging imports (Pomfret, 1981). The pattern for Canadian industrialization behind high tariff walls was firmly set. It began to be eroded only after World War II, but its legacy can still be felt in Canada's modern industrial structure (Williams, 1986).

The tariffs succeeded in giving a boost to Canadian manufacturing, though perhaps at a high cost to the economy as a whole. As Richard Pomfret (1981: 81) concludes:

> Since the protective tariffs remained at high levels for much longer than normal expectations of maturity, it seems probable that the net economic effects were negative. In cases where firms became internationally competitive, they were shielded from competing imports and were able to exploit monopoly positions in the Canadian market. In other cases, inefficient firms could remain in business behind the protective tariff wall. The presumption of net economic costs from the protective tariff is generally accepted by supporters and opponents of the tariff policy alike.

Many of the manufacturing industries established as a result of tariff protection never really outgrew their infancy and continued to need protection for many years. They were generally small and unspecialized firms, producing a wide variety of products in short runs, and hence they were not very efficient. The higher costs of living and the corresponding lower standard of living in Canada caused by this inefficiency played a role in the net emigration to the United States that was a characteristic feature of the period around the turn of the century. The tariffs also had a differential impact on regional economies, favouring central Canada, where manufacturing has been traditionally located, at the expense of the Maritime and western provinces.

The emphasis on tariffs as the main instrument for assisting Canadian manufacturing continued until the end of World War II. The only new development was the greater willingness of the state to own firms directly in order to provide the necessary economic infrastructure. The establishment of Ontario Hydro in 1906 for this purpose was one of the first examples of public enterprise in the English-speaking world. One of the chief reasons for its existence was to provide cheap electricity to manufacturers in Ontario (Nelles, 1974). During World War I the federal government established several firms for the production of armaments and other related products. In 1919 the government established the Canadian National Railway (CNR) through the merger of most of the privately owned railroads in the country (except for those belonging to the CPR), all of which faced bankruptcy because of overexpansion during the previous decades. Over the course of World War II Ottawa established 28 Crown corporations, some new, others through nationalizing privately owned firms. These corporations played a critical role in the economy at the time, employing 12 per cent of the total manufacturing workforce in Canada. At the end of the war, most were either returned to their original owners or sold to the private sector.

In the decade immediately after the war, indications of a significant change in Canada's industrial policy began to appear. While tariffs remained generally high, the acceptance of the terms of the GATT represented a commitment by the Canadian government to their reduction. The period between the end of the war and the late 1950s was marked by the establishment of new social programs rather than economic infrastructure, and the provision of strong incentives to attract foreign investment rather than the creation of public enterprises. Although Canadian governments at the provincial level continued to promote industrial expansion through direct grants, subsidies, and public corporations, at the federal level the government shifted its strategy towards ensuring a sizeable market for Canadian products. In the 1950s and 1960s this process involved augmenting the purchasing power of Canadian consumers. In the 1960s and 1970s, it involved efforts to expand international markets for Canadian goods. In the past two decades the federal government has focused most of its efforts on ensuring access for Canadian goods in those markets through the negotiation of international and bilateral trade treaties, especially with the US.

By the beginning of the 1960s numerous weaknesses had become apparent in the Canadian economy, relating both to Canada's international competitiveness and to the domestic capacity for growth. These weaknesses increased with the passage of time, which led policy-makers to re-evaluate Canada's basic approach to economic and industrial development and rekindled the debate on the need for industrial strategy and the form it should take. The first major concern was the acceleration of the pace of industrial change resulting from the progressive liberalization of international trade and the rapid rate of innovation and diffusion of technology throughout the world in the postwar period. While the growing population and the opening up of export markets enlarged the potential demand for Canadian products, a large proportion of that new demand was filled by increased imports. According to one study of 13 manufacturing industries during the 1967–81 period, increases in domestic demand and exports contributed 5.6 and 2.7 per cent respectively to the total annual average increase in employment in those industries (Robertson and Grey, 1985). But these increases in employment were largely offset by employment losses of 4.1 per cent from increases in imports during the same period. The increases in imports created pressures on Canadian industry to improve its competitiveness, and many in business and government regarded government assistance as indispensable for this initiative.

The second concern related to the slowdown in productivity growth. Between World War II and the early 1970s, productivity growth in manufacturing had been higher in Canada than in most industrialized nations, despite the somewhat higher wages paid in Canada, because of the even higher increase in labour output. The situation deteriorated in the early 1970s when wage increases surpassed the growth in output per hour, leading to higher unit labour costs (Wilkinson, 1980). This situation continued until the early 1980s. As a result, the international competitiveness of Canadian manufacturing suffered.

A third concern arose because, beginning in the early 1960s, Canada came under intense pressure from certain Third World nations in the labour-intensive, standard-technology manufacturing sectors. The Canadian radio and television and rubber footwear industries were all but wiped out by foreign competition, while other sectors such as textiles, clothing, and leather footwear survived only because of the imposition of ad hoc protection from imports. Canadian policy-makers were well aware that the level of protection accorded to many of these vulnerable industries could not be continued forever and that they must either become internationally competitive or be eliminated. Many industrial adjustment programs were devised to modernize or rationalize the industries to equip them to face growing foreign competition.

The fourth cause for concern about Canada's industrial future was the low level of spending on research and development, which is essential for maintaining and increasing competitiveness in the long term. The gross expenditures on R&D as a percentage of the Canadian GNP, after increasing slowly in the 1960s, declined during much of the 1970s (from 1.26 per cent in 1969 to 0.98 per cent in 1977), and then began to rise again, reaching 1.36 per cent of the GNP in 1983 (McFetridge, 1986: 46). Canadian expenditures were low compared to those of other industrialized nations: while Canada spent 1.25 per cent of its GNP on R&D in 1981, the United States spent 2.5 per cent, Japan 2.4 per cent, and France 2 per cent (Macdonald Commission, 1985, II: 98). In fact, Canada had one of the lowest rates of spending on R&D in the OECD. Canadian efforts in this area seemed to be seriously lagging, and the government made many efforts to overcome the perceived shortcomings.

Fifth, the lack of economies of scale in manufacturing was also a source of consternation. Compared to the huge internal markets of the United States, Japan, and the European Community, Canada's domestic market was (and is) small. This problem was aggravated by traditionally high Canadian tariffs that encouraged the establishment of small firms behind protective barriers. Most of these firms were not intended for international trade and were not large enough to be internationally competitive. This led to calls for government assistance towards rationalizing manufacturing and otherwise encouraging larger-scale production.

Sixth, regional economic disparities and the highly regionalized nature of the Canadian industrial structure also occasioned calls for a government response. The per capita income in the Atlantic provinces had dropped to almost 30 per cent lower than the national average and similar disparities were seen in unemployment rates; in fact, in some Atlantic provinces the level of unemployment was twice as high as the national average. Manufacturing activity in Canada was also highly regionalized, being heavily concentrated in Ontario and Quebec. The economies of the western and eastern provinces continued to depend on resource exports and were highly vulnerable to international price fluctuations and continuous boom-and-bust cycles. In addition, the decline of many manufacturing industries because of imports from Third World countries was disproportionately concentrated in Quebec. This resulted in certain regions paying disproportionately high prices for Canada's efforts to reduce trade barriers and rationalize production. Many of the industrial policies adopted in Canada in the early 1970s were directed solely at reducing these regional economic disparities.

The final concern arose from the high level of foreign, especially US, ownership in Canadian manufacturing. From the beginning much Canadian industrial development was financed by foreign capital, at first from Britain and later from the United States. Much of the American investment in Canada was of the direct variety, unlike the earlier British investments, which were primarily portfolio investments. *Portfolio investments* are in the form of ownership of bonds and loans and give no direct control to the investor in the day-to-day management of the borrowing firm. *Direct investments,* in contrast, give the foreign investors ownership and control over the day-to-day management of the recipient firms through the election of representatives of major shareholders to the company's board of directors.

Any investing firm would certainly put its own interests ahead of those of its subsidiaries. The critics of such investments saw the subsidiaries as truncated branch plants that would not undertake sufficient R&D or export efforts, leaving these functions to the parent firms to the disadvantage of the Canadian economy. The 'miniature replica effect' resulting from the inefficient scale of production undertaken by foreign subsidiaries was also seen as damaging to the Canadian economy as a whole. The level of foreign investment began to decline gradually in the late 1970s as a result of numerous government measures to increase Canadian ownership in certain sectors as well as the general deterioration in the international economic position of the United States. By 1980 only 45 per cent of the assets in mining and 48 per cent in manufacturing were foreign-owned (McFetridge, 1986). What was especially disturbing to critics, however, was that much new foreign ownership was financed out of Canadian production. For example, of the total new US investment in 1983, 30 per cent was reinvested profits, 65 per cent was borrowed from Canadian sources, and only 5 per cent came from US sources.

Canadian Industrial Policies after 1960

The concerns about the pattern of Canadian industrial development occasioned numerous government interventions after 1960—so many that an exhaustive list would be difficult to compile. In the first place it is difficult to distinguish industrial policy instruments from other economic policy instruments. Moreover, the range and nature of the programs available during the period underwent numerous changes.

However, it is clear that the primary instruments used to assist industrial development were protection from imports, subsidies (including the subsidy components of loans), and tax benefits. The total cost of protection from imports in the form of tariffs, quotas, and other non-tariff barriers is almost impossible to calculate, but the data available for a few products can provide a rough idea. The aggregate cost to the economy for protecting the dairy industry was $286 million in 1980. For the footwear industry the annual average cost of protection between 1978 and 1983 was $13.9 million, and for the garments industry it was $163 million (Salembier et al., 1987). Similarly, the total cost of federal and provincial subsidies to Canadian industry (excluding agriculture and services) was $98 million in 1978, $223 million in 1981, and $350 million in 1984. The aggregate value of the tax incentives to the manufacturing sector provides a similar picture: in constant (1971) dollars, it was $294.3 million in 1975 and $539.5 million in 1979.

International Trade Measures

Tariffs provided progressively lower protection to Canadian industries after the mid-1960s. In the past, the export orientation of the Canadian economy and the need to secure increased access for foreign markets motivated Canadian governments to reduce tariffs, but at the same time tariffs on certain products were kept high to protect domestic industries and the jobs they provided. After the tariff cuts in 1987, more than two-thirds of imports entered Canada under no tariffs; but for the products that continued to be subject to tariffs, the Canadian rates remained somewhat higher than in other industrialized nations (Nguyen, Perroni, and Wigle, 1996). The phased elimination of tariffs on imports from the United States under the FTA has further reduced the importance of this instrument.

Unable to prevent imports from entering the country, Canada, like most other nations, has shifted its trade strategy to promote its exports. Since 1970 the Export Development Corporation—which replaced the Export Credit Insurance Corporation (1944)—has existed to provide loans, loan guarantees, and export insurance to Canadian exporters. Various kinds of government assistance have also been available to Canadian exporters through the Program for Export Market Development and the Trade Commissioner Service. In recent years, the federal and provincial governments have joined with exporting companies on high-profile 'Team Canada' trade missions to such countries as China and India and regions such as Latin America and East Asia to promote Canadian exports.

Measures to Control Foreign Investment

As uneasiness about the level of foreign ownership in the Canadian economy grew in the 1960s, so, too, did government measures to reduce it and otherwise shape it in accordance with Canadian objectives. In 1966 the government issued the Guidelines of Good Corporate Citizenship to foreign subsidiaries operating in Canada to encourage greater contributions to the Canadian economy. The guidelines were voluntary and had no significant impact on the performance of foreign-owned firms. In 1971 the government established the Canada Development Corporation (CDA) as a holding company to provide venture capital to Canadian-owned firms and to buy back foreign subsidiaries in critical mining and manufacturing industries. By 1981 the renamed Canada Development Investment Corporation (CDIC) provided the largest pool of venture capital in the country and owned several firms in high-technology industries (Morici et al., 1982: 60). In the early 1990s the CDIC was sold in stages to private investors.

The establishment of the Foreign Investment Review Agency in 1974 embodied Canada's strongest effort ever to control foreign investments. It displayed the government's shift in orientation away from buying back foreign-owned firms and towards exercising greater control over their performance. FIRA's approval was required for all new foreign investments and for the purchase of Canadian companies by foreign firms, including the purchase of existing foreign subsidiaries by other foreign firms involving assets of $250,000 or gross revenues of $3 million. The criterion for evaluating the proposed investment was its potential to bring 'significant benefits to Canada'. As a condition of approval, the agency could impose certain performance requirements on foreign firms, such as requiring the use of Canadian products or services or the creation of a specified number of domestic jobs. While FIRA approved well over 80 per cent of the proposals submitted for review during its existence, the figures reveal neither the extent to which foreign firms avoided investments for fear that approval would be denied nor the number of proposals that had to be modified to reflect Canadian priorities.

Immediately after its election in 1984, the Tory government replaced FIRA with Investment Canada, reflecting a more welcoming attitude on the part of the new government towards foreign investments. The new agency was established to court foreign investments rather than restrict them. The threshold value of the assets acquired that were to be subject to review was raised to $5 million, and the criteria for evaluation were relaxed as well. Later, the restrictions on foreign investment were further reduced as a result of the 1989 free trade agreement with the United States.

Perhaps the most dramatic measure towards Canadianization ever undertaken was in the area of energy resources: the establishment of Petro-Canada in 1975 extended Canadian ownership in the industry; the unveiling of the National Energy Program in October 1980 displayed the determination of the government to control critical sectors of the economy. The program's policy objective was to achieve majority Canadian ownership of the oil and gas industry by 1990 regardless of the performance of the foreign firms, which then owned (as they still do) an overwhelming proportion of the industry. The program established a complex tax and subsidy structure to favour domestically owned firms. In addition to enhancing domestic ownership, the program kept Canadian prices of oil below world prices with the purpose of subsidizing Canadian consumers and industrial users located mainly in central Canada. Needless to say, the foreign oil companies, which together form perhaps the single most powerful private economic group in the world, launched a massive campaign against the program. They were assisted in their efforts by the government of Alberta, which wished to capture windfall oil and gas rents and use these revenues to promote the diversification of the provincial economy. The Mulroney government dismantled most of the programs that formed the National Energy Program and undertook the privatization of Petro-Canada—again displaying its more favourable attitude towards foreign investment and its policy orientation of reduced involvement in the domestic economy (Fossum, 1997).

Crown Corporations

While Crown corporations, or public enterprises, enjoy a considerable degree of operating autonomy from the government, they are ultimately responsible to the government and are supposed to operate in a manner that furthers the government's stated objective in establishing and maintaining them. One of the various objectives a government might seek through Crown corporations is industrial development. As Peter Morici and his co-authors put it, state investment in a Crown corporation can be regarded as 'an element of industrial policy only when it is undertaken to establish, maintain or accelerate the growth of a particular industry and/or support the incomes of particular labour-force groups or regions' (Morici et al., 1982: 57). While many Crown corporations make profits for the government, this is not always their primary goal, and their operations quite often run deficits, which are borne by the government. The extent of the shortfall in revenues compared to expenditures (covered by the government) is regarded as a subsidy to the corporation.

Canada has a long history of using Crown corporations as an instrument of industrial policy (Laux and Molot, 1988). Ontario Hydro is one example. Most other provinces own similar utility companies to maintain a stable supply of relatively inexpensive electricity. As we have seen, the federal government has established many public enterprises such as Petro-Canada and the CDC to further the goals of 'Canadianizing' the economy and exploring for new oilfields. Some Crown corporations, whose sole purpose seems to have been to maintain employment, existed in economically depressed regions, such as Sydney Steel and the Cape Breton Development Corporation, which has operated coalmines in Nova Scotia. In some instances, the objective has been to maintain a presence in high-technology sectors—this was the case with Teleglobe Canada, Canadair, and de Havilland, all of which have been sold to private owners in recent years. Numerous other Crown corporations at both the federal and provincial levels have existed for a wide variety of reasons, few of them related to industrial policy.

In 1980 there were 454 Crown corporations in Canada; 242 were owned entirely by the federal government (Economic Council, 1986). They were heavily concentrated in the utilities, transportation, and communication sectors (in which they accounted for 59.5 per cent of total corporate assets in 1980). They had a relatively small presence in the mining (4 per cent) and the manufacturing (5.9 per cent) sectors (McFetridge, 1986a: 25). Canadian governments have recently sold off many highly visible Crown corporations such as Petro-Can and Air Canada as well as less well-known ones such as Northern Transportation Company Limited, Canadair, Teleglobe, and Canadian Arsenals. The net result of this activity was to diminish the public profile of Canadian public enterprises and their overall size in terms of assets controlled. However, between 1984 and 1994 the federal government also created six new Crown corporations in areas such as national museums and galleries (Laux, 1993).

Incentives for Research and Development

While Canada's expenditure on R&D is one of the lowest among industrialized nations, the Canadian government has still spent billions of dollars over the years to encourage industrial R&D undertaken by private firms, universities, and various public and private research institutions. In the late 1970s the R&D conducted directly by the government formed 29 per cent of all such activities in the country, which was a higher rate than in most industrialized nations (Macdonald Commission, 1985, II: 99). In the 1980s the government made attempts to contract out its own R&D, but this did not result in any significant reduction in the government share of the total. The R&D performed at Canadian universities cost $1 billion, funded almost entirely by the federal and provincial governments and forming 20 per cent of the total R&D in the country in 1983 (ibid., 101).

Most R&D in Canada, however, is performed by private firms. Their expenditures formed 55 per cent of the total, which was 14 percentage points higher than in the 1960s (ibid., 102). But the costs were not borne entirely by the firms conducting them; the companies received generous government subsidies and tax benefits. About 13 per cent of the private sector's total R&D expenditures were paid for by government grants and subsidies, excluding tax incentives (the government's share would increase even further if tax incentives were included). In 1983–4 federal R&D payments to Canadian industry, mostly in the form of grants and contracts, amounted to $461.5 million, an increase from $187.6 million in 1977–8 (ibid.). A large proportion of the R&D expenditures has been eligible for tax credits, which meant tax savings of $203.4 million to those firms involved in 1982.

In the late 1980s and early 1990s, government cutbacks to research councils, such as the National Research Council, the Social Sciences and Humanities Research Council, the Medical Research Council, the Natural Sciences and Engineering Research Council, and the International Development Research Council, resulted in less research and development taking place in the country (Stritch, 1997). After an extensive public consultation process in the mid-1990s (Canada, Industry Canada, 1994b), this trend was reversed somewhat as the federal government expanded council budgets and began a new 'education initiative' involving large-scale programs such as the creation of the $800 million Canadian Foundation for Innovation and the $2.5 billion Canadian Millennium Scholarship Fund.

Industrial Adjustment Measures

In the past decade, Canadian industry has faced tremendous adjustment pressures from imports, shifts in demand, and the obsolescence of many domestically manufactured products. Pressures to adjust to changed circumstances affect both capital and labour. While labour finds adjustment more difficult, and hence needs more government assistance, most adjustment programs have been directed at firms. The underlying rationale for this is that the adjustment of private companies will lead automatically to the adjustment of their employees. Adjustment assistance to firms usually takes the form of loans, loan guarantees, and grants, usually available for the purpose of modernizing and rationalizing plants and undertaking additional marketing efforts. While the firms are attempting to adjust the government has sometimes provided quota protection from imports to provide breathing space.

A firm faced with the need for adjustment has three options:

- to exit, by winding down its operation altogether or entering another line of business;
- to revitalize itself, by modernizing and rationalizing its operation to become competitive; or
- to seek government protection to shield it from adjustment pressures.

Exit by firms is a constant feature of any growing economy, and no government seeks to prevent it altogether, despite the social dislocations that result. The Economic Council estimated that 40 per cent of the firms operating in the average manufacturing industry in 1970 had left the industry by 1979 (Economic

Council, 1988a: 7). Revitalization is the preferred option from society's point of view: it preserves jobs without introducing inefficiencies in the economy; and rejuvenation results in enhanced competitiveness. But revitalization is expensive because it involves modernization of plants and adoption of modern management techniques and additional marketing efforts. The costs of modernization may be too high for firms to bear on their own, and hence the government often assists them, financially and otherwise. However, while revitalization is the most desirable objective from society's point of view, the most rational objective for any firm, in the short term, is to seek protection from adjustment and thereby save itself the hardships of exit or the expenses of modernization.

Many of the industrial adjustment programs in Canada are coupled with regional development or R&D expenditures, making them difficult to catalogue. Some industrial adjustment programs have been generally available to all eligible industries, while others are directed specifically at certain industries recognized as needing special attention. The Industrial and Regional Development Program (IRDP), which consolidated a host of similar existing programs, was the most important industrial adjustment program when it was established in 1983. It provided grants, loans, and loan guarantees to needy firms to help cover the costs of innovation, plant establishment or modernization and expansion, marketing, and restructuring. Each proposal was examined against certain specified criteria to determine the nature and amount of assistance. In 1984–5 the estimated government expenditure under this program was $470 million (Macdonald Commission, II: 147).

Industry-specific adjustment programs have included the Pulp and Paper Modernization Program (PPMP), the Shipbuilding Industry Assistance Program (SIAP), and the Canadian Industrial Renewal Program (CIRP). The PPMP, designed to assist in the modernization of pulp and paper plants, cost the government (both federal and provincial, since it was a joint program) $542 million over the 1979–84 period (Economic Council, 1988a: 20). The SIAP was directed at subsidizing construction of new vessels and modernization of shipyards. Between 1975 and 1985 the federal government spent $480 million under the program; $426 million was for vessel construction and only a small amount for modernization (Economic Council, 1988a). The program was discontinued, but other kinds of assistance continue to be available to the industry under various programs. The CIRP was available to the textile, clothing, footwear, and tanning industries between 1981 and 1986. Its main thrust, as indicated by its expenditure pattern, was towards plant modernization and industry restructuring, which received $364 million during the life of the program.

Labour Adjustment Measures

Labour, with its more severe problem of adjustment, faces difficulties not only when employing firms become uncompetitive against imports or when demand for product drops, but also when firms increase their competitiveness by adopting capital-intensive (often labour-displacing) production techniques (Osberg,

Wien, and Grude, 1995). Even at times when the number of jobs in the economy as a whole or in a particular industry is increasing, there are still industries and firms that are reducing employment. Thus, while the annual average growth in employment in trade-sensitive industries was 0.65 per cent during the 1967–81 period, the leather, textiles, knitting, and clothing industries suffered an annual average decline of almost 1 per cent (Robertson and Grey, 1985: 186).

Two broad types of labour adjustment measures are available to Canadian workers: general programs for individuals in need of adjustment assistance (regardless of the region or industrial sector they are located in); and programs directed specifically at individual workers in particular regions or industries faced with an unusual degree of adjustment. The first category covers most of the available programs and includes Employment Insurance, Canada Mobility Programs, Canada Manpower Industrial Training Program, Critical Trade Skills Training Program, and placement services provided by local Canada Employment Centres. These are continuing programs that provide various kinds of assistance to individual workers who meet certain eligibility criteria. In the late 1980s, following the submission of a report on adjustment programs, the deGrandpre report (Advisory Council on Adjustment, 1989), many of these were consolidated into a new Labour Force Development Strategy. In 1991 the government established a new Canadian Labour Force Development Board to co-ordinate public and private labour development and training strategies. This Board, however, foundered on the hostile relations existing between the federal Conservative government and organized labour after the creation of the Canada-US Free Trade Agreement, and on disputes with the provinces surrounding jurisdiction and control over labour market expenditures (Howse and Chandler, 1997).

The specialized programs are directed at workers who need additional assistance that cannot be met by the regular programs. The categories include older workers, workers in economically depressed communities, and workers employed in industries experiencing decline. The Adjustment Assistance Benefits Program was established in 1971 (subsequently modified in 1982 and renamed the Labour Adjustment Benefits Program) to provide pre-retirement benefits to older workers in textiles, clothing, footwear, and tanning industries who would be unable to find employment in different communities, industries, or occupations. In 1981 the government announced its Industry and Labour Adjustment Program (ILAP) designed for workers in designated economically depressed communities. While the program had a significant industrial adjustment component, the labour adjustment component provided enriched (that is, more benefits than those available to all workers) training and mobility assistance, wage subsidies to employers, and direct job creation measures. It was closed down in 1984. Other programs, established in 1981, assisted workers in the textiles, clothing, footwear, and tanning industries regardless of where they were located, unlike the ILAP, which was available only in designated communities.

These special programs were extremely expensive to operate. For instance, the Labour Adjustment Benefits Program entailed an expenditure of $60,000 per recipient (Robertson and Grey, 1985: 191). Similarly, the labour adjustment components of the ILAP entailed the expenditure of $97 million between 1981 and 1983. The federal government of the late 1980s and early 1990s discontinued most of the special labour adjustment programs because of their high costs. However, even then the government was unable to avoid large-scale expenditures related to unforeseen events and occurrences that undermined existing industries and regions. The collapse of the east coast cod fishery in the early 1990s, for example, led to the creation of a new multibillion-dollar Atlantic Groundfish Strategy (TAGS), a set of programs designed to help re-educate and relocate fishermen in the four Atlantic provinces and parts of Quebec affected by the fishery's collapse.

Regional Development Measures

In Canada many of the industrial development programs have had an insepara-ble regional development component. Moreover, there are many regional assis-tance programs whose main purpose is not to aid regional development but to compensate individuals and provincial governments in the poorer regions for their lower income and high unemployment. Programs administered by the Department of Regional Industrial Expansion (DRIE) prior to 1990 and the Department of Regional Economic Expansion (DREE) before 1982 can be broadly regarded as industrial development measures in the economically disadvantaged regions. The average annual expenditure by DREE during the 1968–73 period was $235.2 million; during 1973–81 it was $486.3 million; and between 1981 and 1983 it was $484.4 million (Lithwick, 1987: 150). Many of these expenditures were directed at encouraging new firms to locate in depressed regions or at modernizing and expanding existing firms in the regions. Large as the DREE expenditures were, they are insignificant compared to compensatory fiscal trans-fers to the provinces. DREE expenditures formed only 5.9 per cent (1968–73), 4.3 per cent (1973–81), and 2.5 per cent (1981–5) of the total federal transfers to provinces, municipalities, and individual citizens and families. Thus, compen-satory fiscal transfer payments rather than economic or industrial development have formed the main thrust of the federal regional development programs.

Recognizing this, the federal regional development department was abolished in the late 1980s and replaced by smaller-scale regional 'offices' such as the Atlantic Canada Opportunities Agency. These offices were designed to decentral-ize decision-making on regional issues to the troubled areas themselves, but were accompanied by substantial reductions in the overall regional development expenditure envelope. By 1993, the federal government had virtually abandoned any pretence of developing an 'interventionist' regional development posture. Instead, it resorted to an attempt to offset regional inequities by promoting the free movement of goods, capital, and labour throughout the economy by negoti-ating an Agreement on Internal Trade among Canada's provinces and territories. This agreement, which took effect in July 1995, attempted to extend the princi-ples of economic mobility to provincial government activities and specifically targeted government procurement and regulatory actions as subjects for equal treatment among producers and suppliers from all parts of the country (Trebilcock and Schwanen, 1995).

The agreement promotes the harmonization of government regulations and the principle of non-discrimination against Canadian suppliers, regardless of their province of origin. The general rules of the agreement prohibit signatories from discriminating against another party's goods, services, persons, or investments, restricting movement across provincial boundaries, and maintaining or creating obstacles to internal trade. However, the agreement contains several major loopholes that allow most signatories to continue their existing practices. It includes, among other things, provisions that provinces may have 'legitimate objectives' that allow them to contravene the general rules, that the rules only apply to enumerated sectors in the agreement, and that regional development measures are exempt. In addition, individual chapters on specific sectors also contain multiple exemptions for specific practices (Schwanen, 1995).

Provincial Industrial Policies

The division of powers between the federal and provincial governments and the fragmentation of business and labour along provincial lines are reflected once again in the area of industrial policy. Parallel to the federal government's industrial policies, the provincial governments maintain their own industrial policies to promote development within their borders. While not quite as sophisticated or extensive as Ottawa's policies, these provincial efforts are by no means insignificant. The increase in the provinces' financial capacities and administrative resources in the 1960s and 1970s ensured that they would undertake to expand their industrial bases. Quite often their programs were inspired by their desire to resist what they saw as the adverse effects of national economic policies on their provincial economies. As the Macdonald Commission (1985, II: 143) concluded, 'The provinces' industrial policies varied with their economic conditions and needs, their available resources, the ideologies of their government, and the pressures that private interests brought to bear on their leaders.'

The western provinces' industrial policies were designed to reduce their dependence on exports of unprocessed natural resources and to diversify their economic base. The central Canadian provinces were more concerned with maintaining the competitiveness of their traditional manufacturing industries and with promoting high-tech industries. Quebec has also sought to enhance the Francophone presence in the economy. For the Atlantic provinces, the objective was usually to attract any kind of manufacturing activity. Towards these objectives, the provinces have employed the full panoply of industrial policy instruments, including grants, loans at below-market rates, corporate tax incentives, preferential government procurement from local suppliers, subsidized electricity, and ownership of provincial Crown corporations (Jenkin, 1983). While provincial industrial policies have no doubt added to the incoherence of industrial policies in Canada and introduced economic inefficiencies by vying for industries regardless of their competitiveness, it is generally agreed that their effects, beneficial or otherwise, have been local. The federal government has continued to maintain its dominance in the industrial development field, and its policy has the strongest effects. According to one estimate, by the mid-1980s federal transfers to business for economic development were almost three times as large as those of all 10 provinces combined (McFetridge, 1985: 12).

Canadian Industrial Strategies after 1960

There has been no dearth, then, of industrial policies in Canada. But a collection of policies does not necessarily make an industrial strategy. There is a general consensus among analysts that Canada has no coherent industrial strategy. As one commentator concludes rather bluntly, 'No sane individual would or could construct the barrage of industrial policies that presently exist in Canada, with their duplication, overlap, unknown interaction and unmeasured effect' (McFetridge, 1985: 2). In fact, in the pre-war period, when the phrase 'industrial strategy' was yet to be coined, government policies displayed more coherence than they do now.

Tariffs and the construction of transportation infrastructures were the main vehicles of industrial development until World War I. At the time, however, policy-makers hardly realized that they were engaged in what would later be called an industrial strategy. As Michael Bliss (1982: 16) rightly points out:

> One of the most common views of nineteenth century industrial policies is that the major policies . . . coalesced or cohered into or were planned as part of one grand national development strategy, usually called the National Policy. . . . In fact . . . the term 'National Policy' was used by politicians who invented it to refer to the policy of tariff protection . . . . Throughout the nineteenth century the term did not refer to the other national development policies.

Bliss also notes (p. 18) that the

> aggregation of national policies [by economic historians] into one National Policy tends to obscure the piecemeal, ad hoc, and sometimes contradictory way in which policies were developed by real politicians dealing with real problems on a day-to-day basis. As well, by linking all of the national policies with the prosperity generated in the decades just before World War I, the view shades into a whiggish judgement that late-nineteenth century policy making was vindicated by national economic success.

Whether the policy-makers understood the ramifications of their actions or not, the National Policy tariffs had the effect of nurturing the establishment of indigenous manufacturing industries behind tariff walls and fostered the immigration of foreign companies to evade them. Later historians have categorized this strategy as one of import-substitution industrialization.

While free trade as a major issue died with the 1911 elections, tariff protection of Canadian manufacturing industries continued for many decades to come. There were always some in business and government who supported the lowering of the level of protection, while others supported its continuation. During the 1930s, in the midst of the Depression, there was talk of employing new instruments to boost industrial development, but the debate was not yet conducted in terms of industrial strategy. In the period immediately after World War II, the debate revolved around Keynesian demand management and the need to attract foreign investments to Canada, while the familiar controversies about the wisdom of lowering tariffs, which were slated for reduction under the GATT, declined in significance.

The first serious debate on the need for an industrial strategy began in the late 1950s when the effects of the liberalization of international trade and the emergence of Japan as an aggressive exporter began to be visible. However, the main force behind the debate was the growing concern about US ownership of the Canadian economy. The Gordon Commission's Report in 1957 drew attention to the adverse effects of foreign investments on the Canadian economy and the need to control them. Despite a lot of talk and some feeble attempts, however, little was done to implement the report until the mid-1960s.

In 1968 the Watkins Report argued along the same lines as the Gordon Commission. This was followed by the report of the House of Commons Committee on External Affairs and National Defence (the Wahn Report) in 1970, which also sought restrictions on foreign investment and advocated 51 per cent Canadian ownership of major foreign subsidiaries. In 1972 the Gray Report (named after Herbert Gray, a long-serving cabinet minister in the Trudeau and, later, Chrétien governments) was published, the last of the series of economic policy documents inspired by economic nationalism and concentrating on foreign investment in Canada. It spelled out the dangers of concentrating on staples exports and pointed out that foreign subsidiaries in the manufacturing sector had 'less opportunity for innovation and entrepreneurship, fewer export sales, fewer supporting services, less training of Canadian personnel in various skills, and less specialized product development aimed at Canadian needs or tastes'. It recommended strict screening processes for all foreign investment and the drawing up of government guidelines to compel foreign firms to operate in a manner conducive to Canada's national interest. The federal Liberal government was not sympathetic to most of its proposals. However, relying on NDP support in a minority government situation, the Liberals did establish FIRA to screen foreign investment.

The debate on industrial policy during the 1970s was less obsessed with foreign investment and displayed more understanding of the problems of Canadian manufacturing. The 1972 announcement by Jean-Luc Pepin, the Minister of Industry, Trade and Commerce, that the federal government would develop a general national industrial strategy marked a high point in Canada's efforts to devise such an initiative. Pepin declared: 'My Department and I are committed to try and produce an industrial strategy for Canada. . . . The strategy [will] embrace all sectors of economic activity from resources to services but must emphasize manufacturing and processing' (French, 1980: 105–6). As it turned out, this was no more than a pious hope. Pepin was soon out of the cabinet, and his successors favoured not a comprehensive industrial strategy but rather 'a coherent set of industrial policies', particularly 'strategies for sectors on an industry-to-industry' basis (ibid., 107). The move away from the idea of developing a comprehensive strategy covering all sectors reflected the difficulties of devising a policy that met all the divergent needs and interests.

In the mid-1970s the debate was conducted most vigorously between two semi-autonomous government bodies: the Economic Council and the Science Council of Canada. The Economic Council had by this time concluded that there was little hope for any significant change in Canada's industrial position in the near future and recommended bilateral free trade with the United States and a non-interventionist policy (Economic Council, 1975). In contrast, the Science Council blamed foreign investment for Canada's industrial malaise and recommended a highly interventionist government policy in support of Canadian-owned industries, especially in the high-technology sector (Britton and Gilmour, 1978). The two bodies continued to be rivals in the debate on Canadian industrial strategy until their abolition in the late 1980s.

In 1977 the federal government showed a renewed interest in formulating an industrial strategy. It established 23 task forces, each dealing with a different economic sector (21 in manufacturing, the others in construction and tourism) and consisting of business, labour, academic, federal, and provincial representatives. The reports of these task forces formed the basis of a final report by a so-called 'Tier II' committee, also consisting of representatives from business, labour, and academia. The final report, published in 1982, was no more than a patchwork of compromises among the self-serving demands of the 23 sectors. The government, not surprisingly, made no serious attempt to implement the report.

In the 1980–2 period two other alternative industrial policy documents appeared to compete for acceptance by the government. One was by Herb Gray, now federal Minister of Industry, Trade and Commerce, and it contained many of the same recommendations on foreign investment as in his earlier report, except that it had an additional emphasis on the need to support research and development activity and high-technology industries in the country. The other proposal was contained in the Ministry of State for Economic Development's 'Medium Term Track' position paper put out in 1982. In contrast to the Gray proposal, this paper emphasized the resource sector and recommended a policy that was not particularly interventionist. It argued that Canada had a comparative advantage in extracting and processing resource products and must concentrate only on those products and on the manufacturing industries directly related to them.

The Blair-Carr Committee's Task Force on Major Projects report, *Major Projects for Canada* (1981), also became a serious contender for acceptance. It concentrated on energy and resource-related mega-projects and prepared an inventory of projects spread across all regions. The projects were to be completed by the end of the century at a total cost of $440 billion. The report contained numerous other recommendations to maximize the benefits accruing from resource development, to distribute the development equitably among regions, and to ensure Canadian control in the sectors to be developed (Doern, 1983).

Thus, in 1981, when the government set out to announce its economic development strategy, it had before it a wide variety of recommendations. The strategy that eventually emerged and was presented to Parliament in November 1981 contained three main elements (Canada, 1980). First, it proposed to emphasize the natural resource sector, with the manufacturing sector being encouraged mainly to 'supply machinery, equipment and material needed for resource development and to extend the future processing of resource products beyond the primary state'. Second, it stated that resource development offered better opportunities for equitable regional development than would be possible through development of manufacturing. Third, it recommended that the surplus generated from resource development could be employed to finance the industrial restructuring that would be necessary to make Canadian manufacturing industries internationally competitive.

The government's statement was a classic compromise among the various contending proposals that had been on the table over the decade. It represented a halfway measure between interventionist and free market approaches, between nationalist and continentalist approaches, and between proposals that emphasized manufacturing and those that emphasized the resource sector. However, the onset of economic recession in 1982 (the worst since the Great Depression of the 1930s) and the parallel collapse of international commodity prices made the strategy irrelevant as a policy guide—it had been based on continued high prices for Canadian natural resources, especially for oil and gas, as a means to finance the major project investments. Little was heard of the strategy in subsequent years.

As a result, more than two decades of effort and billions of dollars in state expenditures on promoting industrial development had little to show in terms of coherent and consistent industrial strategy. The Canadian economy remained as dependent as ever on the export of natural resources, and the economically disadvantaged regions remained as dependent as ever on federal transfer payments. The only measure of success was achieved in the area of reducing the level of foreign ownership in the Canadian economy. Even the utility of this achievement, however, appeared dubious as Canada scrambled for investments to boost its economy in the midst of the post-1982 recession. Studies by the Economic Council of Canada and the OECD continued to hammer home the point that the state was incapable of improving the performance of the market and that the best that it could do was to promote 'positive adjustment' to market changes. The same Trudeau government that had displayed tremendous confidence in the state's ability to solve social and economic problems in its early years had run out of ideas in its final years in power.

In this context the government established the Macdonald Commission to report on Canada's economic prospects and the government's role in the economy (Bradford, 1998). The Liberal Party lost the 1984 election, and the Conservatives won on a pro-market platform. When the Macdonald Commission presented its report in 1985, the general thrust of its recommendations was in line with the new government's thinking even though it had apparently arrived at its conclusions independently.

Inspired by the reasoning of liberal political economy, the Macdonald Commission took the promotion of economic efficiency as the primary goal of its recommendations. In the context of industrial development, this meant promoting the domestic and international competitiveness of the Canadian economy. In the commission's words, 'Concern for productivity and competitiveness has been a compelling theme . . . and we are convinced that their significant improvement must be the fundamental objective of our future industrial policy' (Macdonald Commission, 1985, II: 185). Its recommendations were geared towards allowing market forces to determine the allocation of economic resources without state intervention. It was especially opposed to pursuing the strategy of 'picking winners'. It argued: 'In view of the practical difficulties of developing a targeted approach to industrial policy, this Commission does not recommend such an approach to Canada. Rapidly changing international and domestic circumstances demand a highly flexible and adaptive economic system; it is very doubtful whether governments can respond to such situations better than private enterprise can' (ibid., 184).

In line with its commitment to economic efficiency, the commission recommended free trade with the United States. It reasoned: 'Increased competition from the world in general, and the United States in particular, would work powerfully to induce Canadians to allocate our human, capital and natural resources in ways that would improve the country's productivity' (ibid., 201).

The Mulroney government, while not explicitly stating that it was following the commission's recommendations, followed a similar pro-market industrial policy. It privatized several Crown corporations, reduced the level of regulation in certain sectors, did not talk about the need to develop an integrated industrial strategy, and, most importantly, signed the Free Trade Agreement with the United States (McBride and Shields, 1993). Even this government, however, was not able to avoid intervening in the industrial development process. It, too, was forced to establish many programs to meet the special needs of the different regions and different sections of the economy, such as the forestry sector (Howlett, 1989). But such programs were for the most part ad hoc and often unsuccessful, and the government did not try to rationalize them in terms of a general industrial strategy.

This situation changed somewhat when the Liberals re-emerged as the government following the 1993 general election. The Liberal campaign book, *Creating Opportunity*, had promised the development of a new 'jobs and growth' agenda (Liberal Party of Canada, 1993) and soon after taking office the new government released its plan for the industrial sector, *Jobs and Growth: A New Framework for Economic Policy* (Martin, 1993). The government proposed to eschew the microeconomic interventions of its predecessors and to focus on improving productivity through skills training and encouraging new investment. However, it argued that the 'essential condition' for attaining these ends was 'to restore the government to fiscal health'. Despite efforts by the Industry Minister to focus on productivity enhancement through support for technological industries and enhancement of the 'innovative capacity' of Canadian society (Manley, 1994), the government was preoccupied with deficit reduction ('getting government right') throughout its first term in office and did very little in the way of implementing any of the other initiatives laid out in its *New Framework for Economic Policy*.

Constraints on Formulation of Industrial Strategies

The persistent failure to formulate a cohesive industrial strategy in Canada is understandable given the country's institutional and structural constraints on co-ordinated and effective state action. The organization of the Canadian state and society, in addition to the structure of the domestic and international political economy, makes the formulation of a strategy for industrial development an enormously difficult task. Social institutions condition what can or cannot be done, as well as the degree of coherence that can be obtained among the various measures of government.

The first constraint that the formulation of industrial strategy in Canada faces is the structure of the Canadian economy. An industrial strategy that does not give primacy to the export interests of Canada's natural resources industries is unthinkable. It is similarly unthinkable to have a strategy that ignores the manufacturing sector, whose weaknesses have usually occasioned the search for an industrial strategy in the first place. But reconciling the demands of the two sectors is not easy, given the contradictory nature of their interests. The regional nature of the Canadian economy imposes similar constraints on policy-makers, insofar as it is difficult to reconcile the interests of the various regions in a single industrial strategy. Measures to promote industrial development are almost invariably viewed as favouring one region at the expense of others.

The second constraint is rooted in the international political economy. International agreements such as the GATT/WTO regime and NAFTA limit what the government can do to aid its domestic industries. Opting out of the agreements is not a viable option, because although they restrict Canada's options they also protect its access to export markets. Moreover, Canada's middle-power status in the international arena limits its say in shaping the international political economy. The actions of the main actors on the world scene—the United States, the EU, and Japan—can have particularly severe impacts on Canada, given its higher degree of trade dependence. Also, Canada's position as an exporter of primary products, with their highly fluctuating prices determined on the international market, undermines the state's capacity to make predictions on the future, which is essential for the development of a coherent strategy. The first major modern Canadian industrial strategy, announced in 1981, based as it was on optimistic forecasts for the resource sector, floundered as commodity prices collapsed the following year.

The third constraint on policy-makers is the organization of the state. The existence of provinces with their own governments and business and labour interests produces mini-states of sorts, which pursue their own policies and strategies for industrial development. While provincial industrial policies have not posed a major problem so far, the federal government's need to balance the interests, or obtain the agreement, of the various provinces has added to the incoherence of both its sectoral policies and its broader industrial strategy (Howlett, 1989).

The fourth constraint relates to the organization of labour in Canada. The divisions between industrial and craft-based unions, between US and Canadian-affiliated unions, and between the labour employed in exporting industries and the labour employed in the import-competing industries obviously do not make for a unity of interests within the Canadian labour movement. Each has its own sectional interests, which often override the interests of labour as a whole and prevent it from using its collective strength to pressure the state and business to pursue policies beneficial to labour. The lack of a strong trade union central, the localized nature of union activity, and the existence of large numbers of unorganized workers also prevent labour from taking a strong position on many outstanding policy issues or from pursuing the stands it does take in a united and consistent manner.

The fifth constraint shaping the pattern of Canadian industrial policy and its uncohesive nature is the organization of capital. The divisions between finance and industrial capital, between staples-exporting and import-competing businesses, and between foreign-owned subsidiaries and indigenously controlled firms make the formulation of policies to meet joint interests difficult to accomplish. Government policies nevertheless often reflect the intention to satisfy all of them, or at least not to antagonize any of them. The lack of a strong national business organization that could aggregate the competing interests of the conflicting capitalist factions does not help the situation.

Although the Canadian state has participated actively in industrial development since the last century, the purpose of the intervention has been to supplement rather than supplant the market. Huge subsidies—in the form of grants, tax incentives, tariffs and quotas on imports, regulation of foreign investments, and so on—have been directed towards the domestic manufacturing industry to boost its international competitiveness artificially. All the money and effort spent on strengthening the manufacturing sector, however, have produced few results. There has been no significant change in the competitiveness of Canadian manufacturing as a result of the government's assistance. By the 1970s it was recognized that the lack of cohesion, that is, the lack of a consistent strategy, was responsible for the ineffectiveness of many individual government measures. But the ensuing efforts to devise a coherent industrial strategy led to naught—largely thanks to the constraints imposed by the structure of the domestic economy and the international political economy, and the fragmented internal organization of the state, labour, and capital. As a result, Canada has most of the elements of a non-interventionist strategy, but this is due as much to default as it is to conscious policy design or ideological imperative (Howse and Chandler, 1997).

Chapter 12

Conclusion: The Political Economy of Canadian Capitalism

We set out in this text to accomplish two goals: first, to describe the functioning of the Canadian political economy and to discuss why it operates as it does, and, second, to use this information to answer questions about the capacity of Canadian governments to deal with new challenges. Defining political economy as the mix of state and market, we have focused on the historical evolution of ideas and institutions related to the development and working of state and market in Canada.

We soon found that the two general theories in political economy—liberal and socialist—both undertheorize the state, in the sense that they undermine the importance of the state as an independent organization. Both theories construct general models of market-based societies and deductively analyse existing political economies to fulfil their theoretical expectations. It is, therefore, not surprising that their analyses often lead to ill-founded prescriptions for the reorganization of state and market interactions.

Most liberal theorists view the state as an inert institution that is called in to correct the failings of the market. The recent theoretical contributions by neo-conservatives and post-Keynesians bridge this shortcoming to a certain degree but generate other problems in its place. Neo-conservatives regard the democratic state as excessively interventionist, and hence inefficient, and see the solution in restricting the responsiveness of the state to popular pressures. Post-Keynesians diagnose the critical problems in the political economies of the industrialized nations as resting on the organization of both the state and market institutions. They call for concerted action by state, capital, and labour to resolve the problems, although they often fail to realize that this action might not be possible for historical reasons pertaining to the internal fragmentation of these actors.

The socialist theory, by viewing the state as merely an extension of the dominant classes in society, commits the same mistake of not recognizing the autonomous role of the state. Even the neo-Marxists, who do recognize the state's relative autonomy from class interests, are not able to overcome the problem entirely because of their fundamental theoretical precepts, which locate the determinants of state activities in the structural imperatives of a capitalist mode of production. Their argument tends to be remarkably circular: in essence, they say the state is both autonomous and constantly working towards further-ing the long-term interests of capital.

Both the liberal and socialist theories are ideological projects. The chief objec-tive of liberal political economy is to extend the market system and, by implica-tion, to support those who benefit from it the most, the owners of capital. They work to accomplish this by arguing for the superiority of the market and for the restriction of the state's role in it. The most important problems encountered by such a prescriptive, deductive approach is the proclivity to mould the observation of realities to match those projected by theory. Analysis is often manipulated to sustain the elegance of theoretical assumptions and to fit the rules of formal logic rather than to understand the true nature of the phenomenon under consideration.

Socialist political economy has its own problems, since it, too, is a deductive and prescriptive theory. Socialist analyses lead to conclusions that seek to further the interests of labour or, at a minimum, loosely defined anti-capitalist forces. Its ultimate objective is to facilitate the transition from an exploitative capitalist system to a socialist order. As a theory of radical restructuring of the existing order, socialist political economy has had a much larger agenda than liberal polit-ical economy, including the critique of existing society, the theorization of its replacement, and the theorization of the transition from the old to the new. This conceptualization has aroused the ire not only of liberals but also of numerous other theorists who argue that class exploitation is only one form of domination characteristic of capitalist society and that other groups are also oppressed and may in fact be more progressive than the easily co-opted working class—for example, women or members of new social movements concerned with peace, civil rights, or the environment (Cohen, 1982; Roemer, 1986; Kitschelt, 1993a).

Liberal political economy, of course, denies that it furthers the interests of the propertied class. It claims to arrive at universally valid generalizations on the basis of a strictly logical application of immutable principles of human behav-iour. Although usually not willing to engage socialist political economy in direct debate, liberals tend to depict socialist political economy as at best well-inten-tioned and at worst misdirected, ill-informed, and malicious. In the best-case scenario, socialist political economy is portrayed as retaining laudable moral imperatives for such issues as justice, equality, and fairness with which a 'pure science' such as liberal political economy cannot engage (Lindblom, 1977). In this scenario, socialist political economy is usually condemned not for its aims or goals, but for the inadequacy of the means by which it intends to accomplish its stated goals—means such as planning, centralization of decision-making, or a one-party state (Lindblom, 1977; Nove, 1983). In the worst-case scenario, social-ist political economy is portrayed as a partial and ill-conceived analysis that, in replacing the individual with classes as the primary unit of analysis, leads inevitably to the replacement of the general good or public interest by class interests (Flathman, 1966), which inevitably leads to dictatorship and even totalitarianism (Hayek, 1944). Socialist political economists, on the other hand, insist that the socialist project simply replaces the interests of the capitalist class with that of another class, and they tend to reject the concept of a general will or public interest above and beyond class interests (Arendt, 1958; Marcuse, 1958; Fehér et al., 1983).

For the most part staples political economists in Canada have avoided the propensity of socialists and liberals to apply general theories to the examination of the Canadian political economy. While they, too, underestimated the role of the state in the Canadian economy—by viewing it as a by-product of the exigencies of international trade—they advanced the discussion of the market found in liberal and socialist analyses by focusing on the specific nature of production found in Canada, particularly the continued dependence of the economy on the export of natural resources. In doing so they highlighted aspects of the Canadian political economy that had been ignored or glossed over by many liberal and socialist analyses.

The staples approach lost its chief strength, its empirical orientation, when it was revived in the early 1970s, especially when it became linked to dependency theory in its post-Innisian version. The objective of analysis shifted to reducing US control of the Canadian economy rather than to monitoring and detailing the operation of the Canadian political economy itself. The state and capital in Canada were simply assumed to be instruments of American interests, by having aligned themselves with US capital, thus blocking the possibility of an autonomous path of development. This particular staples approach became increasingly untenable as the international economic position of the United States itself began to wane and investment patterns shifted. By the late 1980s, on an annual basis, Canadian investment in the United States began to exceed US investment coming to Canada.

These are difficult times for political economists, in Canada and elsewhere. Socialist theory, and the extended role it prescribes for the state, stands discredited as Eastern Europeans have repudiated their recent past and a still nominally socialist China embraces free markets with a vengeance (Kitschelt, 1994). The staples approach had degenerated into a somewhat crude anti-Americanism and resisted efforts to resurrect it (Clement and Williams, 1989; Pal, 1989). However, in recent years it has been revitalized through analyses that highlight the increasing interpenetration of the Canadian and US political economies as a result of trade liberalization under the GATT/WTO regime and the FTA and NAFTA (McBride and Shields, 1993; Watkins, 1997).

The contemporary discourse in political economy is perhaps more narrowly confined than ever before. Virtually all alternatives on the national policy agenda are grounded in liberal political economy. However, at the theoretical level, the discussion continues on such questions as the primary organizational focus of analysis—identity politics, multiculturalism, individual rights and liberties—or the difficulties involved in moves towards the creation of a political and economic framework for social, cultural, and ecological sustainability.

Regardless of what the various theories of political economy prescribe as the state's appropriate role in society, what matters ultimately is its capacity to arrive at decisions and implement them (Hall and Ikenberry, 1989: 96–7).Certainly, Canada inherited and developed a set of institutions geared towards establishing strong and effective parliamentary governance and élite-driven political leadership. Yet, as we examined the development of Canadian state structures and their activities we could not escape the conclusion that these structures were limited in many ways by the nature of the political community in which they operated and by the fact that they are in a state of change.

What does this tell us about the autonomy of the Canadian state and its ability to rationally and effectively organize and guide economic development at national, provincial, or even sectoral levels? Neoinstitutional analysis holds that the ability of the state to undertake such projects depends on its ability to mobilize societal support—or conversely—whether or not the state is capable of overcoming societal resistance to the paths it chooses to pursue. Support and opposition refer not simply to material interests and objectives, but also to shared and opposing ideas and historical policy legacies that shape conventions of state intervention. Conceived in this fashion, the issue of autonomy is complex because it depends not only on the operation and organization of the state, but also on the similar organizational characteristics of major social actors.

As we addressed the question of the organizational capacity of the state and societal actors—focusing on business and labour, the two major societal actors found in every capitalist political economy—we noted that state-society relations are mediated by parliamentary democracy, federalism, and the unique geopolitical position of the international political economy. Federalism, for Canada, is not simply a tool to overcome space, but the reflection of political society shaped by distinct and often competing nationalisms and regionalisms. Canada is much more a 'political' than 'cultural' nation, and as a result there has been a great deal of ambiguity and conflict about the very nature of Canada. The state is fragmented by divided jurisdictions and the existence of two parallel and distinct parliamentary and administrative structures. The combination of a parliamentary system and federalism has produced an incredible flexibility, based on conventions of élite accommodation, that has continually facilitated state modernization and adjustment to economic and political exigencies. Still, this is a cumbersome process, and the reality is that significant limitations are placed on the capacity of state structures to frame issues and to act on a pan-Canadian basis. Conversely, state structures provide incentives to frame and act within provincial contours.

During the period of globalization the nature of state autonomy and capacity has changed significantly. On one hand, national sovereignty has been both pooled and enhanced within new international trade and investment regimes, and by the establishment of a hemispheric free trade and investment area. On the other hand, the interdependence and common regimes significantly limit the discretionary powers once held by provincial and federal governments.

Domestically, the autonomy of parliamentary and administrative élites has also been reduced through the rise of Charter politics and the disciplining of inter-governmental decision-making by forms of popular participation and referenda.

While our analysis has suggested the state is constrained and much weaker than it sometimes appears, it certainly is not without power or the ability to lead. The reason for this is that labour and capital in Canada are also poorly organized and fragmented. Two-thirds of Canadian wage-earners are not organized within unions and the vast majority do not directly benefit from collective agreements won by the unionized labour force. The remaining one-third are divided into several competing union centrals reflecting Canada's federalism as well as historical splits between industrial and craft and national and international unions. Furthermore, union centrals are limited in their power because the industrial relations regime throughout Canada focuses primarily on decentral-ized bargaining.

Globalization had been difficult for labour. The conventions of industrial relations have effectively changed to discipline the collective bargaining process in the public sector. Fiscal and political imperatives, restructuring, and concerns for economic competitiveness have placed downward pressure on wages and full-time employment growth. Faced with a difficult set of choices, Canadian labour adopted an organizational and political offensive that has rekindled social unionism and allowed it to strengthen its traditional bases. As in the corporate sector, merger and takeover have been part of the political response. Presently, the top 10 Canadian unions contain half the country's organized workforce. Still, labour is significantly limited by decentralization, the exceptional treatment given public-sector wage-earners, and an inability to gain powerful political allies at the federal level. As a result, labour remains weak and negative, capable of mounting specific pressure campaigns on governments and a 'no concessions' bargaining strategy in symbolically important negotiations—but rarely exercising the more positive power that would create opportunities to share in the making of corporate or public policy.

Capital, too, in Canada is highly fragmented, divided by sector and in terms of domestic and foreign ownership. Capital also is directly affected by uneven regional development, the particular specialization of provincial economies, and competition between provinces. These divisions are exacerbated by the existence of a number of business associations claiming to speak for capital. Sometimes, therefore, capital has pressed its interests by means of its own associations and sometimes through clearly aligned or sympathetic provincial administrations. During the modernization period, states were relatively more powerful, and yet business and government were incapable of working together on a pan-Canadian basis to establish an industrial strategy. The absence of broad intersectoral associ-ations left firms to deal directly with the state. The cumulative result of state measures in response to demands by individual firms has been disjointed policies.

In the globalization period, the tables have turned because neo-conservatism has placed the business agenda at the centre of national and international policy.

The terms of new international regimes and conventions of public policy have continually and significantly strengthened the power of capital, and particularly international capital, in state-society relations. Canadian capital has also internationalized to the point where Canadian direct investment abroad is now greater than foreign direct investment in Canada, and these capital flows are not simply following north-south trade. The result is that capital is now much more powerful and autonomous within the political economy. Nevertheless, capital remains fragmented and unorganized. Those regions of the federation in need of fostering development or industrial strategies now have fewer resources with which to pursue any sort of *dirigiste* strategy.

The situation in Canada, then, is one of ambiguous and flexible yet fragmented and constrained state structures, weak and fragmented labour, and powerful yet organizationally weak and fragmented capital. The state has less autonomy than in the modernization period because it is weaker and capital is stronger. Indeed, the rise of neo-conservatism has meant that much public policy is oriented towards enhancing trade, cultivating a healthy business climate, and fostering the structural competitiveness of the economy. Clearly, this privileges the political and material interests of international capital, even though the majority of new employment comes from small firms. The result presents an interesting dilemma for political leaders because it puts them in the position of implementing greater market discipline throughout society, even though such a policy thrust does not enjoy popular support.

The Canadian state's role in the areas of industrial development and fiscal and monetary management illustrates the effects of the organizational weaknesses of state, capital, and labour in Canada and the constraints imposed by the organization of the domestic and international political economies. Efforts to develop forward-looking and cohesive industrial strategies have failed because of the inability of the state to overcome resistance from capital or to fashion some sort of coalition among the different factions of the Canadian business community supporting specific industrial policy measures. Similarly, efforts by the state to develop co-ordinated fiscal and monetary management regimes have failed as a result of divisions between capital and labour over whether the primary aim of such efforts should be the control of inflation or the elimination of unemployment and the preservation of the social wage. They have failed especially because of the inability of the Canadian government to exercise greater control over the conduct of its international economic relations. The result has been that Canadian governmental activities have had an unco-ordinated, ad hoc, and incremental effect on markets, except in wartime when the state has overcome its own divisions and been able to impose its plans on reluctantly acquiescent capital and labour.

The fragmentation of the state and significant political-economic groups, however, bodes ill for meeting the challenges unleashed by globalization. One response is simply to acquiesce to global forces, an option that seems to have been chosen by Canadian policy-makers. However, another, more fruitful response is to take charge of the situation and negotiate the terms of globalization with the purpose of maximizing the opportunities afforded by it while minimizing its adverse effects. The success of the latter strategy, however, is contingent on the pursuit of a coherent set of economic and social policies that enjoy societal support. Unfortunately, both are sorely lacking in Canada.

Over the first 130 years of Confederation, Canada has developed a set of state and market institutions that are highly resistant to change. Although these institutions have performed reasonably well, they have existed within a relatively stable domestic and international political-economic environment, based on more or less open trade in resource commodities. Resource depletion and globalized industrial production and competition are now threatening to undermine the stability of that environment. In this situation there is little doubt that both state and societal actors will become increasingly disenchanted with muddling, reactive, and largely ineffective microeconomic and macroeconomic policy-making.

The future looks uncertain indeed. Since the early 1980s, Canada has already had two severe recessions. Even when economic growth has returned, it has not been accompanied by employment opportunities. Without greater purpose and commitment at the national level, it is probable that the country will simply continue to lurch from recession to recession. While Canada's wealth has been based on resource production, this is not likely to last forever because many resources are finite and others are expensive to renew. The adverse effects of trade liberalization also cannot be taken lightly. Liberalized international trade is a two-edged sword. It allows the importation of goods if they are produced more cheaply abroad, thus benefiting less well-off consumers. At the same time, imports exert downward pressure on wages in domestic labour-intensive industries. This dual process results in increasing income inequities in Canada while, as a consequence, democratically expressed pressures are exerted on governments to shield the populace from the adverse effects of trade liberalization.

At the millennium, change is needed—and being demanded. With the present fragmentation of major political actors, however, it is unlikely that the agenda of any single major actor can be successfully implemented. Fundamental state-based restructuring of the Canadian political economy—whether this would involve radically augmenting or diminishing the role of the state—is unlikely to occur because of the historical development of state and society in Canada. Instead, it is much more likely that the Canadian state will continue to respond to societal problems and concerns in much the same way as it has in the past, that is, through a process of ad hoc, incremental, and reactive change. Still, if any of the major actors in the Canadian political economy can overcome its fragmentation, the situation would be open for major change.

Bibliography

Abella, Irving. 1973. *Nationalism, Communism and Canadian Labour*. Toronto: University of Toronto Press.

Abella, Rosalie Silberman (Commissioner). 1984. *Report of the Commission on Equality in Employment*. Ottawa: Minister of Supply and Services Canada.

Acheson, T.W. 1972. 'The National Policy and the Industrialization of the Maritimes, 1880–1910', *Acadiensis* 1: 3–28.

Adams, Roy J. 1995. 'Canadian Industrial Relations in Comparative Perspective', in Gunderson and Ponek (1995).

Adie, Robert F., and Paul G. Thomas. 1987. *Canadian Public Administration: Problematical Perspectives*. Scarborough, Ont.: Prentice-Hall.

Advisory Council on Adjustment. 1989. *Adjusting to Win*. Ottawa: Ministry of Supply and Services.

Aglietta, Michel. 1979. *A Theory of Capitalist Regulation: The U.S. Experience*. London: New Left Books.

Aitken, Hugh G.J. 1959. *Conference on the State and Economic Growth*. New York: Social Science Research Council.

_____. 1961. *American Capital and Canadian Resources*. Cambridge, Mass.: Harvard University Press.

_____. 1964. 'Government and Business in Canada: An Interpretation', *Business History Review* 38: 4–21.

_____. 1967. 'Defensive Expansionism: The State and Economic Growth in Canada', in Easterbrook and Watkins (1967).

_____ et al. 1959. *The American Economic Impact on Canada*. Durham, NC: Duke University Press.

Alavi, H. 1982. 'The State and Class under Peripheral Capitalism', in H. Alavi and T. Shanin, eds, *Introduction to the Sociology of 'Developing Societies'*. London: Macmillan.

Albert, Michael, and Robin Hahnel. 1981a. *Marxism and Socialist Theory*. Boston: South End Press.

_____ and _____. 1981b. *Socialism Today and Tomorrow*. Boston: South End Press.

Albion, Robert G. 1926. *Forests and Sea-Power: The Timber Problems of the Royal Navy, 1652–1862*. Hamden, Conn.: Archon Books.

Albo, Gregory, and Jane Jenson. 1989. 'A Contested Concept: The Relative Autonomy of the State', in Clement and Williams (1989).

_____ and _____. 1997. 'Remapping Canada: The State in an Era of Globalization', in Clement (1997).

_____, David Langille, and Leo Panitch, eds. 1993. *A Different Kind of State? Popular Power and Democratic Administration*. Toronto: Oxford University Press.

Alexander, David. 1983. *Atlantic Canada and Confederation*. Toronto: University of Toronto Press.

Alford, Robert R., and Roger Friedland. 1985. *Powers of Theory: Capitalism, the State, and Democracy*. Cambridge: Cambridge University Press.

Allen, Robert C. 1985. *Trade Unions and the B.C. Economy*. Vancouver: BC Economic Policy Institute, Pacific Group for Policy Alternatives.

Althusser, Louis, and Etienne Balibar. 1977. *Reading 'Capital'*. London: New Left Books.

Amesse, Fernand, Louise Séquin-Dulude, and Guy Stanley. 1994. 'Northern Telecom: A Case Study in the Management of Technology', in Globerman (1994).

Amin, Samir. 1974. *Accumulation on a World Scale: A Critique of the Theory of Underdevelopment*. New York: Monthly Review Press.

Anderson, F.J. 1985. *Natural Resources in Canada: Economic Theory and Policy*. Toronto: Methuen.

Anderson, John. 1995. 'Trade, Technology and Unions', in Schenk and Anderson (1995).

Anderson, Robert, Theodore Cohn, Chad Day, Michael Howlett, and Catherine Murray, eds. 1998. *Innovation Systems in a Global Context: The North American Experience*. Montreal and Kingston: McGill-Queen's University Press.

Anonymous. 1995–6. 'A Proposed Framework for the Implementation of Monetary Policy in the Large Value Transfer System Environment', *Bank of Canada Review* (Winter): 73–84.

Appleton, Barry. 1994. *Navigating NAFTA: A Concise User's Guide to the North American Free Trade Agreement*. Scarborough, Ont.: Carswell.

Arblaster, Anthony. 1984. *The Rise and Decline of Western Liberalism*. Oxford: Basil Blackwell.

Archer, Keith, Roger Gibbins, Rainer Knopff, and Leslie A. Pal. 1995. *Parameters of Power: Canada's Political Institutions*. Toronto: Nelson.

Arendt, Hannah. 1958. *The Origins of Totalitarianism*. New York: Meridian Books.

Arrighi, Giovanni. 1978. *The Geometry of Imperialism: The Limits of Hobson's Paradigm*. London: New Left Books.

Arscott, Jane, and Linda Trimble, eds. 1996. *In the Presence of Women: Representation of Canadian Governments*. Toronto: Harcourt Brace Canada.

Atkinson, Michael M., ed. 1993. *Governing Canada: Institutions and Public Policy*. Toronto: Harcourt Brace Jovanovich.

_____ and Gerald Bierling. 1998. 'Is There Convergence in Provincial Spending Priorities?', *Canadian Public Policy* 24, 1: 71–89.

_____ and William D. Coleman. 1989. *The State, Business, and Industrial Change in Canada*. Toronto: University of Toronto Press.

Audley, Paul. 1983. *Canada's Cultural Industries: Broadcasting, Publishing, Records and Film*. Toronto: James Lorimer and Co., in association with the Canadian Institute for Economic Policy.

Avakumovic, Ivan. 1975. *The Communist Party in Canada: A History*. Toronto: McClelland & Stewart.

_____. 1978. *Socialism in Canada*. Toronto: McClelland & Stewart.

Avineri, Shlomo, ed. 1968. *Karl Marx on Colonialism and Modernization*. New York: Doubleday.

Bagehot, Walter. 1920. *The English Constitution*. London: K. Paul, Trench, Trubner and Co.

Baggaley, Carmen. 1981. *The Emergence of the Regulatory State in Canada, 1867–1939*. Ottawa: Economic Council of Canada.

Bain, Joe S. 1968. *Industrial Organization*. New York: Wiley.

Baker, Isabella. 1989. 'The Political Economy of Gender', in Clement and Williams (1989).

_____ and Katherine Scott. 1997. 'From the Post-War to the Post-Liberal Keynesian Welfare State', in Clement (1997).

Bakvis, Herman. 1996. 'Federalism, New Public Management, and Labour Market Development', in Fafard and Brown (1996).

_____ and David MacDonald. 1993. 'The Canadian Cabinet: Organization, Decision-Rules, and Policy Impact', in Atkinson (1993).

Baldwin, John R. 1992. *Foreign Multinational Enterprises and Merger Activity in Canada.* Ottawa: Statistics Canada, Analytical Studies Branch No. 42.

_____. 1995a. *Restructuring in the Canadian Manufacturing Sector from 1970 to 1990: Industry and Regional Dimensions of Job Turnover*. Ottawa: Statistics Canada.

_____. 1995b. *Business Strategies in Innovative and Non-Innovative Firms in Canada.* Research Paper No. 73. Ottawa: Statistics Canada, Analytical Studies Branch.

_____ and M. Rafiquzzaman. 1994. *Structural Change in the Canadian Manufacturing Sector 1970–1990*. Ottawa: Statistics Canada.

Bank of Canada. 1996. *Bank of Canada Review, Winter 1995–96*. Ottawa: Bank of Canada.

Banting, Keith G. 1982. *The Welfare State and Canadian Federalism*. Montreal and Kingston: McGill-Queen's University Press.

_____, research coordinator. 1986. *The State and Economic Interests*. Toronto: University of Toronto Press.

_____. 1987. *The Welfare State and Canadian Federalism*, 2nd edn. Montreal and Kingston: McGill-Queen's University Press.

_____. 1996. 'Social Policy', in Doern, Pal, and Tomlin (1996).

_____. 1997. 'The Social Policy Divide: The Welfare State in Canada and the United States', in Banting, Hoberg, and Simeon (1997).

_____ and Charles M. Beach, eds. 1995. *Labour Market Polarization and Social Reform*. Kingston: Queen's University School of Policy Studies.

_____, George Hoberg, and Richard Simeon, eds. 1997. *Degrees of Freedom: Canada and the United States in a Changing World*. Montreal and Kingston: McGill-Queen's University Press.

_____ and Richard Simeon, eds. 1983. *And No One Cheered: Federalism, Democracy and the Constitution Act*. Toronto: Methuen.

Baran, Paul A., and Paul M. Sweezy. 1966. *Monopoly Capital: An Essay on the American Economic and Social Order*. New York: Monthly Review Press.

Barber, C.L. 1957. 'Canada's Post-War Monetary Policy, 1945–54', *Canadian Journal of Economics and Political Science* 23: 349–62.

Barlow, Maude. 1990. *Parcel of Rogues: How Free Trade is Failing Canada*. Toronto: Key Porter Books.

Barnes, Trevor J., and Roger Hayter. 1994. 'Economic Restructuring, Local Development and Resource Towns: Forest Communities in Coastal British Columbia', *Canadian Journal of Regional Science* 17, 3: 289–310 .

Bartholomew, Amy. 1993. 'Democratic Citizenship, Social Rights and the "Reflexive Continuation" of the Welfare State', *Studies in Political Economy* 42: 141–56.

Basran, G.S., and David A. Hay, eds. 1988. *The Political Economy of Agriculture in Western Canada*. Toronto: Garamond Press.

Bealey, Frank. 1988. *Democracy in the Contemporary State*. Oxford: Clarendon Press.

Beetham, David. 1991. *The Legitimation of Power*. London: Macmillan.

Bell, Daniel. 1960. *The End of Ideology: On the Exhaustion of Political Ideas in the Fifties*. Glencoe, Ill.: Free Press.

Bercuson, David J., and David Bright, eds. 1994. *Canadian Labour History: Selected Readings*, 2nd edn. Toronto: Copp Clark Longmans.

Berger, Carl. 1976. *The Writing of Canadian History: Aspects of English-Canadian Historical Writing, 1900–1970*. Toronto: Oxford University Press.

Bernard, Elaine. 1993. 'Labour, the New Democratic Party, and the 1988 Federal Election', in Jenson and Mahon (1993).

Bernard, Mitchell. 1994. 'Post-Fordism, Transnational Production, and the Changing Global Order', in Stubbs and Underhill (1994).

Bernstein, Eduard. 1961 [1899]. *Evolutionary Socialism: A Criticism and Affirmation*. New York: Schocken Books.

Berry, L.Y. 1977. *Planning a Socialist Economy*. Moscow: Progress.

Bertram, Gordon W. 1963. 'Economic Growth and Canadian Industry, 1870–1915: The Staple Model and the Take-Off Hypothesis', *Canadian Journal of Economics and Political Science* 29: 159–84.

_____. 1964. 'Historical Statistics on Growth and Structure of Manufacturing in Canada 1870–1957', in Canadian Political Science Association, *Conference on Statistics, 1962*. Toronto: University of Toronto Press.

Bianco, Anthony. 1997. *The Reichmanns: Family, Faith, Fortune, and the Empire of Olympia & York*. Toronto: Random House.

Bickerton, James. 1990. *Nova Scotia, Ottawa and the Politics of Regional Development*. Toronto: University of Toronto Press.

Biersteker, Thomas J. 1993. 'Evolving Perspectives on International Political Economy: Twentieth-Century Contexts and Discontinuities', *International Political Science Review* 14, 1: 7–33.

Binhammer, H.H. 1977. *Money, Banking and the Canadian Financial System*. Toronto: Methuen.

Bird, Richard M. 1970. *The Growth of Government Spending*. Toronto: Canadian Tax Foundation.

Black, Don, and John Myles. 1986. 'Dependent Industrialization and the Canadian Class Structure: A Comparative Analysis of Canada, the United States, and Sweden', *Canadian Review of Sociology and Anthropology* 23: 157–81.

Blackbourn, Anthony, and Robert G. Putnam. 1984. *Industrial Geography of Canada*. London: Croom Helm.

Bladen, Vincent W. 1956 [1941]. *An Introduction to Political Economy*. Toronto: University of Toronto Press.

Blais, André. 1986a. 'Industrial Policies in Advanced Capitalist Democracies', in Blais, ed., *Industrial Policy*. Toronto: University of Toronto Press.

_____. 1986b. *Political Sociology of Public Aid to Industry*. Toronto: University of Toronto Press.

Bliss, Michael. 1973. 'Another Anti-Trust Tradition: Canadian Anti-Combines Policy, 1889–1910', *Business History Review* 47: 177–88.

_____. 1982. *The Evolution of Industrial Policies in Canada: An Historical Survey*. Ottawa: Economic Council of Canada.

Block, Richard N. 1993. *Unionization, Collective Bargaining and Legal Institutions in Canada and the United States*. Kingston: Industrial Relations Centre.

Block, Walter, and Michael Walker. 1985. *On Employment Equity: A Critique of the Abella Royal Commission Report*. Vancouver: Fraser Institute.

Blomström, Magnus, and Robert E. Lipsey. 1993. 'The Competitiveness of Countries and their Multinational Firms', in Eden and Potter (1993).

Boadway, Robin, ed. 1994. *Defining the Role of Government: Economic Perspectives on the State*. Kingston: Queen's University School of Policy Studies.

Bobbio, Norberto. 1987. *Which Socialism? Marxism, Socialism, and Democracy*. Cambridge: Polity Press.

Boessenkool, Kenneth J., David E.W. Laidler, and William B.P. Robson. 1996. 'Devils in the Details: Improving the Tactics of Recent Canadian Monetary Policy', *Commentary* 79: 1–20.

Boggs, Carl, and David Plotke. 1980. *The Politics of Eurocommunism*. Montreal: Black Rose Books.

Boismenu, G. 1989. *La vraisemblance de la problematique de la regulation pour saisir la realité Canadienne: Étude des indicateurs économique en moyenne periode*. Montreal: Université de Montréal.

_____ and D. Drache, eds. 1990. *Politique et Régulation*. Montreal: Editions du Meridien.

Boivin, Jean, and Esther Déom. 1995. 'Labour-Management Relations in Quebec', in Gunderson and Ponek (1995).

Bolt, Menno. 1993. *Surviving as Indians: The Challenge of Self-Government*. Toronto: University of Toronto Press.

Bottomore, Tom. 1978. *Austro-Marxism*. Oxford: Clarendon Press.

Bourque, Gilles, and Gilles Dostaler. 1980. *Socialisme et indépendance*. Montreal: Boréal Express.

Boyer, R., ed. 1986. *Capitalismes fin de siècle*. Paris: PUF.

Boyer, Robert. 1996. 'State and Market: A New Engagement for the Twenty-First Century?', in Robert Boyer and Daniel Drache, eds, *States Against Markets: The Limits of Globalization*. London: Routledge, 84–116.

_____. 1997. 'The Variety and Unequal Performance of Existing Markets: Farewell to Doctor Pangloss?', in J. Rogers Hollingsworth and Robert Boyer, eds, *Contemporary Capitalism: The Embeddedness of Institutions*. Cambridge: Cambridge University Press, 55–93.

Bradford, Neil. 1998a. *Commissioning Ideas: Canadian National Policy Innovation in Comparative Perspective*. Toronto: Oxford University Press.

_____. 1998b. 'Ontario's Experiment with Sectoral Initiatives: Labour Market and Industrial Policy, 1985–1986', in Gunderson and Sharpe (1998).

_____ and J. Jenson. 1989. *The NDP in Fordism and Post-Fordism: The Impacts of Internal and External Pluralism*. Cambridge, Mass.: Harvard University, Center for European Studies.

Braverman, Harry. 1974. *Labor and Monopoly Capital: The Degradation of Work in the Twentieth Century*. New York: Monthly Review Press.

Brecher, Irving. 1957. *Monetary and Fiscal Thought and Policy in Canada, 1919–1939*. Toronto: University of Toronto Press.

_____. 1981. *Canada's Competition Policy Revisited: Some New Thoughts on an Old Story*. Montreal: Institute for Research in Public Policy.

Breckenridge, R.M. 1910. *The History of Banking in Canada*. Washington: Government Printing Office.

Breen, Richard, and David Rottman. 1995. 'Class Analysis and Class Theory', *Sociology* 29, 3: 453–73.

Brennan, Geoffrey, and James M. Buchanan. 1980. *The Power to Tax: Analytical Foundations of a Fiscal Constitution*. Cambridge: Cambridge University Press.

Brenner, Robert, and Mark Glick. 1991. 'The Regulation Approach: Theory and Practice', *New Left Review* 188: 45–120.

Brewis, T.N. 1965. 'Monetary Policy', in T.N. Brewis, H.E. English, A. Scott, and P. Jewett, eds, *Canadian Economic Policy*. Toronto: Macmillan.

_____. 1968. *Growth and the Canadian Economy*. Toronto: McClelland & Stewart.

Briskin, Linda, and Patricia McDermott. 1993. *Women Challenging Unions: Feminism, Militancy and Democracy*. Toronto: University of Toronto Press.

British Columbia, Ministry of Economic Development. 1978a. *An Economic Strategy for Canada*. Victoria: Crown Publications of Victoria.

_____. 1978b. *An Economic Strategy for Canada: The Industrial Dimension*. Victoria: Crown Publications of Victoria.

Britton, John, and James Gilmour. 1978. *The Weakest Link: A Technological Perspective on Canadian Industrial Underdevelopment*. Ottawa: Science Council of Canada.

Britton, John N.H., ed., 1996. *Canada and the Global Economy: The Geography of Structural and Technological Change*. Montreal and Kingston: McGill-Queen's University Press.

Brodie, Janine. 1990. *The Political Economy of Canadian Regionalism*. Toronto: Harcourt Brace Jovanovich.

_____. 1994. 'Regions and Regionalism', in James Bickerton and Alain-G. Gagnon, eds, *Canadian Politics*, 2nd edn. Peterborough, Ont.: Broadview Press.

_____. 1997. 'The New Political Economy of Regions', in Clement (1997).

_____ and Jane Jenson. 1988. *Crisis, Challenge, and Change: Parties and Class in Canada Revisited*. Ottawa: Carleton University Press.

Brooks, Stephen, and Andrew Stritch. 1991. *Business and Government in Canada*. Scarborough, Ont.: Prentice-Hall.

Brown, Douglas M. 1996. Thinking the 'Unthinkable', in Fafard and Brown (1996).

Browne, Gerald P. 1967. *The Judicial Committee and the BNA Act: An Analysis of the Interpretative Scheme for the Distribution of Legislative Powers*. Toronto: University of Toronto Press.

Brus, Wlodzimierz. 1973. *The Economics and Politics of Socialism*. London: Routledge & Kegan Paul.

_____. 1985. 'Socialism—Feasible and Viable?', *New Left Review* 153: 43–62.

Bryan, Ingrid A. 1994. *Canada in the New Global Economy: Problems and Policies*. Toronto: John Wiley & Sons.

Brym, Robert J., ed. 1985. *The Structure of the Canadian Capitalist Class*. Toronto: Garamond Press.

Buchanan, James M., Gordon Tullock, and Robert Tellison. 1980. *Towards a Theory of the Rent-Seeking Society*. College Station: Texas A & M University Press.

_____ and Richard Wagner. 1977. *Democracy in Deficit: The Political Legacy of Lord Keynes*. New York: Academic Press.

_____ and _____. 1978. *Fiscal Responsibility in Constitutional Democracy*. Boston: Martinus Nijhoff.

Buckley, Kenneth. 1958. 'The Role of Staple Industries in Canada's Economic Development', *Journal of Economic History* 18: 439–50.

_____ and M.C. Urquhart. 1965. *Historical Statistics of Canada*. Toronto: Macmillan.

_____. 1967. 'Capital Formation in Canada, 1896–1930', in Easterbrook and Watkins (1967).

Bull, Martin J. 1993. 'Review Article: The Crisis of European Socialism: Searching for a Really Big Idea', *West European Politics* 16, 3: 413–23.

Burkart, M. Lynn. 1990. *Implementing Pay Equity in Ontario*. Kingston: Industrial Relations Centre, Queen's University.

Cadsby, Charles Bram, and Kenneth Woodside. 1993. 'The Effects of the North American Free Trade Agreement on the Canada-United States Trade Relationship', *Canadian Public Policy* 19, 4: 450–62.

Cairns, Alan C. 1968. 'The Electoral System and the Party System in Canada, 1921–1965', *Canadian Journal of Political Science* 1: 55–80.

_____. 1971. 'The Judicial Committee and Its Critics', *Canadian Journal of Political Science* 4: 301–45.

_____. 1975. 'Political Science in Canada and the Americanization Issue', *Canadian Journal of Political Science* 8: 191–234.

_____. 1983. 'The Politics of Constitutional Conservatism', in Banting and Simeon (1983).

_____. 1991. 'Constitutional Change and the Three Equalities', in Ronald L. Watts and Douglas Brown, eds, *Options for a New Canada*. Toronto: University of Toronto Press.

_____. 1992. *Charter Versus Federalism: The Dilemmas of Constitutional Reform*. Montreal and Kingston: McGill-Queen's University Press.

_____. 1995. 'The Charlottetown Accord: Multinational Canada versus Federalism', in Douglas E. Williams, ed., *Reconfigurations: Canadian Citizenship and Constitutional Change. Selected Essays by Alan C. Cairns*. Toronto: McClelland & Stewart, 280–314.

_____. 1997. 'Constitutional Reform: The God that Failed', in Hayne (1997).

Cameron, Duncan M. 1986. 'The Growth of Government Spending: The Canadian Experience in Comparative Perspective', in Keith Banting, ed., *State and Society: Canada in Comparative Perspective*. Toronto: University of Toronto Press.

_____. 1988. *The Free Trade Deal*. Toronto: James Lorimer.

_____ and F. Houle, eds. 1985. *Canada et la nouvelle division internationale du travail/Canada and the New International Division of Labour*. Ottawa: University of Ottawa Press.

_____ and M. Watkins, eds. 1993. *Canada Under Free Trade*. Toronto: James Lorimer.

Campbell, Bruce. 1993. *Moving in the Wrong Direction: Globalization, the North American Free Trade Agreement and Sustainable Development*. Ottawa: Canadian Centre for Policy Alternatives.

Campbell, Robert M. 1987. *Grand Illusions: The Politics of the Keynesian Experience in Canada, 1945–1975*. Peterborough, Ont.: Broadview Press.

_____. 1995. 'Federalism and Economic Policy', in François Rocher and Miriam Smith, eds. *New Trends in Canadian Federalism*. Peterborough, Ont.: Broadview Press, 187–210.

Canada. 1885. *Report Relative to Manufacturing Industries in Existence in Canada*. Ottawa: King's Printer.

_____. 1968. *Eleventh Report of the Standing Committee on Defence and External Affairs Representing Canada-U.S. Relations*. Ottawa: Minister of Supply and Services.

_____. 1972. *Foreign Direct Investment in Canada*. Ottawa: Information Canada.

_____. 1980. *Statement on Economic Development for Canada in the 1980s*. Ottawa: Minister of Supply and Services.

_____. 1986. *Constitution Act of 1867*. Ottawa: Minister of Supply and Services.

_____. 1992. *North American Free Trade Agreement: An Overview and Description— Canada, Mexico, United States*. Ottawa: Minister of Supply and Services.

_____, Department of Consumer and Corporate Affairs. 1968. *Policies for Price Stability*. Ottawa: Minister of Supply and Services.

_____, Department of External Affairs. 1983. *A Review of Canadian Trade Policy: A Background Document to Canadian Trade Policy of the 1980s*. Ottawa: Minister of Supply and Services.

_____, Department of Finance. 1979, 1980. *Government of Canada Tax Expenditure Account, 1979 and 1980*. Ottawa: Minister of Supply and Services.

_____. 1985. *Account of the Cost of Selective Tax Measures*. Ottawa: Minister of Supply and Services.

_____. 1988a. *The Canada-U.S. Free Trade Agreement: An Economic Assessment*. Ottawa: Minister of Supply and Services.

_____. 1988b. *Quarterly Economic Review: Annual Reference Tables*. Ottawa: Minister of Supply and Services, June.

Canada, Department of Foreign Affairs and International Trade. 1995. *Attracting World Mandates: Perspectives from Canadian CEOs*. Ottawa: Department of Foreign Affairs and International Trade.

_____, Department of Justice. 1965. See Lajoie, P.G.

_____. 1983. *Canada: A Consolidation of the Constitution Acts 1867 to 1982*. Ottawa: Minister of Supply and Services.

Canada, Department of Reconstruction. 1945. *Employment and Income with Special Reference to the Initial Period of Reconstruction*. Ottawa: King's Printer.

_____, Department of Regional Industrial Expansion. 1988. *Canada-U.S. Free Trade Agreement and Industry: An Assessment*. Ottawa: Minister of Supply and Services.

_____, Human Resources Development Canada, Labour Management Partnership Program. 1994. *Labour-Management Innovation in Canada*. Ottawa: Human Resources Development Canada.

_____, Industry Canada. 1994a. *Building a More Innovative Economy*. Ottawa: Minister of Supply and Services.

_____. 1994b. *Building a Federal Science and Technology Strategy*. Ottawa: Minister of Supply and Services.

Canada, National Employment Commission. 1938. *Final Report of the National Employment Commission*. Ottawa: King's Printer.

_____, Parliamentary Task Force on Federal-Provincial Fiscal Arrangements. 1981. *Fiscal Federalism in Canada*. Ottawa: Minister of Supply and Services.

_____, Royal Commission on Aboriginal Peoples. 1996. *People to People, Nation to Nation: Highlights from the Report of the Royal Commission on Aboriginal Peoples*. Ottawa: Minister of Supply and Services.

_____, Royal Commission on Banking and Currency in Canada. 1933. *Report of the Royal Commission on Banking and Currency in Canada*. Ottawa: King's Printer.

_____, Royal Commission on Canada's Economic Prospects (Gordon Commission). 1957. *Report of the Royal Commission on Canada's Economic Prospects*. Ottawa: Queen's Printer.

_____, Royal Commission on Corporate Concentration. 1978. *Report of the Royal Commission on Corporate Concentration*. Ottawa: Minister of Supply and Services.

_____, Royal Commission on Dominion-Provincial Relations (Rowell-Sirois Commission). 1940. *Report of the Royal Commission on Dominion-Provincial Relations: Books I and II*. Ottawa: King's Printer.

_____, Royal Commission on the Economic Union and Development Prospects for Canada (Macdonald Commission). 1985. *Report of the Royal Commission on the Economic Union and Development Prospects for Canada*, 3 vols. Ottawa: Minister of Supply and Services.

Canada, Task Force on Program Review. 1985. *Study Team Reports*. Ottawa: Minister of Supply and Services.

_____, Task Force on the Future of the Canadian Financial Services Sector. 1997. *Discussion Paper*. Ottawa: The Task Force.

_____. 1998. *Final Report: Change, Challenge, Opportunity*. Ottawa: The Task Force.

Canada Year Book. various years. Ottawa: Statistics Canada and Supply and Services.

Canadian Centre for Policy Alternatives. 1996. *Challenging Free Trade in Canada: The Real Story*. Ottawa: Canadian Centre for Policy Alternatives.

Canadian Labour Congress (CLC). 1992. *Justice and Jobs: Full Employment and Equality Action Program*, adopted at the Nineteenth Constitutional Convention, Vancouver, June 1992. Ottawa: Canadian Labour Congress.

_____. 1997. *Women's Work: A Report*. Ottawa: Canadian Labour Congress.

Caragata, Warren. 1979. *Alberta Labour: A Heritage Untold*. Toronto: James Lorimer.

Cardoso, F.H. 1972. 'Dependent Capitalist Development in Latin America', *New Left Review* 74: 83–95.

Carpenter, Michael. 1997. 'Slovakia and the Triumph of Nationalist Populism', *Communist and Post-Communist Studies* 30, 2: 205–20.

Carrillo, Santiago. 1978. *Eurocommunism and the State*. London: Verso.

Carroll, William K. 1986. *Corporate Power and Canadian Capitalism*. Vancouver: University of British Columbia Press.

_____. 1988. 'The Political Economy of Canada', in J. Curtis and L. Tepperman, eds, *Understanding Canadian Society*. Toronto: McGraw-Hill Ryerson.

_____, ed. 1992. *Organizing Dissent: Contemporary Social Movements in Theory and Practice*. Toronto: Garamond Press.

_____, ed. 1997. *Organizing Dissent: Contemporary Social Movements in Theory and Practice. Studies in the Politics of Counter Hegemony*, 2nd edn. Toronto: Garamond Press.

Carter, Donald D. 1991. *The Canadian Charter of Rights and Freedoms: Implications for Industrial Relations and Human Resources Policy Practitioners*. Kingston: Industrial Relations Centre.

_____. 1992. *Canadian Industrial Relations in the Year 2000: Towards a New Order*. Kingston: Industrial Relations Centre.

_____. 1995. 'Collective Bargaining Legislation', in Gunderson and Ponek (1995).

Castells, Manuel. 1980. *The Economic Crisis and American Society*. Princeton, NJ: Princeton University Press.

Caves, Richard E., and Grant L. Reuber. 1969. *Canadian Economic Policy and the Impact of International Capital Flows*. Toronto: University of Toronto Press.

C.D. Howe Institute. 1983. *Flexibility as the Best Protection*. Brief No. 604. Submission to the Royal Commission on the Economic Union and Development Prospects for Canada.

Chambers, Edward J., and Donald F. Gordon. 1966. 'Primary Products and Economic Growth: An Empirical Measurement', *Journal of Political Economy* 74: 315–32.

Chapman, Anthony. 1993. *North American Free Trade Agreement: Rationale and Issues*. Ottawa: Library of Parliament.

Charlesworth, James. 1962. *The Limits of Behavioralism in Political Science*. Philadelphia: American Academy of Political and Social Science.

Chodos, Robert, Rae Murphy, and Eric Hamovitch, 1993. *Canada and the Global Economy: Alternatives to Corporate Strategy for Globalization*. Toronto: James Lorimer.

Chorney, Harold. 1989. *The Deficit and Debt Management: Alternatives to Monetarism*. Ottawa: Canadian Centre for Policy Alternatives.

_____ and Philip Hanson. 1985. 'Neo-Conservatism, Social Democracy and "Province Building": The Experience of Manitoba', *Canadian Review of Sociology and Anthropology* 22: 1–29.

Chow, Franklin. 1994. 'Recent Trends in Canadian Direct Investment Abroad: The Rise of Canadian Multinationals', in Globerman (1994).

Christian, William. 1977a. 'Harold Innis as Political Theorist', *Canadian Journal of Political Science* 10: 21–42.

_____. 1977b. 'The Inquisition of Nationalism', *Journal of Canadian Studies* 12 (Winter): 62–72.

_____ and Colin Campbell. 1974. *Political Parties and Ideologies in Canada*. Toronto: McGraw-Hill.

Clark, J. Matthew. 1996. 'The Bank of Canada, Accountability and Legitimacy: Some Proposals for Reform', *Canadian Public Policy* 22, 4: 330–41.

Clarke, Simon. 1990a. 'Crisis of Socialism or Crisis of the State?', *Capital and Class* 42: 19–29.

_____. 1990b. 'New Utopias for Old: Fordist Dreams and Post-Fordist Fantasies', *Capital and Class* 42: 131–55.

Clarke, Tony. 1992. *Silent Coup: Confronting the Big Business Takeover of Canada*. Toronto: James Lorimer and Canadian Centre for Policy Alternatives.

_____ and Maude Barlow. 1997. *MAI: The Multilateral Agreement on Investment and the Threat to Canadian Sovereignty*. Toronto: Stoddart.

Clark-Jones, Melissa. 1987. *A Staple State: Canadian Industrial Resources in Cold War*. Toronto: University of Toronto Press.

Clarkson, Stephen. 1991. 'Disjunctions: Free Trade and the Paradox of Canadian Development', in Daniel Drache and Meric S. Gertler, eds, *The New Era of Global Competition: State Policy and Market Power*. Montreal and Kingston: McGill-Queen's University Press, 103–26.

Clement, Wallace. 1975. *The Canadian Corporate Elite: An Analysis of Economic Power*. Toronto: McClelland & Stewart.

_____. 1977. *Continental Corporate Power*. Toronto: McClelland & Stewart.

_____. 1981. *Hardrock Mining*. Toronto: McClelland & Stewart.

_____. 1986. *The Struggle to Organize: Resistance in Canada's Fishery*. Toronto: McClelland & Stewart.

_____. 1988. *The Challenge of Class Analysis*. Ottawa: Carleton University Press.

_____, ed. 1997. *Understanding Canada: Building on the New Canadian Political Economy*. Montreal and Kingston: McGill-Queen's University Press, 43–63.

_____ and John Myles. 1994. *Relations of Ruling: Class and Gender in Postindustrial Societies*. Montreal and Kingston: McGill-Queen's University Press.

_____ and Glen Williams, eds. 1989. *The New Canadian Political Economy*. Montreal and Kingston: McGill-Queen's University Press.

_____ and _____. 1997. 'Resources and Manufacturing in Canada's Political Economy', in Clement (1997).

Coates, Ken. 1992. *Aboriginal Land Claims in Canada: A Regional Perspective*. Toronto: Copp Clark Pitman.

Coates, Mary Lou. 1992. *Is There a Future for the Canadian Labour Movement?* Kingston: Industrial Relations Centre.

_____, Gary T. Furlong, and Brian M. Downie. 1997. *Conflict Management and Dispute Resolution Systems in Canadian Nonunionized Organizations*. Kingston: Industrial Relations Centre.

Coats, R.H. 1917. 'The Labour Movement in Canada', in Adam Shortt and Arthur G. Doughty, eds, *Canada and Its Provinces*, vol. 9. Toronto: Glasgow Brook and Company.

Cockburn, Cynthia. 1991. *In the Way of Women: Men's Resistance to Sex Equality in Organizations*. Ithaca, NY: Cornell University Press.

Cohen, Benjamin J. 1983. 'Balance-of-Payments Financing: Evolution of a Regime', in Stephen D. Krasner, ed., *International Regimes*. Ithaca, NY: Cornell University Press, 315–36.

Cohen, Jean. 1982. *Class and Civil Society: The Limits of Marxian Critical Theory*. Lexington, Mass.: University of Massachusetts Press.

Cohen, Marjorie Griffin. 1988. *Women's Work, Markets and Economic Development in Nineteenth-Century Ontario*. Toronto: University of Toronto Press.

_____. 1991. *Women and Economic Structures: A Feminist Perspective on the Canadian Economy*. Ottawa: Canadian Centre for Policy Alternatives.

_____. 1994. 'British Columbia: Playing Safe is a Dangerous Game', *Studies in Political Economy* 43: 149–60.

Colander, David. 1984. *Neo-Classical Political Economy*. Cambridge: Ballinger.

Coleman, William D. 1984. *The Independence Movement in Quebec, 1945–84*. Toronto: University of Toronto Press.

_____. 1985a. 'Analyzing the Associative Action of Business: Policy Advocacy and Policy Participation', *Canadian Public Administration* 28: 413–33.

_____. 1985b. 'The Emergence of Business Interest Associations in Canada: An Historical Overview', paper presented to the Canadian Political Science Association, Montreal.

_____. 1986. 'Canadian Business and the State', in Banting (1986).

_____. 1988. *Business and Politics: A Study of Collective Action*. Montreal and Kingston: McGill-Queen's University Press.

_____ and Geoffrey R.D. Underhill, eds. 1998. *Regionalism and Global Economic Integration*. London and New York: Routledge.

Comisso, Ellen. 1997. 'Is The Glass Half Full or Half Empty? Reflections on Five Years of Competitive Politics in Eastern Europe', *Communist and Post-Communist Studies* 30, 1: 1–21.

Conway, John F. 1983. *The West: The History of a Region in Confederation*. Toronto: James Lorimer.

Cook, Ramsay, John T. Saywell, and John C. Ricker. 1963. *Canada: A Modern Study*. Toronto: Clarke, Irwin & Company.

Copithorne, Lawrence. 1979. *Natural Resources and Regional Disparities*. Ottawa: Economic Council of Canada.

Cornwall, John, and Wendy Maclean. 1984. *Economic Recovery for Canada: A Policy Framework*. Toronto: James Lorimer, in association with the Canadian Institute for Economic Policy.

Coté, Marcel. 1993. 'The Economic Agenda of the Progressive Conservative Party', *Canadian Business Economics* 1, 2.

Coulombe, Serge. 1997. *Regional Disparities in Canada: Characterization, Trends and Lessons for Economic Policy*. Working Paper Number 18. Ottawa: Industry Canada.

Courchene, Thomas J. 1976a. *Monetarism and Controls: The Inflation Fighters*. Montreal: C.D. Howe Institute.

_____. 1976b. *Money, Inflation and the Bank of Canada: Vol. I: An Analysis of Canadian Monetary Policy from 1970 to Early 1975*. Montreal: C.D. Howe Institute.

_____. 1981. *Money, Inflation, and the Bank of Canada: Vol. II: Analysis of Monetary Gradualism, 1975–80*. Montreal: C.D. Howe Institute.

_____. 1982. *Recent Canadian Monetary Policy, 1975–81: Reflections of a Monetary Gradualist*. Montreal and Kingston: McGill-Queen's University Press.

_____. 1983. *No Place to Stand? Abandoning Monetary Targets: An Evaluation*. Montreal: C.D. Howe Institute.

_____. 1986. *Economic Management and the Division of Powers*. Toronto: University of Toronto Press.

_____. 1994. *Social Canada in the Millennium: Reform Imperatives and Restructuring Principles*. Toronto: C.D. Howe Institute.

_____ and Douglas D. Purvis, eds. 1993. *Productivity, Growth and Canada's International Competitiveness*. Kingston: John Deutsch Institute for the Study of Economic Policy.

Craig, Alton W.J., and Norman A. Solomon. 1996. *The System of Industrial Relations in Canada*, 5th edn. Scarborough, Ont.: Prentice-Hall.

Crane, David. 1981. *Beyond the Monetarists: Post-Keynesian Alternatives to Rampant Inflation, Low Growth and High Employment*. Toronto: James Lorimer.

_____. 1992. *The Next Canadian Century: Building a Competitive Economy*. Toronto: Stoddart.

Creese, Gillian. 1995. 'Gender Equity or Masculine Privilege? Union Strategies and Economic Restructuring in a White Collar Union', *Canadian Journal of Sociology* 20, 2: 143–66.

Creighton, Donald. 1956 [1937]. *The Empire of the St. Lawrence*. Toronto: Macmillan.

Cross, Michael S. 1960. 'The Lumber Community in Upper Canada, 1815-1867', *Ontario History* 52: 213–33.

_____. 1973. 'The Shiner's War: Social Violence in the Ottawa Valley in the 1830's', *Canadian Historical Review* 53: 1–26.

Crow, John W. 1988. *The Work of Canadian Monetary Policy*. Edmonton: University of Alberta Eric J. Hanson Memorial Lecture, Microlog Document # 93–08636.

_____. 1993. 'Monetary Policy Under a Floating Rate Regime: The Canadian Experience', *Bank of Canada Review* (Summer): 37–48.

Cuneo, Carl. 1978. 'A Class Perspective on Regionalism', in D. Glenday, H. Guindon, and A. Turowetz, eds, *Modernization and the Canadian State*. Toronto: Macmillan.

_____. 1980. 'State Mediation of Class Contradictions in Canadian Unemployment Insurance', *Studies in Political Economy* 3: 37–65.

Cunningham, Frank. 1987. *Democratic Theory and Socialism*. Cambridge: Cambridge University Press.

Curtis, C.A. 1931. 'Canada and the Gold Standard', *Queen's Quarterly*: 104–20.

_____. 1932. 'The Canadian Monetary System', *Canadian Forum* 12: 207–9.

Curtis, Douglas. 1997. 'Canadian Fiscal and Monetary Policy and Macroeconomic Performance 1984-1993: The Mulroney Years', *Journal of Canadian Studies* 32, 1: 135–52.

Dales, John H. 1957. *Hydro Electricity and Industrial Development in Quebec, 1898–1940*. Cambridge, Mass.: Harvard University Press.

Daniels, Ron. 1991. 'Mergers and Acquisitions and the Public Interest: Don't Shoot the Messenger', in Waverman (1991).

Dasgupta, A.K. 1985. *Epochs of Economic Theory*. Oxford: Basil Blackwell.

Davey, William J. 1996. *Pine and Swine: Canada-United States Trade Dispute Settlement: The FTA Experience and NAFTA Prospects*. Ottawa: Canadian Centre for Trade Policy and Law.

Davies, R.J. 1986. 'The Structure of Collective Bargaining in Canada', in W.C. Riddell, ed., *Canadian Labour Relations*. Toronto: University of Toronto Press.

Davis, H. Craig. 1993. 'Is the Metropolitan Vancouver Economy Uncoupling from the Rest of the Province?', *BC Studies* 98: 1–20.

_____ and Thomas A. Hutton. 1991. 'Producer Services Exports from the Vancouver Metropolitan Region', *Canadian Journal of Regional Sciences* 14, 3: 378–80.

Dawson, Robert M. 1947. *The Government of Canada*. Toronto: University of Toronto Press.

Deane, Phyllis. 1978. *The Evolution of Economic Ideas*. Cambridge: Cambridge University Press.

Della Sala, Vincent. 1994. 'Capital Blight? The Regulation of Financial Institutions in Italy and Canada', *Governance* 7, 3: 244–64.

Denis, Serge. 1976. *Syndicats, parti des travailleurs et parti ouvrier révolutionnaire*. Montreal: PSI.

Deutsch, J.J. 1940. 'War, Finance and the Canadian Economy', *Canadian Journal of Economics and Political Science* 6: 525–42.

Dicey, A.V. 1908. *Introduction to the Study of the Law of the Constitution*. London: Macmillan.

Dobb, Maurice. 1964. *Studies in the Development of Capitalism*. New York: International Publishers.

_____. 1970. *Socialist Planning: Some Problems*. London: Lawrence and Wishart.

Dobell, Rod, and Michael Neufeld, eds. 1993. *Beyond NAFTA: The Western Hemisphere Interface*. Lantzville, BC: Oolichan Books.

Doern, G. Bruce. 1983. 'The Mega-Project Episode and the Formulation of Canadian Economic Development Strategy', *Canadian Public Administration* 26, 2: 219–38.

_____. 1995. *Fairer Play: Canadian Competition: Policy Institutions in a Global Market*. Policy Study No. 25. Toronto: C.D. Howe Institute.

_____, Leslie A. Pal, and Brian W. Tomlin. 1996. *Border Crossings: The Internationalization of Canadian Public Policy*. Toronto: Oxford University Press.

_____ and Brian W. Tomlin. 1991. *Faith and Fear: The Free Trade Story*. Toronto: Stoddart.

Dofny, Jacques. 1968. *Structure et pouvoirs de la Confédération des Syndicats Nationaux*. Ottawa: Privy Council Office Task Force on Labour Relations.

Doherty, Bill. 1991. *Slaves of the Lamp: A History of the Federal Civil Service Organizations 1865–1924*. Victoria, BC: Orca Book Publishers.

Domhoff, G. William. 1967. *Who Rules America?* Englewood Cliffs, NJ: Prentice-Hall.

Donnelly, Michael W. 1994. 'The Political Economy of Japanese Trade', in Stubbs and Underhill (1994).

Dosi, Giovanni, Christopher Freeman, Richard Nelson, Gerald Silverberg, and Luc Soete, eds. 1988. *Technical Change and Economic Theory*. London: Pinter Publishers.

Downie, Brian M., and Mary Lou Coates. 1993. *The Changing Face of Industrial Relations and Human Resources Management in Canada*. Kingston: Industrial Relations Centre.

Drache, Daniel. 1969. 'Harold Innis: A Canadian Nationalist', *Journal of Canadian Studies* 4: 7–12.

_____. 1977. 'Staple-ization: A Theory of Canadian Capitalist Development', in Craig Heron, ed., *Imperialism, Nationalism, and Canada*. Toronto: New Hogtown Press and Between the Lines.

_____. 1978. 'Re-discovering Canadian Political Economy', in W. Clement and D. Drache, eds, *A Practical Guide to Canadian Political Economy*. Toronto: Lorimer.

_____. 1982. 'Harold Innis and Canadian Capitalist Development', *Canadian Journal of Political and Social Theory* 6: 35–60.

_____. 1983. 'The Crisis of Canadian Political Economy: Dependency Theory versus the New Orthodoxy', *Canadian Journal of Political and Social Theory* 7: 25–49.

_____. 1991. 'The Systematic Search for Flexibility: National Competitiveness and New Work Relations', in Drache and Gertler (1991).

_____ and W. Clement. 1985. 'Introduction: Canadian Political Economy Comes of Age', in D. Drache and W. Clement, eds, *The New Practical Guide to Canadian Political Economy*. Toronto: Lorimer.

_____ and Meric S. Gertler, eds. 1991. *The New Era of Global Competition: State Policy and Market Power*. Montreal and Kingston: McGill-Queen's University Press.

_____ and Harry Glasbeek. 1992. *The Changing Workplace: Reshaping Canada's Industrial Relations System*. Toronto: James Lorimer.

_____ and Arthur Kroker. 1983. 'The Labyrinth of Dependency', *Canadian Journal of Political and Social Theory* 7: 5–24.

Drummond, I. 1986. 'Economic History and Canadian Economic Performance since the Second World War', in John Sargent, ed., *Postwar Macroeconomic Development*. Toronto: University of Toronto Press.

Dungan, Peter, and Thomas Wilson. 1985. 'Altering the Fiscal-Monetary Policy Mix: Credible Policies to Reduce the Federal Deficit', *Canadian Tax Journal* 33, 2: 309–18.

Dunk, Thomas, Stephen McBride, and Randle W. Nelson. 1996. *The Training Trap: Ideology, Training and the Wage Labour Market*. Winnipeg: Society for Socialist Studies.

Dunn, Robert M., Jr. 1991. 'Regional and Multilateral Trade Liberalization: Substitutes or Complements?', in Charles F. Doran and Alvin Paul Drischler, eds, *The United States, Canada and the World Economy*. Baltimore: The Johns Hopkins University Foreign Policy Institute.

Dunning, John H. 1993. 'Governments and Multinational Enterprises: From Confrontation to Co-operation?', in Loraine Eden and Evan H. Potter, eds, *Multinationals in the Global Political Economy*. New York: St Martin's Press, 59–83.

Duquette, Michel. 1993. *Énergie et fédéralisme au Canada*. Montreal: Les Presses de l'Université de Montréal.

_____. 1995. 'Conflicting Trends in Canadian Federalism: The Case of Energy Policy', in François Rocher and Miriam Smith, eds., *New Trends in Canadian Federalism*. Peterborough, Ont.: Broadview Press, 391–413.

Duverger, Maurice 1965. *Political Parties*. New York: Wiley.

Dwivedi, O.P. 1982. *Administrative State in Canada: Essays in Honour of J.E. Hodgett*. Toronto: University of Toronto Press.

Dyck, Rand. 1996. 'Relations Between Federal and Provincial Parties', in Alain-G. Gagnon and A. Brian Tanguay, eds, *Canadian Parties in Transition*, 2nd edn. Scarborough, Ont.: Nelson : 160–89.

Easterbrook, W.T. 1959. 'Recent Contributions to Economic History: Canada', *Journal of Economic History* 19: 76–102.

_____ and Hugh G.J. Aitken. 1956. *Canadian Economic History*. Toronto: Macmillan.

_____ and M.H. Watkins. 1967. *Approaches to Canadian Economic History: A Selection of Essays*. Toronto: McClelland & Stewart.

Easton, David. 1965. *A Systems Analysis of Political Life*. New York: Wiley.

Eaton, Curtis B., Richard G. Lipsey, and A. Edward Safarian. 1994. 'The Theory of Multinational Plant Location: Agglomerations and Disagglomerations', in Loraine Eden, ed., *Multinationals in North America*. Calgary: University of Calgary Press, 79–102.

Economic Council of Canada. 1975. *Looking Outwards: A New Trade Strategy for Canada.* Ottawa: Information Canada.

_____. 1979. *Responsible Regulation: An Interim Report.* Ottawa: Minister of Supply and Services.

_____. 1981. *Reforming Regulation.* Ottawa: Minister of Supply and Services.

_____. 1983. *Submission to the Royal Commission on the Economic Union and Development Prospects for Canada.* Ottawa.

_____. 1986. *Minding the Public Business.* Ottawa.

_____. 1987. *Making Technology Work: Innovation and Jobs in Canada.* Ottawa.

_____. 1988a. *Managing Adjustment: Policies for Trade-Sensitive Industries.* Ottawa.

_____. 1988b. *Venturing Forth: An Assessment of the Canada-U.S. Free Trade Agreement.* Ottawa.

Eden, Loraine. 1993. 'Bringing the Firm Back In: Multinationals in the International Political Economy', in Eden and Potter (1993).

_____. 1994a. 'Who Does What After NAFTA? Location Strategies of U.S. Multinationals', in Eden (1994b).

_____, ed. 1994b. *Multinationals in North America.* Calgary: University of Calgary Press.

_____ and Maureen Appel Molot. 1993. 'Canada's National Policies: Reflections on 125 Years', *Canadian Public Policy* 19, 3: 232–51.

_____ and Evan H. Potter, eds. 1993. *Multinationals in the Global Political Economy.* New York: St Martin's Press.

Edquist, Charles, ed. 1997. *Systems of Innovation: Technologies, Institutions and Organizations.* London: Pinter.

Educational Committees of the Confédération des Syndicats Nationaux (CSN) and Centrale de l'enseignement du Québec (CEQ). 1987. *The History of the Labour Movement in Quebec*, trans. Arnold Bennett. Montreal: Black Rose Books.

Edwards, Richard. 1979. *Contested Terrain.* New York: Basic Books.

_____, Michael Reich, and David M. Gordon. 1975. *Labor Market Segmentation.* Lexington, Mass.: D.C. Heath.

Emmanuel, A. 1972. *Unequal Exchange.* New York: Monthly Review Press.

Engels, F. 1972. 'Letters on Historical Materialism', in R.C. Tucker, ed., *The Marx-Engels Reader.* New York: Norton.

Erikson, Richard, and John H. Goldthorpe. 1992. *The Constant Flux: A Study of Class Mobility in Industrial Societies.* Oxford: Clarendon Press.

Esping-Andersen, Gosta. 1980. 'The Political Limits of Social Democracy: State Policy and Party Decomposition in Denmark and Sweden', in Maurice Zeitlin, ed., *Classes, Class Conflict and the State: Empirical Studies in Class Analysis.* Cambridge, Mass.: Winthrop Publishers.

_____. 1981. 'From Welfare State to Democratic Socialism: The Politics of Economic Democracy in Denmark and Sweden', *Political Power and Social Theory* 2: 111–40.

_____. 1985. *Politics Against Markets: The Social Democratic Road to Power.* Princeton, NJ: Princeton University Press.

_____, ed. 1993. *Changing Classes: Stratification and Mobility in Post-Industrial Societies.* Newbury Park, Calif.: Sage.

_____ and R. Friedland. 1982. 'Class Coalitions in the Making of West European Economies', *Political Power and Social Theory* 3: 1–52.

_____, _____, and E.O. Wright. 1976. 'Modes of Class Struggle and the Capitalist State', *Kapitalistate* 4–5: 186–220.

_____ and W. Korpi. 1984. 'Social Policy as Class Politics in Post-War Capitalism: Scandinavia, Austria and Germany', in Goldthorpe (1984).

Evans, P.M., and Wekerle, G.R., eds. 1997. *Women and the Canadian Welfare State: Challenges and Change*. Toronto: University of Toronto Press.

Fafard, Patrick, and Douglas M. Brown, eds. 1996. *Canada: The State of the Federation 1996*. Kingston: Queen's University Institute of Intergovernmental Relations.

Fanon, Frantz. 1965. *The Wretched of the Earth*. New York: Grove Press.

Fay, C.R. 1934. 'The Toronto School of Economic History', *Economic History* 3: 168–71.

Fehér, Ferenc, Agnes Heller, and György Markus. 1983. *Dictatorship over Needs*. Oxford: Basil Blackwell.

Fekete, John. 1994. *Moral Panic: Biopolitics Rising*. Montreal: R. Davies.

Ferguson, Barry. 1993. *Remaking Liberalism: The Intellectual Legacy of Adam Shortt, O.D. Skelton, W.C. Clark, and W.A. Mackintosh, 1890–1925*. Montreal and Kingston: McGill-Queen's University Press.

Fisher, A. 1966. *The March of Progress and Security*. New York: A.M. Kelley.

Flathman, Richard. 1966. *The Public Interest*. New York: Wiley.

Forsey, Eugene. 1974. *The Canadian Labour Movement, 1812–1902*. Ottawa: Canadian Historical Association.

Forster, Jakob. 1986. *A Conjunction of Interests: Business, Politics, and Tariffs, 1825–1879*. Toronto: University of Toronto Press.

Fossum, John. 1997. *Oil, the State, and Federalism: The Rise and Demise of Petro-Canada as a Statist Impulse*. Toronto: University of Toronto Press.

Fowke, Vernon C. 1946. *Canadian Agricultural Policy: The Historical Pattern*. Toronto: University of Toronto Press.

_____. 1952. 'The National Policy—Old and New', *Canadian Journal of Economics and Political Science* 18: 271–86.

Fox, A.B. 1977. *The Politics of Attraction: Four Middle Powers and the United States*. New York: Columbia University Press.

Fox, Bonnie, ed. 1980. *Hidden in the Household: Women's Domestic Labour Under Capitalism*. Toronto: Women's Press.

Fox, R.W., and H.K. Jacobson. 1973. *The Anatomy of Influence: Decision-Making in International Organization*. New Haven, Conn.: Yale University Press.

Frank, André G. 1970. *Latin America: Underdevelopment or Revolution*. New York: Monthly Review Press.

Frank, D., and N. Reilly. 1979. 'The Emergence of the Socialist Movement in the Maritimes, 1899–1916', in R.J. Brym and R.J. Sacouman, eds, *Underdevelopment and Social Movements in Atlantic Canada*. Toronto: New Hogtown Press.

Fraser Institute. 1983. *Submission to the Royal Commission on the Economic Union and Development Prospects for Canada*. Vancouver.

Freeman, John R. 1989. *Democracy and Markets: The Politics of Mixed Economies*. Ithaca, NY: Cornell University Press.

French, Richard. 1980. *How Ottawa Decides: Planning and Industrial Policy-Making, 1968–1980*. Toronto: Lorimer.

_____. 1985. 'Governing without Business: The Parti Québécois in Power', in V.V. Murray, ed., *Theories of Business-Government Relations*. Toronto: Trans-Canada Press.

Friedman, Milton. 1968. 'The Role of Monetary Policy', *American Economic Review* 58.

_____. 1982. *Capitalism and Freedom*. Chicago: University of Chicago Press.

Fudge, Judy, and Patricia McDermott, eds. 1991. *Just Wages: A Feminist Assessment of Pay Equity*. Toronto: University of Toronto Press.

Furtado, Celso. 1964. *Development and Underdevelopment*. Berkeley: University of California Press.

Gagnon, Alain-G., and Guy Lachapelle. 1996. 'Québec Confronts Canada: Two Competing Societal Projects Searching for Legitimacy', *Publius* 26, 3 : 177–91.

_____ and Mary Beth Montcalm. 1990. *Quebec: Beyond the Quiet Revolution*. Scarborough, Ont.: Nelson.

_____ and A. Brian Tanguay, eds. 1996. *Canadian Parties in Transition*, 2nd edn. Scarborough, Ont.: Nelson.

Galbraith, John Kenneth. 1987. *Economics in Perspective: A Critical History*. Boston: Houghton Mifflin.

Gannagé, Charlene. 1995. 'Union Women in the Garment Industry Respond to New Managerial Strategies', *Canadian Journal of Sociology* 20, 4: 469–95.

General Agreement on Tariffs and Trade (GATT). 1969. *Basic Instruments and Selected Documents*. Geneva.

GATT Secretariat. 1987a. *Inventory of Article XIX Actions and Other Measures Which Appear to Serve the Same Purpose*. 12 May.

_____. 1987b. *Drafting History of Article XIX and Its Place in the GATT*. 16 Sept.

_____. 1987c. *Grey-Area Measures: Background Note by the Secretariat*. 16 Sept.

Gera, Surendra, and Kurt Mang. 1998. 'The Knowledge-Based Economy: Shifts in Industrial Output', *Canadian Public Policy* 24, 2: 149–84.

Gettys, Cora L. 1938. *The Administration of Canadian Conditional Grants: A Study in Dominion-Provincial Relationships*. Chicago: Public Administration Service.

Ghalam, Nancy Zukewich. 1993. 'Women in the Workplace', *Canadian Social Trends* 28: 2–7.

Gibson, Gordon. 1994. *Plan B: The Future of the Rest of Canada*. Vancouver: Fraser Institute.

Gillespie, W.I. 1979. 'Postwar Canadian Fiscal Policy Revisited, 1945–1975', *Canadian Tax Journal* 27: 265–76.

_____. 1991. *Tax Borrow and Spend: Financing Federal Spending in Canada 1867–1990*. Ottawa: Carleton University Press.

Gilpin, Robert. 1987. *The Political Economy of International Relations*. Princeton, NJ: Princeton University Press.

Gittins, Susan. 1995. *Behind Closed Doors: The Rise and Fall of Canada's Edper, Bronfman Empires*. Scarborough, Ont.: Prentice-Hall.

Glazebrook, George. 1947. 'The Middle Powers in the United Nations System', *International Organization* 1: 307–15.

Glenday, Daniel. 1989. 'Rich, but Semi Peripheral: Canada's Ambiguous Position in the World Economy', *Review: Fernaud Braudel Centre* 12: 209–61.

Globerman, Steven, ed. 1991. *Continental Accord: North American Economic Integration*. Vancouver: Fraser Institute.

_____, ed. 1994. *Canadian-Based Multinationals*. Calgary: University of Calgary Press.

Golden, Miriam, and Jonas Pontusson, eds. 1992. *Bargaining for Change: Union Politics in North America and Europe*. Ithaca, NY: Cornell University Press.

Goldthorpe, John H., ed. 1984. *Order and Conflict in Contemporary Capitalism*. Oxford: Oxford University Press.

Gonick, Cy. 1987. *The Great Economic Debate: Failed Economies and the Future of Canada*. Toronto: James Lorimer.

_____. 1992. 'Socialism: Past and Future', in J. Roberts and J. Vorst, eds, *Socialism in Crisis? Canadian Perspectives*. Winnipeg: Fernwood Publishing, 199–224.

Gordon, David. 1988. 'The Global Economy: New Edifice or Crumbling Foundations?', *New Left Review* 168: 24–65.

Gordon, H.S. 1966. 'A Twenty Year Perspective: Some Reflections on the Keynesian Revolution in Canada', in S.F. Kaliski, ed., *Canadian Economic Policy Since the War*. Montreal: Canadian Trade Committee.

Gordon, Walter L. 1975. *Storm Signals: New Economic Policies for Canada*. Toronto: McClelland & Stewart.

Gorecki, P.K., and W.T. Stanbury. 1979. *Perspectives on the Royal Commission on Corporate Concentration*. Scarborough, Ont.: Institute for Research in Public Policy.

_____ and _____. 1984. *The Objectives of Canadian Competition Policy, 1888–1983*. Montreal: Institute for Research in Public Policy.

Gough, Ian. 1979. *The Political Economy of the Welfare State*. London: Macmillan.

Grahm, Edward M., and Mark A.A. Warner. 1994. 'Multinationals and Competition Policy in North America', in Eden (1994).

Gramsci, Antonio. 1972. *Selections from the Prison Notebooks*. New York: International Publishers.

Granatstein, J.L. 1967. *The Politics of Survival: The Conservative Party of Canada, 1939–1945*. Toronto: University of Toronto Press.

_____. 1982. *The Ottawa Men: The Civil Service Mandarins, 1935–1957*. Toronto: Oxford University Press.

_____. 1985. 'Free Trade between Canada and the United States: The Issue That Will Not Go Away', in D. Stairs and G. Winham, eds, *The Politics of Canada's Economic Relationship with the United States*.Toronto: University of Toronto Press, 1–51.

Grant, Michel. 1997. *Shifting from Traditional to Mutual Gains Bargaining: Implementing Changes in Canada*. Kingston: Industrial Relations Centre.

Grant, Wyn, and S. Nath. 1984. *The Politics of Economic Policy*. Oxford: Basil Blackwell.

Grayson, John P., ed. 1980. *Class, State, Ideology and Change: Marxist Perspectives on Canada*. Toronto: Holt, Rinehart and Winston.

Grinspun, Ricardo, and Robert Kreklewich. 1994. 'Consolidating Neoliberal Reforms: "Free Trade" as a Conditioning Framework', *Studies in Political Economy* 43: 33–61.

Grubel, Herbert G., and Josef Bonnici. 1986. *Why Is Canada's Unemployment Rate So High?* Vancouver: Fraser Institute.

_____, Douglas D. Purvis, and William M. Scarth. 1992. *Limits to Government: Controlling Deficits and Debt in Canada*. Toronto: C.D. Howe Institute.

Guest, Dennis. 1980. *The Emergence of Social Security in Canada*. Vancouver: University of British Columbia Press.

Gummett, Philip, ed. 1996. *Globalization and Public Policy*. Cheltenham: Edward Elgar.

Gunderson, Morley, Leon Muszynski, and Jennifer Keck. 1990. *Women and Labour Market Poverty*. Ottawa: Canadian Advisory Council on the Status of Women.

_____ and Allen Ponek. 1994. 'Labour Market Implications of Outward Foreign Direct Investment', in Globerman (1994).

_____ and _____, eds. 1995. *Union-Management Relations in Canada*. 3rd edn. Don Mills, Ont.: Addison-Wesley.

_____ and Andrew Sharpe, eds. 1998. *Forging Business-Labour Partnerships: The Emergence of Sector Councils in Canada*. Toronto: University of Toronto Press.

Haggard, Stephan, and Robert R. Kaufman, eds. 1992. *The Politics of Economic Adjustment: International Constraints, Distributive Conflicts, and the State*. Princeton, NJ: Princeton University Press.

Hall, John A., and G. John Ikenberry. 1989. *The State*. Minneapolis: University of Minnesota Press.

Hall, Peter A. 1992. 'The Change from Keynesianism to Monetarism: Institutional Analysis and British Economic Policy in the 1970s', in Sven Steinmo, Kathleen Thelen, and Frank Longstreth, eds, *Structuring Politics: Historical Institutionalism in Comparative Analysis*. Cambridge: Cambridge University Press, 90–114.

Hall, Peter A. 1983. 'Policy Innovation and the Structure of the State: The Politics-Administration Nexus in Britain and France', *The Annals of the American Academy of Political and Social Science* 466 (Mar.): 43–99.

_____. 1986. *Governing the Economy: The Politics of State Intervention in Britain and France*. Cambridge: Polity Press.

_____. 1989. *The Political Power of Economic Ideas: Keynesianism Across Nations*. Princeton, NJ: Princeton University Press.

_____. 1993. 'Policy Paradigms, Social Learning. and the State: The Case of Economic Policymaking in Great Britain', *Comparative Politics* (Apr.): 275–97.

_____ and Rosemary C.R. Taylor. 1996. 'Political Science and the Three New Institutionalisms', *Political Studies* 44: 936–57.

Hamelin, Jean, Paul Larocque, and Jacques Rouillard. 1970. *Repertoire des Grèves dans la Province de Québec au XIXe siècle*. Montreal: Presses de l'École des Hautes Études Commerciales.

Hamilton, Roberta. 1996. 'Feminism and Work', in *Gendering the Vertical Mosaic*. Toronto: Copp Clark, 138–80.

Hammond, Bray. 1957. *Banks and Politics in America: From the Revolution to the Civil War*. Princeton, NJ: Princeton University Press.

Hansen, Phillip. 1994. 'Saskatchewan: The Failure of Political Imagination', *Studies in Political Economy* 43: 161–75.

Harris, Richard G., ed. 1993. *Deficits and Debt in the Canadian Economy*. Kingston: John Deutsch Institute for the Study of Economic Policy.

_____ and William G. Watson. 1993. 'Three Versions of Competitiveness: Porter, Reich and Thurow on Economic Growth and Policy', in Courchene and Purvis (1993).

Hart, Michael, Bill Dymond, and Colin Robertson. 1994. *Decision at Midnight: Inside the Canada-US Free Trade Negotiations*. Vancouver : University of British Columbia Press.

Harvey, Fernand. 1978. *Révolution industrielle et travailleurs: une enquête sur les rapports entre le capital et le travail au Québec à la fin du 19e siècle*. Montreal: Les éditions du Boréal Express.

Hawkes, David C., ed. 1989. *Aboriginal Peoples and Government Responsibility: Exploring Federal and Provincial Roles*. Ottawa: Carleton University Press.

Hayek, Friedrich A. von. 1944. *The Road to Serfdom*. Chicago: University of Chicago Press.

_____. 1960. *The Constitution of Liberty*. Chicago: University of Chicago Press.

_____. 1983. 'The Muddle of the Middle', in Svetozar Pejovich, ed., *Philosophical and Economic Foundations of Capitalism*. Lexington, Mass.: Lexington Books.

Hayne, David M., ed. 1997. *Can Canada Survive? Under What Terms and Conditions?* Transactions of the Royal Society of Canada 1996. Sixth Series. Vol. 7. Toronto: University of Toronto Press.

Haythorne, George. 1973. 'Prices and Incomes Policy: The Canadian Experience, 1969–1972', *International Labour Review*: 485–503.

Hébert, Gérard. 1993. 'Unionism in a Different Context: The Case of Quebec', in Jane Jenson and Rianne Mahon, eds, *The Challenge of Restructuring: North American Labor Movements Respond.* Philadelphia: Temple University Press, 93–111.

Heilbroner, Robert. 1980. *Marxism: For and Against.* New York: Norton.

Helleiner, Eric. 1996. 'Post-Globalization: Is The Financial Liberalization Trend Likely to be Reversed?', in Robert Boyer and Daniel Drache, eds, *States Against Markets: The Limits of Globalization.* London: Routledge, 193–210.

Helleiner, G.D. 1985. 'Underutilized Potential: Canada's Economic Relations with Developing Countries', in John Whalley, ed., *Canada and the Multinational Trading System.* Toronto: University of Toronto Press.

Hellman, Joel S. 1998. 'Winners Take All: The Politics of Partial Reform in Postcommunist Transitions', *World Politics* 50, 2: 203–34.

Heron, Craig. 1989. *The Canadian Labour Movement: A Short History.* Toronto: James Lorimer.

_____. 1996. *The Canadian Trade Union Movement: A Brief History*, 2nd edn. Toronto: James Lorimer.

_____ and Robert Storey. 1986. *On the Job: Confronting the Labour Process in Canada.* Montreal and Kingston: McGill-Queen's University Press.

Hessing, Melody, and Michael Howlett. 1997. *Canadian Natural Resource and Environmental Policy: Political Economy and Public Policy.* Vancouver: University of British Columbia Press.

Hibbs, Douglas A. 1976. 'Industrial Conflict in Advanced Industrial Societies', *American Political Science Review* 70, 4: 1033–58.

_____. 1978. 'On the Political Economy of Long-Run Trends in Strike Activity', *British Journal of Political Sciences* 8: 153–75.

_____. 1987a. *The American Political Economy: Macroeconomics and Electoral Politics.* Cambridge, Mass.: Harvard University Press.

_____. 1987b. *The Political Economy of Industrial Democracies.* Cambridge, Mass.: Harvard University Press.

Higgott, Richard. 1998. 'The International Political Economy of Regionalism: The Asia-Pacific and Europe Compared', in Coleman and Underhill (1998).

Hilferding, Rudolf. 1981. *Finance Capital: A Study of the Latest Phase of Capitalist Development.* London: Routledge & Kegan Paul.

Hill, Michael, and Glen Bramley. 1986. *Analysing Social Policy.* Oxford: Basil Blackwell.

Hiller, James, and Peter Neary, eds. 1980. *Newfoundland in the Nineteenth and Twentieth Centuries.* Toronto: University of Toronto Press.

Himmelstrand, Ulf, G. Ahrne, et al. 1981. *Beyond Welfare Capitalism: Issues, Actors and Forces in Social Change.* London: Heinemann.

Hirschman, Albert O. 1958. *The Strategy of Economic Development.* New Haven, Conn.: Yale University Press.

Hirshhorn, Ronald, and Jean-François Gautrin, eds. 1993. *Competitiveness and Regulation: Government and Competitiveness Seminar Series, Montreal, Quebec, April 1992.* Kingston: Queen's University School of Policy Studies.

Hirst, Paul, and Grahame Thompson. 1992. 'The Problem of "Globalization": International Economic Relations, National Economic Management and the Formation of Trading Blocs', *Economy and Society* 21, 4: 357–96.

Hoberg, George. 1992. *Pluralism by Design: Environmental Policy and the American Regulatory State.* New York: Praeger.

Hodgetts, John E. 1973. *The Canadian Public Service: A Physiology of Government*. Toronto: University of Toronto Press.

Hoekman, Bernard, and Michel Kostecki. 1995. *The Political Economy of the World Trading System: From GATT to WTO*. Oxford: Oxford University Press.

Holden, Barry. 1988. *Understanding Liberal Democracy*. Oxford: Phillip Allen.

Holmes, John, and Pradeep Kumar. 1993. 'Labour Movement Strategies in the Era of Free Trade: The Uneven Transformation of Industrial Relations in the North American Automobile Industry', in Jenson, Mahon, and Benfefeld (1993).

Horowitz, Gad. 1968. *Canadian Labour in Politics*. Toronto: University of Toronto Press.

Horvat, Branko. 1982. *The Political Economy of Socialism: A Marxist Social Theory*. Armonk, NY: M.E. Sharpe.

Houle, François. 1983. 'Economic Strategy and the Restructuring of the Fordist Wage-Labour Relationship in Canada', *Studies in Political Economy* 11: 127–48.

Houseman, Robert F., and Paul Orbuch. 1993. 'Integrating Labor and Environmental Concerns into the North American Free Trade Agreement: A Look Back and A Look Ahead', *American University Journal of International Law and Policy* 8: 719–38.

Houston, Cecil J., and William J. Smyth. 1990. *Irish Immigration and Canadian Settlement: Patterns, Links and Letters*. Toronto and Belfast: University of Toronto Press and Ulster Historical Foundation.

Howitt, Peter. 1986. *Monetary Policy in Transition: A Study of Bank of Canada Policy, 1982–1985*. Toronto: C.D. Howe Institute.

_____. 1990. 'A Skeptic's Guide to Canadian Monetary Policy', *Commentary* 25: 1–16.

Howlett, Michael. 1986. 'Acts of Commission and Acts of Omission: Legal Historical Research and the Intentions of Government in a Federal State', *Canadian Journal of Political Science* 19: 363–70.

_____. 1989. 'The 1987 National Forest Sector Strategy and the Search for a Federal Role in Canadian Forest Policy', *Canadian Public Administration* 32, 4: 545–63.

_____ and Keith Brownsey. 1988. 'The Old Reality and the New Reality: Party Politics and Public Policy in British Columbia', *Studies in Political Economy* 25: 141–76.

_____ and M. Ramesh. 1993. 'Post-Keynesianism in Canada in the 1990s: An Emerging Paradigm or a Hopeless Muddle?', *American Journal of Canadian Studies* 23, 4: 539–64.

Howse, Robert. 1997. 'Searching for Plan A: National Unity and the Chrétien Government's New Federalism', in Harvey Lazar, ed., *Canada: The State of the Federation 1997: Non-Constitutional Renewal*. Kingston: Institute of Intergovernmental Relations, 311–34.

_____ and Marsha Chandler. 1997. 'Industrial Policy in Canada and the United States', in Banting, Hoberg, and Simeon (1997).

Hubbard, Jaimie. 1990. *Public Screening: The Battle for Cineplex Odeon*. Toronto: Lester & Orpen Dennys.

Hum, Derek. 1988. 'Harmonization of Social Programs Under Free Trade', in Glenn Drover, ed., *Free Trade and Social Policy*. Ottawa: Canadian Council on Social Development.

Hunt, E.K. 1979. *History of Economic Thought: A Critical Perspective*. Belmont, Calif.: Wadsworth.

Hurtig, Mel. 1991. *The Betrayal of Canada*. Toronto: Stoddart.

Hutcheson, John. 1978. *Dominance and Dependency*. Toronto: McClelland & Stewart.

Hutton, Thomas A. 1995. *Economic Implications of Environmental Enhancement: A Review and Interpretation of the Contemporary Literature*. Vancouver: University of British Columbia, Centre for Human Settlements, Sept., 25–8.

_____. 1994. *Visions of a 'Post-Staples' Economy: Structural Change and Adjustment Issues in British Columbia.* Vancouver: Centre for Human Settlements.

_____. 1997. 'Vancouver as a Control Centre for British Columbia's Resource Hinterland: Aspects of Linkage and Divergence in a Provincial Staples Economy', in Trevor Barnes and Roger Hayter, eds, *Trouble in the Rainforest: British Columbia's Forest Economy in Transition.* Victoria: Western Geographical Press, 233–62.

Iida, Keisuke. 1993. 'The Political Economy of Exchange-Rate Policy: U.S. and Japanese Intervention Policies, 1977–90', *Journal of Public Policy* 13, 4: 327–50.

Ikenberry, G. John. 1986. 'The Irony of State Strength: Comparative Responses to the Oil Shocks in the 1970s', *International Organization* 40, 1: 106–37.

_____. 1988. 'Conclusion: An Institutional Approach to American Foreign Policy', *International Organization* 42, 1: 219–43.

_____. 1993. 'Creating Yesterday's New World Order: Keynesian "New Thinking" and the Anglo-American Postwar Settlement', in Judith Goldstein and Robert O. Keohane, eds, *Ideas and Foreign Policy: Beliefs, Institutions and Political Change.* Ithaca, NY: Cornell University Press, 57–86.

Innis, Harold A. 1923. *A History of the Canadian Pacific Railway.* London: P.S. King and Sons.

_____. 1937. 'Significant Factors in Canadian Economic Development', *Canadian Historical Review* 18, 4: 374–84.

_____. 1938. *Settlement and the Mining Frontier.* Toronto: Macmillan.

_____. 1940. *The Cod Fisheries: The History of an International Economy.* New Haven, Conn.: Yale University Press.

_____. 1956. *The Fur Trade in Canada: An Introduction to Canadian Economic History.* Toronto: University of Toronto Press.

_____. 1972. *Empire and Communication.* Toronto: University of Toronto Press.

_____. 1982. *Essays in Canadian Economic History*, ed. Mary Q. Innis. Toronto: University of Toronto Press.

_____ et al. 1933. *Problems of Staple Production in Canada.* Toronto: Ryerson.

Instituto del Tercer Mundo. 1995. *The World: A Third World Guide.* Montevideo, Uruguay.

Jackson, Andrew. 1993. *Unions, Competitiveness and Productivity: Towards a Labour Perspective.* Kingston: School of Industrial Relations.

Jamieson, A.B. 1953. *Chartered Banking in Canada.* Toronto: Ryerson.

Jamieson, Stuart. 1968. *Times of Trouble: Labour Unrest and Industrial Conflict in Canada, 1900–66.* Ottawa: Information Canada.

Jay, Martin. 1973. *The Dialectical Imagination: A History of the Frankfurt School and the Institute for Social Research, 1923–1950.* Boston: Little, Brown.

Jenkin, Michael. 1983. *The Challenge of Diversity: Industrial Policy in the Canadian Federation.* Ottawa: Science Council of Canada.

Jenkins, Barbara. 1992. *The Paradox of Continental Production: National Investment Policies in North America.* Ithaca, NY: Cornell University Press.

Jenkins, Rhys. 1981. 'Divisions Over the International Division of Labour', *Capital and Class* 22: 28–58.

Jennings, Ivor. 1952. *Constitutional Laws of the Commonwealth.* Oxford: Clarendon Press.

Jenson, Jane. 1989. 'Different, But Not "Exceptional": Canada's Permeable Fordism', *Canadian Review of Sociology and Anthropology* 26, 1: 69–94.

_____. 1995. 'Citizenship Claims: Routes to Representation in a Federal System', in Karen Knop et al., eds, *Rethinking Federalism: Citizens, Markets, and Governments in a Changing World.* Vancouver: University of British Columbia Press.

_____ and Rianne Mahon, eds. 1993. *The Challenge of Restructuring: North American Labor Movements Respond*. Philadelphia: Temple University Press.

_____, _____, and Manfred Benfefeld, eds. 1993. *Production, Space, Identity: Political Economy Faces the 21st Century*. Toronto: Canadian Scholar's Press.

Jessop, Bob. 1993. 'Towards a Schumpeterian Workfare State? Preliminary Remarks on Post-Fordist Political Economy', *Studies in Political Economy* 40: 7–40.

Jevons, William Stanley. 1965 [1871]. *The Principles of Economics*. New York: A.M. Kelley.

Johnson, Andrew F., Stephen McBride, and Patrick J. Smith, eds. 1994. *Continuities and Dicontinuities: The Political Economy of Social Welfare and Labour Market Policy in Canada*. Toronto: University of Toronto Press.

_____ and Andrew Stritch, eds. 1997. *Canadian Public Policy: Globalization and Political Parties*. Toronto: Copp Clark.

Johnson, David R. 1997. 'Expected Inflation in Canada 1988–1995: An Evaluation of Bank of Canada Credibility and the Effect of Inflation Targets', *Canadian Public Policy* 23, 3: 233–58.

Johnson, Harry. 1963. *The Canadian Quandary: Economic Problems and Policies*. Toronto: McGraw-Hill.

Johnson, Pierre Marc, and André Beaulieu. 1996. *The Environment and NAFTA: Understanding and Implementing the New Continental Law*. Washington: Island Press.

Johnston, Richard. 1980. 'Federal and Provincial Voting: Contemporary Patterns and Historical Evolution', in David Elkins and Richard Simeon, eds, *Small Worlds: Provinces and Parties in Canadian Political Life*. Toronto: Methuen, 131–78.

Jones, Gareth S. 1977. *Western Marxism*. New York: Humanities Press.

Jonsson, Ivar. 1993. 'Regimes of Accumulation, Microeconomies and Hegemonic Politics', *Capital and Class* 50: 49–99.

Kamerman, S.B., and A.J. Kahn, eds. 1989. *Privatization and the Welfare State*. Princeton, NJ: Princeton University Press.

Kaminski, B. 1989. 'The Anatomy of the Directive Capacity of the Socialist State', *Comparative Political Studies* 22: 66–92.

Kaplinsky, Raphael. 1993. 'Post-Fordist Industrial Re-Structuring: Some Policy Implications', in Jenson, Mahon, and Benfefeld (1993).

Kato, Junko. 1996. 'Review Article: Institutions and Rationality in Politics—Three Variants of Neo-Institutionalists', *British Journal of Political Science* 26: 553–82.

Katzenstein, Peter. 1985. *Small States in World Markets: Industrial Policy in Europe*. Ithaca, NY: Cornell University Press.

Kautsky, Karl. 1909. *The Road to Power*. Chicago: S.A. Block.

_____. 1971 [1892]. *The Class Struggle*. New York: Norton.

Kealey, Gregory S. 1973. *Canada Investigates Industrialism*. Toronto: University of Toronto Press.

_____. 1981. 'Labour and Working Class History in Canada: Prospects for the 1980's', *Labour/Le Travail* 7: 67–94.

_____. 1985. 'The Writing of Social History in English Canada, 1970–1984', *Social History* 10: 347–65.

_____. 1995. *Workers and Canadian History*. Montreal and Kingston: McGill-Queen's University Press.

Kearns, Ian. 1994. 'Eastern and Central Europe in the World Political Economy', in Stubbs and Underhill (1994).

Kellogg, Paul. 1989. 'State, Capital and World Economy: Bukharin's Marxism and the "Dependency/Class" Controversy in Canadian Political Economy', *Canadian Journal of Political Science* 22: 337–62.

Keohane, Robert O., and Helen V. Milner. 1996. *Internationalization and Domestic Politics*. Cambridge: Cambridge University Press.

Kernaghan, Kenneth. 1979. 'Power, Parliament and Public Servants in Canada: Ministerial Responsibility Reexamined', *Canadian Public Administration* 3: 383–96.

_____. 1985. 'The Public and Public Servants in Canada', in Kernaghan, ed., *Public Administration in Canada: Selected Readings*. Toronto: Methuen.

_____ and David Siegel. 1987. *Public Administration in Canada: A Text*. Toronto: Methuen.

Keynes, John Maynard. 1936. *The General Theory of Employment, Interest, and Money*. New York: Harcourt, Brace.

Khemani, R.S. 1980. *Concentration in the Manufacturing Industries of Canada: Analysis of Post-War Changes*. Ottawa: Consumer and Corporate Affairs Canada.

_____, D.M. Shapiro, and W.T. Stanbury. 1987. *Mergers, Corporate Concentration and Power in Canada*. Montreal: Institute for Research on Public Policy.

_____ and W.T. Stanbury, eds. 1991. *Historical Perspectives on Canadian Competition Policy*. Halifax: Institute for Research on Public Policy.

Kirichenko, V.N. 1979. *Socialist Long-Term Planning*. Moscow: Progress.

Kitschelt, Herbert. 1993a. 'Social Movements, Political Parties and Democratic Theory', *The Annals* 528: 13–29.

_____. 1993b. 'Class Structure and Social Democratic Party Strategy', *British Journal of Political Science* 23: 299–337.

_____. 1994. *The Transformation of European Social Democracy*. Cambridge: Cambridge University Press.

Kneebone, Ronald D. 1996. 'Four Decades of Deficits and Debt', in Osberg and Fortin (1996).

Knox, Frank A. 1939. *Dominion Monetary Policy, 1929–1939*. Ottawa: Minister of Supply and Services.

Knubley, John, Marc Legault, and Someshwar Rao. 1994. 'Multinationals and Foreign Direct Investment in North America', in Eden (1994).

Kocham, Thomas A. 1992. *Transforming Industrial Relations: A Blueprint for Change*. Kingston: Industrial Relations Centre.

Korpi, Walter. 1983. *The Democratic Class Struggle*. London: Routledge & Kegan Paul.

Krahn, Harvey J., and Graham S. Lowe, eds. 1998. *Work, Industry and Canadian Society*, 3rd edn. Toronto: ITP Nelson.

Kravchuk, Petro. 1996. *Our History: The Ukrainian Labour-Farmer Movement in Canada, 1907–1991*, trans. Mary Skrypnyk. ed. John Boyd. Toronto: Lugus.

Kreklewich, Robert. 1993. 'North American Integration and Industrial Relations: Neoconservatism and Neo-Fordism?', in Ricardo Grinspun and Maxwell A. Cameron, eds, *The Political Economy of North American Free Trade*. Montreal and Kingston: McGill-Queen's University Press, 261–70.

Krugman, Paul R. 1994. 'Competitiveness: A Dangerous Obsession', *Foreign Affairs* 73: 28–44.

Kudrle, Robert Thomas. 1994. 'Regulating Multinational Enterprises in North America', in Eden (1994).

Kumar, Pradeep. 1986. 'Union Growth in Canada: Retrospect and Prospect', in W.C. Riddell, ed., *Canadian Labour Relations*. Toronto: University of Toronto Press.

_____. 1993. *From Uniformity to Divergence: Industrial Relations in Canada and the United States*. Kingston: Industrial Relations Centre, Queen's University.

_____ and Lynn Acri. 1991. *Women's Issues and Collective Bargaining*. Kingston: Industrial Relations Centre, Queen's University.

Kuznets, Simon. 1966. *Modern Economic Growth: Rate, Structure and Spread*. New Haven, Conn.: Yale University Press.

Lacroix, R. 1986. 'Strike Activity in Canada', in W.C. Riddell, ed., *Canadian Labour Relations*. Toronto: University of Toronto Press.

LaForest, Gerard V. 1955. *Disallowance and Reservation of Provincial Legislation*. Ottawa: Department of Justice.

_____. 1981. *The Allocation of Taxing Power under the Canadian Constitution*. Toronto: Canadian Tax Foundation.

Laidler, David, and William B.P. Robson. 1993. *The Great Canadian Disinflation: The Economics and Politics of Monetary Policy in Canada, 1988–93*. Toronto: C.D. Howe Institute.

Lajoie, P.G. 1965. *The Amendment of the Constitution of Canada*. Ottawa: Queen's Printer.

Lambert, Richard, and Paul Pross. 1967. *Renewing Nature's Wealth*. Toronto: Department of Lands and Forest.

Lamy, Paul. 1976. 'The Globalization of American Sociology: Excellence or Imperialism?', *American Sociologist* 11, 2: 104–14.

Landes, Ronald G. 1997. *The Canadian Polity: A Comparative Introduction*, 5th edn. Scarborough, Ont.: Prentice-Hall.

LaSelva, Samuel V. 1996. *The Moral Foundations of Canadian Federalism*. Montreal and Kingston: McGill-Queen's University Press.

Latham, A.B. 1930. *The Catholic and National Labour Unions of Canada*. Toronto: Macmillan.

Laux, Jeanne Kirk. 1993. 'How Private is Privatization?', *Canadian Public Policy* 19, 4: 398–411.

_____ and Maureen A. Molot. 1988. *State Capitalism: Public Enterprise in Canada*. Ithaca, NY: Cornell University Press.

Laxer, Gordon. 1989a. *Open for Business: The Roots of Foreign Ownership in Canada*. Toronto: Oxford University Press.

_____. 1989b. 'The Schizophrenic Character of Canadian Political Economy', *Canadian Journal of Sociology and Anthropology* 26: 178–92.

_____, ed. 1991. *Perspectives on Canadian Economic Development: Class, Staples, Gender, and Elites*. Toronto: Oxford University Press.

_____. 1995. 'Social Solidarity, Democracy and Global Capitalism', *Canadian Review of Sociology and Anthropology* 32, 3: 287–314.

Laxer, James. 1981. *Canada's Economic Strategy*. Toronto: McClelland & Stewart.

_____. 1984. *Rethinking the Economy*. Toronto: New Canada Publications.

Laxer, Robert, ed. 1973. *Canada Ltd.: The Political Economy of Dependency*. Toronto: McClelland & Stewart.

Laycock, David. 1990. *Populism and Democratic Thought in the Canadian Prairies, 1910–1945*. Toronto: University of Toronto Press.

Lazar, Harvey. 1997. 'The Federal Role in a New Social Union', in Lazar, ed., *Canada: The State of the Federation 1997: Non-Constitutional Renewal*. Kingston: Institute of Intergovernmental Relations, 105–36.

Leadbeater, D. 1984. 'An Outline of Capitalist Development in Alberta', in Leadbeater, ed., *Essays on the Political Economy of Alberta*. Toronto: New Hogtown Press.

League for Social Reconstruction. 1935. *Social Planning for Canada*. Toronto: T. Nelson and Sons.

Lecraw, Donald J., and Donald N. Thompson. 1978. *Conglomerate Mergers in Canada*. Ottawa: Royal Commission on Corporate Concentration.

Leier, James Mark. 1990. *Where the Fraser River Flows: The Industrial Workers of the World in British Columbia*. Vancouver: New Star Books.

Lembcke, Jerry, and William Tattam. 1984. *One Union in Wood: A Political History of the International Woodworkers of America*. New York: International Publishers.

Lemco, Jonathan, and William B.P. Robson, eds. 1993. *Ties Beyond Trade: Labor and Environmental Issues under NAFTA*. Toronto: Canadian-American Committee.

Lenin, Vladimir I. 1966. [1902]. *What Is To Be Done? Burning Questions of Our Movement*. Moscow: Progress Publishers.

_____. 1939a. [1917]. *The State and Revolution*. New York: International Publishers.

_____. 1939b. [1916]. *Imperialism, The Highest Stage of Capitalism: A Popular Outline*. New York: International Publishers.

Lermer, George. 1984. *Probing Leviathan: An Investigation of Government in the Economy*. Vancouver: Fraser Institute.

Leslie, Peter. 1997. 'The Economic Framework: Fiscal and Monetary Policy', in Johnson and Stritch (1997).

Levitt, Kari. 1970. *Silent Surrender: The Multinational Corporation in Canada*. Toronto: Macmillan.

Liberal Party of Canada. 1993. *Creating Opportunity*. Toronto: Liberal Party of Canada.

Lindberg, L.N. 1982. 'The Problem of Economic Theory in Explaining Economic Performance', *Annals of the American Academy of Political and Social Sciences* (Jan.): 14–27.

Lindblom, Charles E. 1977. *Politics and Markets: The World's Political Economic Systems*. New York: Basic Books.

Lingard, Charles C. 1946. *Territorial Government in Canada: The Autonomy Question in the Old North-West Territories*. Toronto: University of Toronto Press.

Lipietz, Alain. 1982. 'Towards Global Fordism?', *New Left Review* 132: 33–48.

_____. 1984a. *Accumulation, crises et sorties de crise: Quelques réflexions méthodologiques autour de la motion de 'régulation'*. Paris: CEPREMAP.

_____. 1984b. 'The Globalization of the General Crisis of Fordism, 1967–84', in John Holmes and Colin Leys, eds, *Frontyard Backyard: The Americas in the Global Crisis*. Toronto: Between the Lines.

_____. 1997. 'The Post-Fordist World: Labour Relations, International Hierarchy and Global Ecology', *Review of International Political Economy* 4, 1: 1–41

Lipset, Seymour M. 1959. *Agrarian Socialism*. Berkeley: University of California Press.

_____, ed. 1986. *Unions in Transition: Entering the Second Century*. San Francisco: Institute for Contemporary Studies.

Lipsey, Richard G., Daniel Schwanen, and Ronald J. Wonnacott. 1994. *The NAFTA: What's In, What's Out, What's Next*. Toronto: C.D. Howe Institute.

_____, Peter Steiner, and Douglas Purvis. 1987. *Economics*. New York: Harper and Row.

_____ and R. York. 1988. *Evaluating the Free Trade Deal: A Guided Tour through the Canada-U.S. Agreement*. Scarborough, Ont.: C.D. Howe Institute.

Lipsig-Mummé, Carla. 1993a. 'Quebec Labour, Politics and Economic Crisis: Defensive Accommodation Faces the Future', in Jane Jenson and Rianne Mahon, eds, *The Challenge of Restructuring: North American Labor Movements Respond*. Philadelphia: Temple University Press, 403–21.

_____. 1993b. 'Wars of Position in the Québec Labour Movement', in Jenson, Mahon, and Benfefeld (1993).

_____. 1995. 'Labour Strategies in the New Social Order: A Political Economy Perspective', in Gunderson and Poneks (1995).

Lipton, Charles. 1967. *The Trade Union Movement of Canada, 1827–1959*. Montreal: Canadian Social Publications.

Lithwick, N.H. 1987. 'Regional Development Policies: Context and Consequences', in W.J. Coffey and M. Polese, eds, in *Still Living Together: Recent Trends and Future Directions in Canadian Regional Development*. Montreal: Institute for Research on Public Policy.

Little Bear, Leroy, Menno Boldt, and J. Anthony Long, eds. 1984. *Pathways to Self-Determination: Canada's Indians and the Canadian State*. Toronto: University of Toronto Press.

Littler, Craig R. 1982. *The Development of the Labour Process in Capitalist Societies*. London: Heinemann.

Logan, Harold A. 1928. *The History of Trade-Union Organization in Canada*. Chicago: University of Chicago Press.

_____. 1948. *Trade Unions in Canada: Their Development and Functioning*. Toronto: Macmillan.

Lovink, J.A.A. 1970. 'On Analyzing the Impact of the Electoral System on the Party System in Canada', *Canadian Journal of Political Science* 3: 497–516.

Lowe, Graham S. 1980. *Bank Unionization in Canada: A Preliminary Analysis*. Toronto: Centre for Industrial Relations, University of Toronto.

_____. 1987. *Women in the Administrative Revolution: The Feminization of Clerical Work*. Toronto: University of Toronto Press.

_____ and Harvey J. Krahn, eds. 1993. *Work in Canada: Readings in the Sociology of Work and Industry*, 2nd edn. Scarborough, Ont.: Nelson Canada.

_____ and Herbert C. Northcott. 1993. *Stressful Working Conditions and Union Dissatisfaction*. Kingston: Industrial Relations Centre, Queen's University.

Lower, Arthur R.M. 1936. 'Settlement and the Forest Frontier in Eastern North America', in Lower and H.A. Innis, eds, *Settlement and the Forest Frontier in Eastern Canada*. Toronto: Macmillan of Canada.

_____. 1938. *The North American Assault on the Canadian Forest*. Toronto: Ryerson Press.

_____. 1967. 'The Trade in Square Timber', in Easterbrook and Watkins (1967).

_____. 1973. *Great Britain's Woodyard: British America and the Timber Trade, 1763–1867*. Montreal and Kingston: McGill-Queen's University Press.

_____. 1977 [1946]. *Colony to Nation: A History of Canada*. Toronto: McClelland & Stewart.

Lukacs, György. 1977. *History and Class Consciousness: Studies in Marxist Dialectics*. Cambridge, Mass.: MIT Press.

Lumsden, Ian, ed. 1970. *Close the 49th Parallel etc.: The Americanization of Canada*. Toronto: University of Toronto Press.

Lundrigan, Eugene, and Sari Toll. 1997–8. 'The Overnight Market in Canada', *Bank of Canada Review* (Winter): 27–42.

Luxemberg, Rosa. 1964. *The Accumulation of Capital*. New York: Monthly Review Press.

Luxton, Meg. 1980. *More Than a Labour of Love: Three Generations of Women's Work in the Home*. Toronto: Women's Educational Press.

Lynn, James T. 1967. *Federal-Provincial Fiscal Relations*. Ottawa.

Lyon, Peyton V., and Brian W. Tomlin. 1979. *Canada as an International Actor*. Toronto: Macmillan.

McBride, Stephen. 1992. *Not Working: State, Unemployment and Neo-Conservatism in Canada*. Toronto: University of Toronto Press.

_____ and John Shields. 1993. *Dismantling a Nation: Canada and the New World Order*. Halifax: Fernwood Books.

_____. 1996. 'The Continuity Crisis of Social Democracy: Ontario's Social Contract in Perspective', *Studies in Political Economy* 50.

_____. 1997. 'Investing in People: Labour Market Policy', in Johnson and Stritch (1997).

McCallum, John. 1980. *Unequal Beginnings: Agriculture and Economic Development in Quebec and Ontario Until 1870*. Toronto: University of Toronto Press.

McCormick, P. 1989. 'Provincial Party Systems, 1945–1986', in Gagnon and Tanguay (1989).

Macdonald Commission. 1985. See Canada, Royal Commission on the Economic Union and Development Prospects for Canada.

Macdonald, Laura. 1997. 'Going Global: The Politics of Canada's Foreign Economic Relations', in Clement (1997).

MacDonald, L.R. 1975. 'Merchants Against Industry: An Idea and Its Origin', *Canadian Historical Review* 56: 263–82.

MacDowell, Laurel Sefton, and Ian Radforth, eds. 1992. *Canadian Working Class History: Selected Readings*. Toronto: Canadian Scholars' Press.

McFetridge, D.G. 1986a. 'The Economics of Industrial Structure', in McFetridge, ed., *Canadian Industry in Transition*. Toronto: University of Toronto Press.

_____. 1986b. *The Economics of Industrial Policy and Strategy*. Toronto: University of Toronto Press.

_____. 1994. 'Canadian Foreign Direct Investment, R&D and Technology Transfer', in Globerman (1994).

McIvor, R.C. 1958. *Canadian Monetary, Banking, and Fiscal Development*. Toronto: Macmillan.

_____ and J.H. Panabaker. 1954. 'Canadian Post-War Monetary Policy, 1946–52', *Canadian Journal of Economics and Political Science* 20: 207–26.

Mackintosh, William A. 1934. *Prairie Settlement: The Geographical Setting*. Toronto: Macmillan.

_____. 1939. *The Economic Background of Dominion-Provincial Relations*. Ottawa: King's Printer.

_____. 1966. 'The White Paper on Employment and Income in Its 1945 Setting', in S.F. Kaliski, ed., *Canadian Economic Policy Since the War*. Montreal: Canadian Trade Committee.

_____. 1967. 'Economic Factors in Canadian History', in Easterbrook and Watkins (1967).

MacLachlan, Ian. 1996. 'Organizational Restructuring of U.S.-Based Subsidiaries and Plant Closures', in Britton (1996).

McLellan, David, ed. 1972. *Karl Marx: English Texts*. Oxford: Basil Blackwell.

_____. 1979. *Marxism after Marx*. New York: Harper and Row.

Macmillan, Charles J. 1992. 'Riding on Emotion: Cultural Industries and a NAFTA Accord', in Joseph A. McKinney and M. Rebecca Sharpless, eds, *Implications of a North American Free Trade Region: Multidisciplinary Perspectives*. Ottawa: Carleton University Press, 195–208.

McNally, David. 1981. 'Staple Theory as Commodity Fetishism: Marx, Innis and Canadian Political Economy', *Studies in Political Economy* 6: 35–64.

_____. 1991. 'Beyond Nationalism, Beyond Protectionism: Labour and the Canada-U.S. Free Trade Agreement', *Capital and Class* 43: 233–52.

Macpherson, C.B. 1953. *Democracy in Alberta: Social Credit and the Party System*. Toronto: University of Toronto Press.

_____. 1962. *The Political Theory of Possessive Individualism: Hobbes to Locke*. Oxford: Clarendon Press.

_____. 1974. 'After Strange Gods: Canadian Political Science, 1973', in T.N. Guinsburg and G.L. Reuber, eds, *Perspectives on the Social Sciences in Canada*. Toronto: University of Toronto Press.

_____. 1977. *The Life and Times of Liberal Democracy*. Oxford: Oxford University Press.

_____. 1979. 'By Innis out of Marx: The Revival of Canadian Political Economy', *Canadian Journal of Political and Social Theory* 3: 134–8.

McRoberts, Kenneth. 1993. *Quebec: Social Change and Political Crisis*, 3rd edn with a postscript. Toronto: McClelland & Stewart.

Magder, Ted. 1997. 'Public Discourse and the Structure of Communication', in Clement (1997).

Magnusson, Warren, C. Doyle, et al. 1984. *The New Reality: The Politics of Restraint in British Columbia*. Vancouver: New Star Books.

Mahon, Rianne. 1979. 'Regulatory Agencies: Captive Agents or Hegemonic Apparatuses?', *Studies in Political Economy* 1: 163–200.

_____. 1984. *The Politics of Industrial Restructuring: Canadian Textiles*. Toronto: University of Toronto Press.

_____. 1991. 'Post-Fordism: Some Issues for Labour', in Drache and Gertler (1991).

Mallory, James R. 1971. *The Structure of Canadian Government*. Toronto: Macmillan.

Mandel, Ernest. 1970. *An Introduction to Marxist Economic Theory*. New York: Pathfinder Press.

_____. 1986. 'In Defense of Socialist Planning', *New Left Review* 159: 5–38.

Manfredi, Christopher. 1997. 'The Judicialization of Politics: Rights and Public Policy in Canada and the United States', in Banting, Hoberg, and Simeon (1997).

Manitoba, Task Force on Meech Lake. 1989. *Report on the 1987 Constitutional Accord*. Winnipeg: The Task Force.

Manley, John. 1994. *Industry, Trade, and Technology: The Frontiers for Action*. Ottawa: Industry Canada, Microlog Document no. 9502625.

Mao Tse Tung. 1961. 'On the People's Democratic Dictatorship', in *Selected Works*, vol. 4. Peking: Foreign Languages Publishing House.

Marchak, Patricia. 1975. *Ideological Perspectives on Canada*. Toronto: McGraw-Hill Ryerson.

_____. 1979. *In Whose Interests: An Essay on Multinational Corporations in a Canadian Context*. Toronto: McClelland & Stewart.

_____. 1983. *Green Gold: The Forestry Industry in British Columbia*. Vancouver: University of British Columbia Press.

_____. 1985. 'Canadian Political Economy', *Canadian Review of Sociology and Anthropology* 22: 673–709.

_____. 1986. *British Columbia and the New Reality*. Kingston: Queen's University Program of Studies in National and International Development.

_____. 1996. *Racism, Sexism, and the University: The Political Science Affair at the University of British Columbia*. Montreal and Kingston: McGill-Queen's University Press.

Marcuse, Herbert. 1958. *Soviet Marxism: A Critical Analysis*. New York: Columbia University Press.

Mares, David R. 1988. 'Middle Powers Under Regional Hegemony: To Challenge or Acquiesce in Hegemonic Enforcement', *International Studies Quarterly* 32: 453–71.

Marfels, Christian. 1976. *Concentration Levels and Trends in the Canadian Economy, 1965–1973*. Ottawa: Royal Commission on Corporate Concentration.

Maroney, Heather Jon, and Meg Luxton. 1997. 'Gender at Work: Canadian Feminist Political Economy since 1988', in Clement (1997).

Marshall, Alfred. 1930 [1890]. *Principles of Economics: An Introductory Volume*. London: Macmillan.

Marshall, Herbert, Frank Southard, and Kenneth W. Taylor. 1936. *Canadian-American Industry: A Study in International Investment*. Toronto: Ryerson Press.

Martin, Chester. 1920. *The Natural Resources Question: The Historical Basis of Provincial Claims*. Winnipeg: University of Manitoba Press.

_____. 1973. *Dominion Lands Policy*. Toronto: McClelland & Stewart.

Martin, Paul. 1993. *Agenda: Jobs and Growth: A New Framework for Economic Policy*. Ottawa: Department of Finance.

Marx, Karl. 1962 [1867]. *Capital: A Critique of Political Economy*. London: J.M. Dent and Sons.

_____. 1968 [1848]. *The Manifesto of the Communist Party*. New York: International Publishers.

_____. 1974a. [1859]. 'Preface to a Contribution to the Critique of Political Economy', in Karl Marx and Frederick Engels, *Selected Works*. New York: International Publishers.

_____. 1974b [1871]. 'The Civil War in France', in Karl Marx and Frederick Engels, *Selected Works*. New York: International Publishers.

Maxwell, James A. 1937. *Federal Subsidies to the Canadian Provincial Governments*. Cambridge, Mass.: Harvard University Press.

Maxwell, Judith. 1977. *The Role of the Government: Searching for a Framework*. Montreal: C.D. Howe Institute.

Mellor, John. 1984. *The Company Store: James Bryson McLachlan and the Cape Breton Coal Miners, 1900–1925*. Halifax: Goodread Biographies.

Menger, Karl. 1950 [1871]. *Principles of Economics*. Glencoe, Ill.: Free Press.

Merret, Christopher D. 1996. *Free Trade: Neither Free Nor About Trade*. Montreal: Black Rose Books.

Migdal, Joel. 1988. *Strong Societies and Weak States: State-Society Relations and State Capabilities in the Third World*. Princeton, NJ: Princeton University Press.

Miliband, Ralph. 1990. 'Counter-Hegemonic Struggles', in Miliband, L. Panitch, and J. Saville, eds, *Socialist Register 1990*. London: The Merlin Press, 346–65.

Mills, C.W. 1956. *The Power Elite*. New York: Oxford University Press.

Milner, Helen. 1998. 'Regional Economic Co-operation, Global Markets and Domestic Politics: A Comparison of the NAFTA and Maastricht Treaties', in Coleman and Underhill (1998).

Minville, E., ed. 1944. *La forêt*. Montreal: Fides.

Monahan, Patrick J., and Michael Bryant. 1996. *Coming to Terms with Plan B: Ten Principles Governing Secession*. Commentary 83. Toronto: C.D. Howe Institute.

Moody, Kim. 1997. *Workers in a Lean World: Unions in the International Political Economy*. London: Verso.

Moore, A.M., J.H. Perry, and D. Beach. 1966. *The Financing of Canadian Federation: The First 100 Years*. Toronto: Canadian Tax Foundation.

Moore, Barrington. 1966. *Social Origins of Dictatorship and Democracy*. Boston: Beacon Press.

Moore, Steve, and Debi Wells. 1975. *Imperialism and the National Question in Canada*. Toronto: Moore.

Morici, Peter, et al. 1982. *Canadian Industrial Policy*. Washington: National Planning Association.

Moroz, A. 1985. 'Some Observations on Non-Tariff Barriers in Canada', in J. Whalley, ed., *Canada-United States Free Trade*. Toronto: University of Toronto Press.

Morris-Suzuki, Theresa. 1984. 'Robots and Capitalism', *New Left Review* 147: 109–21.

Morton, Arthur S. 1938. *A History of Prairie Settlement*. Toronto: Macmillan.

Morton, Desmond. 1974. *NDP: The Dream of Power*. Toronto: Hakkert.

_____. 1990. *Working People*, 3rd edn. Toronto: Summerhill Press.

_____. 1995. 'The History of the Canadian Labour Movement', in Gunderson and Ponek (1995).

Morton, William C. 1950. *The Progressive Party in Canada*. Toronto: University of Toronto Press.

Moscovitch, Allan, and Glenn Drover, eds. 1981. *Inequality: Essays on the Political Economy of Social Welfare*. Toronto: University of Toronto Press.

Mundell, R.A. 1963. 'Capital Mobility and Stabilization Policy Under Fixed and Flexible Exchange Rates', *Canadian Journal of Economics* 26: 475–85.

_____. 1993. 'Debts and Deficits in Alternative Macroeconomic Models', in Mario Baldassarri, Robert Mundell, and John McCallum, eds, *Debt, Deficit and Economic Performance*. New York: St Martin's Press, 5–130.

Murphy, Colette, and Doug Olthuis. 1995. 'The Impact of Work Reorganization on Employee Attitudes towards Work, the Company and the Union: Report of a Survey at Walker Exhaust', in Schenk and Anderson (1995).

Murphy, Lawrence, et al. 1977. *Perspectives on the Canadian Economy*. Ottawa: Conference Board of Canada.

Murray, Fergus. 1979. 'The De-centralisation of Production—The Decline of Mass-Collective Worker?', *Capital and Class* 19: 74–99.

Murray, Gregor. 1995. 'Unions: Membership, Structures, and Actions', in Gunderson and Ponek (1995).

Mussati, Giuliano, ed. 1995. *Mergers, Markets and Public Policy*. Boston: Kluwer Academic Publishers.

Myles, J., and D. Forcese. 1981. 'Voting and Class Politics in Canada and the United States', *Comparative Social Research* 4: 3–31.

Myles, John. 1989. 'Understanding Canada: Comparative Political Economy Perspectives', *Canadian Review of Sociology and Anthropology* 26: 1–9.

_____. 1991. 'Post-Industrialism and the Service Economy', in Drache and Gertler (1991).

National Council on Welfare. 1983. *Poverty in Canada: 1981 Preliminary Statistics*. Ottawa: Minister of Supply and Services.

_____. 1997. *Poverty Profile, 1995*. Ottawa: National Council on Welfare.

Naylor, R.T. 1972. 'The Rise and Fall of the Third Commercial Empire of the St. Lawrence', in Teeple (1972).

_____. 1975a. 'Dominion of Capital: Canada and International Investment', in A. Kontos, ed., *Domination*. Toronto: University of Toronto Press.

_____. 1975b. *History of Canadian Business, 1867–1914*, 2 vols. Toronto: Lorimer.

Neatby, H.B. 1969. 'The Liberal Way: Fiscal and Monetary Policy in the 1930's', in V. Hoar, ed., *The Great Depression: Essays and Memoirs from Canada and the United States*. Vancouver: Copp Clark.

Nee, Victor, and David Stark, eds. 1989. *Remaking the Economic Institutions of Socialism: China and Eastern Europe*. Stanford, Calif.: Stanford University Press.

Neis, Bruce, and Douglas D. Purvis. 1984. *Evaluating the Deficit: The Case for Budget Cuts*. Toronto: C.D. Howe Institute.

Nell, Edward. 1988. *Prosperity and Public Spending: Transformational Growth and the Role of Government*. Boston: Allen and Unwin.

Nelles, H.V. 1974. *The Politics of Development: Forests, Mines and Hydro-Electric Power in Ontario*. Toronto: Macmillan.

Nelson, R., and S. Winter. 1982. *An Evolutionary Theory of Economic Change*. Cambridge: Cambridge University Press.

Nelson, Richard R. 1993. *National Innovation Systems: A Comparative Analysis*. New York: Oxford University Press.

Netherton, Alex. 1991. 'Continental Integration: Neo-Liberal Revolution or Social Democratic Consolidation?', in Leslie A. Pal and Rainer Olaf Schultze, eds, *The Nation-State Versus Continental Integration: Canada in North America and Germany in Europe*. Bochum: Universitätsverlag Dr. N. Brockmeyer.

Neufeld, E.P. 1958. *Bank of Canada Operations and Policy*. Toronto: University of Toronto Press.

Nevitte, Neil. 1996. *The Decline of Deference: Canadian Value Change in Cross-National Perspective*. Peterborough, Ont.: Broadview Press.

Newman, Peter C. 1998. *Titans: How the Canadian Establishment Seized Power*. Toronto: Viking.

Nguyen, Trien T., Carlo Perroni, and Randall M. Wigle. 1996. 'Uruguay Round Impacts on Canada', *Canadian Public Policy* 22, 4: 342–55.

Nicholaus, M. 1967. 'Proletariat and the Middle-Class in Marx: Hegelian Choreography and the Capitalist Dialectic', *Studies on the Left* 7: 22–49.

Nicholson, Norman L. 1964. *The Boundaries of Canada: Its Provinces and Territories*. Ottawa: Queen's Printer.

Niosi, Jorge. 1982. *The Economy of Canada: A Study of Ownership and Control*. Montreal: Black Rose Books.

_____. 1983. 'The Canadian Bourgeoisie: Towards a Synthetical Approach', *Canadian Journal of Social and Political Theory* 7 (Fall): 128–49.

_____. 1985. *Canadian Multinationals*. Toronto: Between the Lines.

_____. 1987. *The Rise of the Conglomerate Economy*. Research Paper No. 10. Ottawa: Statistics Canada, Analytical Studies Branch.

_____, ed. 1991a. *Technology and National Competitiveness: Oligopoly, Technological Innovation and International Competition*. Montreal and Kingston: McGill-Queen's University Press.

_____. 1991b. 'Canada's National System of Innovation', *Science and Public Policy* 18, 2: 83–92.

_____. 1994. 'Foreign Direct Investment in Canada', in Eden (1994).

_____ and Bertrand Bellon. 1994. 'The Global Interdependence of National Innovation Systems: Evidence, Limits and Implications', *Technology in Society* 16, 2: 173–97.

Nkrumah, Kwame. 1965. *Neo-Colonialism: The Last Stage of Imperialism*. London: Nelson.

Nordlinger, Eric. 1981. *On the Autonomy of the Democratic State*. Cambridge, Mass.: Harvard University Press.

North, Douglas C. 1961. *The Economic Growth of the United States, 1790–1860*. Englewood Cliffs, NJ: Prentice-Hall.

Nove, Alec. 1975. *Socialist Economics*. Harmondsworth, Middlesex: Penguin.

_____. 1983. *The Economics of Feasible Socialism*. London: Allen and Unwin.

_____. 1986. *The Soviet Economic System*. Boston: Allen and Unwin.

O'Brien, Robert. 1992. 'The Canada-U.S. Subsidy Negotiations: Socio-Economic Harmonization as the Cost of Market Access?', in Gladys L. Symons, John A. Dickinson, and Hans-Josef Niederehe, eds, *Global Re-Structuring: Canada in the 1990s*. Montreal: Association for Canadian Studies.

_____. 1995. 'North American Integration and International Relations Theory', *Canadian Journal of Political Science* 28, 4: 693–724.

O'Connor, James. 1973. *The Fiscal Crisis of the State*. New York: St Martin's Press.

OECD. 1983. *Positive Adjustment Policies*. Paris: Organization for Economic Co-operation and Development.

Offe, Claus. 1987. 'Challenging the Boundaries of Institutional Politics: Social Movements Since the 1960s', in C.S. Maier, ed., *Changing Boundaries of the Political: Essays on the Evolving Balance Between the State and Society, Public and Private in Europe*. Cambridge: Cambridge University Press.

Olmsted, R.A. 1954. *Decisions of the Judicial Committee of the Privy Council Relating to the British North America Act 1867 and the Canadian Constitution 1867–1954*. Ottawa: Queen's Printer.

Olsen, Dennis. 1980. *The State Elite*. Toronto: McClelland & Stewart.

Olson, Mancur. 1965. *The Logic of Collective Action: Public Goods and the Theory of Goods*. Cambridge, Mass.: Harvard University Press.

Ornstein, Michael. 1989. 'The Social Organization of the Canadian Capitalist Class in Comparative Perspective', *Canadian Review of Sociology and Anthropology* 26: 151–77.

Osberg, Lars, and Pierre Fortin, eds. 1996. *Unnecessary Debts*. Toronto: James Lorimer.

_____, Fred Wien, and Jan Grude. 1995. *Vanishing Jobs: Canada's Changing Workplaces*. Toronto: James Lorimer.

Ossowski, Stanislaw. 1963. *Class Structure in the Social Consciousness*. New York: Free Press of Glencoe.

Ostry, Sylvia. 1992. 'The NAFTA: Its International Background', in Stephen J. Randall, Herman Konrad, and Sheldon Silverman, eds, *North America Without Borders? Integrating Canada, the United States, and Mexico*. Calgary: University of Calgary Press, 21–30.

Ouellet, Fernard. 1991. *Economy, Class, and Nation in Quebec: Interpretive Essays*, trans. and ed. Jacques A. Barbier. Toronto: Copp Clark Pitman.

Padoan, Pier Carlo. 1994. 'The Changing European Political Economy', in Richard Stubbs and Geoffrey R.D. Underhill, eds, *Political Economy and the Changing Global Order*. Toronto: McClelland & Stewart, 336–51.

Pal, Leslie A. 1989. 'Political Economy as a Hegemonic Project', *Canadian Journal of Political Science* 22: 827–39.

Palda, Kristian S. 1979. *The Science Council's Weakest Link: A Critique of the Science Council's Technocratic Industrial Strategy for Canada*. Vancouver: Fraser Institute.

_____. 1984. *Industrial Innovation*. Vancouver: Fraser Institute.

Palloix, C. 1976. 'The Labour Process: From Fordism to Neo-Fordism', *Conference of Socialist Economists*. London.

Palmer, Bryan D. 1979–80. 'Working Class Canada: Recent Historical Writing', *Queen's Quarterly* 86: 594–616.

_____. 1983. *Working-Class Experience: The Rise and Reconstitution of Canadian Labour, 1800–1980*. Toronto: Butterworths.

_____. 1992. *Working-Class Experience: Rethinking the History of Canadian Labour, 1800–1991*. Toronto: McClelland & Stewart.

_____ and Gregory S. Kealey. 1982. *Dreaming of What Might Be: The Knights of Labor in Ontario, 1880–1900*. New York: Cambridge University Press.

Panitch, Leo, ed. 1977. *The Canadian State: Political Economy and Political Power*. Toronto: University of Toronto Press.

_____. 1979. 'Corporatism in Canada', *Studies in Political Economy* 1, 1: 43–92.

_____, ed. 1981. 'Dependency and Class in Canadian Political Economy', *Studies in Political Economy* 6: 7–33.

_____. 1992a. 'Beyond Communism and Social Democracy', *Studies in Political Economy* 38: 139–54.

_____. 1992b. 'The NDP in Power: Illusion and Reality', *Studies in Political Economy* 37: 173–88.

_____. 1995. 'Elites, Classes and Power in Canada', in Michael Whittington and Glen Williams, eds, *Canadian Politics in the 1990s*, 4th edn. Toronto: Nelson, 152–75.

_____ and Donald Swartz. 1993. *The Assault on Trade Union Freedoms: From Wage Controls to Social Contract*. Toronto: Garamond.

Parenti, Michael. 1988. *Democracy for the Few*. New York: St Martin's Press.

Parker, Ian. 1977. 'Harold Innis, Karl Marx, and Canadian Political Economy', *Queen's Quarterly* 84: 545–63.

Penner, Norman. 1977. *The Canadian Left: A Critical Analysis*. Scarborough, Ont.: Prentice-Hall.

Pennings, Ray. 1992. *No Rose-Coloured Glasses: The Implications of Competition for the Canadian Workplace*. Mississauga, Ont.: Christian Labour Association of Canada.

Pentland, Clare. 1981. *Labour and Capital in Canada, 1650–1860*. Toronto: James Lorimer.

_____. 1991. 'The Development of a Capitalist Labour Market in Canada', in Laxer (1991).

Percy, Michael B., and Christian Yoder. 1987. *The Softwood Lumber Dispute and Canada-U.S. Trade in Natural Resources*. Halifax: Institute for Research on Public Policy.

Perry, J.H. 1955. *Taxes, Tariffs and Subsidies: A History of Canadian Fiscal Development*. Toronto: Canadian Tax Foundation.

_____. 1982. *Background of Current Fiscal Problems*. Toronto: Canadian Tax Foundation.

_____. 1989. *A Fiscal History of Canada: The Postwar Years*. Toronto: Canadian Tax Foundation.

_____. 1990. *Taxation in Canada*. Toronto: Canadian Tax Foundation.

Phillips, Paul Arthur. 1967. *No Power Greater: A Century of Labour in British Columbia*. Vancouver: BC Federation of Labour and Boag Foundation.

_____. 1991. 'New Staples and Mega-Projects: Reaching the Limits to Sustainable Development', in Drache and Gertler (1991).

_____. 1997. 'Labour in the New Canadian Political Economy', in Clement (1997).

Picard, Robert G., James P.Winter, Maxwell E. McCombs, and Stephen Lacy, eds. 1988. *Press Concentration and Monopoly: New Perspectives on Newspaper Ownership and Operation*. Norwood, NJ: Ablex.

Picot, Garnett, John Myles, and Ted Wannell. 1990. *Good Jobs/Bad Jobs and the Declining Middle, 1967–1986*. Ottawa: Statistics Canada, Analytical Studies Branch.

Pigou, A.C. 1932 [1919]. *The Economics of Welfare*. London: Macmillan.

Piven, F.F., and R.A. Cloward. 1972. *Regulating the Poor: The Functions of Public Welfare*. New York: Pantheon Books.

Plumptre, A.F.W. 1934. 'Canadian Monetary Policy', in H.A. Innis and Plumptre, eds, *The Canadian Economy and Its Problems*. Toronto: Canadian Institute of International Affairs.

_____. 1977. *Three Decades of Decision: Canada and the World Monetary System, 1944–75*. Toronto: McClelland & Stewart.

Polyani, Karl. 1957. *The Great Transformation*. Boston: Beacon Press.

Pomfret, Richard. 1981. *The Economic Development of Canada*. Toronto: Methuen.

Ponek, Allen, and Mark Thompson. 1995. 'Public Sector Collective Bargaining', in Gunderson and Ponek (1995).

Ponting, J. Rick. 1986. *Arduous Journey: Canadian Indians and Decolonization*. Toronto: McClelland & Stewart.

_____ and Roger Gibbins. 1980. *Out of Irrelevance*. Toronto: Butterworths.

Pontusson, Jonas. 1992. 'Introduction', in Golden and Pontusson (1992).

Porter, John. 1965. *The Vertical Mosaic: An Analysis of Social Class and Power in Canada*. Toronto: University of Toronto Press.

Porter, Michael E. 1990. *The Competitive Advantage of Nations*. New York: Free Press.

_____ and the Monitor Company. 1991. *Canada at the Crossroads: The Reality of a New Competitive Environment*. Ottawa: Business Council on National Issues and the Minister of Supply and Services.

Poulantzas, Nicos. 1973. 'On Social Classes', *New Left Review* 78: 27–55.

_____. 1974. 'The Internationalisation of Capitalist Relations and the Nation State', *Economy and Society*: 145–79.

_____. 1980. *State, Power, Socialism*. London: Verso.

Prebisch, Raul. 1968. *Towards a Global Strategy of Development*. New York: United Nations.

Price, Richard. 1984. 'Theories of Labour Process Formation', *Journal of Social History* 18: 91–110.

Prichard, J.R.S. 1983. *Crown Corporations in Canada: The Calculus of Instrument Choice*. Toronto: Butterworths.

Pross, A. Paul 1986. *Group Politics and Public Policy*. Toronto: Oxford University Press.

Przeworski, Adam. 1985. *Capitalism and Social Democracy*. Cambridge: Cambridge University Press.

_____. 1990. *The State and the Economy under Capitalism*. Chur, Switz.: Harwood Academic Publishers.

_____. 1991. *Democracy and the Market: Political and Economic Reforms in Eastern Europe and Latin America*. Cambridge: Cambridge University Press.

Purvis, D.D., and C. Smith. 1986. 'Fiscal Policy in Canada: 1963–84', in J. Sargent, ed., *Fiscal and Monetary Policy*. Toronto: University of Toronto Press.

Quaid, Maeve. 1993. *Job Evaluation: The Myth of Equitable Assessment*. Toronto: University of Toronto Press.

Qualter, Terence. 1970. *The Election Process in Canada*. Toronto: McGraw-Hill.

Radenbaugh, L.H. 1988. 'International Trade in Services: An Overview', in E.H. Fry, ed., *The Canada-U.S. Free Trade Agreement: The Impact on Service Industries*. Provo, Utah: Brigham Young University Press.

Randall, Stephen J. 1997. *Hemispheric Integration, Democratization and Human Rights in the Americas*. Ottawa: Canadian Foundation for the Americas.

Rao, Someshwar, Marc Legault, and Ashfaq Ahmad. 1994. 'Canadian-Based Multinationals: An Analysis of Activities and Performance', in Globerman (1994).

Ray, D. Michael. 1996. 'Employment Creation by Small Firms', in Britton (1996).

Rehny, Nadene, and Stephen McBride. 1997. *Help Wanted: Economic Security for Youth*. Ottawa: Canadian Centre for Policy Alternatives.

Reich, Robert. 1983. *The Next American Frontier*. New York: Time Books.

Resnick, Philip. 1987. 'Montesquieu Revisited, or the Mixed Constitution and the Separation of Powers in Canada', *Canadian Journal of Political Science* 20: 97–129.

_____. 1989. 'From Semi-Periphery to Perimeter of the Core', *Review: Fernand Braudel Centre* 12: 263–97.

Reuber, Grant L. 1962. *The Objectives of Monetary Policy: Working Paper Prepared for the Royal Commission on Banking and Finance*. Ottawa: Queen's Printer.

_____. 1964. 'The Objectives of Canadian Monetary Policy, 1949–61: Empirical "Trade Offs" and the Reaction Function of Authorities', *Journal of Political Economy* 72: 109–32.

_____ and Frank Roseman. 1969. *The Take-Over of Canadian Firms, 1945–1961: An Empirical Analysis*. Ottawa: Queen's Printer.

Rhoads, S.E. 1985. *The Economist's View of the World: Government, Markets, and Public Policy*. Cambridge: Cambridge University Press.

Rich, Edward E. 1960. *The Hudson's Bay Company, 1670–1870*. Toronto: McClelland & Stewart.

Richards, John. 1985. 'The Staple Debate', in Duncan Cameron, ed., *Explorations in Canadian Economic History: Essays in Honour of Irene M. Spry*. Ottawa: University of Ottawa Press.

_____. 1997. 'Reducing the Muddle in the Middle: Three Propositions for Running the Welfare State', in Harvey Lazar, ed., *Canada: The State of the Federation 1997. Non-Constitutional Renewal*. Kingston: Institute of Intergovernmental Relations.

_____, Robert D. Cairns, and Larry Pratt, eds. 1991. *Social Democracy Without Illusions: Renewal of the Canadian Left*. Toronto: McClelland & Stewart.

_____ and Larry Pratt. 1979. *Prairie Capitalism: Power and Influence in the New West*. Toronto: McClelland & Stewart.

Richardson, D. 1985. 'Factor Market Adjustment Policies in Response to Shocks', in J. Whalley, ed., *Domestic Policies and the International Economic Environment*. Toronto: University of Toronto Press.

Richardson, Robin. 1995. 'Inside Canada's Government Debt Problem and the Way Out: 1995 Edition', *Fraser Forum* (Sept.): 7–71.

Richardson, Stephen R., and Kathryn E. Moore. 1995. 'Canadian Experience with the Taxation of Capital Gains', *Canadian Public Policy* 21 (Supp.): S77–S99.

Richer, Stephen, and Lorna Weir, eds. 1995. *Beyond Political Correctness: Toward the Inclusive University*. Toronto: University of Toronto Press.

Riddell, W.C. 1985. 'Canadian Labour Relations: An Overview', in Riddell, ed., *Canadian Labour Relations*. Toronto: University of Toronto Press.

_____. 1993. *Unions in Canada and the United States: A Tale of Two Countries*. Kingston: Industrial Relations Centre, Queen's University.

Riddle, Dorothy I. 1986. *Service-Led Growth: The Role of the Service Sector in World Development*. New York: Praeger.

Risse-Kappen, Thomas, ed. 1995. *Bringing Transnational Relations Back In: Non-State Actors, Domestic Structures and International Institutions*. Cambridge: Cambridge University Press.

Ritchie, Gordon. 1997. *Wrestling with the Elephant: The Inside Story of the Canada-US Trade Wars*. Toronto: Macfarlane Walter & Ross. 1997

Roberts, Bruce. 1995. 'From Lean Production to Agile Manufacturing: A New Round of Quicker, Cheaper, Better', in Schenk and Anderson (1995).

Robertson, M., and A. Grey. 1986. 'Trade-Related Worker Adjustment Policies: The Canadian Experience', in W.C. Riddell, ed., *Canadian Labour Relations*. Toronto: University of Toronto Press.

Robin, Martin. 1968. *Radical Politics and Canadian Labour, 1880–1930*. Kingston: Queen's University Centre for Industrial Relations.

_____. 1972. *The Rush for Spoils*. Toronto: McClelland & Stewart.

_____. 1973. *Pillars of Profit*. Toronto: McClelland & Stewart.

Robinson, Ian. 1993a. *North American Trade as if Democracy Mattered: What's Wrong with NAFTA and What Are the Alternatives?* Ottawa: Canadian Centre for Policy Alternatives.

_____. 1993b. 'Economic Unionism in Trouble: The Origins, Consequences and Prospects of Divergence in Labour-Movement Characteristics', in Jenson and Mahon (1993).

Robles, Alfredo. 1994. *French Theories of Regulation and Conceptions of the International Division of Labour*. London: Macmillan.

Robson, William B.P. 1994. 'Digging Holes and Hitting Walls: Evaluating Canada's Public Debt Crisis', *North American Outlook* 4, 4: 13–43.

_____ and William M. Scarth. 1994. *Deficit Reduction: What Pain, What Gain?* Toronto: C.D. Howe Institute.

Rocher, François, and Christian Roulliard. 1996. 'Using the Concept of Deconcentration to Overcome the Centralization/Decentralization Dichotomy: Thoughts on Recent Constitutional and Political Reform', in Fafard and Brown (1996).

_____ and Miriam Smith, eds. 1995. *New Trends in Canadian Federalism*. Peterborough, Ont.: Broadview Press.

Roemer, John, ed. 1986. *Analytical Marxism*. Cambridge: Cambridge University Press.

Rogers, Joel. 1993. 'Don't Worry, Be Happy: The Postwar Decline of Private Sector Unionism in the United States', in Jenson and Mahon (1993).

Romanow, Roy, John Whyte, and Howard Leeson. 1984. *Canada . . . Notwithstanding: The Making of the Constitution, 1976–82*. Toronto: Carswell/Methuen.

Ropp, Theodore. 1963, 'Politics, Strategy and the Commitment of a Middlepower', in David Deener, ed., *Canada-US Treaty Relations*. Durham, NC: Duke University Press.

Rose, Jeff. 1995. *Beginning to Think About the Next Referendum*. Occasional Paper. Toronto: University of Toronto Faculty of Law.

Rose, Richard. 1968. 'Dynamic Tendencies in the Authority of Regimes', *World Politics* 21, 4: 602–28.

Rosenau, James N. 1988. 'The State in an Era of Cascading Politics', *Comparative Political Studies* 21: 13–44.

Rosenblum, Simon, and Peter Findlay, eds. 1991. *Debating Canada's Future: Views from the Left*. Toronto: James Lorimer.

Rosenbluth, Gideon. 1955. *Business Concentration and Price Policy*. Princeton, NJ: Princeton University Press.

_____. 1957. *Concentration in Canadian Manufacturing Industries*. Princeton, NJ: Princeton University Press.

Ross, George, and Jane Jenson. 1986. 'Post-war Class Struggle and the Crisis of Left Politics', *Socialist Register 1985/86*: 23–49.

Rotstein, Abraham. 1984. *Rebuilding from Within: Remedies for Canada's Ailing Economy*. Toronto: James Lorimer.

Rouillard, Jacques. 1981. *Histoire de la CSN, 1921–1981*. Montreal: Boréal Express.

Rowley, C.K. 1983. 'The Political Economy of the Public Sector', in Rowley, ed., *Perspectives on Political Economy*. Toronto: James Lorimer.

Rowlinson, Michael, and John Hassard. 1994. 'Economics, Politics and Labour Process Theory', *Capital and Class* 53: 65–98.

Rugman, Alan. 1977. 'The Regulation of Foreign Investment in Canada', *Journal of World Trade Law* 11: 322–33.

_____. 1980. *Multinationals in Canada: Theory, Performance and Economic Impact*. Boston: Martinus Nijhoff.

_____. 1990. *Multinationals and Canada-United States Free Trade*. Columbia: University of South Carolina Press.

_____. 1993. 'Drawing the Border for a Multinational Enterprise and a Nation State', in Eden and Potter (1993).

_____. 1994. 'Strategic Management and Canadian Multinationals', in Globerman (1994).

_____ and Joe R. D'Cruz. 1994. 'A Theory of Business Networks', in Eden (1994).

Russell, Bob. 1990. *Back to Work: Labour, State and Industrial Relations in Canada*. Scarborough, Ont.: Nelson.

_____. 1997a. 'Reinventing a Labour Movement', in Carroll (1997).

_____. 1997b. 'Rival Paradigms at Work: Work Reorganization and Labour Force Impacts in a Staple Industry', *Canadian Review of Sociology and Anthropology* 34: 35–52.

Russell, Peter. 1977. 'The Supreme Court's Interpretation of the Constitution from 1949–1960', in P. Fox, ed., *Politics: Canada*. Toronto: McGraw-Hill Ryerson.

_____. 1982. 'The Effect of a Charter of Rights on the Policy-Making Role of the Canadian Courts', *Canadian Public Administration* 25.

_____. 1983. 'The Political Purposes of the Canadian Charter of Rights and Freedoms', *Canadian Bar Review*: 30–54.

_____. 1988. 'The Supreme Court Proposals in the Meech Lake Accord', *Canadian Public Policy* 14 (suppl.): 93–106.

_____. 1994. 'The Three Dimensions of Charter Politics', in James P. Bickerton and Alain-G. Gagnon, eds, *Canadian Politics*, 2nd edn. Peterborough, Ont.: Broadview Press.

_____. 1995. *Constitutional Odyssey*, 2nd edn. Toronto: University of Toronto Press.

Ryerson, Stanley Brehaut. 1963. *The Founding of Canada*. Toronto: Progress Books.

_____. 1968. *Unequal Union: Confederation and the Roots of Conflict in the Canadas, 1815–1873*. Toronto: Progress Books.

Sabel, Charles F. 1982. *Work and Politics: The Division of Labour in Industry*. Cambridge: Cambridge University Press.

Saborio, Sylvia, ed. 1992. *The Premise and the Promise: Free Trade in the Americas*. New Brunswick, NJ: Transaction Publishers.

Sacouman, R.J. 1979. 'The Differing Origins, Organization, and Impact of Maritime and Prairie Co-operative Movements to 1940', in R.J. Brym and Sacouman, eds, *Underdevelopment and Social Movements in Atlantic Canada*. Toronto: New Hogtown Press.

_____. 1981. 'The "Peripheral" Maritimes and Canada-Wide Marxist Political Economy', *Studies in Political Economy* 6: 135–50.

Safarian, A.E. 1966. *Foreign Ownership of Canadian Industry*. Toronto: McGraw-Hill.

_____. 1996. 'The FTA and NAFTA: One Canadian's Perspective', in Charles F. Doran and Alvin Paul Drischler, eds, *A New North America: Cooperation and Enhanced Interdependence*. Westport, Conn.: Praeger.

Sager, Eric. 1987. 'Dependency, Underdevelopment and the Economic History of the Atlantic Provinces', *Acadiensis*: 117–37.

Saint-Pierre, Céline. 1993. 'Recognizing the Working Mother: The Quebec Labour Movement and the Feminization of the Labour Force', in Jenson and Mahon (1993).

Salée, Daniel, and William Coleman. 1997. 'The Challenge of the Quebec Question', in Clement (1997).

Salembier, Gerry E., Andrew R. Moore, and Frank Stone. 1987. *The Canadian Import File: Trade, Protection and Adjustment*. Montreal: Institute for Research on Public Policy.

Samuelson, Paul A., and Anthony Scott. 1971. *Economics*. Toronto: McGraw-Hill.

Saunders, Stanley A. 1939. *The Economic History of the Maritime Provinces*. Ottawa: King's Printer.

Savoie, Donald J. 1986. *Regional Economic Development: Canada's Search for Solutions*. Toronto: University of Toronto Press.

_____. 1992. *Regional Economic Development: Canada's Search for Solutions*, 2nd edn. Toronto: University of Toronto Press.

_____. 1995. 'Regional Development: A Policy for All Seasons', in Rocher and Smith (1995).

Schenk, Christopher, and John Anderson, eds. 1995. *Re-Shaping Work: Union Responses to Technological Change*. Don Mills, Ont.: Ontario Federation of Labour, Technology Adjustment Research Programme.

Schmitter, Philippe, and Gerhard Lehmbruch, eds. 1979. *Trends Towards Corporatist Intermediation*. Beverly Hills, Calif.: Sage Publications.

Schott, J., and M.G. Smith. 1988. 'Services and Investment', in J. Schott, ed., *The Canada-United States Free Trade Agreement*. Washington: Institute for International Economics.

Schott, Kerry. 1984. *Policy, Power and Order: The Persistence of Economic Problems in Capitalist Europe*. New Haven, Conn.: Yale University Press.

Schreiber, E.M. 1980. 'Class Awareness and Class Voting in Canada', *Canadian Review of Sociology and Anthropology* 17: 37–54.

Schumpeter, Joseph A. 1964 [1939]. *Business Cycles: A Theoretical, Historical and Statistical Analysis of the Capitalist Process*. New York: McGraw-Hill.

Schurmann, Franz. 1968. *Ideology and Organization in Communist China*. Berkeley: University of California Press.

Schwanen, Daniel. 1995. 'Overview and Key Policy Issues', in Trebilcock and Schwanen (1995).

_____. 1997. *Trading Up: The Impact of Increased Continental Integration on Trade, Investment, and Jobs in Canada*. Toronto: C.D. Howe Institute Commentary No. 89, Mar.

Schwartz, Herman M. 1994. *States Versus Markets: History, Geography and the Development of the International Political Economy*. New York: St Martin's Press.

Science Council of Canada. 1979. *Forging Links: A Technology Policy for Canada*. Ottawa.

_____. 1984. *Canadian Industrial Development: Some Policy Directions*. Ottawa: Supply and Services Canada.

_____. 1988. *Gearing Up for Global Markets: From Industry Challenge to Industry Commitment*. Ottawa.

Seidle, F. Leslie. 1996. 'The Canadian Electoral System and Proposals for Reform', in Gagnon and Tanguay (1996).

Shalev, M. 1983. 'The Social Democratic Model and Beyond: Two "Generations" of Comparative Research on the Welfare State', *Comparative Social Research* 6: 315–51.

Sheppard, Robert, and Michael Valpy. 1982. *The National Deal: The Fight for a Canadian Constitution*. Toronto: Fleet Books.

Shields, J. 1989. 'British Columbia's New Reality: The Politics of Neo-Conservatism and Defensive Defiance'. Ph.D. thesis, University of British Columbia.

Shortt, A. 1896. *Adam Shortt's History of Canadian Currency and Banking, 1600–1880*, ed. Canadian Bankers Association. Toronto: CBA.

Shrybman, Steven. 1993. 'Trading Away the Environment', in Ricardo Grinspun and Maxwell A. Cameron, eds, *The Political Economy of North American Free Trade*. Montreal and Kingston: McGill-Queen's University Press, 271–96.

Simeon, Richard, and Elaine Willis. 1997. 'Democracy and Performance: Governance in Canada and the United States', in Banting, Hoberg, and Simeon (1997).

Skocpol, Theda. 1985. 'Bringing the State Back In: Strategies of Analysis in Current Research', in P.B. Evans et al., *Bringing the State Back In*. Cambridge: Cambridge University Press.

_____ and Kevin Finegold. 1982. 'State Capacity and Economic Intervention in the Early New Deal'. *Political Science Quarterly* 97.

Smiley, Donald V. 1963. *Conditional Grants and Canadian Federalism: A Study in Constitutional Adaptation*. Toronto: Canadian Tax Foundation.

_____. 1967. 'Contributions to Canadian Political Science Since the Second World War', *Canadian Journal of Economics and Political Science* 33: 569–80.

_____. 1987. *The Federal Condition in Canada*. Toronto: McGraw-Hill Ryerson.

_____ and R. Watts. 1985. *Intrastate Federalism in Canada*. Toronto: University of Toronto Press.

Smith, Adam. 1987 [1776]. *The Wealth of Nations*, Books I-III. Harmondsworth: Penguin.

Smith, David. 1996. 'Canadian Political Parties and National Integration', in Gagnon and Tanguay (1996).

Smith, Doug. 1985. *Let Us Rise! A History of the Manitoba Labour Movement*. Vancouver: New Star Books.

_____. 1996. *We Are Workers Just Like You: The 1996 Manitoba Home-Care Strike*. Winnipeg: Manitoba Government Employees Union.

_____. 1997. *Cold Warrior: C.S. Jackson and the United Electrical Workers*. St John's, Nfld: Canadian Committee on Labour History.

_____, Jock Bates, and Esyllt Jones. 1993. *Lives in the Public Service: A History of the Manitoba Government Employees' Union*. Winnipeg: Manitoba Labour Education Centre.

Smith, Miriam. 1992. 'The Canadian Labour Congress: From Continentalism to Economic Nationalism', *Studies in Political Economy* 38: 35–60.

Smith, Tony. 1979. 'The Underdevelopment of Development Literature: The Case of Dependency Theory', *World Politics* 31: 247–88.

Smith, W. Rand. 1995. 'Industrial Crisis and the Left: Adjustment Strategies in Socialist France and Spain', *Comparative Politics* 28, 1: 1–24.

Snodden, Tracy R. 1998. 'The Impact of the CHST on Interprovincial Redistribution in Canada', *Canadian Public Policy* 24, 1: 49–70.

Sparks, G.R. 1986. 'The Theory and Practice of Monetary Policy in Canada: 1945–83', in J. Sargent, ed., *Fiscal and Monetary Policy*. Toronto: University of Toronto Press.

Srinivasan, T.N. 1985. 'Neoclassical Political Economy: The State and Economic Development', *Asian Development Review* 3: 38–58.

Stanbury, W.T. 1986. *Business-Government Relations in Canada: Grappling with Leviathan*. Toronto: Methuen.

_____, ed. 1996. *Perspectives on the New Economics and Regulation of Telecommunications*. Montreal: Institute for Research on Public Policy.

Staniland, Martin. 1985. *What Is Political Economy? A Study of Social Theory and Underdevelopment*. New Haven, Conn.: Yale University Press.

Statistics Canada. 1983a. *National Income and Expenditure Accounts, 1969–1983*. Cat. No. 13–001. Ottawa: Minister of Supply and Services.

_____. 1983b. *Provincial GDP by Industry*. Cat. No. 61–202. Ottawa: Minister of Supply and Services.

_____. 1983c. *Historical Statistics of Canada*, 2nd edn. Ottawa: Minister of Supply and Services.

_____. 1984. *GDP by Industry, 1984*. Cat. No. 61–213. Ottawa: Minister of Supply and Services.

_____. 1985. *Income Distribution by Size in Canada*. Cat. No. 15–207. Ottawa: Minister of Supply and Services.

_____. 1990. *Women in Canada: A Statistical Report*. Ottawa: Minister of Supply and Services.

_____. 1995a. *Income After Taxes, Distribution by Size in Canada, 1993*. Cat. No. 13–210. Ottawa: Minister of Industry.

_____. 1995b. *Income Distribution by Size in Canada, 1993*. Cat. No. 13–207. Ottawa: Minister of Industry.

_____. 1996a. *Historical Statistical Supplement, 1995/1996*. Cat. No. 11–210–XPB. Ottawa: Minister of Industry.

_____. 1996b. *National Income and Expenditure Accounts, 1984–1995*. Cat. No. 13–201–XPB. Ottawa: Minister of Industry.

_____. 1996c. *The Conceptual Framework of NAICS*. Electronic document available at: *http://www.statscan.ca/english/subjects/Standards/sector.htm*

_____. 1997a. *Canada's International Investment Position, 1926–1996*. Cat. No. 67–202–XPB. Ottawa: Minister of Industry.

_____. 1997b. *Provincial GDP by Industry, 1984–1996*. Cat. No. 15–203–XPB. Ottawa: Minister of Industry.

_____. 1997c. CANSIM, matrices 3685, 3652.

Steinmo, Sven. 1994. 'The End of Redistribution? International Pressures and Domestic Tax Policy Choices', *Challenge* 37, 6: 9–25.

Stevenson, Garth. 1989. *Unfulfilled Union: Federalism and National Unity*, 3rd edn. Toronto: Gage.

Stewart, Ian A. 1990. 'Consensus and Economic Performance', in *Perspective 2000: Proceedings of a Conference Sponsored by the Economic Council of Canada*. Ottawa.

Stewart, J. 1977. *The Canadian House of Commons: Procedure and Reform*. Montreal and Kingston: McGill-Queen's University Press.

Stone, D. 1988. *Policy Paradox and Political Reason*. Glenview, Ill.: Scott, Foresman.

Stone, Frank. 1984. *Canada, the GATT and the International Trade System*. Montreal: Institute for Research on Public Policy.

Stoykp, Peter. 1997. 'Creating Opportunities or Creating Opportunism: The Liberal Labour Market Policy', in Swimmer (1997).

Strange, Susan. 1993. 'Big Business and the State', in Eden and Potter (1993).

Stritch, Andrew. 1997. 'An Innovative Economy: Science and Technology Policy', in Johnson and Stritch (1997).

Stubbs, Richard. 1994. 'The Political Economy of the Asia-Pacific Region', in Stubbs and Underhill (1994).

_____. 1998. 'Asia-Pacific Regionalism versus Globalization: Competing Forms of Capitalism', in Coleman and Underhill (1998).

_____ and Geoffrey R.D. Underhill, eds. 1994. *Political Economy and the Changing Global Order*. Toronto: McClelland & Stewart.

Sutherland, Sharon L. 1993. 'The Public Service and Policy Development', in Atkinson (1993).

_____ and G. Bruce Doern. 1985. *Bureaucracy in Canada: Control and Reform*. Toronto: University of Toronto Press.

Swenarchuk, Michelle. 1993. 'Environment', in Cameron and Watkins (1993).

Swimmer, Gene. 1987. 'Changes to Public Service Labour Relations Legislation: Revitalizing or Destroying Collective Bargaining', in M.J. Prince, ed., *How Ottawa Spends, 1987–88: Restraining the State*. Toronto: Methuen.

_____, ed. 1997. *How Ottawa Spends: Seeing Red: A Liberal Report Card*. Ottawa: Carleton University Press.

Swinton, Katherine. 1988. *Competing Constitutional Visions: The Meech Lake Accord*. Toronto: Carswell.

Tanguay, A. Brian. 1993. 'An Uneasy Alliance: The Parti Québecois and the Unions', in Jenson and Mahon (1993).

Taylor, Malcolm. 1987. *Health Insurance and Canadian Public Policy*. Montreal and Kingston: McGill-Queen's University Press.

Taylor, Wayne D. 1991. *Business and Government Relations: Partners in the 1990s*. Toronto: Gage.

Teeple, Gary, ed. 1972. *Capitalism and the National Question in Canada*. Toronto: University of Toronto Press.

Therborn, Göran. 1977. 'The Rule of Capital and the Rise of Democracy', *New Left Review* 103: 3–41.

_____. 1978. *What Does the Ruling Class Do When It Rules? State Apparatuses and State Power under Federalism, Capitalism and Socialism*. London: Verso.

_____. 1983. 'The Rule of Capital and the Rise of Democracy', in David Held et al., eds, *States and Societies*. Oxford: Robertson.

Thiessen, Gordon G. 1996. 'Monetary and Fiscal Policies: Orientations and Interactions', *Bank of Canada Review* (Spring): 67–72.

Thomas, Paul G., and Orest W. Zajcew. 1993. 'Structural Heretics: Crown Corporations and Regulatory Agencies', in Atkinson (1993).

Thompson, E.P. 1978. *The Poverty of Theory and Other Essays*. London: Merlin Press.

Thorburn, Hugh. 1984. *Planning and the Economy: Building Federal-Provincial Consensus*. Toronto: James Lorimer.

_____. 1985. *Party Politics in Canada*. Scarborough, Ont.: Prentice-Hall.

Tilly, Charles. 1984. *Big Structures, Large Processes, Huge Comparisons*. New York: Sage Foundation.

_____. 1992. 'Prisoners of the State', *International Journal of Social Science* 133: 329–43.

Traves, Tom. 1979. *The State and Enterprise: Canadian Manufacturers and the Federal Government, 1917–1931*. Toronto: University of Toronto Press.

Trebilcock, Michael J., et al. 1982. *The Choice of Governing Instrument*. Ottawa: Canadian Government Pub. Centre.

_____ and Daniel Schwanen, eds. 1995. *Getting There: An Assessment of the Agreement on Internal Trade*. Toronto: C.D. Howe Institute.

Trudeau, Pierre Elliott. 1968. *Federalism and the French Canadians*. Toronto: Macmillan.

Truman, D.B. 1965. 'Disillusion and Regeneration: The Quest for a Discipline', *American Political Science Review* 59, 4: 865–73.

Tucker, R.C., ed. 1972. *The Marx-Engels Reader*. New York: W.W. Norton.

Tuohy, Carolyn. 1992. *Policy and Politics in Canada*. Philadelphia: Temple University Press.

_____. 1993. 'Social Policy: Two Worlds', in Atkinson (1993).

Unger, Brigitte, and Frans Van Waarden, eds. 1995. *Convergence or Diversity? Internationalization and Economic Policy Response*. Brookfield, Vt: Avebury.

United States Congress. 1987. *The GATT Negotiations and U.S. Trade Policy*. Washington: US Government Printing Office, June.

Van Loon, Richard, and Michael Whittington. 1987. *The Canadian Political System: Environment, Structure, and Process*. Toronto: McGraw-Hill.

Veltmeyer, Henry. 1978. 'Dependency and Underdevelopment: Some Questions and Problems', *Canadian Journal of Political and Social Theory* 2: 55–71.

_____. 1979. 'The Capitalist Underdevelopment of Atlantic Canada', in R.J. Brym and R.J. Sacouman, eds, *Underdevelopment and Social Movements in Atlantic Canada*. Toronto: New Hogtown Press.

Verma, Anil. 1995. 'Employee Involvement in the Workplace', in Gunderson and Ponek (1995).

_____ and Joseph M. Weiler. 1994. *Understanding Change in Canadian Industrial Relations: Firm Level Choices and Responses*. Kingston: Industrial Relations Centre, Queen's University.

Vermaeten, Arndt, W. Irwin Gillespie, and Frank Vermaeten. 1995. 'Who Paid the Taxes in Canada, 1951–1988', *Canadian Public Policy* 21, 3: 317–43.

Vernon, Raymond. 1993. 'Sovereignty at Bay: Twenty Years After', in Eden and Potter (1993).

_____. 1994. 'Multinationals and Governments: Key Actors in NAFTA', in Eden (1994).

Vertinsky, Ilan, and Rachana Raizada. 1994. 'MacMillan Bloedel: Foreign Investment Decisions and Their Welfare Consequences', in Globerman (1994).

Vipond, Robert. 1989. '1787 and 1867: The Federal Principle at Canadian Confederation Re-considered', *Canadian Journal of Political Science* 22, 1: 3–25.

Vorst, Jesse, Paul Phillips, and Cy Gonick, eds. 1995. *Labour Gains, Labour Pains: Fifty Years of PC1003*. Winnipeg: Society for Socialist Studies.

Walker, Martin. 1998. 'Transatlantic Trade Deal Placates EU', *Manchester Guardian Weekly*, 24 May: 3.

Walker, Michael, ed. 1984. *On Alberta's Industrial and Science Technology Proposal*. Vancouver: Fraser Institute.

_____, et al., eds. 1976. *The Illusion of Wage and Price Control*. Vancouver: Fraser Institute.

Walras, Leon. 1965 [1874]. *Elements of Pure Economics: Or, the Theory of Social Wealth*. Homewood, Ill.: R.D. Irwin.

Warren, Bill. 1973. 'Imperialism and Capitalist Industrialization', *New Left Review* 81: 3–44.

Watkins, G.C., and M.A. Walker, eds. 1981. *Reaction: The National Energy Program*. Vancouver: Fraser Institute.

Watkins, M.H. 1963. 'A Staple Theory of Economic Growth', *Canadian Journal of Economics and Political Science* 29: 141–58.

_____, ed. 1970. *For an Independent Socialist Canada*. Winnipeg: Canadian Dimension.

_____. 1977. 'The Staple Theory Revisited', *Journal of Canadian Studies* 12: 83–95.

_____. 1982. 'The Innis Tradition in Canadian Political Economy', *Canadian Journal of Political and Social Thought* 6: 12–34.

_____. 1992. *Madness and Ruin: Politics and the Economy in the Neoconservative Age*. Toronto: Between the Lines.

_____. 1994. 'Ontario: Discrediting Social Democracy', *Studies in Political Economy* 43: 139–48.

_____. 1997. 'Canadian Capitalism in Transition', in Clement (1997).

_____, et al. 1968. *Foreign Ownership and the Structure of Canadian Industry*. Ottawa: Privy Council Office.

Watson, William. 1983. *Primer on the Economics of Industrial Policy*. Toronto: Ontario Economic Council.

Watts, George S. 1972. 'The First Phase of the Bank of Canada's Operations', *Bank of Canada Review* (Nov.): 7–21.

_____. 1973a. 'The Bank of Canada during the Period of Postwar Adjustment', *Bank of Canada Review* (Nov.): 3–17.

_____. 1973b. 'The Bank of Canada during the War Years', *Bank of Canada Review* (Apr.): 3–17.

_____. 1974. 'The Bank of Canada from 1948–1952: The Pivotal Years', *Bank of Canada Review* (Nov.): 3–17.

Watts, Ronald L. 1989. 'Executive Federalism: The Comparative Perspective', in David Shugarman and Reg Whitaker, eds, *Federalism and Political Community: Essays in Honour of Donald M. Smiley*. Peterborough, Ont.: Broadview Press, 439–60.

_____. 1996. 'Canada: Three Decades of Periodic Federal Crises', *International Political Science Review* 17, 4: 353–71.

Waverman, Leonard. 1991. 'A Canadian Vision of North American Economic Integration', in Globerman (1991).

_____, ed. 1991. *Corporate Globalization through Mergers and Acquisitions*. Calgary: University of Calgary Press.

Weaver, Sally M. 1981. *Making Canadian Indian Policy: The Hidden Agenda 1968–70*. Toronto: University of Toronto Press.

Webb, M.C., and M.W. Zacher. 1985. 'Canada Export Trade in a Changing International Environment', in D. Stairs and G.R. Winham, eds, *Canada and the International Political/Economic Environment*. Toronto: University of Toronto Press.

Weber, Max. 1958 [1904]. *The Protestant Ethic and the Spirit of Capitalism*. New York: Scribner.

_____. 1978 [1915]. *Economy and Society: An Outline of Interpretive Sociology*. Berkeley: University of California Press.

Weiner, Nan, and Morley Gunderson. 1990. *Pay Equity: Issues, Options and Experiences*. Toronto: Butterworths.

Weiss, Linda. 1997. 'Globalisation and the Myth of the Powerless State', *New Left Review* 225: 3–27.

Weitzman, Martin L. 1993. 'Capitalism and Democracy: A Summing Up of the Arguments', in Samuel Bowles, Herbert Gintis, and Bo Gustafsson, eds, *Markets and Democracy: Participation, Accountability, and Efficiency*. Cambridge: Cambridge University Press, 306–16.

Wejr, Patricia, and Howie Smith, eds. 1978. *Fighting for Labour: Four Decades of Work in British Columbia, 1910–1950*. Victoria, BC: Aural History Program, Provincial Archives of British Columbia.

Weldon, J.C. 1966. 'Consolidations in Canadian Industry, 1900–1948', in L.A. Skeoch, ed., *Restrictive Trade Practices in Canada*. Toronto: McClelland & Stewart.

Wells, Donald M. 1993. 'Recent Innovations in Labour-Management Relations: The Risks and Prospects for Labour in Canada and the United States', in Jenson and Mahon (1993).

Whalley, John. 1985. *Canadian Trade Policies and the World Economy*. Toronto: University of Toronto Press.

_____. 1993. 'Regional Trade Arrangements in North America: CUSTA and NAFTA', in Jaime de Melo and Arvind Panagariya, eds, *New Dimensions in Regional Integration*. Cambridge: Cambridge University Press, 352–82.

_____ and Colleen Hamilton. 1996. *The Trading System After the Uruguay Round*. Washington: Institute for International Economics.

Wheare, K.C. 1964. *Federal Government*. Oxford: Oxford University Press.

Whitaker, Reginald. 1977. *The Government Party: Organizing and Financing the Liberal Party of Canada, 1930–1958*. Toronto: University of Toronto Press.

_____. 1983. 'To Have Insight into Much and Power over Nothing: The Political Ideas of Harold Innis', *Queen's Quarterly* 90: 818–31.

_____. 1997. 'Cruising at 30,000 Feet with a Missing Engine: The Chrétien Government in the Aftermath of the Quebec Referendum', in Swimmer (1997).

Whitehorn, Alan. 1992. *Canadian Socialism: Essays on the CCF-NDP*. Toronto: Oxford University Press.

Wilkinson, Bruce W. 1980. *Canada in the Changing World Economy*. Montreal: C.D. Howe Institute and the National Planning Association.

_____. 1985. 'Canada's Resource Industries', in J. Whalley, ed., *Canada's Resource Industries and Water Export Policy*. Toronto: University of Toronto Press.

Will, Robert M. 1966. *Canadian Fiscal Policy, 1945–63*. Ottawa: Queen's Printer.

Willett, Thomas D. 1988. 'National Macroeconomic Policy Preferences and International Coordination Issues', *Journal of Public Policy* 8, 3/4: 235–63.

Williams, Glen. 1979. 'The National Policy Tariffs: Industrial Development Through Import Substitution', *Canadian Journal of Economics and Political Science* 23, 2.

_____. 1986. *Not for Export: Toward a Political Economy of Canada's Arrested Industrialization*, updated edn. Toronto: McClelland & Stewart.

_____. 1989. 'Canada in the International Political Economy', in Clement and Williams (1989).

_____. 1995. *Not for Export: The International Competitiveness of Canadian Manufacturing*, 3rd edn. Toronto: McClelland & Stewart.

Wilson, Thomas A., and D. Peter Dungan. 1993. *Fiscal Policy in Canada: An Appraisal*. Toronto: Canadian Tax Foundation.

Winter, James. 1997. *Democracy's Oxygen*. Montreal: Black Rose.

Wolf, Charles Jr. 1987. 'Markets and Non-Market Failures: Comparison and Assessment', *Journal of Public Policy* 7, 1: 43–70.

_____. 1988. *Markets or Governments: Choosing between Imperfect Alternatives*. Cambridge, Mass.: MIT Press.

Wolfe, Alan. 1977. *The Limits of Legitimacy: Political Contradictions of Contemporary Capitalism*. New York: Free Press.

Wolfe, David A. 1977. 'The State and Economic Policy in Canada, 1968–75', in L. Panitch, ed., *The Canadian State: Political Economy and Political Power*. Toronto: University of Toronto Press.

_____. 1981. 'Mercantilism, Liberalism, and Keynesianism: Changing Forms of State Intervention in Capitalist Societies', *Canadian Journal of Political and Social Theory* 5, 1–2: 69–96.

_____. 1984. 'The Rise and Demise of the Keynesian Era in Canada: Economic Policy, 1930–1982', in M.S. Cross and G.S. Kealey, eds, *Modern Canada, 1930–1980's*. Toronto: McClelland & Stewart.

_____. 1985. 'The Politics of the Deficit', in G.B. Doern, ed., *The Politics of Economic Policy*. Toronto: University of Toronto Press.

_____. 1989. 'The Canadian State in Comparative Perspective', *Canadian Review of Sociology and Anthropology* 26: 95–126.

_____. 1991. 'Technology and Trade', in Rosenblum and Findlay (1991).

Wolfe, Martin. 1955. 'The Concept of Economic Sectors', *Quarterly Journal of Economics* 69: 402–20.

Wolff, R.D., and S.A. Resnick. 1987. *Economics: Marxian versus Neo-classical*. Baltimore: Johns Hopkins University Press.

Wolfson, M.C., and J.M. Evans. 1996. *Statistics Canada's Low Income Cut-Offs: Methodological Concerns and Possibilities*. Ottawa: Statistics Canada.

Wonnacott, Ronald J. 1991. *The Economics of Overlapping Free Trade Areas and the Mexican Challenge*. Toronto: Canadian-American Committee and C.D. Howe Institute.

Wood, Bernard. 1988. *The Middle Powers and the General Interest*. Ottawa: North-South Institute.

Wood, Louis A. 1975. *A History of Farmers' Movements in Canada*. Toronto: University of Toronto Press.

Wood, N., and E. Wood. 1970. 'Canada and the American Science of Politics', in I. Lumsden, ed., *Close the 49th Parallel, etc.: The Americanization of Canada*. Toronto: University of Toronto Press.

Wood, W.D., and P. Kumar, eds. 1981. *The Current Industrial Relations Scene in Canada*. Kingston: Queen's University Industrial Relations Centre.

Woodside, K. 1983. 'The Political Economy of Policy Instruments: Tax Expenditures and Subsidies in Canada', in M. Atkinson and M. Chandler, eds, *The Politics of Canadian Public Policy*. Toronto: University of Toronto Press.

World Bank. 1997a. *World Development Indicators*, CD-ROM, Washington: World Bank.

_____. 1997b. *World Development Report*. New York: Oxford University Press.

Wright, Eric O. 1985. *Classes*. London: Verso.

Wynn, Graeme. 1981. *Timber Colony: A Historical Geography of Early Nineteenth Century New Brunswick*. Toronto: University of Toronto Press.

Yates, Charlotte A.B. 1993. 'Curtains or Encore: Possibilities for Restructuring in the Canadian Auto Industry', in Jenson and Mahon (1993).

Young, John. 1957. *Canadian Commercial Policy*. Ottawa: Royal Commission on Canada's Economic Prospects.

Young, Oran R. 1980. 'International Regimes: Problems of Concept Formation', *World Politics* 33, 2: 331–57.

Young, Walter. 1969a. *Democracy and Discontent: Progressivism, Socialism and Social Credit in the Canadian West*. Toronto: Ryerson.

_____. 1969b. *The Anatomy of a Party: The National CCF, 1932–1961*. Toronto: University of Toronto Press.

Zakuta, Leo. 1964. *A Protest Movement Becalmed: A Study of Change in the CCF*. Toronto: University of Toronto Press.

Index